RENÉ GIRARD

THE GIRARD READER

Edited by
James G. Williams

A Crossroad Herder Book
The Crossroad Publishing Company
New York

This printing: 2000

The Crossroad Publishing Company
370 Lexington Avenue, New York, NY 10017

Printed in the United States of America

Library of Congress Cataloging-in-Publication Data

Girard, René, 1923-
[Selections. 1996]
The Girard reader / René Girard ; edited by James G. Williams.
p. cm.
"A Crossroad Herder book."
Includes bibliographical references and index.
ISBN 0-8245-1609-5. – ISBN 0-8245-1634-6 (pbk.)
1. Violence – Religious aspects. 2. Religion and culture. 3. Myth. 4. Scapegoat. 5. Sacrifice. 6. Bible. N.T. Gospels – Hermeneutics. 7. Mimesis in literature. 8. Mimesis in the Bible. 9. Girard, René, 1923- – Interviews. I. Williams, James G., 1936- . II. Title.
BL65.V55G572 1996
291.3′4–dc20 96-33185
CIP

Contents

Part V
THE BIBLE, THE GOSPELS, AND CHRIST

Part VI
THE CHALLENGE OF FREUD AND NIETZSCHE

A Note to the Reader

This Reader in René Girard's body of work is intended to present excerpts and articles which cover all the basic aspects of Girard's theory of religion and culture, with special emphasis on his present position on certain questions. Where an excerpt does not represent his present views, this will be indicated in the brief introduction to each chapter. I recommend that the reader previously unacquainted with Girard's work read the selections in the order presented. For many readers, especially students being introduced to Girard's thought, it would be very helpful to read first the biographical sketch of Girard (pp. 1–6) and the interview that concludes the main body of the Reader (pp. 262–288). Then when the selections have been read, it would be useful to go over the biography and interview once more. That is the plan I expect to follow with both undergraduate and graduate students.

The selections are arranged in six parts and an epilogue. The first part offers two selections giving an overview of the mimetic theory. One of these is a journal article which is Girard's own favorite written introduction to his work. The second part focuses on mimetic desire, which is absolutely necessary to understand before proceeding further in Girard's work. Chapter 3 in part 2, on triangular desire from the first chapter of *Deceit, Desire, and the Novel,* is fundamental for sharpening the focus on mimetic desire. Then the beginning reader will be prepared for part 3 on sacrifice and part 4 on the scapegoat and myths as persecution texts. Part 5 provides selections on what Girard considers to be the most important aspect of his work, establishing the place of the Jewish and Christian Bible, especially the Gospels, in the unveiling of the scapegoat mechanism and the unmasking of scapegoaters (including ourselves).

Part 6 will probably be the most difficult for the beginner, although a careful study of the first five parts should prepare the way. For the person with a background in modern philosophical or psychological thought, particularly anyone interested in critical theory or postmodernism, part 6 may be the best place to start. It includes two key selections from the written record of Girard's engagement with Freud and Nietzsche.

The epilogue is the revised written transcription of four hours of conversation which I had with Girard. I had the content of the Reader in mind with the questions I put to him. As I have already remarked, this conversation could provide both an illuminating retrospective view of what is covered in the Reader and an introduction to the whole work.

Girard's mimetic model is the brilliant and elegant expression of a basic set of ideas on the origin and maintenance of culture, the structure and dynamics of the self and human relations, and the transcendent basis of the world and human existence. He "has completely modified the landscape in the social sciences," as Paul Dumouchel has put it.[1] But not only in the social sciences: the humanities, including religious studies and theology, are slowly but surely being affected by Girard's theory. His way of seeing (Greek *theoria*, contemplation, speculation, sight), his approach and his ideas are pioneering, opening up new paths into the understanding of human relations, the formation of nonviolent human community, and the affirmation of faith in the God of the Bible.

But in speaking of theory I do not mean to imply that Girard's thought is inaccessible. He is remarkably clear and very committed to communication with all those who desire to engage in an honest quest for intellectual and spiritual truth. He describes the experience of discovery of truth as the most satisfying thing to him in his work. In the conversation with me that concludes the Reader he recounts three moments or phases of this discovery process. First was the dawning of insight into both how we learn and why we are prone to rivalry and conflict which may, and often does, lead to violence: *we are mimetic, or acquisitively imitational, creatures.* Our objects of desire and our ideas are based on the desires and ideas of others who are our models. This carries the potential of bringing us into conflict, even violence, with the models we imitate, for there always lurks the danger that we might compete with them for the objects of desire we have learned from them. The second moment of discovery for Girard was the discovery of the scapegoat mechanism: *the age-old way of gaining release from the violence or potential violence that mimesis produces is through nonconscious convergence upon a victim.* Scapegoating, in other words. Girard notes in the interview that this gave him a very plausible way of interpreting myth and ritual in ancient cultures. The third great moment of discovery was Girard's encounter with the Bible: *the Jewish and Christian Scriptures, especially the New Testament Gospels, are singular. They represent a revelatory movement away from scapegoating.* The Gospels not only disclose the hidden scapegoat mechanism of human cultures, but witness to the God, the Spirit-Paraclete, who stands with the Innocent Victim and is revealed through him.

Girard's theory of culture, religion, and violence emerged as a series of discoveries made in the investigation of ancient and modern literary

1. Paul Dumouchel, "Ouverture," in Paul Dumouchel, ed., *Violence and Truth: On the Work of René Girard* (Stanford, Calif.: Stanford University Press, 1988), 23.

and religious texts. However, its implications for understanding contemporary popular culture are enormous. Gil Bailie has said, "I have found the interpretive range of Girard's theory to be astonishing. Whether I have tried to understand a piece of literature, an ancient myth, a historical event, or the morning newspaper, I have found Girard's insights invaluable.... In my view, Girard has made the most sweeping and significant intellectual breakthrough of the modern age."[2] Of course, such a claim can properly emerge only out of the personal context of engagement, critical reflection, and broad experience. I hope that the gathering of these selections from Girard's writings and conversations will enable the reader to test this judgment about Girard's breakthrough that I share with Bailie and a number of others who have discovered his work while struggling and stumbling on a journey through what often seems to be a religious and cultural wasteland.

And now one further comment about the selections in this book. Secondary aspects of Girard's theoretical work, or ramifications which are more abstruse, have not been included, although I have given references in his writings on certain subjects. The precognitive or prerepresentational character of mimesis, for example, is not a subject into which the beginner in Girard's thought will need to delve, while those familiar with his work will already know where to look. But for the sake of completeness I have indicated where to find this in his writings in the introduction to chapter 3, "Triangular Desire."

A case could have been made for including texts relating the victimary mechanism and sacrifice to the origin of gods and kings. The logic of this connection is briefly indicated in the introduction to chapter 6, "Sacrifice as Sacral Violence and Substitution." The interested reader should consult chapter 3 of *Violence and the Sacred,* especially pp. 104–10; chapter 3 of *The Scapegoat;* and *Things Hidden since the Foundation of the World,* pp. 51–57.

Both of these issues, mimesis as precognitive and the beginnings of divinity and monarchy, are included in the record of the interview of Girard that concludes the Reader. In this conversation he responds to questions frequently posed and charges commonly made, as, for example, that his theory exhibits male bias or is too forthrightly Christian.

A bibliography is appended, as well as a glossary. The first part of the bibliography, listing Girard's books, chapters in books, and articles, was provided by the Girard Documentation Center of the University of Innsbruck, which was started by Professor Raymund Schwager and which Dietmar Regensburger currently oversees. The second, briefer list-

2. Gil Bailie, *Violence Unveiled: Humanity at the Crossroads* (New York: Crossroad, 1995), 4.

ing brings together recent books in English, French, and German by Girardian scholars. My criterion for "recent" was from 1990, the beginning of this decade. It is a selective list in that I have included only works with which I am acquainted and about which I can attest that their object is to explicate, apply, or criticize Girard's mimetic scapegoat theory, either in whole or in part.

The glossary actually provides a review of aspects of Girard's mimetic scapegoat theory. In the editor's introductions to the chapters of the Reader I have placed an asterisk (*) after the first occurrence of names and terms which may be found in the glossary. In most of the instances only main entries have been so indicated, although some cases I marked subcategories I considered important (e.g., "Internal and External Mediation" under "Model/Mediator").

This book was put together with the continual support and encouragement of Michael Leach of Crossroad, the fine editorial work of John Eagleson of Crossroad, and the expert, sometimes amazing clerical assistance of Deborah Pratt. I thank them warmly. And to Yvonne: once more,

betach bah lev ba'elah (Proverbs 31:11).

Acknowledgments

Permission is gratefully acknowledged to reprint the following articles and excerpts:

René Girard, "Mimesis and Violence: Perspectives in Cultural Criticism," *Berkshire Review* 14 (1979): 9–19. This periodical is no longer published. It is reprinted here by approval of Williams College through Michael Bell, former editor.

René Girard, *Violence and the Sacred,* trans. Patrick Gregory (Baltimore: Johns Hopkins University Press, 1977), 1–18; 39–44; 169–85; 309–14, reprinted by permission of Johns Hopkins University Press and the author.

René Girard, *Deceit, Desire, and the Novel,* trans. Yvonne Freccero (Baltimore: Johns Hopkins University Press, 1965), 1–17; 290–314, reprinted by permission of Johns Hopkins University Press and the author.

René Girard, *The Scapegoat,* trans. Yvonne Freccero (Baltimore: Johns Hopkins University Press, 1986), 1–23, reprinted by permission of Johns Hopkins University Press and the author.

René Girard, "Dionysus versus the Crucified," *Modern Language Notes* 99 (1984): 816–35, reprinted by permission of Johns Hopkins University Press and the author.

"Violence, Difference, Sacrifice: An Interview with René Girard," interview by Rebecca Adams, *Religion and Literature* 25 (1993): 22–26, reprinted by permission of The University of Notre Dame Press.

René Girard, "A Venda Myth Analyzed," in *René Girard and Myth: An Introduction* by Richard J. Golsan (New York and London: Garland Publishing, Inc., 1993), 151–79, reprinted by permission of Richard J. Golsan.

René Girard, *Things Hidden since the Foundation of the World,* trans. Stephen Bann and Michael Metteer (Stanford, Calif.: Stanford University Press, 1987), pages 141–79; 180–82; 205–20), reprinted with the permission of Stanford University Press. English translation copyright

René Girard, "How Can Satan Cast Out Satan?" in Georg Braulik, Walter Gross, and Sean McEvenue, eds., *Biblische Theologie und gesellschaftlicher Wandel* (Freiburg im Breisgau: Verlag Herder, 1993), 125–41, reprinted by permission of Verlag Herder.

René Girard, "Is There Anti-Semitism in the Gospels?" *Biblical Interpretation* 1, no. 3 (1993): 339–49, 351–52, reprinted by permission of E. J. Brill.

Bibliography of René Girard's writings in French and English provided by Girard-Dokumentation, University of Innsbruck.

René Girard: A Biographical Sketch

René Girard was born in 1923, in Avignon on Christmas day. He received his Baccalaureate in Philosophy at the Lycée of Avignon in 1941 and attended the Ecole des Chartres in Paris from 1943 to 1947. He graduated as an archiviste-paléographe, i.e., a specialist in medieval studies. It was in Paris that he had his only brush with the occupying Germans. His primary academic interest at that stage of his life was history and cultural patterns. His thesis was "La vie privée à Avignon dans la seconde moitié du XVe siècle" (Private life in Avignon in the second half of the fifteenth century).

At this point, in 1947, he had an opportunity to spend a year in the United States. It turned out to be forty-nine years and counting. He matriculated at Indiana University in history, where he received his Ph.D. in 1950. His dissertation topic was "American Opinion of France, 1940–1943." It may seem quite removed from his later turn to literature and interdisciplinary research, and in some respects that perception is correct. However, it is related to his later work to the extent that he has always been interested in cultural modes, fashions, and opinions, all of which express and revolve around mimetic desire, the core of his thought. Moreover, as a private citizen he continues to take a lively interest in Franco-American relations specifically and international affairs generally.

The young Girard was assigned to teach courses in French at Indiana. When he was asked to offer courses in literature which he had never read, a fateful period for his career began, although he could not have been clearly aware of this at the time. His doctoral work was in history, but he started to become more and more fascinated with the literature that he was assigned to teach. He would eventually, certainly by the time of his first book, be identified as a literary critic. However, some of Girard's early published research was historiographical (e.g., marriage in Avignon in the second half of the fifteenth century; Voltaire and classical historiography), and one can see in some other early articles that the creative work of writers in relation to their historical circumstances was one of his main concerns (e.g., articles about reflections on art in Malraux's novels; history in the work of Saint-John Perse; the situation of the American poet; Saint-Simon and literary criticism). His *Dostoevsky,* first published in 1963, was composed as a kind of running commentary on Dostoyevsky's life and the intellectual and social movements, as seen through Dostoyevsky's eyes, of that period of Russian history.

But Girard's initial articles did not appear soon enough to win him tenure at Indiana University. He succeeded in publishing a great burst of articles by 1953 (seven in all), but it was too late, as the decision had already been made at Indiana not to keep him. He went to Duke University as an instructor and occupied a position of assistant professor at Bryn Mawr from 1953 to 1957. From there he accepted a position as associate professor at Johns Hopkins University, becoming a full professor in 1961. He served as chair of the Department of Romance Languages from 1965 to 1968.

It was early in this first Johns Hopkins period that he underwent a momentous spiritual change. In the winter of 1959 he experienced a conversion to Christian faith which had been preceded by a kind of intellectual conversion while he was working on his first book. These two conversions are described in the interview at the end of the Reader.[1]

It was during his tenure as chairman of Romance Languages that he facilitated a symposium at Johns Hopkins which was to be important for the emergence of critical theory in America. With Richard Macksey and Eugenio Donato he organized an international conference in October of 1966, "The Languages of Criticism and the Sciences of Man." Participants included Roland Barthes, Jacques Derrida, Lucien Goldman, Jean Hyppolite, Jacques Lacan, Georges Poulet, Tsvetan Todorov, Jean-Pierre Vernant, and others. It was at this symposium that Derrida gave his widely read and cited paper, "La structure, le signe et le jeu dans le discours des sciences humaines" (Structure, sign and play in the discourse of the human sciences). This paper confirmed for Girard that Derrida was a critic to be reckoned with, and he found Derrida's subsequent essay "La pharmacie de Platon" (Plato's pharmacy) to be particularly significant. Girard would develop the *pharmakos* or scapegoat aspect of Derrida's analysis of writing/poison, placing it within history and actual social existence rather than restricting it to language and intertextuality like Derrida.

With his first two books, *Deceit, Desire, and the Novel* and *Dostoievski: du double à l'unité,*[2] Girard had rejected the literary retreat of the 1950s and early 1960s from concern with history, society, and the psyche. However, his first two books did not scandalize the intellectual world like his later writings, beginning with *Things Hidden since*

1. See also *Quand ces choses commenceront,* 190–95, in the bibliography of Girard's writings.

2. Scheduled to be published by Crossroad Publishing Co. in 1997 as *Resurrection from the Underground: Feodor Dostoevsky,* trans. James G. Williams.

the Foundation of the World. These initial works seemed to stay within a literary context and they focused on desire, which enjoyed a vogue by the 1960s. He analyzed the work of Cervantes, Stendhal, Flaubert, Proust, and Dostoyevsky in terms of "triangular" or "mimetic" desire: our desires are copied from models or mediators whose objects of desire become our objects of desire. But the model or mediator we imitate can become our rival if we desire precisely the object he is imagined to have. Or other imitators of the same model may compete with us for the same objects. Jealousy and envy are inevitably aroused in this mimetic situation. The romantic concept of a spontaneous desire is illusory.

As he began to study primitive religions from the standpoint of the mimetic concept, he saw that mimesis usually led to collective violence against a single victim. He turned to the great Greek tragedians. Once the *pharmakos* idea took hold in his thinking, he became more and more convinced of the power and relevance of these dramatists, particularly Sophocles' Oedipus cycle and Euripides with his stunning exposure of mimetic violence in *The Bacchae.* He found fascinating Freud's insight in *Totem and Taboo,* although Freud turned violent origins into a once-and-for-all myth rather than understanding the scapegoat mechanism as a constant factor in human culture and human relations. The mimetic concept, extended to include the scapegoat mechanism and refined by the explication of *The Bacchae* and the critique of Freud: to grasp these developments in his thinking is to grasp the essential argument of *Violence and the Sacred.*

In 1971 Girard accepted a distinguished professor position at the State University of New York at Buffalo, where he remained until 1976. During this period he became a close friend of Cesáreo Bandera, now University Distinguished Professor of Spanish Literature at the University of North Carolina. Bandera was and has remained an important conversation partner for Girard. In 1972 *La violence et le sacré* was published in France (in English *Violence and the Sacred,* 1977). He had published scarcely anything on Christianity and the Bible, but that was about to change, and a new stage of his career was imminent as he left SUNY/Buffalo in 1976.

In 1976 Girard accepted a second appointment at Johns Hopkins University, with the title of John M. Beall Professor of the Humanities. The English translation of *La violence et le sacré* came out in 1977, and for the first time he became the subject of reviews, interviews, and scholarly forums in North America. *Violence and the Sacred* is the one work by Girard that many American scholars have read, although some literary critics have read only *Deceit, Desire, and the Novel.*

The most important book Girard has produced appeared in French in 1978, *Des choses cachées depuis la fondation du monde* (*Things Hidden since the Foundation of the World*). In the form of a dialogue with two psychiatrists, Jean-Michel Oughourlian and Guy Lefort, its format is a triptych: (1) Fundamental Anthropology, (2) The Judeo-Christian Scriptures, (3) Interdividual Psychology. In this book Girard declared himself, in effect, as a Christian and advocated a nonsacrificial reading of the Gospels and the divinity of Christ. In France he was a *cause célèbre* or a *bête noire,* because his argument for a universal anthropological theory, combined with the position that the deepest insights of Western culture stem from biblical revelation, shocked and alienated those who held to the assumption of the all-encompassing nature of language and who tended to ignore Christianity or view it with contempt. However, for many who were seeking a way to affirm the reality of human experience as a referent outside of language or for those who were searching for a way of talking about the biblical God of history, his clear concepts and outspoken positioning of himself against fashionable intellectual modes came across as the discovery of treasure hidden in a field.

This public discussion of Girard's work happened primarily in France, and to some extent in other European countries. Due to the impact of *Things Hidden,* there was a new reading audience for *Violence and the Sacred.* Interest in Girard and the spread of his influence have come about more slowly in North America. The translation of *Things Hidden,* published by Stanford University Press in 1987, was a signal step forward. Another was the formation of the Colloquium on Violence and Religion, to which I will return shortly.

In 1981 Girard accepted his next and last post, that of Andrew B. Hammond Professor of French Language, Literature, and Civilization at Stanford University. These years until his retirement in 1995 saw the appearance of *Le bouc émissaire* (1982), published in English as *The Scapegoat* by Johns Hopkins (1986); *La route antique des hommes pervers* (1985), put out by Athlone and Stanford as *Job: The Victim of His People* (1987); *A Theater of Envy: William Shakespeare* (1991), translated into French as *Shakespeare: Les feux de l'envie,* which actually appeared in 1990, before the English original; and a very important set of interviews, *Quand ces choses commenceront... Entretiens avec Michel Treguer* (When these things will begin... Conversations with Michel Treguer), published by arléa in 1994. Also, as already mentioned, the English version of *Things Hidden since the Foundation of the World* appeared in 1987.

Stanford University was a good setting for Girard in some respects. Stanford University is undoubtedly one of the best research universities in the world, the intelligence and background of its undergraduate students ranks high among American universities, and the graduate students in French were certainly very good. But Stanford's very position as one of the leading universities in the Western world has made it prey to the currents of political correctness that have washed over American education. The problem from Girard's standpoint is the denigration of traditional disciplines and classical learning. Certainly Girard, although well known and highly regarded on campus, became "odd man out" because of his stance toward certain academic fashions and his avowed Christian identity. But he never felt isolated, and his teaching and research were always interdisciplinary.

One of the most important events of this period from the standpoint of Girard's lifetime of work and his intellectual and religious commitments was the formation of the Colloquium on Violence and Religion (COV&R) in 1990. It is characteristic of him that he did not take the initiative to start it, nor has he attempted in any way to manipulate its governance or the topics of meetings and approaches to various issues. He has exemplified the lack of that mimetic obsession with power exhibited by Freud in forming and controlling the inner council of the International Psychoanalytic Association, and Girard's followers and sympathizers in COV&R are noticeably free of the esotericism and cultic exclusivism that have at various times marked disciples of Jung, Heidegger, and Lacan.

The object of COV&R, as stated on behalf of those present at the founding conference at Stanford University, is "to explore, criticize, and develop the mimetic model of the relationship between violence and religion in the genesis and maintenance of culture." This statement presupposes Girard's work as the center and starting point, but the organization includes many people who do not share his religious views or differ with him on certain points of the mimetic theory.

From that first meeting of no more than twenty-five people, there are now more than two hundred members, who are located primarily in the United States and Europe. An annual symposium is held in middle to late spring, and a shorter meeting takes place each year in conjunction with the convention of the American Academy of Religion and the Society of Biblical Literature. A biannual bulletin, *The Bulletin of the Colloquium on Violence and Religion,* features a bibliography of literature on the mimetic theory. The bulletin is financially underwritten by the University of Innsbruck. An annual journal, *Contagion: Journal of Violence, Mimesis, and Culture,* has been published since 1994.

The great majority are academics, many of whom are dissatisfied with the conditions and attitudes they find in academe. They represent not only the usual complaints of lack of interest in humanistic and interdisciplinary studies and the greater support of disciplines which are more closely connected to what is popular and demanded in the marketplace. The deeper dimension of their reaction is a refusal of that very political correctness which pretends to uphold the rights of victims and minorities, but ends by affirming a helter-skelter hodge-podge which undercuts a consistent moral vision and tends to give the upper hand to those who exalt individual self-fulfillment at the one extreme and, at the other extreme, to those who are able to take advantage of the politics of victimization to gain power over others.

But besides academics holding college or university appointments, COV&R's membership includes also some ministers and priests, psychiatrists and psychologists, and others who carry on their vocations in overlapping spheres of academy and church, or academy and the work of conflict resolution in racial, ethnic, and religious relations.

Retired since the summer of 1995, Girard is still actively engaged in thinking and writing. His immediate project is a book on Christianity and myth, which is nearing completion. "Christianity and myth" means for him not primarily the valid points of comparison, which of course must be noted, but above all the differences that disclose the truth of Christianity.

Part I

Overview of the Mimetic Theory

Chapter 1

Mimesis and Violence

The most convenient single summary of Girard's mimetic model, including its relation to the Bible, is this article, "Mimesis* and Violence: Perspectives in Cultural Criticism," which appeared in the now defunct *Berkshire Review* 14 (1979): 9-19. It is essential reading for the beginner in Girard's work, and may be useful to others who are already acquainted with his thought.

If you survey the literature on imitation, you will quickly discover that acquisition and appropriation are never included among the modes of behavior that are likely to be imitated. If acquisition and appropriation were included, imitation as a social phenomenon would turn out to be more problematic than it appears, and above all conflictual. If the appropriative gesture of an individual named A is rooted in the imitation of an individual named B, it means that A and B must reach together for one and the same object. They become rivals for that object. If the tendency to imitate appropriation is present on both sides, imitative rivalry must tend to become reciprocal; it must be subject to the back and forth reinforcement that communication theorists call a positive feedback. In other words, the individual who first acts as a model will experience an increase in his own appropriative urge when he finds himself thwarted by his imitator. And reciprocally. Each becomes the imitator of his own imitator and the model of his own model. Each tries to push aside the obstacle that the other places in his path. Violence is generated by this process; or rather violence is the process itself when two or more partners try to prevent one another from appropriating the object they all desire through physical or other means. Under the influence of the judicial viewpoint and of our own psychological impulses, we always look for some original violence or at least for well-defined acts of violence that would be separate from nonviolent behavior. We want to distinguish the culprit from the innocent and, as a result, we substitute discontinuities and differences for the continuities and reciprocities of the mimetic escalation.

Violence is discussed, nowadays, in terms of aggression. We speak of aggression as an instinct that would be especially strong in certain individuals or in man as a zoological species. It is true, no doubt, that some individuals are more aggressive than others, and that men are more aggressive than sheep, but the problematic of aggression does not go to the root of human conflict. It is unilateral, it seems to suggest that the elimination of something called aggressivity is the problem. Violence is also attributed by many economists to the scarcity of needed objects or to their monopolization by a social élite. It is true that the goods needed by human beings to sustain their lives can be scarce but, in animal life, scarcity also occurs and it is not sufficient, as such, to cause low-ranking individuals to challenge the privileges of the dominant males.

Imitation or mimicry happens to be common to animals and men. It seems to me that a theory of conflict based primarily on appropriative mimicry does not have the drawbacks of one based on scarcity or on aggressivity; if it is correctly conceived and formulated it throws a great deal of light on much of human culture, beginning with religious institutions.

Religious prohibitions make a good deal of sense when interpreted as efforts to prevent mimetic rivalry from spreading throughout human communities. Prohibitions and taboos are often ineffectual and misguided but they are not absurd, as many anthropologists have suggested; they are not rooted primarily in irrational fears, as psychoanalysts have suggested, since they bear on violence, on mimetic behavior, and on the potential objects of mimetic rivalry. Rituals confirm, I believe, that primitive societies are obsessed with the undifferentiation or conflictual reciprocity that must result from the spread of mimetic rivalry. The chaos, the absence of order, and the various disorders that prevail at the beginning of many myths must also be interpreted, I believe, in terms of mimetic rivalry; and so must the natural disasters such as plagues, great floods, or other mythical scourges that often include an element of conflict between mythical partners generally conceived as close relatives, brothers, or identical twins. These themes represent what mythology is unable to conceive rationally, the undifferentiated reciprocity of mimetic conflict.

Many rituals begin with a mimetic free-for-all during which hierarchies disintegrate, prohibitions are transgressed, and all participants become each other's conflictual doubles or "twins." Mimetic rivalry is the common denominator, in my opinion, of what happens in seasonal festivals, of the so-called ordeal undergone by the future initiates in many initiation rituals, as well as of the social breakdown that may follow the death of the sacred king or accompany his enthronement and rejuvenation rituals. The violent demonstrations triggered in many communities by the death of a member must also be interpreted as mimetic rivalry. All these rites amount to a theatrical reenactment of a mimetic crisis in which the differences that constitute the society are dissolved. Why should communities, at certain appointed times and also at times when a crisis threatens, mimic the very type of crisis they dread so much at all times — that generalized mimetic conflict which prohibitions, in normal circumstances, are intended to prevent?

The inability to find a satisfactory solution to the mystery of ritual has spelled the failure of religious anthropology. This failure is not diminished but compounded by the present tendency to deny it as failure, by denying the existence of the problem and minimizing the role of religion in all aspects of human culture.

I believe that the key to the mystery lies in the decisive reordering that occurs at the end of the ritual performance, normally through the mediation of sacrifice. Sacrifice stands in the same relationship to the ritual crisis that precedes it as the death or expulsion of the hero to the undifferentiated chaos that prevails at the beginning of many myths. Real or symbolic, sacrifice is primarily a collective action of the entire community, which purifies itself of its own disorder through the unanimous immolation of a victim, but this can happen only at the paroxysm of the ritual crisis.

I am aware that not all rituals fit that definition exactly, and I do not have enough time to show you that the apparent deviations can be brought back to the single common denominator of the sacrificial immolation. Why should religious communities believe they can be purged of their various ills and primarily of their internal violence through the immolation of a victim? In my opinion, this belief must be taken seriously, and the variations as well as the constants of sacrificial immolation suggests a real event behind blood sacrifice that takes place in all human communities, as a general rule, and that serves as a model for religious ritual. The religious communities try to remember that event in their mythologies, and they try to reproduce it in their sacrifices. Freud was right when he discovered that this model was a collective murder, but he was wrong, I believe, in his interpretation of that murder. The problem is made difficult by the necessary misinterpretation and transfiguration of the event by the religious communities themselves. This misinterpretation is an essential aspect of the collective murder itself insofar as it effectively resolves and terminates crises of mimetic rivalry among human groups.

Sacrifice is the resolution and conclusion of ritual because a collective murder or expulsion resolves the mimetic crisis that ritual mimics. What kind of mechanism can this be? Judging from the evidence, direct and indirect, this resolution must belong to the realm of what is commonly called a scapegoat effect.

The word "scapegoat" means two things: the ritual described in Leviticus 16 or similar rituals which are themselves imitations of the model I have in mind. I distinguish between scapegoat as ritual and scapegoat as effect. By a scapegoat effect I mean that strange process through which two or more people are reconciled at the expense of a third party who appears guilty or responsible for whatever ails, disturbs, or frightens the scapegoaters. They feel relieved of their tensions and they coalesce into a more harmonious group. They now have a single purpose, which is to prevent the scapegoat from harming them, by expelling and destroying him.

Scapegoat effects are not limited to mobs, but they are most conspicuously effective in the case of mobs. The destruction of a victim can make a mob more furious, but it can also bring back tranquility. In a mob situation, tranquility does not return, as a rule, without some kind of victimage to assuage the desire for violence. That collective belief appears so absurd to the detached observer, if there is one, that he is tempted to believe the mob is not duped by its own identification of the scapegoat as a culprit. The mob appears insincere and hypocritical. In reality, the mob really believes. If we understand this, we also understand that a scapegoat effect is real; it is an unconscious phenomenon, but not in the sense of Freud.

How can the scapegoat effect involve real belief? How can such an effect be generated without an objective cause, especially with the lightning speed that can often be observed in the case of the scapegoating mobs? The answer is that scapegoat effects are mimetic effects; they are generated by mimetic rivalry itself, when it reaches a certain degree of intensity. As an object becomes the focus of mimetic rivalry between two or more antagonists, other members of the group tend to join in, mimetically attracted by the presence of mimetic desire. Mimesis is mimetically attractive, and we can assume that at certain stages, at least in the evolution of human communities, mimetic rivalry can spread to an entire group. This is what is suggested by the acute disorder phase with which many rituals begin. The community turns into a mob under the effect of mimetic rivalry. The phenomena that take place when a human group turns into a mob are identical to those produced by mimetic rivalry, and they can be defined as that loss of differentiation which is described in mythology and reenacted in ritual.

We found earlier that mimetic rivalry tends toward reciprocity. The model is likely to be mimetically affected by the desire of his imitator. He becomes the imitator of his own imitator, just as the latter becomes the model of his own model. As this feedback process keeps reinforcing itself, each constitutes in the other's path a more and more irritating obstacle and each tries to remove this obstacle more and more forcefully. Violence is thus generated. Violence is not originary; it is a by-product of mimetic rivalry. Violence is mimetic rivalry itself becoming violent as the antagonists who desire the same object keep thwarting each other and desiring the object all the more. Violence is supremely mimetic.

The antagonists are caught in an escalation of frustration. In their dual role of obstacle and model, they both become more and more fascinated by each other. Beyond a certain level of intensity they are totally absorbed and the disputed object becomes secondary, even irrelevant. Judging from many rituals, their mutual fascination can reach the level of a hypnotic trance. That particular condition becomes the principal goal of certain religious practices under the name of possession.

At this paroxystic level of mimetic rivalry, the element of mimicry is still around, more intense than ever. It has to focus on the only entities left in the picture, which are the antagonists themselves. This means that the selection of an antagonist depends on the mimetic factor rather that on previous developments. Transfers of antagonism must take place, therefore, for purely mimetic reasons. Mimetic attraction is bound to increase with the number of those who converge on one and the same antagonist. Sooner or later a snowball effect must occur that involves the entire group minus, of course, the one individual, or the few against whom all hostility focuses and who become the "scapegoats," in a sense analogous to but more extreme than our everyday sense of the word "scapegoat." Whereas mimetic appropriation is inevitably divisive, causing the contestants to fight over an object they cannot all appropriate together, mimetic antagonism is ultimately unitive, or rather reunitive since it provides the antagonists with an object they can really share, in the sense that they can all rush against that victim in order to destroy it or drive it away.

If I am right, the contradiction between prohibitions and rituals is only apparent. The purpose of both is to spare the community another mimetic perturbation. In normal circumstances, this purpose is well served by the prohibitions. In abnormal circumstances, when a new crisis seems impending, the prohibitions are of no avail anymore. Once the contagion of mimetic violence is reintroduced into the community, it cannot be contained. The community, then, changes its tactic entirely. Instead of trying to roll back mimetic violence it tries to get rid of it by encouraging it and by bringing it to a climax that triggers the happy solution of ritual sacrifice with the help of a substitute victim. There is no difference of purpose between prohibitions and rituals. The behavior demanded by the first and the behavior demanded by the disorderly phase of ritual are in opposition, of course, but the mimetic reading makes this opposition intelligible. In the absence of this reading, anthropologists have either minimized the opposition or viewed it as an insoluble contradiction that ultimately confirmed their conception of religion as utter nonsense. Others, under the influence of psychoanalysis, have viewed the transgressive aspect of ritual, in regard to prohibitions, as an end in itself, in keeping, of course, with the contemporary ethos and its predilection for disorder, at least among intellectuals who feel, perhaps, they do not have enough of it in their own lives.

Religion is different, and the purpose of ritual is reconciliation and reordering through sacrifice. The current views of ritual as essentially transgressive are given a semblance of credibility by the fact that long before anthropologists and psychoanalysts showed up on the scene, the religious believers themselves had often lost touch with the unity of purpose of their various religious practices and begun to perceive the opposition between prohibitions and ritual as an unintelligible contradiction. And they normally tried to cope with this contradiction either by minimizing it and making their prohibitions less stringent as well as their rituals less disorderly or on the contrary by emphasizing and "maximizing" so to speak the opposition and turning their rites into the so-called festival that presents itself explicitly as a period of time in which the social rules and taboos of all kinds do not apply.

Modern theorists have some support from late religious developments, in other words, when they try to elude or give trivial answers to the problem posed by the behavioral opposition between prohibitions and rituals. This is the wide road of modern interpretation, and it has turned out to be an impasse. We will not take that road, therefore, and we will face the contrast between ritual and prohibition in all its sharpness, not to espouse some psychoanalytical view, of course, but to perceive the true paradox of ritual — which is the genesis and regeneration as well as degeneration of the cultural order through paroxystic disorder.

Mythology and religious cults form systems of representation necessarily untrue to their own genesis. The episode of mimetic violence and reconciliation is always recollected and narrated, as well as reenacted, from the perspective of its beneficiaries, who are also its puppets. From the standpoint of the scapegoaters and their inheritors — the religious community — there is no such thing as scapegoating in our sense. A scapegoat effect that can be acknowledged as such by the scapegoaters is no longer effective, it is no longer a scapegoat *effect*. The victim must be perceived as truly responsible for the troubles that come to an end when it is collectively put to death. The community could not be at peace with itself once more if it doubted the victim's enormous capacity for evil. The belief in this same victim's enormous capacity for doing good is a direct consequence of that first belief. The peace seems to be restored as well as destroyed by the scapegoat himself.

An arbitrary victim would not reconcile a disturbed community if its members realized they are the dupes of a mimetic effect. I must insist on this aspect because it is crucial and often misunderstood. The mythic systems of representation obliterate the scapegoating on which they are founded, and they remain dependent on this obliteration. Scapegoating has never been conceived by anyone as an activity in which he himself participates and may still be participating even as he denounces the scapegoating of others. Such denunciation can even become a precondition of successful scapegoating in a world like ours, where knowledge of the phenomenon is on the rise and makes its grossest and most violent forms obsolete. Scapegoating can continue only if its victims are perceived primarily as scapegoaters.

Traces of an act of collective scapegoating that has effectively reconciled a community are elusive since the phenomenon is necessarily recollected from the deluded standpoint it generates. At first sight, this situation seems discouraging, but in reality it is highly favorable to the demonstration of my thesis: features that characterize the deluded standpoint of the scapegoaters are easily ascertainable. Once they are ascertained, we can verify that they are really present in primitive mythology; they constitute the constants or near constants of that mythology, in contradistinction to the variables, which are quite significant as well but demand lengthier analysis. The victim cannot be perceived as innocent and impotent; he (or she, as the case may be) must be perceived if not necessarily as a culprit in our sense, at least as a creature truly responsible for all the disorders and ailments of the community, in other words for the mimetic crisis that has triggered the mimetic mechanism of scapegoating. We can verify, indeed, that the victim is usually presented in that fashion. He is viewed as subversive of the communal order and as a threat to the well-being of the society. His continued presence is therefore undesirable and it must be destroyed or driven away by other gods, perhaps, or by the community itself.

The Oedipus myth does not tell us Oedipus is a mimetic scapegoat. Far from disproving my theory, this silence confirms it as long as it is surrounded by the telltale signs of scapegoating as, indeed, it is. The myth reflects the standpoint of the scapegoaters, who really believe their victim to be responsible for the plague in their midst, and they connect that responsibility with anti-natural acts, horrendous transgressions that signify the total destruction of the social order. All the themes of the story suggest we must be dealing with the type of delusion that has always surrounded and still surrounds victimage by mobs on the rampage. In the Middle Ages, for instance, when the Jews were accused of spreading the plague during the period of the Black Death, they were also accused of unnatural crimes à la Oedipus.

The most interesting question is: Why are we able to see through this type of delusion in some instances, and unable in others, especially in the case of that vast corpus of mysterious *récits* we call mythology? Why are the greatest specialists in the field still fooled by themes which historians of the Western world have long ago recognized as indicative of persecution in their own areas of research? Historians are working in areas with which they feel more at ease and are more knowledgeable because they are culturally closer, but this is part of the story; it may account for the tortuous nature of our progress toward a greater understanding of persecution everywhere but not for the progress itself. So-called primitive or archaic people are fooled by their own myths as much or even more than by the myths of others. The amazing thing about us is not that so many are still fooled but that many are not and that suspicion, as a whole, is on the increase. Our sterility as creators of myth must not be deplored because it is one and the same with our inability to transfigure our victims, with our growing ability, therefore, to see through the collective delusions of scapegoating. This ability has grown enormously in the last centuries and, in my opinion, it is still growing. The recognition of mimetic victimage as the major "referent" behind mythology is about to occur, and it will be only one more step in an advance that began a long time ago and that is not yet over.

The views I am now expressing seem paradoxical because purely formal, structural, and nonreferential readings are now in vogue, but this state of affairs is only the most visible and limited consequence of a development which had to take place before the mimetic victimage hypothesis could appear, and it is the radical critique of all efforts so far to ground mythology in psychosocial phenomena. The current vogue is short-sighted only in its failure to realize that mythological systems as a whole may be amenable to an entirely new type of hypothesis regarding their ultimate origin. These structuralists and poststructuralists who describe my hypothesis as theoretically regressive have not fully assessed its nature and its significance.

If a society's growing awareness of victimage effects and the weakening of these effects are correlated, the phenomena we are dealing with are ruled by something like an "uncertainty principle." As our knowledge of them increases, they tend, if not to disappear, at least to become marginalized, and that is the reason why some people object to my thesis on the grounds that victimage phenomena are not effective enough to account for the religious practices and beliefs of primitive people. This is true, indeed, of the victimage phenomena we ourselves can observe. At the root of primitive religion, phenomena must be postulated that are analogous to but not identical with those still taking place around us. If phenomena completely identical with those we must postulate were still present among us, they would still generate primitive religion and could not be scientifically observed; they would appear to us only in the transfigured and unrecognizable shape of religion.

Victimage is still present among us, of course, but in degenerate forms that do not produce the type of mythical reconciliation and ritual practice exemplified by primitive cults. This lack of efficiency often means that there are more rather than fewer victims. As in the case of drugs, consumers of sacrifice tend to increase the doses when the effect becomes more difficult to achieve.

This last metaphor is not quite satisfactory, of course, if victimage and sacrifice are the means through which human societies have always been created and perpetuated. In our world, sacrificial means have degenerated more and more as victimage, oppression, and persecution have become predominant issues. No return to the rigidities of prohibition and ritual is in sight, and some very special cause must be found to account for this unique evolution.

I have an answer to propose, and it is the presence of the biblical text in our midst. This answer is bound to surprise and even scandalize an intellectual world for which the complete exclusion of that text is a prerequisite of rationality and scientific research. No one is disturbed when religious texts that are not specifically our own are assumed to be important for our modern psyche and for our modern society. But believers and unbelievers alike tend to become upset when our own religious texts are brought into the picture.

The biblical tendency to "side with the victims" is obvious, but modern students of the Bible tend to limit its consequences to ethical and purely "religious" considerations. If the preceding is true, this tendency must have epistemological consequences as well. Even in the most archaic texts, the collective violence that constitutes the hidden infrastructure of all mythology begins to emerge, and it emerges as unjustified or arbitrary. Behind the story told by the eleven brothers to their father Jacob, after they violently expel from their midst their twelfth brother, Joseph, there is the vengeful consensus of this violent group. Unlike mythology, the biblical text rejects that perspective and sees Joseph as an innocent scapegoat, a victim of his brothers' jealousy, the biblical formulation of our mimetic desire. Later on, in Egypt, the same mimetic consensus reappears when Joseph is imprisoned. Everybody believes Joseph has betrayed his adoptive father, Potiphar, and committed with the latter's wife an action analogous to the incest of Oedipus. The biblical text, unlike the Oedipus myth, disbelieves this accusation, recognizing in it the kind of story that can be expected from a community that, for a number of possible reasons, happens to be disturbed and is mimetically, i.e., unconsciously, looking for scapegoat relief.

The scapegoat in that story is the main subject under investigation, as in countless other stories, as in the book of Job, as in many of the psalms, and a profound reflection is at work, everywhere in the Bible, regarding the ethical demands that a revelation of victimage and its refusal places upon human beings. In the Joseph story, again, this time in the last episode, we see the hero himself engineer a scapegoat *mise en scène* in order to test the possibility of a change of heart in his brothers.

These had come a first time to beg for grain, and Joseph, now the most powerful man in Egypt, had warned them that they would not be supplied with it a second time unless they brought with them their youngest brother, Benjamin. Besides Joseph, Benjamin is the only other son of Jacob by his most cherished wife, Rachel.

The famine becomes so serious that the brothers come back, this time with Benjamin. On Joseph's orders a precious cup that belongs to him is placed in Benjamin's bag. When the eleven brothers are searched on their way back to Palestine, the youngest appears guilty of theft and Joseph announces he will be detained. At this point, Judah, one of the ten brothers, offers to take Benjamin's place as a prisoner of Joseph, for fear, he says, that his father might die of grief. This dedication of Judah stands in symmetrical opposition to the original deed of collective violence which it cancels out and reveals. As he hears Judah, Joseph is moved to tears and identifies himself.

Unique in many of its features, of course, this story is nevertheless typical of the Bible in the sense that it exemplifies its counter-mythical thrust in the treatment of victimage. This thrust is also present not only in other similar stories, but in countless other texts that espouse the perspective of the victim rather than the mythical perspective of the persecutors, such as the penitential psalms or the book of Job. Prophetic inspiration focuses on the revelation of victimage and the famous songs of the Servant in Second Isaiah constitute its summit; they provide a complete revelation of collective victimage as the founding mechanism of human culture. The responsibility for the victim's death is placed squarely upon the community even though in other parts of the same text God is presented as responsible. The same ambiguity or even contradiction remains in Christian theology but not in the text of the Gospels, which replaces the violent God of the past with a nonviolent one whose demand is for nonviolence rather than sacrifice. The Christ of the Gospels dies against sacrifice, and through his death, he reveals its nature and origin by making sacrifice unworkable, at least in the long run, and bringing sacrificial culture to an end. The word "sacrifice" is not important in itself, but the singularity of the Passion is obscured if the same word is used for the Passion and for what takes place in sacrificial rituals.[1] Can we use the same word for the deed that is committed at the beginning of Joseph's story, when the eleven brothers expel their own brother, and for Judah's willingness to die, if necessary, in order to prevent the sacrifice of his brother?

The sacrificial misreading common to Christians and non-Christians alike has obscured the nonsacrificial significance of the Judeo-Christian Scriptures but not entirely suppressed its impact. Thus, our society could

---

1. See the introduction to chapter 6. –*J. W.*

result from a complex interaction between the Judeo-Christian and the sacrificial. Acting upon the latter as a force of disruption — as new wine in old wine-skins — the former would be responsible for our constantly increased awareness of victimage and for the decadence of mythology in our world.

Chapter 2

The Surrogate Victim

This excerpt is the conclusion to *Violence and the Sacred*, trans. P. Gregory (Baltimore: Johns Hopkins University Press, 1977), 309-18. In it Girard does not develop his concept of mimetic desire* as such, but focuses on the surrogate victim as the cultural antidote to violence that is represented in sacrifice,* scapegoating,* Greek drama, and other great literary texts. His understanding of sacrifice has been modified since the publication of *Violence and the Sacred*. On this shift see the introduction to chapter 6.

A theory of the nature of primitive religion has emerged from the foregoing inquiry into the origins of myth and ritual....

My theory depends on a number of basic premises. Even if innumerable intermediary stages exist between the spontaneous outbursts of violence and its religious imitations, even if it is only these imitations that come to our notice, I want to stress that these imitations had their origin in a real event. The actuality of this event, over and above its existence in rite and record, must be kept in mind. We must also take care not to restrict this event to any one context, any one dominant intellectual framework, whether semantic or symbolic, which lacks a firm basis in reality. The event should be viewed as an absolute beginning, signifying the passage from nonhuman to human, as well as a relative beginning for the societies in question.

The theory of the surrogate victim is paradoxical in that it is based on facts whose empirical characteristics are not directly accessible. These facts can be drawn exclusively from texts that invariably offer distorted, fragmentary, or indirect testimony. We can gain access to the generative event only through constant reference to these enigmatic sources, which constitute at once the foreground in which our theory situates itself and the background against which its accuracy must be tested.

The theory of evolution depends on the comparison and linkage of evidence — the fossil remains of living creatures — corresponding, in the case of my hypothesis, to religious and cultural texts. No single anatomical fact studied in isolation can lead to the concept of evolution. No direct observation is possible, nor form of empirical verification even conceivable, because evolution occurred over a span of time entirely out of scale with the span of human existence.

In the same way no single text — mythic, religious, or tragic — will yield the operating procedures of violent unanimity. Here, too, the comparative method is the only one possible. If this method has not been successful to date, that is because there are so many variables at work; it is hard to locate the single underlying scheme that controls them all. The theory of evolution, too, constitutes a hypothesis.

The surrogate victim theory presents, as a theory, a distinct superiority over the theory of evolution. The inaccessible character of the generative event is not merely an obstacle unrelated to the theory, an aspect that contributes nothing of positive value; rather, it is an essential part of that theory, something we cannot do without. In order to retain its structuring influence the generative violence must remain hidden; misapprehension is indispensable to all religious or postreligious structuring. And the hidden nature of the event corresponds to the researcher's inability to attribute a satisfactory function to religious practices. My theory is the first to offer an explanation of the primordial role that religion plays in primitive societies, as well as of man's ignorance of this role.

This hidden nature is much less problematic than a notion like the unconscious of Freud.[1] A comparison of certain myths and rituals, viewed in the light of Greek tragedy, leads to the theory of the surrogate victim and violent unanimity through a path much more direct than that of "verbal slips" to such psychoanalytic concepts as suppressed desires and the unconscious. Surely such slips can be attributed to many different causes. But the surrogate victim theory is the only hypothesis that accounts for all features of the cultural phenomena presented here. Unlike the psychoanalytical explanations, it leaves no areas in shadow and neglects no major aspects.

Although generative violence is invisible, it can logically be deduced from myths and rituals once their real structures have been perceived. The further one advances along this path and the more transparent the true nature of religious thought appears, the clearer it becomes that there is nothing here to suppress or to hide. There is no justification for the idea that religious thought either represses or deliberately refuses to acknowledge a threatening self-awareness. Such awareness does not yet

1. See chapter 15, "Freud and the Oedipus Complex." –*J.W.*

present any threat to religion. It is we who are threatened by it, we who flee from it.

If religious misapprehensions were to be regarded in the same light as psychoanalysis regards its material, we should require some religious equivalent to the Freudian repression of the patricide/incest desire, something that must be hidden and kept hidden. Yet such is hardly the case. To be sure, there are many details of the generative event that have dropped out, many elements that have become so warped, misshapen, and transfigured as to be unrecognizable when reproduced in mythical or ritualistic form. Yet no matter how gaping the lacunae may appear, no matter how grotesque the deformations, they are not ultimately indispensable to the religious attitude, the religious misapprehension. Even if it were brought face to face with the inner workings of the mechanism, the religious mind would be unable to conceive of the transformation of bad into good, of violence into culture, as a spontaneous phenomenon calling for a positive approach.

It is natural to assume that the best-concealed aspect of the generative mechanism will be the most crucial element, the one most likely to render the sacrificial system nonfunctional if it becomes known. This aspect will be the arbitrary selection of the victim, its essential insignificance, which contradicts the meaning accumulated upon its head by the scapegoat projections.

Close examination will reveal that even this aspect is not really hidden; it can be readily detected once we know what we must look for. Frequently the rituals themselves are engineered so that they include an element of chance in the choice of the victim, but mythologies have never taken this into account.

Although we have already called attention to those rites designed to give a role to chance in the selection of the victim, it may be that we have not put sufficient stress on this essential aspect.

Sporting contests and games of chance appear to modern man most incongruous as ritual practices. The Uitoto Indians, for example, incorporate a balloon game into their ritual; and the Kayans of Borneo use a top in the course of their religious ceremonies.

Even more remarkable, apparently even more incongruous, is the game of dice that figures in the funeral rites of the Canelos Indians. Only the men participate in this game. Divided into two rival groups and lined up on either side of the deceased, they take turns casting their dice *over* the corpse. The sacred spirit, in the person of the dead man, determines the outcome of each throw. The winner is awarded one of the dead man's domestic animals, which is slaughtered on the spot, and the women prepare a meal from it for the assembled mourners.

Jensen, in citing these facts, remarks that the games are not simply additions to established religious practices.[2] If one were to say that the Canelos Indians "play at dice during the funeral rites of their parents," one would be conveying the wrong idea of the ceremonies. For this game takes place only in conjunction with these funeral rites. It is modern man who thinks of games of this sort as exclusively secular, and we must not project that idea onto the Canelos Indians. This is not to say that our own games have nothing to do with rites; in fact, they originate in rites. But, as usual, we have got things reversed. For us, games of chance are a secular activity upon which a religious meaning has been superimposed. The true state of affairs is precisely the opposite: games originate in rites that have been divested, to a greater or lesser degree, of their sacred character. Huizinga's famous theory of play should be inverted. It is not play that envelops the sacred, but the sacred that envelops the notion of play.

Death, like any passage, entails violence. The passage into the beyond by a member of the community may provoke (among other difficulties) quarrels among the survivors, for there is always the problem of how to redistribute the dead man's belongings. In order to meet the threat of maleficent contagion the community must have recourse to the universal model, to generative violence; it must attend to the advice of the sacred itself. In this particular case, the community has perceived and retained the role of choice in the liberating decision. If violence is given free play, chance alone is responsible for the ultimate resolution of the conflict; and the rite tries to force the hand of chance before violence has had the opportunity to act. The rite aims straight at the final result, achieving, as it were, a minimum expenditure of violence.

The Canelos dice game offers a clue to the reason why the theme of chance recurs so frequently in folklore, myth, and fable. Oedipus, it will be remembered, refers to himself as the son of *Tychè* — that is, Fortune or Chance. There were towns in the ancient world in which the selection of magistrates was made by drawing lots, for the power bestowed by ritually regulated chance always contains a sacred element, the sacred "fusion of opposites." Indeed, the more we reflect on this theme of Chance, the more universal it appears. In popular legend and fairy tale Chance is often invoked to "find" kings or, conversely (and the converse is always the other face of the same coin), to designate someone to undertake a difficult or perilous mission, a mission that might involve self-sacrifice for the general good — someone, in short, to assume the role of surrogate victim:

> On tira-t à la courte paille
> Pour savoir qui serait mangé

2. Jensen, *Mythes et cultes chez les peuples primitifs,* trans. M. Metzger and J. Goffinet (Paris: Payot, 1954), 77–83.

(One drew for the short straw
to know who would be eaten.)[3]

Yet is there any way of proving that the motif of Chance has its origin in the arbitrary nature of the violent resolution? There are numerous instances in which the drawing of lots so clearly supports the meaning proposed here that it is virtually impossible to doubt the connection. One such example is the Old Testament Book of Jonah. God tells Jonah to go forth and warn the people of Nineveh that their city will be destroyed if they do not repent of their ways. Hoping to evade this thankless task, the reluctant prophet embarks on a ship sailing for Tarshish:

> But the Lord sent out a great wind into the sea, and there was a mighty tempest in the sea, so that the ship was like to be broken.
>
> Then the mariners were afraid, and cried very man unto his god, and cast forth the wares that were in the ship into the sea, to lighten it of them. But Jonah was gone down into the sides of the ship; and he lay, and was fast asleep.
>
> So the shipmaster came to him, and said unto him, What meanest thou, O sleeper? Arise, call upon thy God, if so be that God will think upon us, that we perish not.
>
> And they said every one to his fellow, Come, and let us cast lots, that we may know for whose cause this evil is upon us. So they cast lots, and the lot fell upon Jonah. (Jonah 1:4–7)

The ship represents the community, the tempest the sacrificial crisis. The jettisoned cargo is the cultural system that has abandoned its distinctions. The fact that everybody calls out to his own particular god indicates a breakdown in the religious order. The floundering ship can be compared to the city of Nineveh, threatened with destruction unless its people repent. The forms may vary, but the crisis is always the same.

The passengers cast lots to determine who is responsible for the crisis. Chance can always be trusted to reveal the truth, for it reflects the will of the divinity. The lot designates Jonah, who proceeds to confess his culpability:

> Then the men were exceedingly afraid, and said unto him, Why hast thou done this? For the men knew that he fled from the presence of the Lord, because he had told them.
>
> Then they said unto him, What shall we do unto thee, that the sea may be calm unto us? for the sea wrought, and was tempestuous.

3. From "Il était un petit navire," folkloric French song. –*Ed.*

> And he said unto them, Take me up, and cast me forth into the sea; so shall the sea be calm unto you: for I know that for my sake this great tempest is upon you. (Jonah 1:10–12)

The sailors attempt to gain the shore by their own efforts; they would like to save Jonah's life. But they finally recognize the futility of their efforts, and address themselves to the Lord—even though he is Jonah's Lord and not their own:

> Wherefore they cried unto the Lord, and said, We beseech thee, O Lord, we beseech thee, let us not perish for this man's life, and lay not upon us innocent blood: for thou, O Lord, hast done as it pleased thee.
>
> So they took up Jonah, and cast him forth into the sea; and the sea ceased from her raging.
>
> Then the men feared the Lord exceedingly, and offered a sacrifice unto the Lord, and made vows. (Jonah 1:14–16)

What we see here is a reflection of the sacrificial crisis and its resolution. The victim is chosen by lot; his expulsion saves the community, as represented by the ship's crew; and a new god is acknowledged through the crew's sacrifice to the Lord whom they did not know before. Taken in isolation this story tells us little, but when seen against the backdrop of our whole discussion, each detail acquires significance.

Modern man flatly rejects the notion that Chance is the reflection of divine will. Primitive man views things differently. For him, Chance embodies all the obvious characteristics of the sacred. Now it deals violently with man, now it showers him with gifts. Indeed, what is more capricious in its favors than Chance, more susceptible to those rapid reversals of temper that are invariably associated with the gods?

The sacred nature of Chance is reflected in the practice of the lottery. In some sacrificial rites the choice of victim by means of a lottery serves to underline the relationship between Chance and generative violence. In an essay entitled "Sur le symbolisme politique: le Foyer commun," Louis Gernet cites a particularly revealing ritual, which took place in Cos during a festival dedicated to Zeus:

> The choice of victim was determined by a sort of lottery in which all the cattle, which were originally presented separately by each division of each tribe, were mixed together in a common herd. The animal ultimately selected was executed on the following day, having first been "introduced to Hestia," and undergone various rites. Immediately prior to the ritual presentation, Hestia herself receives homage in the form of an animal sacrifice.[4]

---

4. Gernet, *Anthropologie de la Grèce antique* (Paris: Maspero, 1968), 393.

Hestia, the common hearth, in all probability marked the place where the original act of communal violence was perpetrated. It seems more than likely, therefore, that the selection of the victim by lottery was meant to simulate that original violence. The selection is not made by men, but left to divine Chance, acting through violence. The mixing together of the cattle that had originally been identified by tribe or by division of tribe is particularly revealing. This deliberate confusion of distinctions, this merger into a communal togetherness, constitutes an obligatory preamble to the lottery; clearly it was introduced to reproduce the exact order of the original events. The arbitrary and violent resolution that serves as a model for the lottery takes place at the very height of the sacrificial crisis, when the distinctions delegated to the members of society by the cultural order succumb to the reciprocal violence and are merged into a communal mass.

A traditional discussion of Dionysus involves a demonstration of how he differs from Apollo or from the other gods. But is it not more urgent to show how Dionysus and Apollo share the same characteristics, why the one and the other should be called divine? Surely all the gods, despite their differences, have something in common, something from which all their distinctive qualities spring. Without such a common basis, the differences become meaningless.

Scholars of religion devote themselves to the study of gods and divinity. They should be able to provide clear and concise definitions of these concepts, but they do not. They are obliged, of course, to decide what falls within their field of study and what falls outside it, yet they leave the crucial and most decisively scientific task of *defining* their subject to uninformed public opinion. Even assuming that it is possible — or justifiable — to stretch the concept of divinity to include each and everybody's idea of the divine, the so-called science of religion can neither do without this approach nor provide a convincing defense of it.

There is no true science of religion, any more that there is a science of culture. Scholars are still disputing about which cult Greek tragedy should be ascribed to. Were the ancients correct in assigning tragedy to Dionysus, or does it rightfully belong to another god? Undoubtedly this is a genuine problem; but it is also, I think, a secondary one. Far more important, but far less discussed, is the relationship between tragedy and the divine, between the theater in general and religion.

Whether my theory proves to be true or false, it can, I believe, lay claim to being "scientific," if only because it allows for a rigorous definition of such terms as "divinity," "ritual," "rite," and "religion." Any phenomenon associated with the acts of remembering, commemorating, and perpetuating a unanimity that springs from the murder of a surrogate victim can be termed "religious."

The surrogate victim theory avoids at once the impressionism of the positivist approach and the arbitrary and "reductivist" schemata of psychoanalysis. Although this theory brings together many crucial aspects of man's experience, it offers no simple substitute for the "wondrous profusion" of the world's religious systems. Indeed, one ought perhaps to ask whether this "profusion" is really as wondrous as all that; in any case, the mechanism proposed here carries us beyond the mere cataloging of characteristics. The endless diversity of myths and rituals derives from the fact that they all seek to recollect and reproduce something they never succeed in comprehending. There is only one generative event, only one way to grasp its truth: by means of my hypothesis. On the other hand, there are innumerable ways of missing it; hence the multiplicity of religious systems. My thesis results from an eminently positive line of inquiry. I have a certain confidence in language—contrary to some modern thinkers who, at the very moment when truth becomes accessible in language, declare that language is incapable of expressing truth. This absolute distrust of language, in a period of mythic dilapidation like our own, may well serve the same purpose as the excessive confidence that prevailed before the dilapidation, when no decisive truth was in sight.

Our theory should be approached, then, as one approaches any scientific hypothesis. The reader must ask himself whether it actually takes into account all the items it claims to cover; whether it enables him to assign to primitive institutions an origin, function, and structure that cohere to one another as well as to their overall context; whether it allows him to organize and assess the vast accumulation of ethnological data, and to do so in a truly economical manner, without recourse to "exceptions" and "aberrations." Above all, he must ask himself whether this theory applies not in single, isolated instances but in every conceivable situation. Can he see the surrogate victim as that stone initially rejected by the builders, only to become the cornerstone of a whole mythic and ritualistic edifice? Or as the key that opens any religious text, revealing its innermost workings and rendering it forever accessible to the human intellect?

❧

That incoherence traditionally attributed to religious ideas seems to be particularly associated with the theme of the scapegoat. Frazer treats this subject at length; his writing is remarkable for its abundance of description and paucity of explanation. Frazer refuses to concern himself with the formidable forces at work behind religious significations, and his openly professed contempt for religious themes protects him from all unwelcome discoveries:

> The notion that we can transfer our guilt and sufferings to some other being who will bear them for us is familiar to the savage mind. It arises from a very obvious confusion between the physical and the mental, between the material and the immaterial. Because it is possible to shift a load of wood, stones, or what not, from our own back to the back of another, the savage fancies that it is equally possible to shift the burden of his pains and sorrows to another, who will suffer them in his stead. Upon this idea he acts, and the result is an endless number of very unamiable devices for palming off upon someone else the trouble which a man shrinks from bearing himself. In short, the principle of vicarious suffering is commonly understood and practiced by races who stand on a low level of social and intellectual culture.[5]

However, the disrepute in which he is held today is far from justifiable, for few scholars have labored so diligently in the field or set forth their findings with such admirable clarity. And many later writers have in effect done little more than repeat in somewhat different form Frazer's own profession of ignorance.

Anyone who tries to subvert the sacrificial principle by turning it to derision invariably becomes its unwitting accomplice. Frazer is no exception. His work contributes to the concealment of the violent impulse that lurks within the rite of sacrifice. Such phrases as "physical loads" and "bodily and mental ailments" recall nothing so much as the platitudes of second-rate theologians; and Frazer treats the act of sacrificial substitution as if it were pure fantasy, a nonphenomenon. Yet authors closer to our time have done the same and with considerably less excuse, for the Freudian notion of transference, inadequate as it is in some respects, should at least have alerted us that something vital is missing from the picture.

The modern mind still cannot bring itself to acknowledge the basic principle behind that mechanism which, in a single decisive movement, curtails reciprocal violence and imposes structure on the community. Because of this willful blindness, modern thinkers continue to see religion as an isolated, wholly fictitious phenomenon cherished only by a few backward peoples or milieus. And these same thinkers can now project upon religion alone the responsibility for a violent projection of violence that truly pertains to all societies including our own. This attitude is seen at its most flagrant in the writing of that gentleman-ethnologist Sir James

5. J. G. Frazer, *The Golden Bough,* 1 vol., abridged (New York: Macmillan, 1963), 624.

Frazer. Frazer, along with his rationalist colleagues and disciples, was perpetually engaged in a ritualistic expulsion and consummation of religion itself, which he used as a sort of scapegoat for all human thought. Frazer, like many another modern thinker, washed his hands of all the sordid acts perpetrated by religion and pronounced himself free of all taint of superstition. He was evidently unaware that this act of handwashing has long been recognized as a purely intellectual, nonpolluting equivalent of some of the most ancient customs of mankind. His writing amounts to a fanatical and superstitious dismissal of all the fanaticism and superstition he had spent the better part of a lifetime studying.

The *sacrificial* character of this misunderstanding should remind us that today, more than ever before, we will encounter resistance when we try to rid ourselves of ignorance — even though the time has come for this ignorance to yield to knowledge. This resistance is similar to what Freud calls resistance, but is far more formidable. We are not dealing with the sort of repressed desires that everyone is really eager to put on public display, but with the most tenacious myths of modernism; with everything, in short, that claims to be free of all mythical influence.

What I have said of Freud holds true for all modes of modern thought; most particularly for ethnology, to which Freud was irresistibly drawn. That ethnology is alive today, when the traditional modes of interpretation are sick unto death, is evidence of a new sacrificial crisis. This crisis is similar but not identical to previous ones. We have managed to extricate ourselves from the sacred somewhat more successfully than other societies have done, to the point of losing all memory of the generative violence; but we are now about to rediscover it. The essential violence returns to us in a spectacular manner — not only in the form of a violent history but also in the form of subversive knowledge. This crisis invites us, for the very first time, to violate the taboo that neither Heraclitus nor Euripides could ever quite manage to violate, and to expose to the light of reason the role played by violence in human society.

Part II

Triangular Desire

Chapter 3

Triangular Desire

"Mimesis" or "mimetic desire" is the single most important concept for understanding Girard's thought. His main reason for using the Greek word rather than "imitation" is that it "makes the conflictual aspect of mimesis conceivable," something not possible with the drained and feeble imitation (Girard, *Things Hidden*, 18). "Triangular Desire" is an excerpt taken from the first chapter of Girard's first book, *Deceit, Desire, and the Novel* (1-17). It includes the triangular structure of desire: self, other as mediator* (later he would switch to "model"*), and the object that the self or subject desires because he or she knows, imagines, or suspects the mediator desires it. Internal* and external* mediation (see under Model/Mediator),* rivalry, resentment, envy, and vanity are discussed in the course of Girard's argument that the romantic concept of a spontaneous desire is illusory. The only essential aspect of mimesis that Girard did not emphasize in this early analysis is the reality of mimesis as a capacity and force which operates prior to cognition and representation, although of course it becomes intertwined with representation in all the forms of human culture.* For further reading on mimesis as precognitive and prerepresentational, see *Things Hidden*, 1-23, and *"To Double Business Bound,"* 200-203, as well as the interview that constitutes the epilogue to the Reader.

"I want you to know, Sancho, that the famous Amadis of Gaul was one of the most perfect knight errants. But what am I saying, one of the most perfect? I should say the only, the first, the unique, the master and lord of all those who existed in the world.... I think... that, when a painter wants to become famous for his art he tries to imitate the originals of the best masters he knows; the same rule applies to most important jobs or exercises which

> contribute to the embellishment of republics; thus the man who wishes to be known as careful and patient should and does imitate Ulysses, in whose person and works Homer paints for us a vivid portrait of carefulness and patience, just as Virgil shows us in the person of Aeneas the valor of a pious son and the wisdom of a valiant captain; and it is understood that they depict them not as they are but as they should be, to provide an example of virtue for centuries to come. In the same way Amadis was the post, the star, the sun for brave and amorous knights, and we others who fight under the banner of love and chivalry should imitate him. Thus, my friend Sancho, I reckon that whoever imitates him best will come closest to perfect chivalry."

Don Quixote has surrendered to Amadis the individual's fundamental prerogative: he no longer chooses the objects of his own desire — Amadis must choose for him. The disciple pursues objects which are determined for him, or at least seem to be determined for him, by the model of all chivalry. We shall call this model the *mediator* of desire. Chivalric existence is the *imitation* of Amadis in the same sense that the Christian's existence is the imitation of Christ.

In most works of fiction, the characters have desires which are simpler than Don Quixote's. There is no mediator; there is only the subject and the object. When the "nature" of the object inspiring the passion is not sufficient to account for the desire, one must turn to the impassioned subject. Either his "psychology" is examined or his "liberty" invoked. But desire is always spontaneous. It can always be portrayed by a simple straight line which joins subject and object.

The straight line is present in the desire of Don Quixote, but it is not essential. The mediator is there, above that line, radiating toward both the subject and the object. The spatial metaphor which expresses this triple relationship is obviously the triangle. The object changes with each adventure but the triangle remains. The barber's basin or Master Peter's puppets replace the windmills; but Amadis is always present.

The triangle is no *Gestalt*. The real structures are intersubjective. They cannot be localized anywhere; the triangle has no reality whatever; it is a systematic metaphor, systematically pursued. Because changes in size and shape do not destroy the identity of this figure, as we will see later, the diversity as well as the unity of the works can be simultaneously illustrated. The purpose and limitations of this structural geometry may become clearer through a reference to "structural models." The triangle is a model of a sort, or rather a whole family of models. But these models are not "mechanical" like those of Claude Lévi-Strauss. They always allude to the mystery, transparent yet opaque, of human relations. All types of structural thinking assume that human reality is intelligible;

it is a *logos* and, as such, it is an incipient *logic,* or it degrades itself into a logic. It can thus be systematized, at least up to a point, however unsystematic, irrational, and chaotic it may appear even to those, or rather especially to those who operate the system. A basic contention of this essay is that the great writers apprehend intuitively and concretely, through the medium of their art, if not formally, the system in which they were first imprisoned together with their contemporaries. Literary interpretation must be systematic because it is the continuation of literature. It should formalize implicit or already half-explicit systems. To maintain that criticism will never be systematic is to maintain that it will never be real knowledge. The value of a critical thought depends not on how cleverly it manages to disguise its own systematic nature or on how many fundamental issues it manages to shirk or to dissolve but on how much literary substance it really embraces, comprehends, and makes articulate. The goal may be too ambitious but it is not outside the scope of literary criticism. It is the very essence of literary criticism. Failure to reach it should be condemned, but not the attempt. Everything else has already been done.

Don Quixote, in Cervantes's novel, is a typical example of the victim of triangular desire, but he is far from being the only one. Next to him the most affected is his squire, Sancho Panza. Some of Sancho's desires are not imitated, for example, those aroused by the sight of a piece of cheese or a goatskin of wine. But Sancho has other ambitions besides filling his stomach. Ever since he has been with Don Quixote he has been dreaming of an "island" of which he would be governor, and he wants the title of duchess for his daughter. These desires do not come spontaneously to a simple man like Sancho. It is Don Quixote who has put them into his head.

This time the suggestion is not literary, but oral. But the difference has little importance. These new desires form a new triangle of which the imaginary island, Don Quixote, and Sancho occupy the angles. Don Quixote is Sancho's mediator. The effects of triangular desire are the same in the two characters. From the moment the mediator's influence is felt, the sense of reality is lost and judgment paralyzed.

Since the mediator's influence is more profound and constant in the case of Don Quixote than in that of Sancho, romantic readers have seen in the novel little more than the contrast between Don Quixote the *idealist* and the *realist* Sancho. This contrast is real but secondary; it should not make us overlook the analogies between the two characters. Chivalric passion defines a desire *according to the Other,* opposed to this desire *according to Oneself* that most of us pride ourselves on enjoying. Don Quixote and Sancho borrow their desires from the Other in a movement which is so fundamental and primitive that they completely confuse it with the will to be Oneself.

One might object that Amadis is a fictitious person — and this we must admit, but Don Quixote is not the author of this fiction. The mediator is imaginary but not the mediation. Behind the hero's desires there is indeed the suggestion of a third person, the inventor of Amadis, the author of the chivalric romances. Cervantes's work is a long meditation on the baleful influence that the most lucid minds can exercise upon one another. Except in the realm of chivalry, Don Quixote reasons with a great deal of common sense. Nor are his favorite writers mad: perhaps they do not even take their fiction seriously. The illusion is the fruit of a bizarre marriage of two lucid consciousnesses. Chivalric literature, ever more widespread since the invention of the printing press, multiplies stupendously the chances of similar unions.

Desire according to the Other and the "seminal" function of literature are also found in the novels of Flaubert. Emma Bovary desires through the romantic heroines who fill her imagination. The second-rate books which she devoured in her youth have destroyed all her spontaneity. We must turn to Jules de Gaultier for the definition of this "bovarysm" which he reveals in almost every one of Flaubert's characters: "The same ignorance, the same inconsistency, the same absence of individual reaction seem to make them fated to obey the suggestion of an external milieu, for lack of an auto-suggestion from within." In his famous essay, entitled *Bovarysm,* Gaultier goes on to observe that in order to reach their goal, which is to "see themselves as they are not," Flaubert's heroes find a "model" for themselves and "imitate from the person they have decided to be, all that can be imitated, everything exterior, appearance, gesture, intonation, and dress."

The external aspects of imitation are the most striking; but we must above all remember that the characters of Cervantes and Flaubert are imitating, or believe they are imitating, the *desires* of models they have freely chosen. A third novelist, Stendhal, also underscores the role of suggestion and imitation in the personality of his heroes. Mathilde de la Mole finds her models in the history of her family; Julien Sorel imitates Napoleon. *The Memoirs of Saint-Helena* and *Bulletins* of the Grand Army replace the tales of chivalry and the romantic extravagances. The prince of Parma imitates Louis XIV. The young Bishop of Agde practices the benediction in front of a mirror; he mimics the old and venerable prelates whom he fears he does not sufficiently resemble.

Here history is nothing but a kind of literature; it suggests to all Stendhal's characters feelings and, especially, desires that they do not experience spontaneously. When he enters the service of the Rênal family, Julien borrows from Rousseau's *Confessions* the desire to eat at his master's table rather than at that of the servants. Stendhal uses the word "vanity" (*vanité*) to indicate all these forms of "copying" and imitating." The *vaniteux* — vain person — cannot draw his desires from his own resources; he must borrow them from others. Thus the *vaniteux* is brother to Don Quixote and Emma Bovary. And so in Stendhal we again find triangular desire.

In the first pages of *The Red and the Black* we take a walk through Verrières with the mayor of the village and his wife. Majestic but tormented, M. de Rênal strolls along his retaining walls. He wants to make Julien Sorel the tutor of his two sons, but not for their sake nor from the love of knowledge. His desire is not spontaneous. The conversation between husband and wife soon reveals the mechanism: "Valenod has no tutor for his children — he might very well steal this one from us."

Valenod is the richest and most influential man in Verrières, next to M. de Rênal himself. The mayor of Verrières always has the image of his rival before his eyes during his negotiations with old Mr. Sorel, Julien's father. He makes the latter some very favorable propositions but the sly peasant invents a brilliant reply: "We have a better offer." This time M. de Rênal is completely convinced that Valenod wishes to engage Julien and his own desire is redoubled. The ever-increasing price that the buyer is willing to pay is determined by the imaginary desire which he attributes to his rival. So there is indeed an imitation of this imaginary desire, and even a very scrupulous imitation, since everything about the desire which is copied, including its intensity, depends upon the desire which serves as model.

At the end of the novel, Julien tries to win back Mathilde de la Mole and, on the advice of the dandy Korasof, resorts to the same sort of trick as his father. He pays court to the Maréchale de Fervacques; he wishes to arouse this woman's desire and display it before Mathilde so that the idea of imitating it might suggest itself to her. A little water is enough to prime a pump; a little desire is enough to arouse desire in the creature of vanity.

Julien carries out his plan and everything turns out as expected. The interest which the Maréchale takes in him reawakens Mathilde's desire. And the triangle reappears — Mathilde, Mme. de Fervacques, Julien — M. de Rênal, Valenod, Julien. The triangle is present each time that Stendhal speaks of vanity, whether it is a question of ambition, business, or love. It is surprising that the Marxist critics, for whom economic structures provide the archetype of all human relations, have not as yet pointed out the analogy between the crafty bargaining of old man Sorel and the amorous maneuvers of his son.

A *vaniteux* will desire any object so long as he is convinced that it is already desired by another person whom he admires. The mediator here is a *rival,* brought into existence as a rival by vanity, and that same vanity demands his defeat. The rivalry between mediator and the person who desires constitutes an essential difference between this desire and that of Don Quixote, or of Emma Bovary. Amadis cannot vie with

Don Quixote in the protection of orphans in distress; he cannot slaughter giants in his place. Valenod, on the other hand, can steal the tutor from M. de Rênal; the Maréchale de Fervacques can take Julien from Mathilde de la Mole. In most of Stendhal's desires, the mediator himself desires the object, or could desire it: it is even this very desire, real or presumed, which makes this object infinitely desirable in the eyes of the subject. The mediation begets a second desire exactly the same as the mediator's. This means that one is always confronted with two *competing* desires. The mediator can no longer act his role of model without also acting or appearing to act the role of obstacle. Like the relentless sentry of the Kafka fable, the model shows his disciple the gate of paradise and forbids him to enter with one and the same gesture. We should not be surprised if the look cast by M. de Rênal on Valenod is vastly different from that raised by Don Quixote toward Amadis.

In Cervantes the mediator is enthroned in an inaccessible heaven and transmits to his faithful follower a little of his serenity. In Stendhal, this same mediator has come down to earth. The clear distinction between these two types of relationship between mediator and subject indicates the enormous spiritual gap which separates Don Quixote from the most despicably vain of Stendhal's characters. The image of the triangle cannot remain valid for us unless it at once allows this distinction and measures this gap for us. To achieve this double objective, we have only to vary the *distance,* in the triangle, separating the mediator from the desiring subject.

Obviously this distance is greatest in Cervantes. There can be no contact whatsoever between Don Quixote and his legendary Amadis. Emma Bovary is already closer to her Parisian mediator. Travelers' tales, books, and the press bring the latest fashions of the capital even to Yonville. Emma comes still closer to her mediator when she goes to the ball at the Vaubyessards'; she penetrates the holy of holies and gazes at the idol face to face. But this proximity is fleeting. Emma will never be able to desire that which the incarnations of her "ideal" desire; she will never be able to be their rival; she will never leave for Paris.

Julien Sorel does all that Emma cannot do. At the beginning of *The Red and the Black* the distance between the hero and his mediator is as great as in *Madame Bovary.* But Julien spans this distance; he leaves his province and becomes the lover of the proud Mathilde; he rises rapidly to a brilliant position. Stendhal's other heroes are also close to their mediators. It is this which distinguishes Stendhal's universe from those we have already considered. Between Julien and Mathilde, between Rênal and Valenod, between Lucien Leuwen and the nobles of Nancy, between Sansfin and the petty squires of Normandy, the distance is always small enough to permit the rivalry of desires. In the novels of Cervantes and

Flaubert, the mediator remained beyond the universe of the hero; he is now within the same universe.

Romantic works are, therefore, grouped into two fundamental categories — but within these categories there can be an infinite number of secondary distinctions. We shall speak of *external mediation* when the distance is sufficient to eliminate any contact between the two spheres of *possibilities* of which the mediator and the subject occupy the respective centers. We shall speak of *internal mediation* when this same distance is sufficiently reduced to allow these two spheres to penetrate each other more or less profoundly.

Obviously it is not physical space that measures the gap between mediator and the desiring subject. Although geographical separation might be one factor, the *distance* between mediator and subject is primarily spiritual. Don Quixote and Sancho are always close to each other physically but the social and intellectual distance which separates them remains insuperable. The valet never desires what his master desires. Sancho covets the food left by the monks, the purse of gold found on the road, and other objects which Don Quixote willingly lets him have. As for the imaginary island, it is from Don Quixote himself that Sancho is counting on receiving it, as the faithful vassal holds everything in the name of his lord. The mediation of Sancho is therefore an external mediation. No rivalry with the mediator is possible. The harmony between the two companions is never seriously troubled.

The hero of external mediation proclaims aloud the true nature of his desire. He worships his model openly and declares himself his disciple. We have seen Don Quixote himself explain to Sancho the privileged part Amadis plays in his life. Mme. Bovary and Léon also admit the truth about their desires in their lyric confessions. The parallel between *Don Quixote* and *Madame Bovary* has become classic. It is always easy to recognize analogies between two novels of external mediation.

Imitation in Stendhal's work at first seems less absurd since there is less of that divergence between the worlds of disciple and model which makes a Don Quixote or an Emma Bovary so grotesque. And yet the imitation is no less strict and literal in internal mediation than in external mediation. If this seems surprising it is not only because the imitation refers to a model who is "close," but also because the hero of internal mediation, far from boasting of his efforts to imitate, carefully hides them.

The impulse toward the object is ultimately an impulse toward the mediator; in internal mediation this impulse is checked by the mediator himself since he desires, or perhaps possesses, the object. Fascinated by his model, the disciple inevitably sees, in the mechanical obstacle which he puts in his way, proof of the ill will borne him. Far from declaring himself a faithful vassal, he thinks only of repudiating the bonds of mediation. But these bonds are stronger than ever, for the mediator's apparent hostility does not diminish his prestige but instead augments it. The subject is convinced that the model considers himself too superior to accept him as a disciple. The subject is torn between two opposite feelings toward his model—the most submissive reverence and the most intense malice. This is the passion we call *hatred.*

Only someone who prevents us from satisfying a desire which he himself has inspired in us is truly an object of hatred. The person who hates first hates himself for the secret admiration concealed by his hatred. In an effort to hide this desperate admiration from others, and from himself, he no longer wants to see in his mediator anything but an obstacle. The secondary role of the mediator thus becomes primary, concealing his original function of a model scrupulously imitated.

In the quarrel which puts him in opposition to his rival, the subject reverses the logical and chronological order of desires in order to hide his imitation. He asserts that his own desire is prior to that of his rival; according to him, it is the mediator who is responsible for the rivalry. Everything that originates with this mediator is systematically belittled, although still secretly desired. Now the mediator is a shrewd and diabolical enemy; he tries to rob the subject of his most prized possessions; he obstinately thwarts his most legitimate ambitions.

All the phenomena explored by Max Scheler in *Ressentiment*[1] are, in our opinion, the result of internal mediation. Furthermore, the word *ressentiment* itself underscores the quality of reaction, of repercussion which characterizes the experience of the subject in this type of mediation. The impassioned admiration and desire to emulate stumble over the unfair obstacle with which the model seems to block the way of his disciple, and then these passions recoil on the disciple in the form of impotent hatred, thus causing the sort of psychological self-poisoning so well described by Scheler.

As he indicates, *ressentiment* can impose its point of view on even those whom it does not dominate. It is *ressentiment* which prevents us, and sometimes prevents Scheler himself, from recognizing the part played by imitation in the birth of desire. For example, we do not see that jealousy and envy, like hatred, are scarcely more than traditional names given to internal mediation, names which almost always conceal their true nature from us.

---

1. The author quotes from the French translation, *L'Homme du Ressentiment.* There is an English translation by William H. Holdheim, *Ressentiment* (New York: Free Press, 1960). The word *ressentiment* is used by Scheler in the original German text as the most accurate term for the feeling described. –*Trans.*

Jealousy and envy imply a third presence: object, subject, and a third person toward whom the jealousy or envy is directed. These two "vices" are therefore triangular; however, we never recognize a model in the person who arouses jealousy because we always take a jealous person's attitude toward the problem of jealousy. Like all victims of internal mediation, the jealous person easily convinces himself that his desire is spontaneous, in other words, that it is deeply rooted in the object and in this object alone. As a result he always maintains that his desire preceded the intervention of the mediator. He would have us see him as an intruder, a bore, a *terzo incomodo* who interrupts a delightful tête-à-tête. Jealousy is thus reduced to the irritation we all experience when one of our desires is accidentally thwarted. But true jealousy is infinitely more profound and complex; it always contains an element of fascination with the insolent rival. Furthermore, it is always the same people who suffer from jealousy. Is it possible that they are all the victims of repeated accidents? Is it *fate* that creates for them so many rivals and throws so many obstacle in the way of their desires? We do not believe it ourselves, since we say that these chronic victims of jealousy or of envy have a "jealous temperament" or an "envious nature." What exactly then does such a "temperament" or "nature" imply if not an irresistible impulse to desire what Others desire, in other words to imitate the desires of others?

Max Scheler numbers "envy, jealousy, and rivalry" among the sources of *ressentiment.* He defines envy as "a feeling of impotence which vitiates our attempt to acquire something because it belongs to another." He observes, on the other hand, that there would be no envy, in the strong sense of the word, if the envious person's imagination did not transform into concerted opposition the passive obstacle which the possessor puts in his way by the mere fact of possession. "Mere regret at not possessing something which belongs to another and which we covet is not enough in itself to give rise to envy, since it might also be an incentive for acquiring the desired object or something similar. . . . *Envy* occurs only when our efforts to acquire it fail and we are left with a feeling of impotence."

The analysis is accurate and complete; it omits neither the envious person's self-deception with regard to the cause of his failure, nor the paralysis that accompanies envy. But these elements remain isolated; Scheler has not really perceived their relationship. On the other hand everything becomes clear, everything fits into a coherent structure if, in order to explain envy, we abandon the object of rivalry as a starting point and choose instead the rival himself, i.e., the mediator, as both a point of departure for our analysis and its conclusion. Possession is a merely passive obstacle; it is frustrating and seems a deliberate expression of contempt only because the rival is secretly revered. The demigod seems to answer homage with a curse. He seems to render evil for good. The subject would like to think of himself as the victim of an atrocious injustice but in his anguish he wonders whether perhaps he does not deserve his apparent condemnation. Rivalry therefore only aggravates mediation; it increases the mediator's prestige and strengthens the bond which links the object to this mediator by forcing him to affirm openly his right or desire of possession. Thus the subject is less capable than ever of giving up the inaccessible object: it is on this object and it alone that the mediator confers his prestige, by possessing or wanting to possess it. Other objects have no worth at all in the eyes of the envious person, even though they may be similar to or indeed identical with the "mediated" object.

Everything becomes clear when one sees that the loathed rival is actually a mediator. Max Scheler himself is not far from the truth when he states in *Ressentiment* that "the fact of choosing a model for oneself" is the result of a certain tendency, common to all men, to compare oneself with others, and he goes on to say, "all jealousy, all ambition, and even an ideal like the 'imitation' of Christ is based on such comparisons." But this intuition remains isolated. Only the great artists attribute to the mediator the position usurped by the object; only they reverse the commonly accepted hierarchy of desire.

In *The Memoirs of a Tourist,* Stendhal warns his readers against what he calls the *modern* emotions, the fruits of universal vanity: "envy, jealousy, and impotent hatred." Stendhal's formula gathers together the three triangular emotions; it considers them apart from any particular object; it associates them with that imperative need to imitate by which, according to the novelist, the nineteenth century is completely possessed. For his part, Scheler asserts, following Nietzsche — who acknowledged a large debt to Stendhal — that the romantic state of mind is pervaded by *ressentiment.* Stendhal says precisely this, but he looks for the source of this spiritual poison in the passionate imitation of individuals who are fundamentally our equals and whom we endow with an arbitrary prestige. If the *modern* emotions flourish, it is not because "envious natures" and "jealous temperaments" have unfortunately and mysteriously increased in number, but because *internal* mediation triumphs in a universe where the differences between men are gradually erased.

The great novelists reveal the imitative nature of desire. In our days its nature is hard to perceive because the most fervent imitation is the most vigorously denied. Don Quixote proclaimed himself the disciple of Amadis and the writers of his time proclaimed themselves the disciples of the Ancients. The romantic *vaniteux* does not want to be anyone's disciple. He convinces himself that he is thoroughly *original.* In the nineteenth century spontaneity becomes a universal dogma, succeeding imitation. Stendhal warns us at every step that we must not be fooled by these individualisms professed with fanfare, for they merely hide a new form of imitation. Romantic revulsion, hatred of society, nostalgia for the desert, like gregariousness, usually conceal a morbid concern for the Other.

In order to camouflage the essential role which the Other plays in his desires, Stendhal's *vaniteux* frequently appeals to the clichés of the reigning ideology. Behind the devotion, the mawkish altruism, the hypocritical *engagement* of the *grandes dames* of 1830, Stendhal finds not the generous impulse of a being truly prepared to give itself but rather the tormented recourse of vanity at bay, the centrifugal movement of an ego powerless to desire by itself. The novelist lets his characters act and speak; then, in the twinkling of an eye, he reveals to us the mediator. He reestablishes covertly the true hierarchy of desire while pretending to believe in the weak reasoning advanced by his character in support of the contrary hierarchy. This is one of the perpetual methods of Stendhal's irony.

The romantic *vaniteux* always wants to convince himself that his desire is written into the nature of things, or which amounts to the same thing, that it is the emanation of a serene subjectivity, the creation *ex nihilo* of a quasi-divine ego. Desire is no longer rooted in the object perhaps, but it is rooted in the subject; it is certainly not rooted in the Other. The objective and subjective fallacies are one and the same; both originate in the image which we all have of our own desires. Subjectivisms and objectivisms, romanticisms and realisms, individualisms and scientisms, idealisms and positivisms appear to be in opposition but are secretly in agreement to conceal the presence of the mediator. All these dogmas are the aesthetic or philosophic translation of worldviews peculiar to internal mediation. They all depend directly or indirectly on the lie of spontaneous desire. They all defend the same illusion of autonomy to which modern man is passionately devoted.

It is this same illusion which the great novel does not succeed in shattering although it never ceased to denounce it. Unlike the romantics and neo-romantics, a Cervantes, a Flaubert, and a Stendhal reveal the truth of desire in their great novels, but this truth remains hidden even at the heart of its revelation. The reader, who is usually convinced of his own spontaneity, applies to the work the meanings he already applies to the world. The nineteenth century, which failed completely to understand Cervantes, continually praised the "originality" of his hero. The romantic reader, by a marvelous misinterpretation which fundamentally is only a superior truth, identifies himself with Don Quixote, the supreme imitator, and makes of him the *model individual.*

Thus is should not surprise us that the term "romanesque"[2] still re-

2. In the French original, constant association and opposition of *romantique* and *ro-*

flects, in its ambiguity, our unawareness of all mediation. The term denotes the chivalric romances and it denotes *Don Quixote;* it can be synonymous with "romantic" and it can indicate the destruction of romantic pretensions. In the future we shall use the term "romantic" for the works which reflect the presence of a mediator without ever revealing it and the term "novelistic" for the works which reveal this presence. It is to the latter that this book is primarily devoted.

---

manesque, with their same radical and different endings, tried to convey something of an essential, yet elusive, difference between the works which passively reflect and those which actively reveal "mediated" desire. The two words are not interchangeable, to be sure, but their opposition alone is fully significant. The essay must not be read as the indictment of a narrowly, or even broadly defined literary *school.* Neither is it an effort to circumscribe the *genre* of the novel. The author is aware that *Jean Santeuil* is a novel and should be classified as such if classifications were the order of the day. *Jean Santeuil* can nevertheless be viewed as "romantic" within the context of the essay, in other words by contrast with the "romanesque" — novelistic — *Remembrance of Things Past.* Similarly, Chateaubriand's *Mémoires d'outre-Tombe* is not a novel but it partakes somewhat of the "romanesque" by contrast with the romantic *René.* Unlike the categories of literary historians, which are mechanistic and positivistic, the present categories, even though they are not Hegelian, are still dialectical. They are not independent labels stuck once and for all on a fixed amount of static and objective literary material. Neither are they literature-proof receptacles in which that same material would be contained. They have no value in themselves; no single category can be appraised separately. Oppositions are essential; their terms should not be dissociated. The whole *system* alone is truly significant and self-sufficient, in accordance with a *structural* hypothesis.

Chapter 4

Desire and the Unity of Novelistic Conclusions

This selection is the concluding chapter of *Deceit, Desire, and the Novel*. Here Girard summarizes his argument that in the best work of the great novelists such as Cervantes, Stendhal, Flaubert, Proust, and Dostoyevsky, the novelistic (nonromantic) conclusions represent conversions from the death to which rivalrous desire leads. In the great novels the authors attain a profound communion of Self and Other, intuit in their protagonists their own similarity to the Other who is a model-rival (see under Model/Mediator)* or even a model-obstacle (see under Model/Mediator),* and find liberation from the pride of romantic individualism. The climax of this conversionary discovery occurs above all in Dostoyevsky, whose *Notes from the Underground* "is the turning point between romanticism and the novel," and whose conclusion to *The Brothers Karamazov* affirms the reality of the death and resurrection to which the agnostic Proust gives literary expression in *The Past Recaptured* and *Remembrance of Things Past*.

The ultimate meaning of desire is death but death is not the novel's ultimate meaning. The demons like raving madmen throw themselves into the sea and perish. But the patient is cured. Stepan Trofimovitch on his deathbed recalls the miracle: "But the sick man will be healed and 'will sit at the feet of Jesus,' and all will look upon him with astonishment."

These words are applicable not only to Russia but to the dying man himself. Stepan Trofimovitch is this sick man who is healed in death and whom death heals. Stepan let himself be carried away by the wave of scandal, murder, and crime which engulfed the town. His flight has its roots in the universal madness but as soon as it is undertaken its significance changes—it is transformed into a return to the mother earth and to the light of day. His roaming finally leads the old man to a wretched bed in an inn where a Gospel woman reads him the words of St. Luke. The dying man sees the truth in the parable of the swine of Gerasa. Out of supreme disorder is born supernatural order.

The closer Stepan comes to death, the more he withdraws from lying: "I've been telling lies all my life. Even when I told the truth I never spoke for the sake of the truth, but always for my own sake. I knew it before, but I only see it now." In these words Stepan *clearly contradicts his former ideas.*

The apocalypse would not be complete without a positive side. There are two antithetical deaths in the conclusion of *The Possessed:* one death which is an extinction of the spirit and one death which is spirit; Stavrogin's death is only death, Stepan's death is life. This double ending is not unusual in Dostoyevsky. We find it in *The Brothers Karamazov* where the madness of Ivan Karamazov is contrasted with the redeeming conversion of Dmitri. We find it in *Crime and Punishment* where Svidrigailov's suicide is contrasted with the redeeming conversion of Raskolnikov. The Gospel woman who watches at Stepan's bedside plays a similar role to Sonia's though less pronounced. She is the mediator between the sinner and the Scriptures.

Raskolnikov and Dmitri Karamazov do not die a physical death but they are nonetheless restored to life. All Dostoyevsky's conclusions are fresh beginnings; a new life commences, either among men or in eternity.

But perhaps it would be better not to push this analysis any further. Many critics refuse to accept Dostoyevsky's religious conclusions. They find them artificial, ill-considered, and superficially imposed on the novel. The novelist is supposed to have written them when he ran out of novelistic inspiration, in order to give his work an appearance of religious orthodoxy.

So let us leave Dostoyevsky and turn to the conclusions of other novels, such as *Don Quixote.* The hero's death is very like that of Stepan Trofimovitch. His passion for chivalry is portrayed as an actual possession of which the dying man sees himself fortunately, though somewhat belatedly, delivered. The clarity of vision that he regains enables Don Quixote, like Stepan Trofimovitch, to reject his former existence.

> At this time my judgment is free and clear and no longer covered with a thick blanket of ignorance woven by my sad and constant reading of detestable books of chivalry. I recognize their extravagance and trickery. My only regret is that my disillusionment has come too late and that I do not have time to make up for my mistake by reading other books which would help to enlighten my soul.

The Spanish *desengaño* has the same meaning as Dostoyevsky's conversion. But again there are many writers who advise us not to dwell on this conversion in death. The conclusion of *Don Quixote* is almost as unappreciated as Dostoyevsky's conclusions, and strangely enough the same faults are found in it. It is considered artificial, conventional, and superimposed on the novel. Why should two such great novelists both consider it proper to disfigure the final pages of their masterpieces? As we have seen, Dostoyevsky is considered the victim of self-imposed censure. The Inquisition was hostile to books of chivalry. The critics remain convinced that *Don Quixote* is a book of chivalry. Cervantes therefore was obliged to write a "conformist" conclusion which would allay ecclesiastical suspicions.

Let us then leave Cervantes, if we must, and turn to a third novelist. Stendhal was not a Slavophile and had no reason to fear the church, at least during the period when he wrote *The Red and the Black*. But the conclusion of that novel is nevertheless a third *conversion in death*. Julien also utters words which *clearly contradict* his former ideas. He repudiates his will to power, he makes a break with the world which fascinated him; his passion for Mathilde disappears; he flies to Mme. de Rênal and refuses to defend himself.

All these analogies are remarkable. But again we are asked not to attach any importance to this conversion in death. Even the author, who seems ashamed of his own lyricism, conspires with the critics to discredit his own text. He tells us we should not take Julien's meditations seriously for "the lack of exercise was beginning to affect his health and give him the exalted and weak character of a young German student."

Let Stendhal say what he likes. We can no longer be put off the scent. If we are still blind to the unity displayed in novelistic conclusions, the unanimous hostility of romantic critics should be enough to open our eyes.

It is the hypotheses of the critics that are insignificant and artificial, not the conclusions. One would have to have little esteem for Cervantes to think him capable of betraying his own thought. The hypothesis of self-censure is not even worth discussing, for the beauty of the text alone is enough to demolish it. The solemn adjuration of the dying Don Quixote is addressed to us, the readers, just as much as to his friends and relatives gathered about him: "In the extremity which I have reached I must not make light of my soul."

It is easy to understand the hostility of the romantic critics. All the heroes, in the conclusion, utter words which *clearly contradict their former ideas,* and those ideas are always shared by the romantic critics. Don Quixote renounces his knights, Julien Sorel his revolt, and Raskolnikov his superhumanity. Each time the hero denies the fantasy inspired by his pride. And it is that fantasy which the romantic interpretation always exalts. The critics do not want to admit that they have been mistaken; thus they have to maintain that the conclusion is unworthy of the work it crowns.

The analogies between the conclusions of the great novels destroy *ipso facto* all interpretations that minimize their importance. There is a single phenomenon and it must be accounted for by one principle.

The unity of novelistic conclusions consists in the renunciation of metaphysical desire. The dying hero repudiates his mediator: "I am the enemy of Amadis of Gaul and of all the infinite battalions of his kind.... Today, through God's mercy, having been made wise at my own expense, I loathe them."

Repudiation of the mediator implies renunciation of divinity, and this means renouncing pride. The physical diminution of the hero both expresses and conceals the defeat of pride. One sentence with a double meaning in *The Red and the Black* expresses beautifully the link between death and liberation, between the guillotine and the break with the mediator: "What do *Others* matter to me," exclaims Julien Sorel, "my relations with others are going to be abruptly cut off."

In renouncing divinity the hero renounces slavery. Every level of his existence is inverted, all the effects of metaphysical desire are replaced by contrary effects. Deception gives way to truth, anguish to remembrance, agitation to repose, hatred to love, humiliation to humility, mediated desire to autonomy, deviated transcendency to vertical transcendency.

This time it is not a false but a genuine conversion. The hero triumphs in defeat; he triumphs because he is at the end of his resources; for the first time he has to look his despair and his nothingness in the face. But this look which he has dreaded, which is the death of pride, is his salvation. The conclusions of all the novels are reminiscent of an oriental tale in which the hero is clinging by his finger-tips to the edge of a cliff; exhausted, the hero finally lets himself fall into the abyss. He expects to smash against the rocks below but instead he is supported by the air: the law of gravity is annulled.

All novelistic conclusions are conversions; it is impossible to doubt this. But can one go further? Can one maintain that all these conversions have the same meaning? Two fundamental categories seem to be distinguishable from the outset: those conclusions which portray a solitary hero who rejoins other men and those which portray a "gregarious" hero gaining solitude. Dostoyevsky's novels belong to the first category, Stendhal's to the second. Raskolnikov rejects solitude and embraces Others, Julien Sorel rejects Others and embraces solitude.

The opposition seems insurmountable. Yet it is not. If our interpretation of the conversion is correct, if it puts an end to triangular desire, then its effects cannot be expressed either in terms of absolute solitude or in terms of a return to the world. Metaphysical desire brings into being a certain relationship to others and to oneself. True conversion engenders a new relationship to others and to oneself. The mechanical oppositions of solitude and gregariousness, involvement and noninvolvement are the result of romantic interpretations.

If we examine Stendhal's and Dostoyevsky's conclusions more closely we find that the two aspects of true conversion are always present but that they are not equally developed. Stendhal places more emphasis on the subjective aspect and Dostoyevsky more on the intersubjective aspect. The neglected aspect is never completely suppressed. Julien wins solitude but he triumphs over isolation. His happiness with Mme. de Rênal is the supreme expression of a profound change in his relationship with Others. When the hero finds himself surrounded by a crowd at the beginning of his trial, he is surprised to find that he no longer feels his old hatred for Others. He wonders whether Others are as bad as he once thought them. When he no longer envies people, when he no longer wishes to seduce or dominate them, then Julien no longer hates them.

Similarly Raskolnikov, in the conclusion, triumphs over his isolation but he also gains solitude. He reads the Gospel; he recovers the peace which has so long escaped him. Solitude and human contact exist only as functions of each other; they cannot be isolated without lapsing into romantic abstraction.

The differences between novelistic conclusions are negligible. It is less a question of opposition than of a shift of accent. The lack of balance between the various aspects of the metaphysical cure reveal that the novelist has not rid himself entirely of his own "romanticism"; he remains the prisoner of formulas whose function of pure justification he does not perceive. Dostoyevsky's conclusions are not completely purified of the tendency to wallow in misery. In Stendhal's conclusions can be found traces of the middle-class romanticism which was rampant in the Delécluze salon. In the process of underlining these *differences* it is easy to lose sight of the unity of novelistic conclusions. The critics ask no better, for unity in their languages means banality, and banality is the worst charge of all. If the critics do not reject the conclusion outright, they try to prove that it is *original,* that it contradicts the conclusions of other novels. They always trace the author back to his romantic origins. They think they are doing his work a good service. And this is doubtless true according to the romantic taste of the educated public. But on a more profound level they are doing it a disservice. They are exalting that in it which is contrary to novelistic truth.

Romantic criticism rejects what is essential; it refuses to go beyond metaphysical desire to the truth of the novel which shines beyond death. The hero succumbs as he achieves truth and he entrusts his creator with the heritage of his clairvoyance. The title of hero of a novel must be reserved for the character who triumphs over metaphysical desire in a tragic conclusion and thus becomes *capable of writing the novel.* The hero and his creator are separated throughout the novel but come together in the conclusion. Approaching death, the hero looks back on his lost existence. He sees it with the "breadth and depth of vision" which suffering, sickness, and exile gave to Mme. de Clèves and which is that of the novelist himself. This "breadth and depth of vision" is not so different from the "telescope" mentioned by Marcel Proust in *The Past Recaptured,* and from the supereminent position which Stendhal's hero attains in his prison. All these images of distance and elevation are the expression of a new and more detached vision, which is the creator's own vision. This ascending movement must not be confused with pride. The aesthetic triumph of the author is one with the joy of the hero who has renounced desire.

Therefore the conclusion is always a memory. It is the eruption of a memory which is more true than the perception itself. It is a "panoramic vision" like Anna Karenina's. It is a "revivification of the past." The expression is Proust's but he is not speaking of *The Past Recaptured,* as one would immediately imagine, but of *The Red and the Black.* The inspiration always comes from memory and memory springs from the conclusion. Every novelistic conclusion is a beginning.

Every novelistic conclusion is a *Past Recaptured.*

Marcel Proust in his own conclusion merely uncovered a meaning that had previously been hidden by a transparent veil of fiction. The narrator of *Remembrance of Things Past* makes his way to the novel through the novel. But all the heroes of previous novels did the same. Stepan Trofimovitch moves toward the Gospel which summarizes the meaning of *The Possessed.* Mme. de Clèves moves toward the "breadth and depth of vision," that is, toward novelistic vision. Don Quixote, Julien Sorel, and Raskolnikov have the same spiritual experience as Marcel in *The Past Recaptured.* Proust's aesthetics do not consist of a number of formulas and percepts; they are indissolubly united with the escape from metaphysical desire. All of the characteristics of novelistic conclusions mentioned above may be found in *The Past Recaptured,* but here they are represented as exigencies of creation. The novel's inspiration springs from the break with the mediator. The absence of desire in the present makes it possible to recapture past desires.

In *The Past Recaptured* Proust emphasizes that *self-centeredness* is a barrier to novelistic creation. Proustian self-centeredness gives rise to *imitation* and makes us live *outside ourselves.* This self-centeredness is other-centeredness as well; it is not one-sided egotism; it is an impulse in two contradictory directions which always ends by tearing the individual apart. To triumph over self-centeredness is to get away from oneself and make contact with others, but in another sense it also imposes a greater intimacy with oneself and a withdrawal from others. A self-centered person thinks he is choosing himself but in fact he shuts himself out as much as others. Victory over self-centeredness allows us to probe deeply into the Self and at the same time yields a better knowledge of Others. At a certain depth there is no difference between our own secret and the secret of Others. Everything is revealed to the novelist when he penetrates this Self, a truer Self than that which each of us displays. This Self imitates constantly, on its knees before the mediator.

This profound Self is also a universal Self. The dialectic of metaphysical pride alone can help us understand and accept Proust's attempt to reconcile the particular and universal. In the context of the romantic's mechanical opposition between Self and Others, such an attempt would be absurd.

This logical absurdity no doubt struck Proust, and he occasionally gives up his attempt at reconciliation and slips back into the clichés of twentieth-century romanticism. In a few isolated passages of *The Past Recaptured* he declares that the work of art must permit us to grasp our "differences" and makes us delight in our "originality."

These scattered passages are the result of Proust's lack of theoretic vocabulary. But the attempt at logical coherence is quickly swept away by inspiration. Proust knew that in describing his own youth he was describing ours as well. He knew that the true artist no longer has to choose between himself and Others. Because it is born of renunciation, great novelistic art loses nothing and regains everything.

But this renunciation is very painful. The novelist can write his novel only if he recognizes that *his* mediator is a person like himself. Marcel, for example, has to give up considering his beloved a monstrous divinity and seeing himself in the role of an eternal victim. He has to recognize that his beloved's lies are similar to his own.

This victory over a self-centeredness which is other-centered, this renunciation of fascination and hatred, is the crowning moment of novelistic creation. Therefore it can be found in all the great novelists. Every novelist sees his similarity to the fascinating Other *through the voice of his hero.* Mme. de la Fayette recognizes her similarity to the women for whom love has been their undoing. Stendhal, the enemy of hypocrites, recognizes at the end of *The Red and the Black* that he is also a hypocrite. Dostoyevsky, in the conclusion of *Crime and Punishment,* gives up seeing himself alternately as a superhuman and as a subhuman. The novelist recognizes that he is guilty of the sin of which he is accusing his mediator. The curse which Oedipus hurls at Others falls on his own head.

This is the meaning of Flaubert's famous cry: "Mme Bovary, c'est moi!" Flaubert first conceived Mme. Bovary as that despicable Other whom he had sworn to deal with. Mme. Bovary originally was Flaubert's enemy, as Julien Sorel was Stendhal's enemy and Raskolnikov Dostoyevsky's enemy. But while remaining that Other, the hero of the novel gradually merges with the novelist in the course of creation. When Flaubert cries, "Mme Bovary, c'est moi," he is not trying to say that Mme. Bovary has become one of those flattering doubles with whom romantic writers love to surround themselves. He means that the Self and the Other have become one in the miracle of the novel.

Great novels always spring from an obsession that has been transcended. The hero sees himself in the rival he loathes; he renounces the "differences" suggested by hatred. He learns, at the expense of his pride, the existence of the psychological circle. The novelist's self-examination merges with the morbid attention he pays to his mediator. All the powers of a mind freed of its contradictions unite in one creative impulse. Don Quixote and Emma Bovary and Charlus would not be so great were they not the result of a synthesis of the two halves of existence which pride usually succeeds in keeping separate.

This victory over desire is extremely painful. Proust tells us that we must forego the fervent dialogue endlessly carried on by each one of us at the superficial levels of our being. One must "give up one's dearest illusions." The novelist's art is a phenomenological *epochē*. But the only authentic *epochē* is never mentioned by modern philosophers; it is always victory over desire, victory over Promethean pride.

Some texts written shortly before Marcel Proust's great creative period throw a brilliant light on the connection between *The Past Recaptured* and classical novelistic conclusions. Perhaps the most important of them is an article published in *Le Figaro* in 1907 entitled "The Filial Sentiments of a Parricide." The article is devoted to the drama of a family whom the Prousts knew slightly. Henri Van Blarenberghe had killed himself after murdering his mother. Proust gives a short account of this double tragedy concerning which he seems to have no special information. At the conclusion there is a widening of the perspective and the tone becomes more personal. The Van Blarenberghe affair becomes a symbol of the mother-son relationship in general. The vices and ingratitude of children make their parents age prematurely. This theme is already present in the conclusion of *Jean Santeuil*. After describing in his article how terribly decrepit a mother, worn-out by suffering, seems to her son, Proust writes:

> Perhaps women who could see that, *in that belated moment of lucidity which may occur even in lives completely obsessed by illusions, since it happened even to Don Quixote,* perhaps that someone, like Henri Van Blarenberghe after he stabbed his mother to death, would recoil from the horror of his life and snatch up a

> gun, in order to put an immediate end to his existence. [Emphasis added.]

The parricide recovers his lucidity in the course of expiating crime, and expiates his crime in the course of recovering his lucidity. His terrifying vision of the past is a vision of truth; it stands in direct opposition to his life "obsessed by illusions." The "Oedipal" atmosphere of these lines is quite striking. It is the year 1907, Proust has just lost his mother and is obsessed with remorse. In this brief paragraph we are given a glimpse of the process which enables a Stendhal, Flaubert, Tolstoy, or Dostoyevsky to give expression to his experience as a man and a writer in an ordinary news item.

In his "belated moment of lucidity" the parricide joins the ranks of all the heroes of previous novels. How can we deny this *when Proust himself compares this death to that of Don Quixote?* "The Filial Sentiments of a Parricide" provides the missing link between classical conclusions and *The Past Recaptured.* This attempt will have no immediate sequel. Proust will discard the classical method of transposition in the novel. His hero will not kill himself; rather he will become a novelist. But nevertheless the inspiration will come from death, that death which Proust is in the process of living in 1907, and whose horror is reflected in all his writing of that period.

Is this giving too much importance to a few forgotten lines? Perhaps it will be objected that the text has no literary value, that it is written in a hurry for a daily newspaper, and that its conclusion wallows in melodramatic clichés. That may be, but such considerations carry little weight in the face of Proust's own evidence. In a letter of Calmette, which accompanied the article, Proust gave *Le Figaro* full permission to edit and cut his text — except for the last paragraphs, which he demanded should be published in their entirety.

The allusion to Don Quixote's belated lucidity is all the more precious since it reappears in the notes which were published in an appendix to *Contre Sainte-Beuve,* and this time in a purely literary context. The many comments on Stendhal, Flaubert, Tolstoy, George Eliot, and Dostoyevsky in these same notes show us Proust's awareness of the unity of novelistic genius. Proust notes that all Dostoyevsky's and Flaubert's works could be entitled *Crime and Punishment.* The principle of the unity of all the great works is clearly stated in the chapter on Balzac: "All the writers come together at certain points and they seem like different and sometimes contradictory elements of a single genius."

There can be no question that Proust was aware of the connection between *The Past Recaptured* and the classical novelistic conclusions. He could have written the one book on the unity of novelistic genius which would have been worthy of such a great topic.

Under the circumstances it is surprising that Proust never broached the theme of novelistic unity in his own conclusion, *The Past Recaptured,* which broadens into a meditation on novelistic creation. His silence on the topic of other novels is all the more surprising when we consider the number of literary references he makes. He acknowledges forerunners of the "affective memory" in Jean-Jacques Rousseau, Chateaubriand, and Gérard de Nerval. But he does not mention a single novelist. The intuitions of *Contre Sainte-Beuve* are never taken up and developed. What happened?

In Proust, as in all persons who experience a very intense and solitary spiritual experience, the fear of appearing extravagant is superseded only by that of seeming ridiculous by repeating universally accepted truths. The wish to avoid both of these opposite dangers would seem to have suggested to Proust the compromise he finally adopted. Fearing that he would be accused on the one hand of leaving the royal paths of literature, and on the other of plagiarizing the great novels, Proust picks out some literary ancestors but scrupulously avoids the novelists.

Proust, we know, lived only for his work. Léon-Pierre Quint has demonstrated the forces he could marshal in the art of literary strategy. This final "idolatry" does not blemish the perfection of *The Past Recaptured,* but it somewhat limits its universality. The author of *Remembrance of Things Past* is not interested in indicating similarities of structure among the great novels. He is afraid of putting his critics on a track that would lead to too many discoveries. He knows the importance given to *originality* in his time, and he is afraid of having some of his literary glory taken from him. He emphasizes and brings into relief the most "original" elements of his novel's revelation, especially the affective memory which we discover upon examination to play a much less central role in the works which precede *The Past Recaptured* than that assigned to it in this final novel.[1]

What explanation other than "literary strategy" can be given for Proust's silence? How are we to explain the omission, in his reflections of the art of the novel, of Stendhal's conclusion whose every characteristic we had pointed out in his *Contre Sainte-Beuve,* characteristics which can be found in *The Past Recaptured:* "An exclusive taste for sensations of the soul, revivification of the past, detachment from ambition and lack of interest in intrigue." How can we not be impressed by the fact that Proust is the only one to have seen the part played by memory in

1. We are far from seeing in that central position given to the affective memory a "fault" of the novelist or a betrayal of the original experience. This position is justified by reasons of economy in the novel. We wish only to note that Proust managed to combine very cleverly the superior demands of revelation in the novel with the practical demands of "literary strategy."

Julien's death, and that he perceived this role at the very moment he was preparing to write *The Past Recaptured?*

Proust was also very interested, at the same time and in that same conclusion, in the visit paid to Julien by the Abbé Chélan, very much weakened by age. "The weakening of a great intelligence and a great heart linked to that of the body. The old age of a virtuous man: moral pessimism." Julien's lucid death stands out marvelously against the background of this slow and terrible decomposition of the flesh.

Again the attention given by Proust to this episode is not disinterested. He builds the whole of *The Past Recaptured* on a similar contrast between two antithetical deaths. The hero is lucid when he dies to be reborn in the work, but around him people continue to die without hope of resurrection. The spiritually fertile death of the narrator is contrasted with the cruel spectacle of the Guermantes's soirée with the horrible and useless aging of the members of high society. This contrast is already to be found in "The Filial Sentiments of a Parricide," but from now on it gains its classically novelistic meaning and achieves unity with the Dostoyevskian apocalypse. In fact we must see in *The Red and the Black* and *The Past Recaptured* the two inseparable and opposed faces of the novelistic apocalypse as they were first revealed in the work of Dostoyevsky. In all genuine novelistic conclusions death as spirit is victoriously opposed to death of the spirit.

Are we being carried away by our imagination? To dispel any doubts we will introduce a final witness in favor of the unity of novelistic conclusions: Balzac. This novelist has not been included in our group, but his creative experience is just as close in certain points to those which we have been considering. For proof of these analogies we need only look at the following passage taken from the conclusion of *Cousin Pons.* Balzac is describing his hero's death and in doing so he defines the double face of the novelistic apocalypse:

> Ancient and modern sculptors have often placed on either side of the tomb genies holding flaming torches. These flames illuminate for the dying their faults, their errors, as they light up the paths of Death. Sculpture there represents great ideas, it formulates a human fact. Death has its wisdom. Often simple girls, at a very tender age, are found to have the wisdom of old men, become prophets, judge their family and not be taken in by any deception. This is the poetry of Death! But it is a strange thing and should be noticed that one dies in two different ways. This poetry of prophecy, this gift of penetration, whether before or after, is only found in those who are merely dying in the flesh, who are dying through the destruction of the organs of carnal life. Thus people suffering, like Louis XIV, from gangrene, consump-

> tion, people who die of fever like Pons, or of a stomach ailment like Mme de Mortsauf, enjoy this sublime lucidity, and achieve amazing and admirable deaths; whereas people who die of intellectual sicknesses, as it were, where the trouble is in the brain, in the nervous system which serves as an intermediary for the body to provide it with the brain's fuel; these die in entirety. In them, body and mind founder together. The first, souls without bodies, become biblical spirits; the others are corpses. This virgin, this unascetic Cato, [Pons, the hero] this just and almost innocent man eventually penetrated the pockets of gall which made up the heart of the magistrate's wife. He understood the world as he was about to leave it. Several hours before he had resigned himself to the inevitable, like a joyful artist for whom everything is a pretext for caricature and raillery. The last ties binding him to life, the chains of admiration, the powerful knots which link the connoisseur to the masterpieces of art had been broken in the morning. When he saw that he had been robbed by the Cibot woman he made a Christian farewell to the pomp and vanity of art.

We must not begin from reality as we see it and subject novelistic creation to the standards of this vision. In this conclusion, historical figures like Louis XIV are put side by side with fictional creation like Pons and Mme. de Mortsauf. Behind the veil of pseudo-physiology, as elsewhere beneath phrenology, Martinism, or magnetism, Balzac is incessantly telling us about his novelistic experience. Here in a few sentences he sums up the essential characteristics of the novelistic conclusion: the double face of death, the role of suffering, the detachment of passion, the Christian symbolism, and that *sublime lucidity* which is both memory and prophecy, and which throws an equal light on the soul of the hero and the soul of the other characters.

In Balzac, as in Cervantes, Stendhal, and Dostoyevsky, the tragic event expresses the advent of a new vision, the novelist's vision. This is why Balzac compares the dying man's state of soul to that of a "joyful artist." The conclusion of *Cousin Pons* is a *Past Recaptured.*

It is easy to prove the unity of novelistic conclusions if we compare texts. But in theory, at least, this last proof is not necessary. Our analyses inevitably lead to the message unanimously proclaimed by all the great conclusions. When he renounces the deceptive divinity of pride, the hero frees himself from slavery and finally grasps the truth about his unhappiness. There is no distinction between this renunciation and the creative renunciation. It is a victory over metaphysical desire that transforms a romantic writer into a true novelist.

Up to this point this truth had only been hinted at, but at last we have reached it; we can grasp and possess it here in the last pages of the novel. All we needed was the author's permission, and this we now have: "I loathe Amadis of Gaul and all the infinite number of his kind." The novelists themselves, through the medium of their heroes, confirm what we have been asserting all the way through this book: the sickness is rooted in pride and the universe of the novel is a universe of people possessed. The conclusion is the stationary axle around which the wheel of the novel turns. The whole kaleidoscope of appearances depends on it. The conclusion of novels is also the conclusion of our present investigation.

Truth is active throughout the great novel but its primary location is in the conclusion. The conclusion is the temple of that truth. The conclusion is the site of the presence of truth, and therefore a place avoided by error. If error cannot destroy the unity of novelistic conclusions it tries to render it powerless. It attempts to sterilize it by calling it a *banality*. We should not deny that banality but loudly proclaim it. In the body of the novel, novelistic unity is mediate, but it becomes immediate in the conclusion. Novelistic conclusions are bound to be banal since they all quite literally repeat the same thing.

This banality of novelistic conclusions is not the local and relative banality of what used to be considered "original" and could again be given oblivion followed by a "rediscovery" and a "rehabilitation." It is the absolute banality of what is essential in Western civilization. The novelistic dénouement is a reconciliation between the individual and the world, between man and the sacred. The multiple universe of passion decomposes and returns to simplicity. Novelistic conversion calls to mind the *analusis* of the Greeks and the Christian rebirth. In this final moment the novelist reaches the heights of Western literature; he merges with the great religious ethics and the most elevated forms of humanism, those which have chosen the least accessible part of man.

The theme of reconciliation has been so constantly harped on by unworthy authors that it is easy to become convinced, in this time given to indignation and scandal, that it never did and never could have any concrete content. It seems to emanate from the most superficial areas of novelistic consciousness. To put reconciliation in its proper perspective we must look on it as the conquest of a possibility that has long been denied the writer. The conclusion must be considered as a successful effort to overcome the inability to conclude. The criticism of Maurice Blanchot can help us in this task. Maurice Blanchot portrays Franz Kafka as the exemplary representative of a literature doomed to inconclusiveness. Like Moses, Kafka's hero will never see the promised land. This inability to conclude, Blanchot tells us, is an inability to die in the work and to free oneself in death.

The impossible conclusion defines a "literary space" which is not beyond but this side of reconciliation. The fact that this space is the only one accessible to our own time of anguish is disquieting but not surprising to anyone who bears in mind the evolution of the structure of the novel. The fact would not have surprised Dostoyevsky, who has already given us characters doomed to inconclusiveness and was traversing Maurice Blanchot's "literary space" at the time he wrote *Notes from the Underground*. This story, like so many of Kafka's and those of writers after Kafka, has no conclusion:

> The notes of this paradoxialist do not end here, however. He could not refrain from going on with them, but it seems to us that we may stop here.

Notes from the Underground is the turning point between romanticism and the novel, between the preceding inauthentic reconciliations and the authentic reconciliations which follow. The great novelists cross the literary space defined by Blanchot but they do not stay there. They push beyond that space toward the infinity of a liberating death.

In contrast to the incompleteness of the contemporary narrative, an incompletion which in the best writers reflects not a passing fashion but a particular historical and metaphysical situation, the conclusion of the novelistic work embodies not only a historical but an individual possibility finally and triumphantly actualized.

The great novelistic conclusions are banal but they are not conventional. Their lack of rhetorical ability, even their clumsiness, constitute their true beauty and clearly distinguish them from the deceptive reconciliations which abound in second-rate literature. Conversion in death should not seem to us the easy solution but rather an almost miraculous descent of novelistic grace.

The truly great novels are all born of that supreme moment and return to it the way a church radiates from the chancel and returns to it. All the great works are composed like cathedrals: once again the truth of *Remembrance of Things Past* is the truth of all the great novels.

We carry within us a whole hierarchy of the superficial and the profound, the essential and the subordinate, and we apply it instinctively to the novel. This hierarchy, which is often "romantic" and "individualist" in character, conceals from us certain essential aspects of artistic creation. For example, we are in the habit of never taking Christian symbolism seriously, perhaps because it is common to many works both mediocre and sublime. We attribute a purely decorative function to the symbolism when the author is not a Christian, and a purely apologetic function when he is a Christian. Truly "scientific" criticism would discard all these a priori judgments and would note the amazing points of similarity among all the different novelistic conclusions. If only our prejudices *pro* and *con* did not erect a watertight barrier between aesthetic experience and religious experience, we would see the problems of creation in a new light. We would not cut off Dostoyevsky's work from all its religious meditations. In *The Brothers Karamazov,* for example, we would discover texts as important for the study of novelistic creation as those of *The Past Recaptured.* And we would at last realize that Christian symbolism is universal, for it alone is able to give form to the experience of the novel.

We must therefore look at this symbolism from the point of view of the novel. The task is all the more difficult since the author himself sometimes tries to throw us off the scent. Stendhal attributes Julien Sorel's "German mysticism" to the extreme dampness of his prison cell. But the conclusion of *The Red and the Black* remains a meditation on Christian themes and symbols. In it the novelist reaffirms his skepticism, but the themes and symbols are nonetheless present in order to be clothed in negations. They play exactly the same role as in Proust or Dostoyevsky. We shall see everything which touches on these themes, including the monastic vocation of Stendhal's heroes, in a fresh light which the author's irony cannot hide from us.

Here, as before, we must interpret the novelists by comparing them to one another. We should not treat the religious question externally but if possible look on it as a purely novelistic problem. The question of Christianity in Stendhal, the question of "mysticism" in Proust and in Dostoyevsky can be understood only through comparisons.

"If the seed does not die after it has been sown, it will remain alone, but if it dies it will bear much fruit." The verse from St. John reappears in several crucial episodes of *The Brothers Karamazov.* It expresses the mysterious connections between the two deaths in the novel, the link between the prison and Dmitri's spiritual healing, the link between the mortal sickness and the redeeming confession of the "unknown visitor," the link between Ilusha's death and the charitable work of Alyosha.

Proust has recourse to the same verse from the Gospel of St. John when he wants to explain to us the part played by sickness, that younger sister of death, in his own creation. "When sickness, like a harsh spiritual director, caused me to die to the social world, it did me a good service for if the seed does not die after it is sown it will remain alone and will not bear much fruit."

Mme. de la Fayette too could have quoted St. John, for one finds in *The Princess of Clèves* the sickness of Proust's narrator. This sickness comes at the same point in the novel's development as in Proust and has exactly the same spiritual consequences: "The necessity of dying, which she saw was very near, made her used to detachment and the length of her illness made it a habit.... Worldly passions and activities appeared to her in the same way as to people who have broader and deeper vision." This *breadth and depth of vision* belongs to the new being who is literally born of the death.

The verse from St. John serves as an epigraph for *The Brothers Karamazov,* and it could serve as an epigraph for all novelistic conclusions. Repudiation of a human mediator and renunciation of deviated transcendency inevitably call for symbols of vertical transcendency whether the author is Christian or not. All the great novelists respond to this fundamental appeal, but sometimes they manage to hide from themselves the meaning of their response. Stendhal uses irony. Proust masks the true face of novelistic experience with romantic commonplaces but he gives the stale symbols a profound and secret brilliance. In his work symbols of immortality and resurrection appear in a purely aesthetic context and only surreptitiously do they transcend the banal meaning to which romanticism reduces them. They are not operetta princes; they are true princes disguised as operetta princes.

These symbols make their appearance long before *The Past Recaptured,* in all the passages which are both an echo and annunciation of the original experience. One of these passages is devoted to the death and funeral of the great writer Bergotte:

> They buried him, but all through the night of mourning, in the lighted windows, his books arranged three by three kept watch like angels with outspread wings and seemed, for him who was no more, the symbol of his resurrection.

Bergotte is famous and Proust obviously is thinking of his posthumous glory, to that *consolatrice affreusement laurée* which so irritated Valéry. But this romantic cliché is no more than a pretext in this passage: it is merely an excuse to introduce the word "resurrection," without disturbing the external positive and "realist" order. The death and resurrection of Bergotte foreshadow the death and resurrection of the author himself, the second birth from which *Remembrance of Things Past* springs. The true resonance of the sentence just quoted is derived from the expectance of that resurrection. Along with the images of deviated transcendency we can discern the outlines of the symbolism of vertical transcendency. Contrasted with the demoniacal idols who drag the narrator down into the abyss are angels with outspread wings. We must interpret this symbolism in the light of *The Past Recaptured:* "The greatness of Proust," André Malraux correctly notes, "became evident when the publication of *The Past Recaptured* revealed the significance of a literary achievement which, up to that point, did not seem to surpass that of Dickens."

It was *The Past Recaptured,* to be sure, which gave Proust's creation its meaning, but other novelistic conclusions contributed to that meaning as well. *The Brothers Karamazov* makes it impossible for us to consider the resurrection of Bergotte simply a romantic commonplace. And in the same way, *The Past Recaptured,* which Proust first entitled *Perpetual Adoration,* makes it impossible for us to see in the religious meditations of *The Brothers Karamazov* merely religious propaganda, external to the novel itself. If Dostoyevsky suffered so much while writing those pages it is not because he found it a boring task but because he considered them of prime importance.

In the second part of *The Brothers Karamazov* little Ilusha dies for the sake of all the heroes of Dostoyevsky's novels, and the communion which springs from that death is Balzac's and Proust's *sublime lucidity* shared by many. The structure of crime and redeeming punishment transcends the solitary consciousness. Never did a novelist make such a radical break with romantic and Promethean individualism.

The conclusion of *The Brothers Karamazov* is borne on the highest crest of Dostoyevsky's genius. The last distinctions between novelistic and religious experience are abolished. But the structure of experience has not changed. It is easy to recognize in the words " memory," "death," "love" and "resurrection" found in the mouths of the children of this novel the themes and symbols that inspired the creative ardor of the agnostic author of *The Past Recaptured:*

> "We love you, we love you!" they all caught it up.
>
> There were tears in the eyes of many of them.
>
> "Hurrah for Karamazov!" Kolya shouted ecstatically.
>
> "And may the dear boy's memory live for ever!" Alyosha added again with feeling.
>
> "For ever!" the boys chimed in again.
>
> "Karamazov," cried Kolya, "can it be true what's taught us in religion, that we shall all rise again from the dead and shall live and see each other again, all, Ilusha too?"
>
> "Certainly we shall all rise again, certainly we shall see each other and shall tell each other with joy and gladness all that has happened!" Alyosha answered, half laughing, half enthusiastic.

Chapter 5

The Goodness of Mimetic Desire

This is an excerpt from an interview of Girard conducted by Rebecca Adams in November of 1992 and published as "Violence, Difference, Sacrifice: A Conversation with René Girard" in *Religion and Literature* 25, no. 2 (1993): 9-33. This selection is taken from pages 22-26. It is important as one of Girard's recent clarifications that mimetic desire is good in itself; it is the basis of love even though it often—and inevitably in terms of the history of the human race—takes destructive forms. It cannot be renounced by the Christian because what Jesus advocates is imitation of himself just as he imitates God the Father. This clarification is found also in *Quand ces choses commenceront . . . Entretiens avec Michel Treguer* (Paris: arléa, 1994), 70-71, 76.

— ❧ —

Rebecca Adams: Let's go on with some more theological implications of your arguments. At the end of *Things Hidden,* then, you make the statement that to follow Christ means to "give up" or renounce mimetic desire, yet the hominization section implies that mimetic desire is the only kind of desire there is. There seems to be a covert suspicion, throughout the theory, of real agency. The theory of mimetic desire itself seems to entail an — again, almost Augustinian — idea of the bondage of the will. Freedom of the will is an illusion which must be renounced. But in your thought, it's not even as if we once had real agency before the "fall," as Calvin, for instance, believed.

René Girard: No, that impression is not true. I believe in freedom of the will. Jesus says that scandals must happen, and he tells his disciples that they will all be scandalized when he is arrested; but at the same time he says: happy are those to whom I will not be a scandal. So there are nevertheless a few who are not scandalized. That scandals must happen might sound like determinism, but it is not.

RA: So are you saying that mimesis, imitation and the violence it engenders, is extremely seductive and powerful like a current in a river, but it is not as if a person cannot resist it?

R.G.: Even if persons cannot resist it, they can convert away from it.

R.A.: But again, that's the idea of renunciation of the will, isn't it?

R.G.: The idea of renunciation has, no doubt, been overdone by the Puritans and the Jansenists, but the blanket hostility that now prevails against it is even worse. The idea that renunciation in all its forms should be renounced once and for all may well be the most flagrant nonsense any human culture has ever devised. But as to whether I am advocating "renunciation" of mimetic desire, yes and no. Not the renunciation of mimetic desire itself, because what Jesus advocates *is* mimetic desire. Imitate me, and imitate the father through me, he says, so it's twice mimetic. Jesus seems to say that the only way to avoid violence is to imitate me, and imitate the Father. So the idea that mimetic desire itself is bad makes no sense. It is true, however, that occasionally I say "mimetic desire" when I really mean only the type of mimetic desire that generates mimetic rivalry and, in turn, is generated by it.

R.A.: This is an important clarification. It seems that it wouldn't make sense, in light of your theory itself, to say mimetic desire should be renounced, because mimetic desire is itself a *pharmakon* — a medicine or a poison. The claim at the end of *Things Hidden* that to "give up" or renounce mimetic desire is what we must do is, I think, particularly misleading in this regard. Perhaps mimetic desire per se is not to be done away with, but is to be fulfilled — transformed, "converted."

R.G.: A simple renunciation of desire I don't think is Christian; it's more Buddhist. Undoubtedly there are similarities between what I am saying and Buddhism. If you read the descriptions of Buddhism, they are very profound; they are very aware of mimetic desire, and of contagion, and of all the things that matter in human relations. Like all great religious writing. The thing that is unique about Christianity is that it wants to go back to the origin, to the sacrificial origin, and uncover it. Buddhism is not interested in doing this at all. And Buddhism advocates getting out of the world altogether. Christianity never does that. Christianity says, the Cross will be there for you, inevitably. But that kind of renunciation is very different.

R.A.: What you are advocating, actually, is not renunciation of desire but imitation of a positive model. St. Paul, too, says "imitate me." He also says, think upon these *positive* things, the fruits of the spirit: love, joy, peace, and so forth. In his book *The Peace of the Present: An Unviolent Way of Life,* John S. Dunne has a short section in which he has an exchange with you over this issue of desire. His concept of "heart's desire" seems initially to be very similar to what you mean when speaking of "imitating" Christ; if the heart's desire is indeed mimetic, in other words, it would express itself in imitating Christ, or God through Christ. But Dunne doesn't talk about desire in mimetic terms. He speaks as if we have an active, positive agency to desire the good, the capacity and choice to desire nonviolently.

R.G.: But I would say that mimetic desire, even when bad, is intrinsically good, in the sense that far from being merely imitative in a small sense, it's the opening out of oneself.

R.A.: Openness to others.

R.G.: Yes. Extreme openness. It is everything. It can be murderous, it is rivalrous; but it is also the basis of heroism, and devotion to others, and everything.

R.A.: And love for others and wanting to imitate them in a good sense?

R.G.: Yes, of course. And the fact that novelists and playwrights, and that primitive religion, are inevitably concerned with rivalry — conflictual mimetic desire, which is always in the way and is a huge problem for living together — doesn't mean it is the only thing there is. Now writers are what I would call "hypermimetic," which cannot be considered necessarily pathological. Literature shifts into hypermimeticism, and therefore writers are obsessed with bad, conflictual mimetic desire, and that's what they write about — that's what literature is about. I agree with Gide that literature is about evil. That doesn't mean evil is the whole of life. I hear this question all the time: "Is all desire mimetic?" Not in the bad, conflictual sense. Nothing is more mimetic than the desire of a child, and yet it is good. Jesus himself says it is good. Mimetic desire is also the desire for God.

R.A.: For those who would not a priori accept a religious framework, nor a concept of the "imitation of Christ" as you employ it, it might be understood also as the desire for love, for creativity, for community.

R.G.: Cultural imitation is a positive form of mimetic desire.

R.A.: In *Saints and Postmodernism: Revisioning Moral Philosophy,* Edith Wyschogrod, a contemporary moral philosopher, talks about excessive desire on behalf of the Other as the basis for ethics: desiring for the other because of the otherness of the other. Note how this would look in terms of mimetic desire. Positive mimetic desire works out to recapitulate the Golden Rule: we desire for the other *what the other desires for her or himself.* This kind of desire is therefore neither colonialist, nor does it scapegoat. Wyschogrod calls for a new postmodern sainthood based on this excessive desire and the genuine valuing of difference. I guess I'm wondering whether it's possible within your theory to fully account for this desire on behalf of the Other — for nonviolent, saintly desire — as an excess of desire rather than as a renunciation of desire.

R.G.: Your question makes sense to me, and more so these days since I no longer hesitate to talk about theology. Wherever you have that desire, I would say, that really active, positive desire for the other, there is some kind of divine grace present. This is what Christianity unquestionably tells us. If we deny this we move into some form of optimistic humanism.

R.A.: Divine grace is present, you would say, whether or not it is recognized as such?

R.G.: Whether or not it is recognized as such.

Part III

Sacrifice

Chapter 6

Sacrifice as Sacral Violence and Substitution

Mimetic desire may be contained and routed through the differences of language and culture if these are effectively conveyed in religious and cultural traditions. It may lead to human redemption if the mimesis is a conversionary, non-violent imitation of divine love (see chapter 5 and chapters 11 and 12). Cultural traditions stem from the disorder, the actual or potential violence that is experienced when mimetic desire gets out of hand and the hominids in the process of becoming human, which includes a sense of community, tradition, symbolic universe, etc., discover that convergence upon a victim brings them unanimity and thus relief from violence. (See chapter 1 of this Reader and *Things Hidden*, book 1, esp. pp. 84-104.) Both sacrifice and rituals of scapegoating represent, in camouflaged form, the disorder resulting in the originary violence of immolation or expulsion of the victim and the order stemming from the newly found relief from conflict and violence. This disorder and order are the function of the *double transference* (see under Scapegoat/Scapegoating)* of the scapegoat* effect: those involved in the collective violence transfer the disorder and the offenses producing it to the victim, but they transfer also their newly found peace to the victim, ascribing to him or her the power that brings it about. From this double transfer Girard hypothesizes the origin of the gods and kingship (see "A Note to the Reader" and the concluding interview).

Sacrifice, the act of making the offered victim or object sacred (note Latin *sacrificare*), is thus sacred violence. In this selection from *Violence and the Sacred*, 1-18, 39-44, Girard focuses on sacrifice as sacred violence in relation to its essential elements and other aspects of given cultural systems: substitution, particularly of an animal for a human victim; the cultural necessity of *méconnaissance*; the role of vengeance; the primitive character of sacrifice as compared to the emergence of judicial systems; and the sacrificial crisis that occurs when sacrifice fails to perform one of its main functions, which is to distinguish or maintain the distinction between "good" and "bad" violence. As for *méconnaissance*, it is translated in this text as "misunderstanding," but it has the connotation of unconscious distortion and concealment in ritual and myth (see under Scapegoat/Scapegoating).* In the context of Girard's research it often connotes "delusion," and has been translated as such in some of his writings. As delusion it would be a cultural assumption concealing a generative mechanism (see Scapegoat Mechanism under Scapegoat)* which is blind or extremely resistant to ordinary reason.

It should be noted that already in *Violence and the Sacred* Girard recognized and indicated that sacrifice is not simply violence; it is violence that is limited for the sake of achieving or maintaining order. But in recent years he has become much more positive about sacrifice and the use of the adjective "sacrificial." It is not only that the violence underlying institutions and rituals* of sacrifice is preferable to the alternative of widespread violence, but that the vision of nonsacrificial and nonviolent relationships must be understood and held in tension with the sacrificial context out of which the vision arises. To forget or dismiss this fact of our biblical and postbiblical traditions is to be doomed to repeat it in some new guise. In keeping with the tension between the empirical and historical grounding of sacrifice and the revealing of a new way in the biblical prophets, especially the Suffering Servant in Isaiah 52-53, and Jesus Christ in the Gospels, he affirms a positive, derived sense of "sacrificial" as the willingness to give of oneself to others and to commit oneself to God, not for sadomasochistic purposes (i.e., to inflict injury on others or oneself, ostensibly for the sake of faith*), but out of love and faithfulness to the other. See the citations in the introduction to chapter 5; also Girard, "Mimetische Theorie und Theologie," in *Vom Fluch und Segen der Sündenböcke: Raymund Schwager zum 60. Geburtstag*, ed. J. Niewiadomski and W. Palaver (Thaur, Austria: Kulturverlag, 1995), 15-29.

— ❧ —

In many rituals the sacrificial act assumes two opposing aspects, appearing at times as a sacred obligation to be neglected at grave peril, at other times as a sort of criminal activity entailing perils of equal gravity.

To account for this dual aspect of ritual sacrifice — the legitimate and the illegitimate, the public and the all but covert — Henri Hubert and Marcel Mauss, in their "Essay on the Nature and Function of Sacrifice,"[1] adduce the sacred character of the victim. Because the victim is sacred, it is criminal to kill him — but the victim is sacred only because he is to be killed. Here is a circular line of reasoning that at a somewhat later date would be dignified by the sonorous term *ambivalence*. Persuasive and authoritative as that term still appears, it has been so extraordinarily abused in our century that perhaps we may now recognize how little light it sheds on the subject of sacrifice. Certainly it provides no real explanation. When we speak of ambivalence, we are only pointing out a problem that remains to be solved.

If sacrifice resembles criminal violence, we may say that there is, inversely, hardly any form of violence that cannot be described in terms of sacrifice — as Greek tragedy clearly reveals. It has often been observed that the tragic poets cast a glimmering veil of rhetoric over the sordid realities of life. True enough — but sacrifice and murder would not lend themselves to this game of reciprocal substitution if they were not in some way related. Although it is so obvious that it may hardly seem worth mentioning, where sacrifice is concerned first appearances count for little, are quickly brushed aside — and should therefore receive special attention. Once one has made up one's mind that sacrifice is an institution essentially if not entirely symbolic, one can say anything whatsoever about it. It is a subject that lends itself to insubstantial theorizing.

Sacrifice contains an element of mystery. And if the pieties of classical humanists lull our curiosity to sleep, the company of the ancient authors keeps it alert. The ancient mystery remains as impenetrable as ever. From the manner in which the moderns treat the subject of sacrifice, it would be hard to know whether distraction, detachment, or some sort of secret discretion shapes their thinking. There seems to be yet another mystery here. Why, for example, do we never explore the relationship between sacrifice and violence?

Recent studies suggest that the physiology of violence varies little from one individual to another, even from one culture to another. According to Anthony Storr, nothing resembles an angry cat or man so much as another angry cat or man.[2] If violence did indeed play a role

1. Henri Hubert and Marcel Mauss, *Sacrifice: Its Nature and Function* (Chicago: University of Chicago Press, 1968).

2. Anthony Storr, *Human Aggression* (New York: Bantam Books, 1968).

in sacrifice, at least at one particular stage of the ritual, we would have a significant clue to the whole subject. Here would be a factor to some extent independent of those cultural variables that are often unknown to us, or only dimly known, or perhaps less familiar than we like to think.

Once aroused, the urge to violence triggers certain physical changes that prepare men's bodies for battle. This set toward violence lingers on; it should not be regarded as a simple reflex that ceases with the removal of the initial stimulus. Storr remarks that it is more difficult to quell an impulse toward violence than to rouse it, especially within the normal framework of social behavior.

Violence is frequently called irrational. It has its reasons, however, and can marshall some rather convincing ones when the need arises. Yet these reasons cannot be taken seriously, no matter how valid they may appear. Violence itself will discard them if the initial object remains persistently out of reach and continues to provoke hostility. When unappeased, violence seeks and always finds a surrogate victim. The creature that excited its fury is abruptly replaced by another, chosen only because it is vulnerable and close at hand.

There are many indications that this tendency to seek out surrogate objects is not limited to human violence. Konrad Lorenz makes reference to a species of fish that, if deprived of its natural enemies (the male rivals with whom it habitually disputes territorial rights), turns its aggression against the members of its own family and destroys them.[3] Joseph de Maistre discusses the choice of animal victims that display human characteristics—an attempt, as it were, to deceive the violent impulse: "The sacrificial animals were always those most prized for their usefulness: the gentlest, most innocent creatures, whose habits and instincts brought them most closely into harmony with man.... From the animal realm were chosen as victims those who were, if we might use the phrase, the most *human* nature."[4]

Modern ethnology offers many examples of this sort of intuitive behavior. In some pastoral communities where sacrifice is practiced, the cattle are intimately associated with the daily life of the inhabitants. Two peoples of the Upper Nile, for example—the Nuer, observed by E. E. Evans-Pritchard, and the Dinka, studied at a somewhat later date by Godfrey Lienhardt—maintain a bovine society in their midst that parallels their own and is structured in the same fashion.[5]

The Nuer vocabulary is rich in words describing the ways of cattle

3. Konrad Lorenz, *On Aggression,* trans. Marjorie Kerr Wilson (New York: Harcourt Brace Jovanovich, 1966).

4. Joseph de Maistre, "Eclaircissement sur les sacrifices," in *Les Soirées de Saint-Pétersbourg* (Lyons, 1890), 2:341–42. Here, and throughout the book, translations are by Patrick Gregory unless an English-language reference is cited.

5. E. E. Evans-Pritchard, *The Nuer* (Oxford: Oxford University Press, 1940); God-

and covering the economic and practical, as well as the poetic and ritualistic, aspects of these beasts. This wealth of expression makes possible a precise and finely nuanced relationship between the cattle, on the one hand, and the human community on the other. The animals' color, the shape of their horns, their age, sex, and lineage are all duly noted and remembered, sometimes as far back as five generations. The cattle are thereby differentiated in such a way as to create a scale of values that approximates human distinctions and represents a virtual duplicate of human society. Among the names bestowed on each man is one that also belongs to the animal whose place in the herd is most similar to the place the man occupies in the tribe.

The quarrels between various subgroups of the tribes frequently involve cattle. All fines and interest payments are computed in terms of head of cattle, and dowries are apportioned in herds. In fact, Evans-Pritchard maintains that in order to understand the Nuer, one must "*chercher la vache*" — "look to the cows." A sort of "symbiosis" (the term is also Evans-Pritchard's) exists between this tribe and their cattle, offering an extreme and almost grotesque example of the closeness that characteristically prevails between pastoral peoples and their flocks.

Fieldwork and subsequent theoretical speculation lead us back to the hypothesis of substitution as the basis for the practice of sacrifice. This notion pervades ancient literature on the subject — which may be one reason, in fact, why many modern theorists reject the concept out of hand or give it only scant attention. Hubert and Mauss, for instance, view the idea with suspicion, undoubtedly because they feel that it introduces into the discussion religious and moral values that are incompatible with true scientific inquiry. And to be sure, Joseph de Maistre takes the view that the ritual victim is an "innocent" creature who pays a debt for the "guilty" party. I propose a hypothesis that does away with this moral distinction. As I see it, the relationship between the potential victim and the actual victim cannot be defined in terms of innocence or guilt. There is no question of "expiation." Rather, society is seeking to deflect upon a relatively indifferent victim, a "sacrificeable" victim, the violence that would otherwise be vented on its own members, the people it most desires to protect.

The qualities that lend violence its particular terror — its blind brutality, the fundamental absurdity of its manifestations — have a reverse side. With these qualities goes the strange propensity to seize upon surrogate victims, to actually conspire with the enemy and at the right moment toss him a morsel that will serve to satisfy his raging hunger. The fairy tales of childhood in which the wolf, ogre, or dragon gobbles

frey Lienhardt, *Divinity and Experience: The Religion of the Dinka* (Oxford: Oxford University Press, 1961).

up a large stone in place of a small child could well be said to have a sacrificial cast.

Violence is not to be denied, but it can be diverted to another object, something it can sink its teeth into. Such, perhaps, is one of the meanings of the story of Cain and Abel. The Bible offers us no background on the two brothers except the bare fact that Cain is a tiller of the soil who gives the fruits of his labor to God, whereas Abel is a shepherd who regularly sacrifices the first-born of his herds. One of the brothers kills the other, and the murderer is the one who does not have the violence-outlet of animal sacrifice at his disposal. This difference between sacrificial and nonsacrificial cults determines, in effect, God's judgment in favor of Abel. To say that God accedes to Abel's sacrificial offerings but rejects the offerings of Cain is simply another way of saying — from the viewpoint of the divinity — that Cain is a murderer, whereas his brother is not.

A frequent motif in the Old Testament, as well as in Greek myth, is that of brothers at odds with one another. Their fatal penchant for violence can only be diverted by the intervention of a third party, the sacrificial victim or victims. Cain's "jealousy" of his brother is only another term for his one characteristic trait: his lack of a sacrificial outlet.

According to Moslem tradition, God delivered to Abraham the ram previously sacrificed by Abel. This ram was to take the place of Abraham's son Isaac; having already saved one human life, the same animal would now save another. What we have here is no mystical hocus-pocus, but an intuitive insight into the essential function of sacrifice, gleaned exclusively from the scant references in the Bible.

Another familiar biblical scene takes on new meaning in the light of our theory of sacrificial substitution, and it can serve in turn to illuminate some aspects of the theory. The scene is that in which Jacob receives the blessing of his father Isaac.

Isaac is an old man. He senses the approach of death and summons his elder son, Esau, on whom he intends to bestow his final blessing. First, however, he instructs Esau to bring back some venison from the hunt, so as to make a "savory meat." This request is overheard by the younger brother, Jacob, who hastens to report it to his mother, Rebekah. Rebekah takes two kids from the family flock, slaughters them, and prepares the savory meat dish, which Jacob, in the guise of his elder brother, then presents to his father.

Isaac is blind. Nevertheless Jacob fears he will be recognized, for he is a "smooth man," while his brother Esau is a "hairy man." "My father peradventure will feel me, and I shall seem to him as a deceiver; and

I shall bring a curse upon me, not a blessing." Rebekah has the idea of covering Jacob's hands and the back of his neck with the skins of the slaughtered goats, and when the old man runs his hands over his younger son, he is completely taken in by the imposture. Jacob receives the blessing that Isaac had intended for Esau.

The kids served in two different ways to dupe the father — or, in other terms, to divert from the son the violence directed toward him. In order to receive his father's blessing rather than his curse, Jacob must present to Isaac the freshly slaughtered kids made into a "savory meat." Then the son must seek refuge, literally, in the skins of the sacrificed animals. The animals thus interpose themselves between father and son. The serve as a sort of insulation, preventing the direct contact that could lead only to violence.

Two sorts of substitution are telescoped here: that of one brother for another, and that of an animal for a man. Only the first receives explicit recognition in the text; however, this first one serves as the screen upon which the shadow of the second is projected.

Once we have focused attention on the sacrificial victim, the object originally singled out for violence fades from view. Sacrificial substitution implies a degree of misunderstanding. Its vitality as an institution depends on its ability to conceal the displacement upon which the rite is based. It must never lose sight entirely, however, of the original object, or cease to be aware of the act of transference from that object to the surrogate victim; without that awareness no substitution can take place and the sacrifice loses all efficacy. The biblical passage discussed above meets both requirements. The narrative does not refer directly to the strange deception underlying the sacrificial substitution, nor does it allow this deception to pass entirely unnoticed. Rather, it mixes the act of substitution with another act of substitution, permitting us a fleeting, sidelong glimpse of the process. The narrative itself, then, might be said to partake of a sacrificial quality; it claims to reveal one act of substitution while employing this first substitution to half-conceal another. There is reason to believe that the narrative touches upon the mythic origins of the sacrificial system.

The figure of Jacob has long been linked with the devious character of sacrificial violence. In Greek culture Odysseus plays a similar role. The story of Jacob's benediction can be compared to the episode of the Cyclops in the *Odyssey,* where a splendidly executed ruse enables the hero to escape the clutches of a monster.

Odysseus and his shipmates are shut up in the Cyclops' cave. Every day the giant devours one of the crew; the survivors finally manage to blind their tormentor with a flaming stake. Mad with pain and anger, the Cyclops bars the entrance of the cave to prevent the men from escaping. However, he lets pass his flock of sheep, which go out daily to pasture. In a gesture reminiscent of the blind Isaac, the Cyclops runs his hands over the back of each sheep as it leaves the cave to make sure that it carries no passenger. Odysseus, however, has outwitted his captor, and he rides to freedom by clinging to the thick wool on the underside of one of the rams.

A comparison of the two scenes, one from Genesis and the other from the *Odyssey,* lends credence to the theory of their sacrificial origins. In each case an animal intervenes at the crucial moment to prevent violence from attaining its designated victim. The two texts are mutually revealing: the Cyclops of the *Odyssey* underlines the fearful menace that hangs over the hero (and that remains obscure in the Genesis story); and the slaughter of the kids in Genesis, along with the offering of the "savory meat," clearly implies the sacrificial character of the flock, an aspect that might go unnoticed in the *Odyssey.*

❧

Sacrifice has often been described as an act of mediation between a sacrificer and a "deity." Because the very concept of a deity, much less a deity who receives blood sacrifices, has little reality in this day and age, the entire institution of sacrifice is relegated by most modern theorists to the realm of the imagination. The approach of Hubert and Mauss leads to the judgment of Claude Lévi-Strauss in *La Pensée sauvage:* because sacrificial rites have no basis in reality, we have every reason to label them meaningless.

The attempt to link sacrifice to a nonexistent deity brings to mind Paul Valéry's description of poetry as a purely solipsistic activity practiced by the more able solely out of love for art, while the less able persist in the belief that they are actually communicating with someone!

The two ancient narratives examined above make unmistakable reference to the act of sacrifice, but neither makes so much as a passing mention of a deity. If a god had intervened in either incident, its significance would have been diminished rather than increased, and the reader would have been led to conclude, in accordance with the beliefs common to late antiquity and to the modern world, that sacrifice has no real function in society. Divine intervention would have meant the elimination of the pervasive aura of dread, along with its firmly structured economy of violence. We would have then been thrown back upon a formalistic critical approach that would in no way further our understanding.

As we have seen, the sacrificial process requires a certain degree of *misunderstanding*. The celebrants do not and must not comprehend the true role of the sacrificial act. The theological basis of the sacrifice has a crucial role in fostering this misunderstanding. It is the god who supposedly demands the victims; he alone, in principle, who savors the smoke from the altars and requisitions the slaughtered flesh. It is to appease his anger that the killing goes on, that the victims multiply. Interpreters who think they question the primacy of the divine sufficiently by declaring the whole affair "imaginary" may well remain the prisoners of the theology they have not really analyzed. The problem then becomes, how can a real institution be constructed on a purely illusory basis? It is not astonishing that the illusion finally makes it give way, bringing down with it even the most solid aspects of the institution.

Instead of rejecting the theological basis outright, qua abstraction (which is the same, in effect, as passively accepting it), let us expose its assumptions to a critical examination. Let us try to uncover the societal conflicts that the sacrificial act and its theological interpretations at once dissimulate and appease. We must break with the formalistic tradition of Hubert and Mauss.

The interpretation of sacrifice as an act of violence inflicted on a surrogate victim has recently been advanced once again. Godfrey Lienhardt (in *Divinity and Experience*) and Victor Turner (in a number of works, especially *The Drums of Affliction*), drawing from fieldwork, portray sacrifice as practiced among the Dinka and the Ndembu as a deliberate act of collective substitution performed at the expense of the victim and absorbing all the internal tensions, feuds, and rivalries pent up within the community.

Sacrifice plays a very real role in these societies, and the problem of substitution concerns the entire community. The victim is not a substitution for some particularly endangered individual, nor is it offered up to some individual of particularly bloodthirsty temperament. Rather, it is a substitute for all the members of the community, offered up by the members themselves. The sacrifice serves to protect the entire community from *its own* violence; it prompts the entire community to choose victims outside itself. The elements of dissension scattered throughout the community are drawn to the person of the sacrificial victim and eliminated, at least temporarily, by its sacrifice.

If we turn our attention from the theological superstructure of the act — that is, from an interpretive version of the event that is often accepted as the final statement on sacrifice — we quickly perceive yet another level of religious discourse, in theory subordinated to the theological dimension, but in reality quite independent of it. This has to do with the social function of the act, an aspect far more accessible to the modern mind.

It is easy to ridicule a religion by concentrating on its more eccentric rites, rites such as the sacrifices performed to induce rain or bring fine weather. There is in fact no object or endeavor in whose name a sacrifice cannot be made, especially when the social basis of the act has begun to blur. Nevertheless, there is a common denominator that determines the efficacy of all sacrifices and that becomes increasingly apparent as the institution grows in vigor. This common denominator is internal violence — all the dissensions, rivalries, jealousies, and quarrels within the community that the sacrifices are designed to suppress. The purpose of the sacrifice is to restore harmony to the community, to reinforce the social fabric. Everything else derives from that. If once we take this fundamental approach to sacrifice, choosing the road that violence opens before us, we can see that there is no aspect of human existence foreign to the subject, not even material prosperity. When men no longer live in harmony with one another, the sun still shines and the rain falls, to be sure, but the fields are less well tended, the harvests less abundant.

The classic literature of China explicitly acknowledges that propitiatory function of sacrificial rites. Such practices "pacify the country and make the people settled.... It is through the sacrifices that the unity of the people is strengthened" (CH'U YU II, 2). The *Book of Rites* affirms that sacrificial ceremonies, music, punishments, and laws have one and the same end: to unite society and establish order.[6]

In attempting to formulate the fundamental principles of sacrifice without reference to the ritualistic framework in which the sacrifice takes place, we run the risk of appearing simplistic. Such an effort smacks strongly of "psychologizing." Clearly, it would be inexact to compare the sacrificial act to the spontaneous gesture of the man who kicks his dog because he dares not kick his wife or boss. However, there are Greek myths that are hardly more than colossal variants of such gestures. Such a one is the story of Ajax. Furious at the leaders of the Greek army, who refused to award him Achilles' weapons, Ajax slaughters the herd of sheep intended as provisions for the army. In his mad rage he mistakes these gentle creatures for the warriors on whom he means to vent his rage. The slaughtered animals belong to a species traditionally utilized by the Greeks for sacrificial purposes; but because the massacre takes place outside the ritual framework, Ajax is taken for a madman. The myth is not, strictly speaking, about the sacrificial process; but it is certainly not irrelevant to it. The institution of sacrifice is based on effects analogous to those produced by Ajax's anger — but structured, channeled, and held in check by fixed laws.

In the ritualistic societies most familiar to us — those of the Jews and of the Greeks of the classical age — the sacrificial victims are almost always animals. However, there are other societies in which human victims are substituted for the individuals who are threatened by violence.

Even in fifth-century Greece — the Athens of the great tragedians — human sacrifice had not, it seems, completely disappeared. The practice

6. A. R. Radcliffe-Brown, *Structure and Function in Primitive Society* (Glencoe, Ill.: Free Press, 1952), 158.

was perpetuated in the form of the *pharmakos,* maintained by the city at its own expense and slaughtered at the appointed festivals as well as at a moment of civic disaster. If examined closely for traces of human sacrifice, Greek tragedy offers some remarkable revelations. It is clear, for example, that the story of Medea parallels that of Ajax on the sacrificial level, although here we are dealing with human rather than animal sacrifice. In Euripides' *Medea* the principle of human substitution of one victim for another appears in its most savage form. Frightened by the intensity of Medea's rage against her faithless husband, Jason, the nurse begs the children's tutor to keep his charges out of their mother's way:

> I am sure her anger will not subside until it has found a victim. Let us pray that the victim is at least one of our enemies.[7]

Because the object of her hatred is out of reach, Medea substitutes her own children. It is difficult for us to see anything resembling a religious act in Medea's insane behavior. Nonetheless, infanticide has its place among ritualistic practices; the practice is too well documented in too many cultures (including the Jewish and the ancient Greek) for us to exclude it from consideration here. Medea's crime is to ritual infanticide what the massacre of the sheep in the *Ajax* is to animal sacrifice. Medea prepares for the death of her children like a priest preparing for a sacrifice. Before the fateful act, she issues the traditional ritual announcement: all those whose presence might in any way hinder the effectiveness of the ceremony are requested to remove themselves from the premises.

Medea, like Ajax, reminds us of a fundamental truth about violence; if left unappeased, violence will accumulate until it overflows its confines and floods the surrounding area. The role of sacrifice is to stem this rising tide of indiscriminate substitutions and redirect violence into "proper" channels.

Ajax has details that underline the close relationship between the sacrificial substitution of animals and of humans. Before he sets upon the flock of sheep, Ajax momentarily contemplates the sacrifice of his own son. The boy's mother does not take this threat lightly; she whisks the child away.

In a general study of sacrifice there is little reason to differentiate between human and animal victims. When the principle of the substitution is *physical resemblance* between the vicarious victim and its prototypes, the mere fact that both victims are human beings seems to suffice. Thus, it is hardly surprising that in some societies whole categories of human

---

7. Here, and throughout the book, quotations from the Greek plays have been translated by Patrick Gregory, from the original Greek.

beings are systematically reserved for sacrificial purposes in order to protect other categories.

I do not mean to minimize the gap that exists between the societies that practice human sacrifice and those that do not. However, this gap should not prevent us from perceiving what they have in common. Strictly speaking, there is no essential difference between animal sacrifice and human sacrifice, and in many cases one is substituted for the other. Our tendency to insist on differences that have little reality when discussing the institution of sacrifice — our reluctance, for example, to equate animal with human sacrifice — is undoubtedly a factor in the extraordinary misunderstandings that still persist in that area of human culture.

This reluctance to consider all forms of sacrifice as a single phenomenon is nothing new. Joseph de Maistre, having defined the principle of sacrificial substitution, makes the bold and wholly unsubstantiated assertion that this principle does not apply to human sacrifice. One cannot, he insists, kill a man to save a man. Yet this assertion is repeatedly contradicted by Greek tragedy, implicitly in a play like *Medea,* and explicitly elsewhere in Euripides.

In Euripides' *Electra,* Clytemnestra explains that the sacrifice of her daughter Iphigenia would have been justified if it had been performed to save human lives. The tragedian thus enlightens us, by way of Clytemnestra, on the "normal" function of human sacrifice — the function de Maistre had refused to acknowledge. If, says Clytemnestra, Agamemnon had permitted his daughter to die:

> ...in order to prevent the sack of the city, to help his home, to rescue his children, sacrificing one to save the others, I could then have pardoned him. But for the sake of brazen Helen!...

Without ever expressly excluding the subject of human sacrifice from their research — and indeed, on what grounds could they do so? — modern scholars, notably Hubert and Mauss, mention it but rarely in their theoretical discussions. On the other hand, the scholars who do concern themselves with human sacrifice tend to concentrate on it to the exclusion of everything else, dwelling at length on the "sadistic" or "barbarous" aspects of the custom. Here, again, one particular form of sacrifice is isolated from the subject as a whole.

This dividing of sacrifice into two categories, human and animal, has itself a sacrificial character, in a strictly ritualistic sense. The division is based in effect on a value judgment, on the preconception that one category of victim — the human being — is quite unsuitable for sacrificial purposes, while another category — the animal — is eminently sacrificeable. We encounter here a survival of the sacrificial mode of thinking that perpetuates a misunderstanding about the institution as a whole.

It is not a question of rejecting the value judgment on which this misunderstanding is based, but of putting it, so to speak, in a parentheses, of recognizing that as far as the institution is concerned, such judgments are purely arbitrary. All reduction into categories, whether implicit or explicit, must be avoided; all victims, animal or human, must be treated in the same fashion if we wish to apprehend the criteria by which victims are selected (if indeed such criteria exist) and discover (if such a thing is possible) a universal principle for their selection.

We have remarked that all victims, even the animal ones, bear a certain *resemblance* to the object they replace; otherwise the violent impulse would remain unsatisfied. But this resemblance must not be carried to the extreme of complete assimilation, or it would lead to disastrous confusion. In the case of animal victims the difference is always clear, and no such confusion is possible. Although they do their best to empathize with their cattle, the Nuer never quite manage to mistake a man for a cow — the proof being that they always sacrifice the latter, never the former. I am not lapsing into the trap of Lévy Bruhl's "primitive mentality." I am not saying that primitive man is less capable of making distinctions than we moderns.

In order for a species or category of living creature, human or animal, to appear suitable for sacrifice, it must bear a sharp resemblance to the *human* categories excluded from the ranks of the "sacrificeable," while still maintaining a degree of difference that forbids all possible confusion. As I have said, no mistake is possible in the case of animal sacrifice. But it is quite another case with human victims. If we look at the extremely wide spectrum of human victims sacrificed by various societies, the list seems heterogeneous, to say the least. It includes prisoners of war, slaves, small children, unmarried adolescents, and the handicapped; it ranges from the very dregs of society, such as the Greek *pharmakos,* to the king himself.

Is it possible to detect a unifying factor in this disparate group? We notice at first glance beings who are either outside or on the fringes of society: prisoners of war, slaves, *pharmakos.* In many primitive societies children who have not yet undergone the rites of initiation have no proper place in the community; their rights and duties are almost nonexistent. What we are dealing with, therefore, are exterior or marginal individuals, incapable of establishing or sharing the social bonds that link the rest of the inhabitants. Their status as foreigners or enemies, their servile condition, or simply their age prevents these future victims from fully integrating themselves into the community.

But what about the king? Is he not at the very heart of the community? Undoubtedly — but it is precisely his position at the center that serves to isolate him from his fellow men, to render him casteless. He escapes from society, so to speak, via the roof, just as the *pharmakos* escapes through the cellar. The king has a sort of foil, however, in the person of his fool. The fool shares his master's status as an outsider — an isolation whose literal truth is often of greater significance than the easily reversible symbolic values often attributed to it. From every point of view the fool is eminently "sacrificeable," and the king can use him to vent his own anger. But it sometimes happens that the king himself is sacrificed, and that (among certain African societies) in a thoroughly regulated and highly ritualistic manner.[8]

It is clearly legitimate to define the difference between sacrificeable and nonsacrificeable individuals in terms of their degree of integration, but such a definition is not yet sufficient. In many cultures women are not considered full-fledged members of their society; yet women are never, or rarely, selected as sacrificial victims. There may be a simple explanation for this fact. The married woman retains her ties with her parents' clan even after she has become in some respects the property of her husband and his family. To kill her would be to run the risk of one of the two groups' interpreting her sacrifice as an act of murder, committing it to a reciprocal act of revenge. The notion of vengeance casts a new light on the matter. All our sacrificial victims, whether chosen from one of the human categories enumerated above or, *a fortiori,* from the animal realm, are invariably distinguishable from the nonsacrificeable beings by one essential characteristic: between these victims and the community a crucial social link is missing, so they can be exposed to violence without fear of reprisal. Their death does not automatically entail an act of vengeance.

The considerable importance this freedom from reprisal has for the sacrificial process makes us understand that sacrifice is primarily an act of violence without risk of vengeance. We also understand the paradox — not without is comic aspects on occasion — of the frequent references to vengeance in the course of sacrificial rites, the veritable obsession with vengeance when no chance of vengeance exists:

> For the act they were about to commit elaborate excuses were offered; they shuddered at the prospect of the sheep's death, they wept over it as though they were its parents. Before the blow was struck, they implored the beast's forgiveness. They then addressed themselves to the species to which the beast belonged, as if addressing a large family clan, beseeching it not to seek vengeance for the act that was about to be inflicted on one of its members. In the same vein the actual murderer was punished in some manner, either beaten or sent into exile.[9]

8. The sacrifice of the monarch is treated in chapter 4, 104–10 of *Violence and the Sacred. Ed.*

9. Hubert and Mauss, *Sacrifice,* 33.

It is the entire species *considered as a large family clan* that the sacrificers beseech not to seek vengeance. By incorporating the element of reprisal into the ceremony, the participants are hinting broadly at the true function of the rite, the kind of action it was designed to circumvent, and the criteria that determined the choice of victim. The desire to commit an act of violence on those near us cannot be suppressed without a conflict; we must divert that impulse, therefore, toward the sacrificial victim, the creature we can strike down without fear of reprisal, since he lacks a champion.

Like everything that touches on the essential nature of the sacrificial act, the true distinction between the sacrificeable and the nonsacrificeable is never clearly articulated. Oddities and inexplicable anomalies confuse the picture. For instance, some animal species will be formally excluded from sacrifice, but the exclusion of members of the community is never mentioned. In constantly drawing attention to the truly maniacal aspects of sacrifice, modern theorists only serve to perpetuate an old misunderstanding in new terms. Men can dispose of their violence more efficiently if they regard the process not as something emanating from within themselves, but as a necessity imposed from without, a divine decree whose least infraction calls down terrible punishment. When they banish sacrificial practices from the "real," everyday world, modern theorists continue to misrepresent the violence of sacrifice.

The function of sacrifice is to quell violence within the community and to prevent conflicts from erupting. Yet societies like our own, which do not, strictly speaking, practice sacrificial rites, seem to get along without them. Violence undoubtedly exists within our society, but not to such an extent that the society itself is threatened with extinction. The simple fact that sacrificial practices, and other rites as well, can disappear without catastrophic results should in part explain the failure of ethnology and theology to come to grips with these cultural phenomena, and explain as well our modern reluctance to attribute a real function to them. After all, it is hard to maintain that institutions for which, as it seems, we have no need are actually indispensable.

It may be that a basic difference exists between a society like ours and societies imbued with religion—a difference that is partially hidden from us by rites, particularly by rites of sacrifice, that play a compensatory role. This difference would help explain why the actual function of sacrifice still eludes us.

When internal strife, previously sublimated by means of sacrificial practices, rises to the surface, it manifests itself in interfamily vendettas or blood feuds. This kind of violence is virtually nonexistent in our own culture. And perhaps it is here that we should look for the fundamental difference between primitive societies and our own; we should examine the specific ailments to which we are immune and which sacrifice manages to control, if not to eliminate.

Why does the spirit of revenge, wherever it breaks out, constitute such an intolerable menace? Perhaps because the only satisfactory revenge for spilt blood is spilling the blood of the killer; and in the blood feud there is no clear distinction between the act for which the killer is being punished and the punishment itself. Vengeance professes to be an act of reprisal, and every reprisal calls for another reprisal. The crime to which the act of vengeance addresses itself is almost never an unprecedented offense; in almost every case it has been committed in revenge for some prior crime.

Vengeance, then, is an interminable, infinitely repetitive process. Every time it turns up in some part of the community, it threatens to involve the whole social body. There is the risk that the act of vengeance will initiate a chain reaction whose consequences will quickly prove fatal to any society of modest size. The multiplication of reprisals instantaneously puts the very existence of a society in jeopardy, and that is why it is universally proscribed.

Curiously enough, it is in the very communities where the proscription is most strictly enforced that vengeance seems to hold sway. Even when it remains in the background, its role in the community unacknowledged, the specter of vengeance plays an important role in shaping the relationships among individuals. That is not to say that the prohibition against acts of vengeance is taken lightly. Precisely because murder inspires horror and because men must be forcibly restrained from murder, vengeance is inflicted on all those who commit it. The obligation never to shed blood cannot be distinguished from the obligation to exact vengeance on those who shed it. If men wish to prevent an interminable outbreak of vengeance (just as today we wish to prevent nuclear war), it is not enough to convince their fellows that violence is detestable — for it is precisely because they detest violence that men make a duty of vengeance.

In a world still haunted by the specter of vengeance it is difficult to theorize about vengeance without resorting to equivocations or paradoxes. In Greek tragedy, for instance, there is not — and cannot be — any consistent stand on the subject. To attempt to extract a coherent theory of vengeance from the drama is to miss the essence of tragedy. For in tragedy each character passionately embraces or rejects vengeance depending on the position he occupies at any given moment in the scheme of the drama.

Vengeance is a vicious circle whose effect on primitive societies can only be surmised. For us the circle has been broken. We owe our good fortune to one of our social institutions above all: our judicial system, which serves to deflect the menace of vengeance. The system does not suppress vengeance; rather, it effectively limits it to a single act of reprisal, enacted by a sovereign authority specializing in this particular function. The decisions of the judiciary are invariably presented as the final word on vengeance.

Vocabulary is perhaps more revealing here than judicial theories. Once the concept of interminable revenge has been formally rejected, it is referred to as *private* vengeance. The term implies the existence of a *public* vengeance, a counterpart never made explicit. By definition, primitive societies have only private vengeance. Thus, public vengeance is the exclusive property of well-policed societies, and our society calls it the judicial system.

Our penal system operates according to principles of justice that are in no real conflict with the concept of revenge. The same principle is at work in all systems of violent retribution. Either the principle is just, and justice is therefore inherent in the idea of vengeance, or there is no justice to be found anywhere. He who exacts his own vengeance is said to "take the law into his own hands." There is no difference of principle between private and public vengeance; but on the social level, the difference is enormous. Under the public system, an act of vengeance is no longer avenged; the process is terminated, the danger of escalation averted.

The absence of a judicial system in primitive societies has been confirmed by ethnologists. Malinowski concludes that "the 'criminal' aspect of law in savage communities is perhaps even vaguer than the civil one; the idea of 'justice' in our sense [is] hardly applicable and the means of restoring a disturbed tribal equilibrium [are] slow and cumbersome."[10]

Radcliffe-Brown's conclusions are identical, and summon up, as such conclusions must, the specter of perpetual vengeance:

> Thus, though the Andaman Islanders had a well-developed social conscience, that is, a system of moral notions as to what is right and wrong, there was no such thing as punishment of a crime by the society. If one person injured another it was left to the injured one to seek vengeance if he wished and if he dared. There were probably always some who would side with the criminal, their attachment to him overcoming their disapproval of his actions.[11]

The anthropologist Robert Lowie speaks of the "administering of justice" in reference to primitive societies. He distinguishes two types of societies, those that possess a "central authority" and those that do not. Among the latter it is the parental group, he declares, that exercises the judicial power, and *this group confronts the other group in the same*

---

10. Bronislaw Malinowski, *Crime and Custom in Savage Society* (Totowa, N.J.: Littlefield, Adams & Co., 1967), 94.

11. A. R. Radcliffe-Brown, *The Andaman Islanders* (New York: Free Press, 1964), 52.

way that a sovereign state confronts the outside world. There can be no true "administering of justice," no judicial system without a superior tribunal capable of arbitrating between even the most powerful groups. Only that superior tribunal can remove the possibility of blood feud or perpetual vendetta. Lowie himself recognizes that this condition is not always met:

> From the supreme law of group solidarity it follows that when an individual has injured a member of another group, his own group shield him while the opposing group support the injured man's claims for compensation or revenge. Thence there may develop blood-feuds and civil wars. . . . The Chukchi generally make peace after the first act of retribution, but among the Ifugao the struggle may go on almost interminably.[12]

To speak here of the "administering of justice" is to abuse the meaning of the words. The desire to find in primitive societies virtues equal or superior to our own as regards the control of violence must not lead us to minimize the difference. Lowie's terminology simply perpetuates a widely accepted way of thinking by which the right to vengeance *takes the place* of a judicial system wherever such a system is lacking. This theory, which seems securely anchored to common sense, is in fact erroneous and gives rise to an infinite number of errors. Such thinking reflects the ignorance of a society—our own—that has been the beneficiary of a judicial system for so many years that it is no longer conscious of the system's real achievements.

If vengeance is an unending process it can hardly be invoked to restrain the violent impulses of society. In fact, it is vengeance itself that must be restrained. Lowie bears witness to the truth of this proposition every time he gives an example of the "administering of justice," even in those societies that, according to him, possess a "central authority." It is not the lack of any abstract principle of justice that is important, but the fact that the so-called legal reprisals are always in the hands of the victims themselves and those near to them. As long as there exists no sovereign and independent body capable of taking the place of the injured party and taking upon itself the responsibility for revenge, the danger of interminable escalation remains. Efforts to modify the punishment or to hold vengeance in check can only result in a situation that is precarious at best. Such efforts ultimately require a spirit of conciliation that may indeed be present, but may equally well be lacking. As I have said, it is inexact to speak of the administering of justice, even in connection with such institutional concepts as "an eye for an eye" or the various forms of trial by combat. In such cases it seems wise to adhere

12. Robert Lowie, *Primitive Society* (New York: Liveright, 1970), 400.

to Malinowski's conclusion: "The means of restoring a disturbed tribal equilibrium [are] slow and cumbersome.... We have not found any arrangement or usage which could be classed as a form of 'administration of justice,' or according to a code and by fixed methods."[13]

If primitive societies have no tried and true remedies for dealing with an outbreak of violence, no certain cure once the social equilibrium has been upset, we can assume that *preventive* measures will play an essential role. Here again I return to the concept of sacrifice as I earlier defined it: an instrument of prevention in the struggle against violence.

In a universe where the slightest dispute can lead to disaster—just as a slight cut can prove fatal to a hemophiliac—the rites of sacrifice serve to polarize the community's aggressive impulses and redirect them toward victims that may be actual or figurative, animate or inanimate, but that are always incapable of propagating further vengeance. The sacrificial process furnishes an outlet for those violent impulses that cannot be mastered by self-restraint; a partial outlet, to be sure, but always renewable, and one whose efficacy has been attested by an impressive number of reliable witnesses. The sacrificial process prevents the spread of violence by keeping vengeance in check.

In societies that practice sacrifice there is no critical situation to which the rites are not applicable, but there are certain crises that seem to be particularly amenable to sacrificial mediation. In these crises the social fabric of the community is threatened; dissension and discord are rife. The more critical the situation, the more "precious" the sacrificial victim must be.

It is significant that sacrifice has languished in societies with a firmly established judicial system—ancient Greece and Rome, for example. In such societies the essential purpose of sacrifice has disappeared. It may still be practiced for a while, but in diminished and debilitated form. And it is precisely under such circumstances that sacrifice usually comes to our notice, and our doubts as to the "real" function of religious institutions are only reinforced.

Our original proposition stands: ritual in general, and sacrificial rites in particular, assume essential roles in societies that lack a firm judicial system. It must not be assumed, however, that sacrifice simply "replaces" a judicial system. One can scarcely speak of replacing something that never existed to begin with. Then, too, a judicial system is ultimately irreplaceable, short of a unanimous and entirely voluntary renunciation of all violent actions.

When we minimize the dangers implicit in vengeance we risk losing sight of the true function of sacrifice. Because revenge is rarely encountered in our society, we seldom have occasion to consider how societies

13. Malinowski, *Crime and Custom in Savage Society,* 94, 98.

lacking a judicial system of punishment manage to hold it in check. Our ignorance engages us in a false line of thought that is seldom, if ever, challenged. Certainly we have no need of religion to help us solve a problem, runaway vengeance, whose very existence eludes us. And because we have no need for it, religion itself appears senseless. The efficiency of our judicial solution conceals the problem, and the elimination of the problem conceals from us the role played by religion.

The Sacrificial Crisis

As we have seen, the proper functioning of the sacrificial process requires not only the complete separation of the sacrificed victim from those beings for whom the victim is a substitute but also a similarity between both parties. This dual requirement can be fulfilled only through a delicately balanced mechanism of associations.

Any change, however slight, in the hierarchical classification of living creatures risks undermining the whole sacrificial structure. The sheer repetition of the sacrificial act—the repeated slaughter of the same type of victim — inevitably brings about such change. But the inability to adapt to new conditions is a trait characteristic of religion in general. If, as is often the case, we encounter the institution of sacrifice either in an advanced state of decay or reduced to a relative insignificance, it is because it has already undergone a good deal of wear and tear.

Whether the slippage in the mechanism is due to "too little" or "too much" contact between the victim and those whom the victim represents, the results are the same. The elimination of violence is no longer effected; on the contrary, conflicts within the community multiply, and the menace of chain reactions looms ever larger.

If the gap between victim and the community is allowed to grow too wide, all similarity will be destroyed. The victim will no longer be capable of attracting the violent impulses to itself; the sacrifice will cease to serve as a "good conductor," in the sense that metal is a good conductor of electricity. On the other hand, if there is *too much* continuity the violence will overflow its channels. "Impure" violence will mingle with the "sacred" violence of the rites, turning the latter into a scandalous accomplice in the process of pollution, even a kind of catalyst in the propagation of further impurity.

These are postulates that seem to take form a priori from our earlier conclusions. They can also be discerned in literature — in the adaptations of certain myths in classical Greek tragedy, in particular in Euripides' version of the legend of Heracles.

Euripides' *Heracles* contains no tragic conflict, no debate between declared adversaries. The real subject of the play is the failure of a sacrifice, the act of sacrificial violence that suddenly *goes wrong*. Heracles, returning home after the completion of his labors, finds his wife and children in the power of a usurper names Lycus, who is preparing to offer them as sacrificial victims. Heracles kills Lycus. After this most recent act of violence, committed in the heart of the city, the hero's need to purify himself is greater than ever, and he sets about preparing a sacrifice of his own. His wife and children are with him when Heracles, suddenly seized by madness, mistakes them for his enemies and *sacrifices* them.

Heracles' misidentification of his family is attributed to Lyssa, goddess of madness, who is operating as an emissary of two other goddesses, Iris and Hera, who bear Heracles ill will. The preparations for the sacrifice provide an imposing setting for the homicidal outburst; it is unlikely that their dramatic significance passed unnoticed by the author. In fact, it is Euripides himself who directs or attention to the ritualistic origins of the onslaught. After the massacre, Heracles' father, Amphitryon, asks his son: "My child, what happened to you? How could this horror have taken place? Was it perhaps the spilt blood that turned your head?" Heracles, who is just returning to consciousness and remembers nothing, inquires in turn: "Where did the madness overtake me? Where did it strike me down?" Amphitryon replies: "Near the altar, where you were purifying your hands over the sacred flames."

The sacrifice contemplated by the hero succeeded only too well in polarizing the forces of violence. Indeed, it produced a superabundance of violence of a particularly virulent kind. As Amphitryon suggested, the blood shed in the course of the terrible labors and in the city itself finally turned the hero's head. Instead of drawing off the violence and allowing it to ebb away, the rites brought a veritable flood of violence down on the victim. The sacrificial rites were no longer able to accomplish their task; they swelled the surging tide of impure violence instead of channeling it. The mechanism of substitutions had gone astray, and those whom the sacrifice was designed to protect became its victims.

The difference between sacrificial and nonsacrificial violence is anything but exact; it is even arbitrary. At times the difference threatens to disappear entirely. There is no such thing as truly "pure" violence. Nevertheless, sacrificial violence can, in the proper circumstances serve as an agent of purification. That is why those who perform the rites are obliged to purify themselves at the conclusion of the sacrifice. The procedure followed is reminiscent of atomic power plants; when the expert has finished decontaminating the installation, he must himself be decontaminated. And accidents can always happen.

The catastrophic inversion of the sacrificial act would appear to be an essential element in the Heracles myth. The motif reappears, thinly concealed behind secondary themes, in another episode of his story, in Sophocles' *The Women of Trachis.*

Heracles had mortally wounded the centaur Nessus, who had assaulted Heracles' wife, Deianira. Before dying, the centaur gave the young woman a shirt smeared with his sperm — or, in Sophocles' version, smeared with his blood mixed with the blood of a Hydra. (Once again, as in the *Ion,* we encounter the theme of the two kinds of blood mingling to form one.)

The subject of the tragedy, as in Euripides' *Heracles,* is the return of the hero. In this instance Heracles is bringing with him a pretty young captive, of whom Deianira is jealous. Deianira sends a servant to her husband with a welcoming gift, the shirt of Nessus. With his dying breath the centaur had told her that the shirt would assure the wearer's eternal fidelity to her; but he cautioned her to keep it well out of the way of any flame or source of heat.

Heracles puts on the shirt, and soon afterward lights a fire for the rites of sacrificial purification. The flames activate the poison in the shirt; it is the rite itself that unlooses the evil. Heracles, contorted with pain, presently ends his life on the pyre he has begged his son to prepare. Before dying, Heracles kills the servant who delivered the shirt to him; this death, along with his own and the subsequent suicide of his wife, contributes to the cycle of violence heralded by Heracles' return and the failure of the sacrifice. Once again, violence has struck the beings who sought the protection of sacrificial rites.

A number of sacrifice motifs intermingle in these two plays. A special sort of impurity clings to the warrior returning to his homeland, still tainted with the slaughter of war. In the case of Heracles, his sanguinary labors render him particularly impure.

The returning warrior risks carrying the seed of violence into the very heart of his city. The myth of Horatius, as explicated by Georges Dumézil, illustrates this theme: Horatius kills his sister before any ritual purification has been performed. In the case of Heracles the impurity triumphs over the rite itself.

If we examine the mechanism of violence in these two tragedies, we notice that when the sacrifice goes wrong it sets off a chain reaction. The murder of Lycus is presented in the Euripides play as a last "labor" of the hero, a still-rational prelude to the insane outburst that follows. Seen from the perspective of the ritualist, it might well constitute a first link of impure violence. With this incident, as we have noted, violence invades the heart of the city. This initial murder corresponds to the death of the old servant in *The Women of Trachis.*

Supernatural intervention plays no part in these episodes, except perhaps to cast a thin veil over the true subject: the sacrificial celebration that has gone wrong. The goddess Lyssa, Nessus's shirt — these add nothing to the meaning of the two stories; rather, they act as a veil, and as soon as the veil is drawn aside we encounter the same theme of "good" violence turning into "bad." The mythological accompaniments of the stories can be seen as redundant. Lyssa, the goddess of madness, sounds more like a refugee from an allegorical tale than a real goddess, and Nessus's shirt joins company with all the acts of violence that Heracles carries on his back.

The theme of the Warrior's Return is not, strictly speaking, mythological, and readily lends itself to sociological or psychological interpretations. The conquering hero who threatens to destroy the liberty of his homeland belongs to history, not myth. Certainly that is the way Corneille seems to approach the subject in *Horace,* although in his version of the tale the ideology is somewhat reversed — the returning warrior is rightly shocked by his sister's lack of patriotism. We could easily translate the "case histories" of Heracles and Horatius into psychological or psychoanalytical terms and come up with numerous working theories, each at variance with the other. But we should avoid this temptation, for in debating the relative merits of each theory we would lose sight of the role played by ritual — a subject that has nothing to do with such debates, even though it may, as we shall see, open the way to them. Being more *primitive,* ritualistic action is hospitable to all ideological interpretations and dependent on none. It has only one axiom: the contagious nature of the violence encountered by the warrior in battle — and only one prescription: the proper performance of ritual purification. Its sole purpose is to prevent the resurgence of violence and its spread throughout the community.

The two tragedies we have been discussing present in anecdotal form, as if dealing exclusively with exceptional individuals, events that are significant because they affect the community as a whole. Sacrifice is a social act, and when it goes amiss the consequences are not limited to some "exceptional" individual singled out by Destiny.

Historians seem to agree that Greek tragedy belonged to a period of transition between the dominance of an archaic theocracy and the emergence of a new, "modern" order based on statism and laws. Before its decline the archaic order must have enjoyed a certain stability; and this stability must have reposed on its religious element — that is, on the sacrificial rites.

Although they predate the tragedians, the pre-Socratics are often regarded as the philosophers of classical tragedy. In their writings we can find echoes of the religious crisis we are attempting to define. The fifth fragment of Heraclitus quite clearly deals with the decay of sacrificial rites, with their inability to purify what is impure. Religious beliefs are compromised by the decadent state of the ritual:

> In vain do they strive for purification by besmirching themselves with blood, as the man who has bathed in the mire seeks to clean himself with mud. Such antics can only strike the beholder as utter folly! In addressing their prayers to images of the gods, they might just as well be speaking to the walls, without seeking to know the true nature of gods or heroes.

The difference between blood spilt for ritual and for criminal purposes no longer holds. The Heraclitus fragment appears in even sharper relief when compared to analogous passages in the Old Testament. The preexilian prophets Amos, Isaiah, and Micah denounce in vehement terms the impotence of the sacrificial process and ritual in general. In the most explicit manner they link the decay of religious practices to the deterioration of contemporary behavior. Inevitably, the eroding of the sacrificial system seems to result in the emergence of reciprocal violence. Neighbors who had previously discharged their mutual aggressions on a third party, joining together in the sacrifice of an "outside" victim, now turn to sacrificing one another. Empedocles' *Purifications* brings us even closer to the problem:

> 135. When will the sinister noise of this carnage cease? Can you not see that you are devouring another with your callous hearts?
>
> 137. The father seizes hold of the son, who has changed form; in his mad delusion he kills him, murmuring prayers. The son cries out, imploring his insane executioner to spare him. But the father hears him not, and cuts his throat, and spreads a great feast in his palace. In the same way the son takes hold of the father, the children their mother, one slaughtering the other and devouring their own flesh and blood.

The concept of a "sacrificial crisis" may be useful in clarifying certain aspects of Greek tragedy. To a real extent it is a sacrificial religion that provides the language for these dramas; the criminal in the play sees himself not so much as a righter-of-wrongs as a performer-of-sacrifices. We always view the "tragic flaw" from the perspective of the new, emergent order, never from that of the old order in the final stages of decay. The reason for this approach is clear: modern thought has never been able to attribute any real function to the practice of sacrifice, and because the nature of the practice eludes us, we naturally find it difficult to determine when and if this practice is in the process of disintegration. In the case of Greek tragedy it is not enough merely to believe in the existence of the old order; we must look deeper if we hope to discover the religious problems of the era. Unlike the Jewish prophets, whose viewpoint was historical, the Greek tragedians evoked their own sacrificial crisis in terms of legendary figures whose forms were fixed by tradition.

All the bloody events that serve as background to the plays — the plagues and pestilences, civil and foreign wars — undoubtedly reflect the contemporary scene, but the images are unclear, as if viewed through a glass darkly. Each time, for example, a play of Euripides deals with the collapse of a royal house (as in *Heracles, Iphigenia in Aulis,* or *The Bacchae*), we are convinced that the poet is suggesting that the scene before our eyes in only the tip of the iceberg, that the real issue is the fate of the entire community. At the moment when Heracles is slaughtering his family offstage, the chorus cries out: "Look, look! The tempest is shaking the house; the roof is falling in."

Part IV

The Scapegoat and Myths as Texts of Persecution

Chapter 7

The Scapegoat as Historical Referent

Girard has consistently maintained that mythical texts do not characteristically present an explicit *theme* of scapegoating; myth camouflages scapegoating even as it represents patterns of meaning in stories of gods, ancient heroes, foundations of social order and ritual, etc. However, even if much of any myth or legend may be fantastic or unbelievable to modern critical thinking, particularly within the scholarly disciplines of the humanities and social sciences, the stories and texts that seem incredible do have empirical or historical referents at the generative level. The two chief referents are a social or cultural *crisis* and collective violence against a victim (or victims) who are both blamed for the crisis and, in archaic societies, credited with the peace and harmony that are restored once the lynching has taken place. In this excerpt, which is the first chapter of *The Scapegoat*, Girard uses a fourteenth-century text by Guillaume de Machaut, *Judgment of the King of Navarre*, as a test case for showing that texts in which persecution is accepted or justified have the same structure as myths. Every historian or comparative religionist reading Guillaume's epic poem will easily discern its unbelievable mythical elements, but none of them will doubt that a severe crisis occasioned by the bubonic plague occurred in France in the late 1340s and that an untold number of Jews were accused of causing the plague and murdered in paroxysms of mob violence.

Guillaume de Machaut was a French poet of the mid-fourteenth century. His *Judgment of the King of Navarre* deserves to be better known. The main part of the work is a long poem in the conventional, courtly style, but its opening is striking. Guillaume claims that he participated in a confusing series of catastrophic events before he finally closeted himself in his house in terror to await death or the end of the indescribable ordeal. Some of the events he describes are totally improbable, others only partially so. Yet the account leaves the impression that something must actually have happened.

There are signs in the sky. People are knocked down by a rain of stones. Entire cities are destroyed by lightning. Men die in great numbers in the city where Guillaume lives (he doesn't tell us its name). Some of these deaths are the result of the wickedness of the Jews and their Christian accomplices. How did these people cause such huge losses among the local population? They poisoned the rivers that provided the drinking water. Heaven-sent justice righted these wrongs by making the evildoers known to the population, who massacred them all. People continued to die in ever greater numbers, however, until one day in spring when Guillaume heard music in the street and men and women laughing. All was over, and courtly poetry could begin again.

Modern criticism, since its origin in the sixteenth and seventeenth centuries, has not relied blindly on texts. Many scholars today believe their critical insight develops in proportion to increasing skepticism. Texts that were formerly thought to contain real information are now suspect because they have been constantly reinterpreted by successive generations of historians. On the other hand, epistemologists and philosophers are experiencing an extreme crisis, which is undermining what was once called historical science. Scholars who used to sustain themselves on their texts now doubt the certainty of any interpretation.

At first glance, Guillaume de Machaut's text may seem susceptible to the prevailing skepticism concerning historical certainty. But after some moments' reflection even contemporary readers will find some real events among the unlikely occurrences of the story. They will not believe in the signs in the sky or in the accusations against the Jews, but neither will they treat all the unlikely themes in the same way, or put them on the same level. Guillaume did not invent a single thing. He is credulous, admittedly, and he reflects the hysteria of public opinion. The innumerable deaths he tallies are nonetheless real, caused presumably by the famous Black Death, which ravaged the north of France in 1349 and 1350. Similarly, the massacre of the Jews was real. In the eyes of the massacrers the deed was justified by the rumors of poisoning in circulation everywhere. The universal fear of disease gives sufficient weight to the rumors to unleash the massacres described. The following is the passage from the *Judgment of the King of Navarre* that deals with the Jews:

> After that came a false, treacherous and contemptible swine: this was shameful Israel, the wicked and disloyal who hated good and loved everything evil, who gave so much gold and silver and prom-

> ises to Christians, who then poisoned several rivers and fountains that had been clear and pure so that many lost their lives; for whoever used them died suddenly. Certainly ten times one hundred thousand died from it, in country and in city. Then finally this mortal calamity was noticed.
>
> He who sits on high and sees far, who governs and provides for everything did not want this treachery to remain hidden; he revealed it and made it so generally known that they lost their lives and possessions. Then every Jew was destroyed, some hanged, others burned; some were drowned, others beheaded with an ax or sword. And many Christians died together with them in shame.[1]

Medieval communities were so afraid of the plague that the word alone was enough to frighten them. They avoided mentioning it as long as possible and even avoided taking the necessary precautions at the risk of aggravating the effects of the epidemic. So helpless were they that telling the truth did not mean facing the situation but rather giving in to its destructive consequences and relinquishing all semblance of normal life. The entire population shared in this type of blindness. Their desperate desire to deny the evidence contributed to their search for "scapegoats."[2] La Fontaine, in *Animals Sickened by the Plague,* gives an excellent description of this almost religious reluctance to articulate the terrifying term and thereby unleash some sort of evil power on the community: The plague (since it must be called by its name)....[3]

La Fontaine introduces us to the process of collective bad faith which recognizes the plague as a divine punishment. The angry god is annoyed by a guilt that is not equally shared. To avert the plague the guilty must be identified and punished, or rather, as La Fontaine writes, "dedicated" to the god. The first to be interrogated in the fable are the beasts of prey, who describe their bestial behavior, which is immediately excused. Last comes the ass, the least bloodthirsty of them all, and therefore the weakest and least protected. It is the ass that is finally designated.

According to historians, in some cities Jews were massacred at the mere mention of the plague being in the area, even before it had actually arrived. Guillaume's account could fit this sort of phenomenon, because the massacre occurred well before the height of the epidemic. But the number of deaths the author attributes to the Jews' poisoning suggests another explanation. If the deaths are real — and there is no reason to

1. Guillaume de Machaut, *Oeuvres,* Société des anciens textes français, vol. 1, *Le jugement du Roy de Navarre* (Paris: Ernest Hoeppfner, 1908), 144–45.

2. J.-N. Biraben, *Les Hommes et la peste en France et dans les pays européens et mediterranéens,* 2 vols. (Paris, The Hague: Mouton, 1975–76); Jean Delumeau, *La Peur en Occident* (Paris: Fayard, 1978).

3. Jean La Fontaine, *Les Animaux malades de la peste* (Paris: Libraire Larousse, n.d.), book 7, no.1.

think they are imagined — they might well be the first victims of that same plague. But Guillaume does not think so even in retrospect. In his eyes the traditional scapegoats remain the cause of *the first stages of the epidemic.* Only in the later stages does the author recognize the presence of a properly pathological phenomenon. Ultimately, the disaster is so great that it casts doubt on the likelihood of a single explanation of a conspiracy of poisoners, though Guillaume does not then reinterpret the whole chain of events from a rational perspective.

In fact, we might well ask to what extent the poet recognizes the existence of the plague, since he avoids writing the fatal word until the very end. At the climactic moment he solemnly introduces the word of Greek origin, *epydimie,* which was uncommon at the time. The word obviously does not function in his text in the same way as it would in ours; it is not really a synonym for the dreaded word but rather a sort of euphemism, a new way of not calling the plague by its name. It is in fact a new but purely linguistic scapegoat. Guillaume tells us it was never possible to determine the nature and the cause of the disease from which so many people died in such a short time:

> Nor was there any physician or doctor who really knew the cause or origin, or what it was (nor was there any remedy), yet this malady was so great that it was called an epidemic.

On this score Guillaume prefers to refer to public opinion rather than to think for himself. The word *epydimie* in the fourteenth century had a certain scientific flavor which helped to ward off anxiety, somewhat like the vapors of the fumigation carried out at street corners to reduce the wave of pestilence. A disease with a name seems on the way to a cure, so uncontrollable phenomena are frequently renamed to create the impression of control. Such verbal exorcisms continue to appeal wherever science remains illusory or ineffective. By the refusal to name it, the plague itself becomes "dedicated" to the god. This linguistic sacrifice is innocent compared with the human sacrifices that accompany or precede it, but its essential structure is the same.

Even in retrospect, all the real and imaginary collective scapegoats, the Jews and the flagellants, the rain of stones and the *epydimie,* continue to play such an effective role in Guillaume's story that he never perceives in them the single entity that we call the "Black Death." The author continues to see a number of more or less independent disasters, linked only by their religious significance, similar in a way to the ten plagues of Egypt.

Almost everything I have said so far is obvious. We all understand Guillaume's text in the same way and my readers have no need of me. It is not useless, however, to insist on this reading, of which the boldness and forcefulness elude us, precisely because it is accepted by everyone and is uncontroversial. There has been agreement about it literally for centuries, all the more remarkable in that it involves a radical reinterpretation. We reject without question the meaning the author gives his text. We declare that he does not know what he is saying. From our several centuries' distance we know better than he and can correct what he has written. We even believe that we have discovered a truth not seen by the author and, with still greater audacity, do not hesitate to state that he provides us with this truth even though he does not perceive it himself.

What is the source of our amazing confidence in the statement that Jews were really massacred? An answer comes immediately to mind. We are not reading this text in a vacuum. Other texts exist from the same period; they deal with the same subjects; some of them are more valuable than Guillaume's. Their authors are less credulous. They provide a tight framework of historical knowledge in which Guillaume's text can be placed. Thanks to this context, we can distinguish true from false in the passage quoted.

It is true that the facts about the anti-Semitic persecutions during the plague are quite well known. There is an already recognized body of knowledge that arouses certain expectations in us. Guillaume's text is responding to those expectations. This perspective is not wrong from the point of view of our individual experience and our immediate contact with the text, but it does not justify us from the theoretical point of view.

Although the framework of historical knowledge does exist, it consists of documents that are no more reliable than Guillaume's text, for similar or different reasons. And we cannot place Guillaume exactly in this context because we lack knowledge of where exactly the events he describes took place. It may have been in Paris or Reims or even another city. In any case the context is not significant; even without that information the modern reader would end up with the reading I have given. He would conclude that there were probably victims who were unjustly massacred. He would therefore think the text is false, since it claims that the victims were guilty, but true insofar as there really were victims. He would, in the end, distinguish the true from the false exactly as we do. What gives us this ability? Would it not be wise to be guided systematically by the principle of discarding the whole basket of apples because of the few rotten ones among them? Should we not suspect a certain lapse of caution or remnant of naïveté that, given the opportunity, will be attacked by overzealous contemporary critics? Should we not admit that all historical knowledge is uncertain and that nothing can be taken from a text such as ours, not even the reality of a persecution?

All these questions must be answered categorically in the negative. Out-and-out skepticism does not take into account the real nature of the text. There is a particular relationship between the likely and the unlikely characteristics of this text. In the beginning the reader cannot of course distinguish between true and false. He sees only themes that are incredible as well as others that are quite credible. He can believe in the increasing number of deaths; it could be an epidemic. But the massive scale of the poisonings described by Guillaume is scarcely credible. There were no substances in the fourteenth century capable of producing such harmful effects. The author's hatred for the supposedly guilty people is explicit and makes his thesis extremely suspect.

These two types of characteristics cannot be recognized without at least implicitly acknowledging that they interact with each other. If there really is an epidemic, then it might well stir up latent prejudices. The appetite for persecution readily focuses on religious minorities, especially during a time of crisis. On the other hand a real persecution might well be justified by the sort of accusation that Guillaume credulously echoes. Such a poet is not expected to be particularly sanguinary. If he believes in the stories he tells us, no doubt they are believed by the people around him. The text suggests that public opinion is overexcited and ready to accept the most absurd rumors. In short it suggests a propitious climate for massacres which the author confirms actually took place.

In a context of improbable events, those that are possible become probable. The reverse is also true. In a context of probable events, the unlikely ones cannot be ascribed to an imagination operating freely for the pleasure of inventing fiction. We are aware of the imaginary element, but it is the very specific imagination of people who crave violence. As a result, among the textual representations there is a mutual confirmation. This correspondence can be explained by only one hypothesis. The text we are reading has its roots in a real persecution described from the perspective of the persecutors. The perspective is inevitably deceptive since the persecutors are convinced that their violence is justified; they consider themselves judges, and therefore they must have guilty victims, yet their perspective is to some degree reliable, for the certainty of being right encourages them to hide nothing of their massacres.

Faced with a text such as Guillaume de Machaut's, it is legitimate to suspend the general rule by which the text as a whole is never worth more, as far as real information goes, than the least reliable of its features. If the text describes circumstances favorable to persecution, if it presents us with victims of the type that persecutors usually choose, and if, in addition, it represents these victims as guilty of the type of crimes which persecutors normally attribute to their victims, then it is very likely that the persecution is real. If this reality is confirmed by the text itself then there is little scope for doubt.

When one begins to understand the perspective of the persecutors, the absurdity of their accusations strengthens rather than compromises the informational value of the text, but only in reference to the violence that it echoes. If Guillaume had added stories of ritual infanticide to the episodes of poisoning, his account would be even more improbable without, however, in the least diminishing the accuracy of the massacres it reports. The more unlikely the accusations in this genre of text the more they strengthen the probability of the massacres: they confirm for us the psychosocial context within which the massacres must have taken place. Conversely, if the theme of massacres is placed alongside the theme of an epidemic it provides the historical context within which even the most precise scholar could take this account of poisoning seriously.

The accounts of persecutions are no doubt inaccurate, but in a way they are so characteristic of persecutors in general, and of medieval persecutors in particular, that the text can be believed in all the areas in which conjectures are prompted by the very nature of the inaccuracy. When potential persecutors describe the reality of their persecutions, they should be believed.

The combination of the two types of characteristics generates certainty. If the combination were only to be found in rare examples we could not be so certain. But its frequency is too great to allow doubt. Only actual persecution seen from the perspective of the persecutors can explain the regular combination of these characteristics. Our interpretation of all the texts is confirmed statistically.

The fact that certainty is statistically verifiable does not mean it is based only on an accumulation of equally uncertain documents. All documents like Guillaume de Machaut's are of considerable value because in them the probable and improbable interact in such a way that each explains and justifies the presence of the other. If there is a statistical character to our certainty it is because any document studied in isolation could be forged. This is unlikely, but not impossible, in the case of a single document. And yet it is impossible where a great number of documents are concerned.

The modern Western world chooses to interpret "texts of persecution" as real, this being the only possible way to demystify them. This solution is accurate and perfect because it makes allowance for all the characteristics found in this type of text. Solid intellectual reasoning is the basis, rather than humanitarianism or ideology. This interpretation has not usurped the almost unanimous agreement granted it. For the social historian reliable testimony, rather than the testimony of someone who shares Guillaume de Machaut's illusions, will never be as valuable as the unreliable testimony of persecutors, or their accomplices, which reveals more because of its unconscious nature. The conclusive document belongs to persecutors who are too naïve to cover the traces of their crimes, in contrast to modern persecutors who are too cautious to leave behind documents that might be used against them.

I call those persecutors naïve who are still convinced that they are right and who are not so mistrustful as to cover up or censor the fundamental characteristics of their persecution. Such characteristics are either clearly apparent in the text and are directly revealing or they remain hidden and reveal indirectly. They are all strong stereotypes and the combination of both types, one obvious and one hidden, provides us with information about the nature of these texts.

We are all able today to recognize the stereotypes of persecution. But what is now common knowledge scarcely existed in the fourteenth century. Naïve persecutors *are unaware of what they are doing*. Their conscience is too good to deceive their readers systematically, and they present things as they see them. They do not suspect that by writing their accounts they are arming posterity against them. This is true of the infamous "witch-hunts" of the sixteenth century. It is still true today in the backward regions of the world. We are, then, dealing with the commonplace, and my readers may be bored by my insistence on these first obvious facts. The purpose will soon be seen. One slight displacement is enough to transform what is taken for granted, in the case of Guillaume de Machaut, into something unusual and even inconceivable.

My readers will have already observed that in speaking as I do I contradict certain principles that numerous critics hold as sacrosanct. I am always told one must never do violence to the text. Faced with Guillaume de Machaut the choice is clear: one must either do violence to the text or let the text forever do violence to innocent victims. Certain principles universally held to be valid in our day, because they seem to guard against the excesses of certain interpretations, can bring about disastrous consequences never anticipated by those who, thinking they have foreseen everything, consider the principles inviolable. Everyone believes that the first duty of the critic is to respect the meaning of texts. Can this principle be sustained in the face of Guillaume de Machaut's work?

Another contemporary notion suffers in the light of Guillaume de Machaut's text, or rather from the unhesitating way we read it, and that is the casual way in which literary critics dismiss what they call the "referent." In current linguistic jargon the referent is the subject of the text; in our example it is the massacre of the Jews, who were seen as responsible for the poisoning of Christians. For some twenty years the referent has been considered more or less inaccessible. It is unimportant, we hear, whether we are capable or not of reaching it; this naïve notion of the referent would seem only to hamper the latest study of textuality. Now the only thing that matters is the ambiguous and unreliable relationships of language. This perspective is not to be rejected wholesale, but in applying it in a scholarly way we run the risk that only Ernest Hoeppfner, Guillaume's editor in the venerable Société des anciens textes, will be seen as the truly ideal critic of that writer. His introduction does in fact speak of courtly poetry, but there is never any mention of the massacre of the Jews during the plague.

The passage from Guillaume provides a good example of what I have called in *Things Hidden since the Foundation of the World* "persecution texts."[4] By that I mean accounts of real violence, often collective, told from the perspective of the persecutors, and therefore influenced by characteristic distortions. These distortions must be identified and corrected in order to reveal the arbitrary nature of the violence that the persecution text presents as justified.

We need not examine at length the accounts of witch trials to determine the presence of the same combination of real and imaginary, though not gratuitous, details that we found in the text of Guillaume de Machaut. Everything is presented as fact, but we do not believe all of it, nor do we believe that everything is false. Generally we have no difficulty in distinguishing fact from fiction. Again, the accusations made in trials seem ridiculous, even though the witch may consider them true and there may be reason to suspect her confession was not obtained by torture. The accused may well believe herself to be a witch, and may well have tried to harm her neighbors by magical proceedings. We still do not consider that she deserves the death sentence. We do not believe that magic is effective. We have no difficulty in accepting that the victim shares her torturers' ridiculous belief in the efficacy of witchcraft but this belief does not affect us; our skepticism is not shaken.

During the trial not a single voice is raised to reestablish or, rather, to establish the truth. No one is capable of doing so. This means that not only the judges and witnesses but also the accused are not in agreement with our interpretation of their own texts. This unanimity fails to influence us. The authors of these documents were there and we were not. We have access to no information that did not come from them. And yet, several centuries later, one single historian or even the first person to read the text feels he has the right to dispute the sentence pronounced on the witches.[5]

Guillaume de Machaut is reinterpreted in the same extreme way, the same audacity is exercised in overthrowing the text, the same intellectual operation is in effect with the same certainty, based on the same type of reasoning. The fact that some of the details are imagined does not persuade us to consider the whole text imaginary. On the contrary, the

4. Girard, *Things Hidden,* 126–38.

5. J. Hansen, *Zauberwahn, Inquisition und Hexenprozess im Mittelalter und die Entstehung der grossen Hexenverfolgung* (Munich, Leipzig: Scientia, 1900); Delumeau, *La Peur en Occident,* vol. 2, chap. 2. On the end of the witchcraft trials, see Robert Mandrou, *Magistrats et sorciers* (Paris: Plon, 1968). See also Natalie Zemon Davis, *Society and Culture in Early Modern France* (Stanford, Calif.: Stanford University Press, 1975).

incredible accusations strengthen rather than diminish the credibility of the other facts.

Once more we encounter what would seem to be, but is not, a paradoxical relationship between the probable and improbable details that enter into the text's composition. It is in the light of this relationship, not yet articulated but no less apparent to us, that we will evaluate the quantity and quality of the information that can be drawn from our text. If the document is of a legal nature, the results are usually as positive or even more positive than in the case of Guillaume de Machaut. It is unfortunate that most of the accounts were burned with the witches. The accusations are absurd and the sentence unjust, but the texts have been edited with the care and clarity that generally characterize legal documents. Our confidence is therefore well placed. There is no suspicion that we secretly sympathize with those who conducted the witch-hunts. The historian who would consider all the details of a trial equally fantastic, on the excuse that some of them are tainted by the distortions of the persecutors, is no expert, and his colleagues would not take him seriously. The most effective criticism does not consist in rejecting even the believable data on the ground that it is better to sin by excess rather than lack of distrust. Once again the principle of unlimited mistrust must give way to the golden rule of persecution texts: the mind of a persecutor creates a certain type of illusion and the traces of his illusion confirm rather than invalidate the existence of a certain kind of event, the persecution itself in which the witch is put to death. To distinguish the true from the false is a simple matter, since each bears the clear mark of a stereotype.

In order to understand the reasons behind this extraordinary assurance evidenced in persecution texts, we must enumerate and describe the stereotypes. This is also not a difficult task. It is merely a question of articulating an understanding we already possess. We are not aware of its scope because we never examine it in a systematic fashion. The understanding in question remains captive in the concrete examples to which we apply it, and these always belong to the mainly Western historical domain. We have never yet tried to apply this understanding beyond that domain, for example, to the so-called ethnological universe. To make this possible I am now going to sketch, in summary fashion, a typology of the stereotypes of persecution.[6]

6. This sketch of stereotypes of persecution, chapter 2 of *The Scapegoat,* is presented in the next chapter of the Reader. –*J. W.*

Chapter 8

Stereotypes of Persecution

In the second chapter of *The Scapegoat*, which is presented here, Girard offers a kind of "grammar" of persecution in his delineation of stereotypes of persecution. These stereotypes are: a crisis of the loss of the distinctions felt to be necessary to social order; accusations made against victims onto whom the alleged crimes undermining law and order are transferred; and the signs of victims, both those within the cultural system who are weak or marginal and those who exist outside the system, such as foreigners. Every culture is a differential system, which means that it coheres as a unitary complex of differences or distinctions. Those bearing the signs of victims do not differ in the right way—in a way in keeping with the system's complex of differences; they are thus always potentially threatening and may be the object of persecution and mob violence, or they may be set aside as a pool of sacrificial victims.

I shall confine my discussion to collective persecutions and their resonances. By collective persecutions I mean acts of violence committed directly by a mob of murderers such as the persecution of the Jews during the Black Death. By collective resonances of persecutions I mean acts of violence, such as witch-hunts, that are legal in form but stimulated by the extremes of public opinion. The distinction is not, however, essential. Political terrors, such as the French Revolution, often belong to both types. The persecutions in which we are interested generally take place in times of crisis, which weaken normal institutions and favor *mob* formation. Such spontaneous gatherings of people can exert a decisive influence on institutions that have been so weakened, and even replace them entirely.

These phenomena are not always produced by identical circumstances. Sometimes the cause is external, such as an epidemic, a severe drought, or a flood followed by famine. Sometimes the cause is internal—political disturbances, for example, or religious conflicts. Fortunately, we do not have to determine the actual cause. No matter what circumstances trigger great collective persecutions, the experience of those who live through them is the same. The strongest impression is without question an extreme loss of social order evidenced by the disappearance of the rules and "differences" that define cultural divisions. Descriptions of these events are all alike. Some of them, especially descriptions of the plague, are found in our greatest writers. We read them in Thucydides and Sophocles, in Lucretius, Boccaccio, Shakespeare, Defoe, Thomas Mann, Antonin Artaud, and many others. Some of them are also written by individuals with no literary pretensions, and there is never any great difference. We should not be surprised since all the sources speak endlessly of the absence of difference, the lack of cultural differentiation, and the confusion that results. For example the Portuguese monk Fco de Santa Maria writes in 1697:

> As soon as this violent and tempestuous spark is lit in a kingdom or a republic, magistrates are bewildered, people are terrified, the government thrown into disarray. Laws are no longer obeyed; business comes to a halt; families lose coherence, and the streets their lively atmosphere. Everything is reduced to extreme confusion. Everything goes to ruin. For everything is touched and overwhelmed by the weight and magnitude of such a horrible calamity. People regardless of position or wealth are drowning in mortal sadness.... Those who were burying others yesterday are themselves buried today.... No pity is shown to friends since every sign of pity is dangerous....
>
> All the laws of love and nature are drowned or forgotten in the midst of the horrors of such great confusion; children are suddenly separated from their parents, wives from their husbands, brothers and friends from each other.... Men lose their natural courage and, not knowing any longer what advice to follow, act like desperate blind men, who encounter fear and contradictions at every step.[1]

Institutional collapse obliterates or telescopes hierarchical and functional differences, so that everything has the same monotonous and monstrous aspect. The impression of difference in a society that is not in a state of crisis is the result of real diversity and also of a system of exchange that "differentiates" and therefore conceals the reciprocal elements it contains by its very culture and by the nature of the exchange. Marriages for example, or consumer goods, are not clearly perceived

1. Fco de Santa Maria, *Historia de sagradas concregaçøes* ... (Lisbon: M. L. Ferreyra, 1697); quoted by Delumeau, *La Peur en Occident,* 112.

as exchanges. When a society breaks down, time sequences shorten. Not only is there an acceleration of the tempo of positive exchanges that continue only when absolutely indispensable, as in barter for example, but also the hostile or "negative" exchanges tend to increase. The reciprocity of negative rather than positive exchanges becomes foreshortened as it becomes more visible, as witnessed in the reciprocity of insults, blows, revenge, and neurotic symptoms. That is why traditional cultures shun a too immediate reciprocity.

Negative reciprocity, although it brings people into opposition with each other, tends to make their conduct uniform and is responsible for the predominance of the *same*. Thus, paradoxically, it is both conflictual and solipsistic. This lack of differentiation corresponds to the reality of human relations, yet it remains mythic. In our own time we have had a similar experience which has become absolute because it is projected on the whole universe. The text quoted above highlights this process of creating uniformity through reciprocity: "Those who were burying others yesterday are themselves buried today.... No pity is shown to friends since every sign of pity is dangerous ... children are suddenly separated from their parents, wives from husbands, brother and friends from each other." The similarity of behavior creates confusion and a universal lack of difference: "People regardless of position or wealth are drowning in mortal sadness.... Everything is reduced to an extreme."

The experience of great social crisis is scarcely affected by the diversity of their true causes. The result is great uniformity in the descriptions that relate to the uniformity itself. Guillaume de Machaut is no exception. He sees in the egotistical withdrawal into the self and in the series or reprisals that result — the paradox of reciprocal consequences — one of the main causes of the plague. We can then speak of a stereotype of crisis which is to be recognized, logically and chronologically, as the first stereotype of persecution. Culture is somehow eclipsed as it becomes less differentiated. Once this is understood it is easier to understand the coherence of the process of persecution and the sort of logic that links all the stereotypes of which it is composed.

Men feel powerless when confronted with the eclipse of culture; they are disconcerted by the immensity of the disaster but never look into the natural causes; the concept that they might affect those causes by learning more about them remains embryonic. Since cultural eclipse is above all a social crisis, there is a strong tendency to explain it by social and, especially, moral causes. After all, human relations disintegrate in the process and the subjects of those relations cannot be utterly innocent of this phenomenon. But, rather than blame themselves, people inevitably blame either society as a whole, which costs them nothing, or other people who seem particularly harmful for easily identifiable reasons. The suspects are accused of a particular category of crimes.

Certain accusations are so characteristic of collective persecution that their very mention makes modern observers suspect violence in the air. They look everywhere for other likely indications — other stereotypes of persecution — to confirm their suspicion. At first sight the accusations seem fairly diverse but their unity is easy to find. First there are violent crimes which choose as object those people whom it is most criminal to attack, either in the absolute sense or in reference to the individual committing the act: a king, a father, the symbol of supreme authority, and in biblical and modern societies the weakest and most defenseless, especially young children. Then there are sexual crimes: rape, incest, bestiality. The ones most frequently invoked transgress the taboos that are considered the strictest in the society in question. Finally there are religious crimes, such as profanation of the host. Here, too, it is the strictest taboos that are transgressed.

All these crimes seem to be fundamental. They attack the very foundation of cultural order, the family and the hierarchical differences without which there would be no social order. In the sphere of individual action they correspond to the global consequences of an epidemic of the plague or of any comparable disaster. It is not enough for the social bond to be loosened; it must be totally destroyed.

Ultimately, the persecutors always convince themselves that a small number of people, or even a single individual, despite his relative weakness, is extremely harmful to the whole of society. The stereotypical accusation justifies and facilitates this belief by ostensibly acting the role of mediator. It bridges the gap between the insignificance of the individual and the enormity of the social body. If the wrongdoers, even the diabolical ones, are to succeed in destroying the community's distinctions, they must either attack the community directly, by striking at its heart or head, or else they must begin the destruction of difference within their own sphere by committing contagious crimes such as parricide and incest.

We need not take time to consider the ultimate causes of this belief, such as the unconscious desires described by psychoanalysts, or the Marxist concept of the secret will to oppress. There is no need to go that far. Our concern is more elementary; we are only interested in the mechanism of the accusation and in the interaction between representation and acts of persecution. They comprise a system, and, if knowledge of the cause is necessary to the understanding of the system, then the most immediate and obvious causes will suffice. The terror inspired in people by the eclipse of culture and the universal confusion of popular uprisings are signs of a community that is literally undifferentiated, deprived of all that distinguishes one person from another in time and space. As a result all are equally disordered in the same place and at the same time.

The crowd tends toward persecution since the natural causes of what troubles it and transforms it into a *turba*[2] cannot interest it. The crowd by definition seeks action but cannot affect natural causes. It therefore looks for an accessible cause that will appease its appetite for violence. Those who make up the crowd are always potential persecutors, for they dream of purging the community of the impure elements that corrupt it, the traitors who undermine it. The crowd's act of becoming a crowd is the same as the obscure call to assemble or mobilize, in other words to become a "mob." Actually this term comes from "mobile," which is as distinct from the word "crowd" as the Latin *turba* is from *vulgus*. The word "mobilization" reminds us of a military operation, against an already identified enemy or one soon to be identified by the mobilization of the crowd.

All the stereotypes of accusation were made against the Jews and other scapegoats during the plague. But Guillaume de Machaut does not mention them. As we have seen, he accuses the Jews of poisoning the rivers. He dismisses the most improbable accusations, and his relative moderation can perhaps be explained by the fact that he is an "intellectual." His moderation may also have a more general significance linked to intellectual development at the end of the Middle Ages.

During this period belief in occult forces diminished. Later we shall ask why. The search for people to blame continues but it demands more rational crimes; it looks for a material, more substantial cause. This seems to me to be the reason for the frequent references to *poison*. The persecutors imagined such venomous concentrations of poison that even very small quantities would suffice to annihilate entire populations. Henceforth the clearly lightweight quality of magic as a cause is weighted down by materiality and therefore "scientific" logic. Chemistry takes over from purely demoniac influence.

The objective remains the same, however. The accusation of poisoning makes it possible to lay the responsibility for real disasters on people whose activities have not been really proven to be criminal. Thanks to poison, it is possible to be persuaded that a small group, or even a single individual, can harm the whole society without being discovered. Thus poison is both less mythical and just as mythical as previous accusations or even the ordinary "evil eye," which is used to attribute almost any evil to almost any person. We should therefore recognize in the poisoning of drinking water a variation of a stereotypical accusation. The fact that these accusations are all juxtaposed in the witch trials is proof that they all respond to the same need. The suspects are always convicted of nocturnal participation is the famous *sabbat*. No alibi is possible since

2. Girard here uses the Latin *turba* in the sense of "confused crowd," a crowd on the verge of becoming a mob. –*J. W.*

the physical presence of the accused is not necessary to establish proof. Participation in criminal assemblies can be purely spiritual.

The crimes and their preparation with which the sabbat is associated have a wealth of social repercussions. Among them can be found the abominations traditionally attributed to the Jews in Christian countries, and before them to the Christians in the Roman Empire. They always include ritual infanticide, religious profanation, incestuous relationships, and bestiality. Food poisoning as well as offenses against influential or prestigious citizens always play a significant role. Consequently, despite her personal insignificance, a witch is engaged in activities that can potentially affect the whole of society. This explains why the devil and his demons are not disdainful of such an alliance. I will say no more about stereotypical accusations. It is easy to see their character and their link to the first stereotype, the crisis of undifferentiation.

I turn now to a third stereotype. The crowd's choice of victims may be totally random; but it is not necessarily so. It is even possible that the crimes of which they are accused are real, but that sometimes the persecutors choose their victims because they belong to a class that is particularly susceptible to persecution rather than because of the crimes they have committed. The Jews are among those accused by Guillaume de Machaut of poisoning the rivers. Of all the indications he gives us this is for us the most valuable, the one that most reveals the distortion of persecution. Within the context of other imaginary and real stereotypes, we know that this stereotype must be real. In fact, in modern Western society Jews have frequently been persecuted.

Ethnic and religious minorities tend to polarize the majorities against themselves. In this we see one of the criteria by which victims are selected, which, though relative to the individual society, is transcultural in principle. There are very few societies that do not subject their minorities, all the poorly integrated or merely distinct groups, to certain forms of discrimination and even persecution. In India the Moslems are persecuted, in Pakistan the Hindus. There are therefore universal signs for the selection of victims, and they constitute our third stereotype.

In addition to cultural and religious there are purely *physical* criteria. Sickness, madness, genetic deformities, accidental injuries, and even disabilities in general tend to polarize persecutors. We need only look around or within to understand the universality. Even today people cannot control a momentary recoil from physical abnormality. The very word "abnormal," like the word "plague" in the Middle Ages, is something of a taboo; it is both noble and cursed, *sacer* in all senses of the word. It is considered more fitting in English to replace it with the word "handicapped." The "handicapped" are subject to discriminatory measures that make them victims, out of all proportion to the extent to which their presence disturbs the ease of social exchange. One of the great qualities of our society is that it now feels obliged to take measures for their benefit.

Disability belongs to a large group of banal signs of a victim, and among certain groups — in a boarding school, for example — every individual who has difficulty adapting, someone from another country or state, an orphan, an only son, someone who is penniless, or even simply the latest arrival, is more or less interchangeable with a cripple. If the disability or deformity is real, it tends to polarize "primitive" people against the afflicted person. Similarly, if a group of people is used to choosing its victims from a certain social, ethnic, or religious category, it tends to attribute to them disabilities or deformities that would reinforce the polarization against the victim, were they real. This tendency is clearly observable in racist cartoons.

The abnormality need not be only physical. In any area of existence or behavior abnormality may function as the criterion for selecting those to be persecuted. For example there is such a thing as social abnormality; here the average defines the norm. The further one is from normal social status of whatever kind, the greater the risk of persecution. This is easy to see in relation to those at the bottom of the social ladder.

This is less obvious when we add another marginal group to the poor and outsiders — the marginal insider, the rich and powerful. The monarch and his court are often reminiscent of the *eye* of the hurricane. This double marginality is indicative of a social organization in turmoil. In normal times the rich and powerful enjoy all sorts of protection and privileges which the disinherited lack. We are concerned here not with normal circumstances but with periods of crisis. A mere glance at world history will reveal that the odds of a violent death at the hands of a frenzied crowd are statistically greater for the privileged than for any other category. Extreme characteristics ultimately attract collective destruction at some time or other, extremes not just of wealth or poverty, but also of success and failure, beauty and ugliness, vice and virtue, the ability to please and to displease. The weakness of women, children, and old people, as well as the strength of the most powerful, becomes weakness in the face of the crowd. Crowds commonly turn on those who originally held exceptional power over them.

No doubt some people will be shocked to find the rich and powerful listed among the victims of collective persecution under the same title as the poor and weak. The two phenomena are not symmetrical in their eyes. The rich and powerful exert an influence over society which justifies the acts of violence to which they are subjected in times of crisis. This is the holy revolt of the oppressed.

The borderline between rational discrimination and arbitrary persecution is sometimes difficult to trace. For political, moral, and medical reasons certain forms of discrimination strike us as reasonable today, yet they are similar to the ancient forms of persecution; for example, the quarantine of anyone who might be contagious during an epidemic. In the Middle Ages doctors were hostile to the idea that the plague could spread through physical contact with the diseased. Generally, they belonged to the enlightened group and any theory of contagion smacked too much of a persecutor's prejudice not to be suspect. And yet these doctors were wrong. For the idea of contagion to become established in the nineteenth century in a purely medical context, devoid of any association with persecution, it was necessary for there to be no suspicion that it was the return of prejudice in a new disguise.

This is an interesting question but has nothing to do with our present work. My only goal is to enumerate the qualities that tend to polarize violent crowds against those who possess them. The examples I have given unquestionably belong in this category. The fact that some of these acts of violence might even be justifiable today is not really important to the line of analysis I am pursuing.

I am not seeking to set exact boundaries to the field of persecution; nor am I trying to determine precisely where injustice begins or ends. Contrary to what some think, I am not interested in defining what is good and bad in the social and cultural order. My only concern is to show that the pattern of collective violence crosses cultures and that its broad contours are easily outlined. It is one thing to recognize the existence of this pattern, another to establish its relevance. In some cases this is difficult to determine, but the proof I am looking for is not affected by such difficulty. If a stereotype of persecution cannot be clearly recognized in a particular detail of a specific event, the solution does not rest only with this particular detail in an isolated context. We must determine whether or not the other stereotypes are present along with the detail in question.

Let us look at two examples. Most historians consider that the French monarchy bears some responsibility for the revolution in 1789. Does Marie Antoinette's execution therefore lie outside our pattern? The queen belongs to several familiar categories of victims of persecution; she is not only a queen but a foreigner. Her Austrian origin is mentioned repeatedly in the popular accusations against her. The court that condemns her is heavily influenced by the Paris mob. Our first stereotype can also be found; all the characteristics of the great crisis that provoke collective persecution are discernible in the French Revolution. To be sure historians are not in the habit of dealing with the details of the French Revolution as stereotypes of the one general pattern of persecution. I do not suggest that we should substitute this way of thinking in all our ideas about the French Revolution. Nonetheless it sheds interesting light on an accusation which is often passed over but which figures explicitly in the queen's trial, that of having committed incest with her son.[3]

Let's look at another example of a condemned person, someone who has actually committed the deed that brings down on him the crowd's violence: a black male who actually rapes a white female. The collective violence is no longer arbitrary in the most obvious sense of the term. It is actually sanctioning the deed it purports to sanction. Under such circumstances the distortions of persecution might be supposed to play no role and the existence of the stereotypes of persecution might no longer bear the significance I give it. Actually, these distortions of persecution are present and are not incompatible with the literal truth of the accusation. The persecutor's portrayal of the situation is irrational. It inverts the relationship between the global situation and the individual transgression. If there is a causal or motivational link between the two levels, it can only move from the collective to the individual. The persecutor's mentality moves in the reverse direction. Instead of seeing in the microcosm a reflection or imitation of the global level, it seeks in the individual the origin and cause of all that is harmful. The responsibility of the victims suffers the same fantastic exaggeration whether it is real or not. As far as we are concerned there is very little difference between Marie Antoinette's situation and that of the persecuted black male.

We have seen the close relationship that exists between the first two stereotypes. In order to blame victims for the loss of distinctions resulting from the crisis, they are accused of crimes that eliminate distinctions. But in actuality they are identified as victims for persecution because they bear the signs of victims. What is the relationship of the third type to the first two stereotypes? At first sight the signs of a victim are purely differential. But cultural signs are equally so. There must therefore be two ways of being different, two types of differences.

No culture exists within which everyone does not feel "different" from others and does not consider such "differences" legitimate and necessary. Far from being radical and progressive, the current glorification of difference is merely the abstract expression of an outlook common to all cultures. There exists in every individual a tendency to think of himself not only as different from others but as extremely different, because every culture entertains this feeling of difference among the individuals who compose it.

The signs that indicate a victim's selection result not from the difference within the system but from the difference outside the system, the

3. I am grateful to Jean-Claude Guillebaud for drawing my attention to this accusation of incest.

potential for the system to differ from its own difference, in other words not to be different at all, to cease to exist as a system. This is easily seen in the case of physical disabilities. The human body is a system of anatomic differences. If a disability, even as the result of an accident, is disturbing, it is because it gives the impression of a disturbing dynamism. It seems to threaten the very system. Efforts to limit it are unsuccessful; it disturbs the differences that surround it. These in turn become *monstrous,* rush together, are compressed and blended together to the point of destruction. Difference that exists outside the system is terrifying because it reveals the truth of the system, its relativity, its fragility, and its mortality.

The various kinds of victims seem predisposed to crimes that eliminate differences. Religious, ethnic, or national minorities are never actually reproached for their difference, but for not being as different as expected, and in the end for not differing at all. Foreigners are incapable of respecting "real" differences; they are lacking in culture or in taste, as the case may be. They have difficulty in perceiving exactly what is different. The *barbaros* is not the person who speaks a different language but the person who mixes the only truly significant distinctions, those of the Greek language. In all the vocabulary of tribal or national prejudices hatred is expressed, not for difference, but for its absence. It is not the other *nomos* that is seen in the other, but anomaly, nor is it another norm but abnormality; the disabled becomes deformed; the foreigner becomes the *apatride.* It is not good to be a cosmopolitan in Russia. Aliens imitate all the differences because they have none. The mechanisms of our ancestors are reproduced unconsciously, from generation to generation, and, it is important to recognize, often at a less lethal level than in the past. For instance today anti-Americanism pretends to "differ" from previous prejudices because it espouses all differences and rejects the uniquely American virus of uniformity.

We hear everywhere that "difference" is persecuted. This is the favorite statement of contemporary pluralism, and it can be somewhat misleading in the present context.

Even in the most closed cultures men believe they are free and open to the universal; their differential character makes the narrowest cultural fields seem inexhaustible from within. Anything that compromises this illusion terrifies us and stirs up the immemorial tendency to persecution. This tendency always takes the same direction; it is embodied by the same stereotypes and always responds to the same threat. Despite what is said around us persecutors are never obsessed by difference but rather by its unutterable contrary, the lack of difference.

Stereotypes of persecution cannot be dissociated, and remarkably most languages do not dissociate them. This is true of Latin and Greek, for example, and thus of French or English, which forces us constantly in our study of stereotypes to turn to words that are related: "crisis," "crime," "criteria," "critique," all share a common root in the Greek verb *krino,* which means not only to judge, distinguish, differentiate, but also to accuse and condemn a victim. Too much reliance should not be placed on etymology, nor do I reason from that basis. But the phenomenon is so constant it deserves to be mentioned. It implies an as yet concealed relationship between collective persecutions and the culture as a whole. If such a relationship exists, it has never been explained by any linguist, philosopher, or politician.

Chapter 9

Python and His Two Wives: An Exemplary Scapegoat Myth

The myth of Python and his wives, which belongs to the Venda, a people of South Africa, is a typical instance of a witchcraft persecution text. In this analysis of a Venda myth, which was first published as an appendix to Richard J. Golsan, *René Girard and Myth: An Introduction* (New York and London: Garland Publishing, Inc., 1993), 151-79, Girard offers a more extended version of the methodology presented in *The Scapegoat.* He holds that Python and his wives may eventually be understood as an important piece of evidence for determining the primary generative features of the original myths of the Psyche type, prior to their Greek and German versions.

— ❧ —

According to the mimetic theory, myths reflect a contagious process of disorder that culminates with the death or expulsion of a victim.

The escalations of mimetic rivalry to which archaic societies are prone stir up all kinds of disorders until their very intensity produces a unanimous polarization against a more or less random victim. Mimetically carried away, the entire community joins in, and as a result, mutual suspicions are extinguished; peace returns.

The scapegoaters do not understand their own scapegoat mechanism and they project upon their victim both their dissensions and their reconciliation. This is the double transference of the sacred which appears as both a source of disorder and a source of order. Its mythical embodiments are both malefactors and benefactors.

It follows from this that mythical heroes can never appear *as scapegoats* in their own myths. Those who try to turn this absence of a *scapegoat theme* into an instant refutation of the mimetic theory simply do not understand the *genetic* role of scapegoating in these texts.

I use the word "scapegoat" in the modern sense, of course, necessarily different from the Leviticus ritual which it implicitly demystifies. No one tries to indict scapegoaters on the basis of what they say about their own scapegoats. They cannot be expected to beat their breasts and proclaim loudly: "Our victim is only a scapegoat." When we suspect scapegoating we cannot verify our suspicion directly; we must rely on indirect clues.

Students of myth too must rely on indirect clues. In the myths easiest to analyze, the ones upon which I have focused most attention, and will once again in this essay, they are as follows:

1. A theme of disorder or undifferentiation, which does not always come first since it is seen as a consequence of the scapegoat's misdeed, rather than as a cause. The expressions of this theme may range from original chaos, or a catastrophe of cosmic proportions, to almost any kind of disaster. It may be a plague epidemic, a fire, a flood, a drought, a quarrel between relatives, preferably twin brothers. It may be any disturbance or state of incompletion from which the community suffers. It may be other things as well. They all express some mimetic disturbances in the community that generate the myth. They may be symbolic, real, or simultaneously symbolic and real.

2. One particular individual stands convicted of some fault. It may be a heinous crime and it may be a mere misdemeanor, even an accidental faux-pas. Regardless of how trivial or dreadful the incriminating action is, its consequences are catastrophic: they are none other than the state of chaos, crisis, or incompletion from which the community suffers. The hero or heroine is really seen as the cause of the crisis. This is scapegoat projection.

3. The identification of the scapegoat is often facilitated by what I call preferential signs of victimage. They are the very diverse characteristics or attributes that tend to arouse the hostility of a crowd against their possessors. They testify to the objective arbitrariness of the victim's selection. Mythical scapegoats are often physically, morally, or socially impaired; they may be strangers, cripples, outcasts, persons of very low or very high standing, etc. These signs do not constitute a separate theme and they may be completely absent.

4. The "culprit" is killed, expelled, or otherwise eliminated, either by the whole community acting like one man or by a single individual, one of the brothers, for instance, if brothers are involved. This is scapegoating *stricto sensu,* the violent deed, the fruit of the mimetic polarization triggered by the mimetic crisis.

5. As soon as the violence against the victim is consummated, peace returns; order is (re)generated. This, too, is projected onto the scapegoat who is revealed as a founding ancestor or a divinity. This is the second transference of the sacred.

For an illustration of such a myth and its mimetic analysis, I will now go to a very transparent example that belongs to the Venda, a people of South Africa. For the purpose of this presentation I have amalgamated and slightly condensed the two versions reproduced by Luc de Heusch in his *Le Roi ivre ou l'origine de l'état* (Gallimard, 1972, 61–62):

> Python, the water snake, had two wives. The first knew who he was but the second wife did not know and she was not supposed to know. In the middle of the night, she would wake up drenched. The first wife tried to protect her husband's secret but her rival was curious and, after a good deal of spying on him she discovered the truth. Then, all the rivers dried up. The only water left was in the lake at the bottom of which Python had taken refuge.
>
> When they learned from the first wife the reason for Python's disappearance, the old men decided that a beer offering should be prepared. Divination revealed that Python desired the company of his second wife. While the men were playing the flute, the young woman entered the water, carrying the beer offering in a basket. As the music grew louder, she disappeared, and the rain began to fall; the rivers filled up and all the people rejoiced.

The woman designated as the *second wife* is indicted for scaring away a divine snake and thus causing a drought. The drought is the real and/or symbolic crisis and the fault that supposedly causes it is the scapegoat accusation. The victim dies by drowning in front of the assembled community, a typical scapegoat death.

This death is presented as a *beer offering*, a sacrificial rite that should fully appease the offended god since it simultaneously punishes the offender and returns his favorite wife to a loving husband. Since the drought ends as a result of her death, the victim partakes of the sacred. The insignificant troublemaker of the beginning has become the savior of the community, together with her beloved husband, Python, the water god. The double transference of the sacred is not defined explicitly but its presence is unmistakable.

The victim is a woman and also a second wife, hierarchically inferior to the first. These determinations can be regarded as preferential signs of victimage, not particularly spectacular, to be sure, but we do not really need them. The identification of the scapegoat relies primarily on the idea that the drought is caused by the fantastic misconduct of the second wife with her fantastic husband, and on the fact that the drought is ended by her death. My analysis will soon make it evident that these themes and their arrangement *demand* a real victim.

Insofar as it pertains to the internal peace of a community, unanimous scapegoating is self-fulfilling; it really concludes the crisis. The same cannot be true in regard to a drought. Do I assume that the death of a young woman can favorably influence a drought? Certainly not. All we have to believe is that the victim died just before the natural end of the drought, assuming, once again, that the drought was a real one.

We may suppose that the "beer offering" recorded in our myth was not the only one during the whole mimetic crisis in which this myth is rooted. If this mimetic crisis was not a purely internal phenomenon, if it was caused by a real drought, we can also suppose that the particular "beer offering" portrayed in it happened to coincide with the natural end of the drought. What generated the myth was the conjunction of the mimetic reconciliation against the scapegoat, plus the natural end of the drought. This chance timing made this particular episode of scapegoating a long-range success, memorable enough to generate a myth.

❧

Most students of myth will reject out of hand the interpretation I have just outlined. Knowing that I regard the myth as the trace of an extratextual drama, a real scapegoat phenomenon, they will quit listening. The assertion that the victim must be real seems irresponsible. They see a theoretical impossibility to which I must be blind.

These critics dismiss my work a priori, without examining my demonstration. They are absolutely certain that I cannot be right. The failure of my interpretation is too obvious, they feel, to require a complete refutation.

This conviction relies essentially on the fantastic aspect of myth, which is seen as an insurmountable obstacle to the realism, or referentiality, of my interpretation. In the present example, for instance, we have a divine snake, a water god that causes a drought because the excessive curiosity of his wife drives him into hiding. Even interpreters free from the currently fashionable anti-referential bias will find it incredible that a text with such a nonsensical theme in it could ever become a source of extratextual information.

Two themes in our myth, the drought and the death by drowning, could *possibly* yield extratextual information but only in a nonfantastic context. Their potential in that respect seems nullified by the story of the divine snake which is inextricably entangled with the rest of the myth. "Tell me what company you keep and I will tell you who you are."

When I say that there must be a real victim behind our Venda myth, and other similar myths, I blatantly disregard, it seems, what everybody agrees must be the most basic principle of critical prudence. No text can be more reliable than the least reliable of its components. Let us call it the *law of contamination by the unbelievable.* Even interpreters unaffected by the interpretive nihilism of our time will see no possible compromise on this point. I certainly violate this law. But my reasons for doing so are legitimate. Critics will retort that there cannot be any legitimate reason for such a violation. They think that the law is absolute, that it suffers no exception. They are wrong.

I am going to show that there are exceptions to the law of contamination by the fantastic, and everybody tacitly agrees that they are legitimate. I will then show that, even though they are not included among these exceptions, foundational myths should be.

❧

The texts I have in mind are thematically and structurally similar to our Venda myths. They are stereotyped modalities of collective persecution and their interpretation rightfully violates the law of contamination by the unbelievable. They relate the violent actions performed by deluded persecutors, witch hunters for instance, and they believe that the women accused of witchcraft are truly guilty. They include unbelievable features, therefore, presented as solid evidence against the accused, *bona fide* truth.

In *The Scapegoat* I have shown that we interpret these medieval texts *against* their own superstitious and violent spirit, in a manner that closely parallels my interpretation of myth.[1] In order to understand these texts we must realize that the authors mistake the unbelievable for the truth because they participate in the scapegoating of the victims. The French poet Guillaume de Machaut, for instance, believed that the Jews really contributed to the Black Death epidemic by poisoning the sources of drinking water and committing all sorts of crimes.

Even though these texts take at face value the fantastic material they contain, modern historians do not regard them as necessarily useless from the standpoint of objective information. They understand the reason for the author's credulity. They have no trouble detecting a magical accusation behind the fantastic theme and they realize that, dreadful as its consequences are, the author's blindness does not necessarily extend to all data in his text and does not invalidate the entire account, especially insofar as the other data relate to the violent consequences of scapegoating. If the author reports that the accused have been killed or otherwise punished, there is a good chance that, on this point at least, he is saying the truth.

These texts reflect a mimetic polarization broadly similar to the one I think can also be deduced from the themes and structure of all myths of the type exemplified by our Venda myth.

❧

Let us first find out a little more in detail how our myth responds to the possibility that, like the medieval texts, it might reflect a scapegoat mechanism triggered by a magical accusation.

---

1. See chapters 7 and 8 of this Reader. —*J.W.*

The longish first part of our myth is initially a little confusing, but as soon as we examine it from the standpoint of a witchcraft accusation, the confusion clears up.

The second wife is presented as the *rival* of the first. In reality, as her husband's favorite, she has no reason to be jealous or envious of anyone. The first wife, on the contrary, has a good reason to regard the second as a rival. The myth seems to espouse the viewpoint of the first wife in this affair. This is only one of the signs that designate the first wife as the accuser of the second.

To their husbands, second wives are usually more attractive than first wives, at least for a while. First wives have more authority, however, not only in their household, but with the community. They are in a good position to make life difficult for second wives, and even, it seems, to exact a dreadful vengeance for the humiliation of being supplanted by a younger woman. It is for a husband to decide which wife he chooses for the night. Just before the drama, the husband of our two wives, it seems, was spending all his nights with wife number two, and part of his days as well.

Wife number one was incensed. Being in charge during the day, she would try to prevent additional rendezvous between the two lovers. Apparently she was not very successful.

The situation perfectly accounts for the peculiarities of the accusation against the second wife. As a wife, she is just as legitimate as the first and she cannot be indicted simply for being her husband's favorite. Having no special rights to claim, the first wife must concoct a more arcane transgression, and she elaborated the myth of a divine status for her husband, of which she alone is supposed to be informed.

Even this most fantastic aspect of our myth must not be fiction in the sense that our literary critics demand. Their fabrication *ex nihilo* probably does not exist at all. The mimetic theory suggests an explanation for the divinity of the husband. It must go back to the mimetic rivalry between the wives which, as usual, magnifies the value of the disputed object so much that it seems divine. Imagination and imitation are one and the same thing.

The dreaded secret, we are told, could not be kept away from the second wife for long. She discovered the "truth" about her husband even though or perhaps because her rival was trying very hard to prevent that discovery.

This catastrophic disclosure too must be a mythical reading of the mimetic escalation that any rivalry tends to generate. The obstacles that the two women place in each other's path finally turn the husband into a divinity not only in the eyes of the most frustrated first wife, but in the eyes of the other as well, whose frustration must grow as a result of the first wife's behavior. Being perpetually crossed by this jealous woman, the second wife finally surrenders to the spirit of the rivalry, the spirit of her rival.

Our myth sounds like a malevolent fantasizing of mimetic rivalry, triggered by a husband's preference for a younger wife, the twisted expression of a jealousy that finds the triumph of a rival intolerable.

The first part of our myth seems merely to repeat what the first wife told the elders about the origin of the drought. This means that first these elders and then the whole people mimetically embraced these mad rantings, thus turning them into the truth of the myth, the sacred dogma of the entire tribe.

The second wife is too insignificant to be regarded as the direct and principal cause of the drought. She belongs in the "sorcerer's apprentice" category. She was too simple and flighty to realize that her pestering of the god — what her enemy interprets as such — could harm the whole community. Even a beloved favorite can abuse her privileges and make herself obnoxious in the eyes of an easily offended divinity.

The first wife showed genius when she linked her rival to the drought. Or is it the community's obsession that created that link? We cannot tell and it does not matter. All we need to remember is that everywhere in the world, even today, any natural or man-made disaster intensifies the appetite for victims and causes accusations to proliferate. Even in our world, when a crisis breaks out, accusations border on the magical and, regardless of the facts, politicians have to pay the price.

The myth says, of course, that the second wife's alleged indiscretion with her divine husband came first, not the drought. This is obvious nonsense, but in the light of our hypothesis, highly significant nonsense. The mythical sequence is a scapegoat inspired reversal of cause and effect. The jealousy of the first wife has nothing to do with the drought but the drought provides the ideal terrain for it and it spreads like wildfire.

If our myth first seemed like a heterogeneous collection of themes, this impression is now entirely dissipated, replaced by something so coherent that the reality of the drama reflected in it becomes highly probable. Just as in the case of Machaut, or of medieval witch-hunting, we are led to believe that a real victim must have perished.

All the themes dovetail in such a way as to confirm the scapegoat interpretation of the whole text. What clinches the case is the very theme that made the myth look like inextricable nonsense when we first read it, the snake god. The role of this deity fits too perfectly with the rivalry of the two women, with the killing of the victim and finally with the end of the drought, not to compel the reasonably attentive reader to perceive the scapegoat reading as the only commonsensical solution to the riddle of this text.

Let us go back to the law of contamination by the fantastic. Just as in the case of medieval texts, we can and we must suspend its application because the magical accusation hypothesis works too well to be rejected. The story of the snake is no longer the sole affair of the first wife but that which everybody believes, the consensus of the whole community, the content of the scapegoat accusations. We can well understand, therefore, why the myth handles this nonsense as if it were the truth.

As soon as we see this, we no longer have to assume that the myth is necessarily valueless from the standpoint of extratextual information. If the second wife is the target of a scapegoat polarization, the probability of a real victim, treated just as the myth suggests, is very high.

The scapegoaters truly cannot distinguish the true from the false. It is not poetic imagination or the Freudian unconscious that generated our Venda myth but the jealousy of the first wife, authenticated by the unanimous scapegoating of the community. The myth-makers are deluded scapegoaters in very much the same sense as medieval witch-hunters.

Our reading of the myth can reach this conclusion because the scapegoat hypothesis turns the fantastic theme into a magical accusation similar to a witchcraft accusation in a medieval text. This hypothesis enables us to sort out the fantastic theme in our myth and keep it separate from the other themes. The idea of a magical accusation functions like a *cordon sanitaire* that prevents the fantastic data from contaminating the nonfantastic ones and destroying their credibility. The same idea also disentangles the believable from the unbelievable in the case of medieval texts. Looking at each detail separately we have been doing step by step and quite deliberately what the readers of medieval texts do so rapidly and instinctively that it hardly reaches their consciousness. They *discount* the magical theme because they immediately realize that it is a magical accusation.

Far from being an outlandish and farfetched invention, "my theory" of myth is not even "mine." It is patterned after the historians' interpretation of texts we long ago learned to demystify. It is the application to myth of a critical practice that seems unproblematic as long as it remains confined to our own cultural context. If this practice were examined for its own sake, the theory of it would be mimetic in the sense of my mimetic theory.

Let us forget for a while that our Venda myth is called a myth and let us pretend that it originated somewhere in Europe in the fifteenth century. Let us shift the language to medieval Latin or some French or German dialect. To do a credible job, we must modify some themes but very slightly. The general tenor and the structure of our text will remain the same.

The beer offering and the flute playing have no place in the medieval world and we eliminate them. The snake can remain but not as a legitimate husband and not as a divinity. We must turn him into a demon, or the devil himself. The idea that a woman can make love to a snake who is really Satan in disguise poses no problem *as a witchcraft accusation.*

We would not be surprised to see that this charge leads to the drowning of the accused. It is presented as true, just as true as the drowning itself, because everybody involved believed that it was true. The inability of the text to distinguish the unbelievable from the believable does not mean that it should be regarded as unbelievable *in toto,* it means that a mimetic scapegoat genesis should be inferred. With a few minor changes, we almost instantly transform our myth into an example of medieval witch hunting that is too *transparent* not to be convincing.

Fire was the most popular way of dealing with witches but drowning was not uncommon. And, just as in the case of the second wife, the death of a witch was regarded as beneficial to the community, not to the extent that a mythical drama is, no doubt, but to a degree sufficient for us to realize that the principle of the transfiguration is the same. If a witch is accused of causing a drought, and if she dies for it, we can be sure that her death will be credited with the return of the rain, provided of course, that the account comes from true believers.

If our myth were a *bona fide* historical text, not even the most ardent textual nihilist would dare reject the realistic and referential explication that I just gave. Everybody would agree that there must be a real woman behind the text and that she is a scapegoat.

Everybody would understand that the conjunction of themes in our Venda text cannot be fortuitous. It can only result from a collective appetite for real victims, stirred up no doubt, by a severe drought and by the tensions that it stirs up in the community.

If some would-be interpreter insisted that the accounts on which we base our certainty of real victims are too contaminated with fantastic data to be regarded as a plausible source of information on any subject, he would be regarded as naïve or worse still, he would be suspected of sympathy for the witch hunters.

Is it possible to say that, even though our Venda myth and a medieval record of deluded witch-hunting may be quite alike in regard to both the themes and the organization of these themes, the differences between the contexts in which medieval texts on the one hand and myths on the other are situated justifies the different interpretation of the two texts?

Are the differences so important between the application of the scapegoat theory inside our culture and its application outside that the second becomes illegitimate?

I already mentioned the first difference and main difference. Myths contain material more fantastic and less circumscribed than the material contained in medieval texts, and the language in which they are couched is more alien to our rationality than the language of even the most fantastic witchcraft accusations in the Western world.

True as this may be, a detailed examination will show that the nature of the fantastic material is similar at bottom in both types of texts and that many myths, among which I would include our Venda example, are less fantastic than many medieval texts that we find intelligible as traces of scapegoat persecution.

A second difference is that, in the case of medieval Europe, we have a great deal of historical background which helps us place the text in a light favorable to the type of interpretation that faces up to the probable reality of the victims and of the violence they suffered. In the case of myth we have practically no background information.

It is true, of course, that we know a great deal about the Middle Ages and almost nothing about the societies from which myths originate. This difference is clearly the reason why we do not dare interpret similar texts in a similar way when they come from the second rather than from the first context.

Our knowledge of what the historians call the witchcraft epidemic of the late Middle Ages certainly plays a role *in our readiness* to bring forward the magical accusation hypothesis. In a medieval context, historians are always willing to read the various themes and their structural arrangement as clues to a scapegoat polarization. In a mythical context, this willingness is not there. The hypothesis of a magical accusation is never mentioned by the students of myth.

But this readiness does not really depend on precise historical information. It is easy to show that our reading of historical witch-hunting, or analogous persecutions, is not always based on detailed knowledge of when and where the document originated, or in what circumstances. In the case of Guillaume de Machaut, for instance, we have no indication of place or time; we do not even know in which city the poet resided during the Black Death epidemic.

The reading in terms of a scapegoat polarization requires no background knowledge except for a general awareness of a rampant fear of witchcraft in the society where Machaut was writing.

If that awareness is always there, at the ready, in the back of our mind, when we are confronted by the right kind of text, such as our Venda myth, we cannot fail to wonder if the interpretation of the fantastic material in terms of a fantastic accusation might not click with the other themes and provide us with the perfect explanation, the one that makes everything intelligible.

Our little experiment with the Venda myth demonstrates that in our refusal to go to scapegoating as an explication of our Venda myth, the context is everything. We refuse the right interpretation because we have no historical background to back it up. But the context is everything not because it is really useful but because it modifies our willingness to read the text as it can be read. The medieval context provides no information that is not available as well in the case of myth-making societies.

In order to generate myth, the fear of witchcraft does not have to reach the acute level that it did at the end of the Middle Ages. All we have to assume is that this fear was present in the societies from which myths originate. This is a most reasonable assumption. In the more specific case of the Venda people, we know for sure that magic is an important part of their belief-system and that even today, witchcraft accusations are widespread and a major cause of violent crime.

The law of contamination by the unbelievable is not merely suspended: it is reversed. There is now a law of contamination by the believable.

The fact that the author presents the fantastic accusations as true makes him, in principle, less reliable as a man and therefore as the author of the text we are reading. This is true, and yet, paradoxically but logically, it makes the text that he produced under the influence of scapegoating more rather than less reliable in the portion of it that is potentially reliable, the material that relates to the "punishment" of the "culprit," or "culprits," i.e., that violence inflicted on the victims.

How can that be? The very credulity of our author suggests the existence of a mood in the community, conducive to violence against the victims. The probability that the violence really occurred is increased rather than decreased by the presence of the fantastic elements in the text. This is an essential point that is always ignored and that I have not defined properly until now.

The conjunction of themes is too significant to be fortuitous. There is still a chance that it could be fortuitous if we only had one example of such a text, or even a few. The more we have, the more a fortuitous assemblage of themes seems unlikely. If this reasoning is sound, and I doubt very much that it can be challenged, our next question will be the following: Why, in the case of historical texts, are we willing to resort to the scapegoat explication and not in the case of myths?

The decisive difference between medieval historians and students of myth is not in the texts they interpret. It is not the presence or absence of historical knowledge. It is that the first are willing and the second unwilling to entertain the possibility that an accusation and scapegoat mechanism might be involved in the genesis of thematically and structurally similar texts.

First, is the reading of historians really certain? They suffer from a bad reputation among interpreters influenced by the radical skepticism of our age. Is it really certain that real victims lie behind the medieval texts? Are not the historians too easily satisfied with a sloppy handling of their texts, are they not more credulous than they should be, more credulous than the students of myth who, under the influence of radical thinking and literary theory, deny all possible referentiality to their texts? Are they a little soft on the referent, perhaps too easily satisfied with a naïve view of the relationship between a text and an extratextual reality?

In order to show that the historians' certainty of reaching real dramas behind their texts is well founded, we must go back briefly to the arrangement of themes that characterizes both myths and medieval texts of persecution.

Why am I convinced that the fantastic theme of our Venda myth is a magical accusation of the first wife mimetically embraced by the whole community? The explication is convincing because it explains not merely the long first paragraph of our myth, the accusation itself, but the other themes of the myth, the drought, the drowning of the woman, the consequences of that drowning.

The interpretation is so complete and perfect that it suspends the law of contamination by the fantastic. Or rather what happens here is more drastic and paradoxical than a mere suspension. The law is turned upside down. While still unbelievable in the absolute, the divine snake and the whole story of the first wife are so believable as a magical accusation that it makes the other themes more believable than they would be in and by themselves, in the absence of the magical accusation. Instead of being diminished by the fantastic theme, the likelihood that an innocent woman really died by drowning is increased. The potential referentiality of the myth as a whole is considerably increased.

Instead of a contamination by the unbelievable, we now have the very reverse, a contamination by the believable. As we realize that the drought provides the ideal terrain for the first wife's accusation, the drought becomes more believable. And so does the drowning of the woman. And so do the beneficial consequences of that drowning. The more we look at any one of these themes in the light of all the others, the more believable everything becomes.

All this believability adds up to an extremely coherent interpretation, but the anti-referential critics will not be satisfied that it adds up to a certainty. Good interpretations are a dime a dozen, they say, and of no interpretation can it be said that it is the one and only true interpretation. There is no such thing as an authoritative interpretation.

This may well be true for a poem of Mallarmé, but our Venda myth is not a literary text and, against those who want to assimilate all texts to poems, we must assert that the interpretation I just gave is not hermeneutical in the ordinary sense if we deny hermeneutics the ability to reach what I do not hesitate to call the truth of the text, its absolute truth. We can and must say that the scapegoat explication is true without reservations of any kind. We must reject interpretive pluralism as absurd and dangerous nonsense, at least in this one domain, potentially destructive of a certainty on which our very essential liberties depend.

In order to validate this affirmation, I will first show that historians are right to regard as absolutely certain the reality of victims whose existence we know only through testimony of texts fundamentally unreliable since they embrace fantastic data as if they were the truth.

The reality of the Jews and the non-Jews mentioned by Machaut and others as having been killed at the outset of the Black Death epidemic is a historical certainty, even though the victims are presented as guilty and all the texts we have must be regarded as untrustworthy, the work of untrustworthy authors.

The "even though" is really a "because." Far from making the account of the violent deeds reported by them untrustworthy, the untrustworthiness of the authors paradoxically increases the probability that they are speaking the truth.

In order to see that this paradox is not really a paradox, we must reflect on the specific nature of the believable and unbelievable data in the texts at issue, and the relationship between the two.

When large numbers of human beings become hysterical enough to regard as entirely truthful the grotesque accusations against would-be witches, or the Jews during plague epidemics, the consequences are quite predictable. Once awakened, the crowd's appetite for violence demands to be nourished. The best possible nourishment, of course, consists in the presumed culprits and, even in the eventuality that they be protected by the authorities, the crowd is numerous enough to take justice into its own hands in order to destroy the people in whose guilt it believes.

In the historical world the logic of the fantastic accusation that results in some form of violence against the accused is so logical that, when we find it in a text we automatically assume that it may well correspond to a real sequence of events.

Let us imagine two texts. The first one tells us simply that some violent disturbances have occurred because of alleged facts of witchcraft and that some people have been killed. The author does not even mention the accusations against the victims. He seems rational and his account must be taken seriously, but no more seriously and perhaps a little less, given the temper of the times, than a very similar account in which typical witchcraft accusations would be included and would be treated as absolutely convincing evidence, unquestionable truth. This second author may well be less reliable than the first in an absolute sense, but he is just as reliable and even more reliable relative to the affair that he reports. The reason for his greater reliability is what we can infer from his own text. When he wrote it, his mental attitude and his mood were precisely the ones that the judges had to share with him, if there was a trial, or the violent mob, if there was no trial, in order to behave as violently with the presumed culprits as the text claims that they did.

Between the events reported by the author and his attitude toward the possible victims there is a mutual fit, an appropriateness that reinforces the probability of the reported violence having really occurred and therefore the victims being real.

The texts mystified by a faith in witchcraft reveal that their authors, and those who inspired them, were, at the time of writing, in the state of anguish, indignation, and credulity most conducive to the violent actions that they tell us were really committed.

In conjunction with the other themes of the text, the very theme that does make these authors unreliable as individuals, because it reveals a surrender to the spirit of the mob, makes them especially good informants in regard to the effects of that same mob spirit, if the reported effects are those which we know are likely to occur.

The skeptics will still not be satisfied, and they have a right not to be. This is well and good, they will say; the probability that these texts speak the truth is quite high, but it still is no more than a probability. It is not a certainty. To this one must answer that the objection would be valid if there existed only one text of the type I am now discussing, or at the most a few.

As long as scapegoat-generated texts are few in number, a possibility remains that the tell-tale arrangement of themes in these texts is purely fortuitous, a matter of chance, or some kind of hoax, a deliberate forgery.

Since the probability can never turn itself into a certainty in the case of one individual text, of no individual text can we assert with complete certainty that there is a real victim behind it. But this is unimportant if the number of texts is large enough. The uncertainty turns into complete certainty if the number of texts is large enough. And in the case of our medieval texts it certainly is.

Because we have a large number of texts that report the murder of presumed witches as if they were really guilty, we can say with absolute certainty that there was an epidemic of witch-hunting at the end of the Middle Ages.

Our certainty is due to the fact that these texts are too similar in their themes and structures and they originate in too many different places and at too many different times for them to be the fruit of a chance assemblage of themes, or of gratuitous invention, or of a fabrication for the purpose of faking a witchcraft epidemic that, in reality, would never have taken place.

With each individual text none of these hypotheses can be entirely discounted but, with all of them together, they must be. Our individual doubts regarding each text do not add up to a statistically significant doubt regarding the whole. It is statistically impossible that forgery, the poetic imagination, or any other explication could satisfactorily account for the vast number of texts that contain tell-tale signs of many so-called witches being scapegoated, and they contain such signs because the authors themselves partake in the scapegoating and therefore write about the victims in part falsely, insofar as they agree with the accusers, and in part truthfully, insofar as they faithfully report what happened to these real victims. Being convinced that the violence against them was justified, they had no motivation for hiding from each other or from us the violence that these victims suffered.

The only rational hypothesis is that most of these texts reflect scapegoat phenomena triggered by the last convulsions of magical thought at the end of the Middle Ages. Historians are not "soft on the referent." They are one hundred percent right to regard these texts as trustworthy not, I repeat, as individual texts but in their mass, statistically.

No one, I believe, has ever observed this most remarkable ability of certain texts crammed full with nonsensical material, the sabbath of medieval witches, to give the lie to a major law of interpretive prudence, the law that forces us to refrain from trying to extract from these texts any reliable information about the possible events from which they sprang.

Is all this applicable to mythology as well? Our main question now is one of numbers. Are there other myths composed of such themes arranged in such a fashion that they could be the tell-tale signs of scapegoating? I answered that question at the very beginning of this essay when I grouped the themes of foundational myths in five categories suggestive of scapegoating, the five categories which our Venda myth nicely illustrates.

As I said before, I agree that the traces of scapegoating are often more confusing in myth than in medieval texts of a similar stripe. I also agree as well that the lack of historical background makes the extension of the historical decrypting to myths intimidating. But these obstacles are obviously minor and the time has come to overcome them.

The structure of this myth is the standard one for etiological myths. This structural regularity makes it difficult to doubt that the mechanism at work in medieval witch-hunting is not also at work in all of them.

I have no time to multiply examples. As I always do, however, I will say a word about the best known of all Greek myths, the Oedipus myth, in relation to our Venda myth.

At first glance, it would seem that our Venda myth is not closely related to the Oedipus myth, but, as soon as the themes are grouped in the manner that I advocate, we can see that the two myths are very close to each other. The Oedipus myth, too, glaringly exemplifies the crisis, which here is a plague instead of a drought, the witchcraft accusation, the patricide and incest that cause the plague, and the spontaneous conviction patter, the inability of the Thebans to question the story that incriminates Oedipus, even though it involves a single culprit rather than the "many murderers of Laius."

The oracle is the voice of successful scapegoating. Its message is that the plague will be cured if and when the Thebans expel from their midst the right victim, the individual about whom they can all agree that he is the one who brought them the plague.

The message of the Venda myth is thematically different but not significantly so because it is structurally identical. The drought will be cured when the community rids itself of the right victim, the woman who supposedly brought it about by marrying a snake and then putting it to flight. The key to the mythical enigma is none other than the extension to mythology of a method which historians routinely use but which is not historical in the sense of relying on historical knowledge. It is a purely internal analysis of the data which is no less applicable to myths than to deluded accounts of persecution in our historical world and which will produce the same certainty as it is applied to more and more myths.

The same restrictions apply in the case of myth as in the case of historical texts. It is only a remote possibility but a possibility nevertheless that any particular text, our Venda myth for instance, was invented by the native informants of the anthropologist who transmitted this myth to us. Maybe they wanted to fool these anthropologists. Maybe the myth is an invention of the anthropologist themselves, as the fashionable contemporary suspicion demands, because all anthropologists are colonialists, etc. Even if this were true, however, it would still be impossible that not only our Venda myth, but the Oedipus myth, the Tikarau myth, the Dogrib myth about the birth of mankind, and countless other myths would have been fabricated for the purpose of fooling us. There are just too many myths of this type and the only reasonable explanation for the traces of scapegoating they exhibit is that they truly originate in actual scapegoating. Myths are the textual product of generative scapegoating. At the level of the individual text, I repeat, it is impossible to eliminate all doubt, and I do not claim that the "second wife" really exists or that any detail of our myth or this myth as a whole truly reflects an actual episode of scapegoating. All I claim is that, statistically, there must be real victims behind most myths with these types of themes, similarly arranged.

The overall nature of the themes and their arrangement is so similar to what we have in countless other myths of the same type that the scapegoat mechanism, each time, must be the cause of the recurrence. Without it nothing makes sense, with it everything does.

The mimetic theory does not say that the myth is a faithful representation of what happened. It simply claims that the probability of a real victim behind such themes as we found in our myth, arranged in the manner that they are, is very, very high.

Is it believable that the perpetual juxtaposition of a social scourge, a magical accusation, and collective violence against the accused would *always* mean arbitrary persecution in our society and *never* mean any such thing in the case of myth? If the answer is no, the mimetic theory of myth deserves the serious hearing that it has never received.

Historians — God bless them! — have not given up on the referentiality of their texts. In their search for hidden persecution, they implicitly if not explicitly realize that they can and must transgress the law of contamination by the fantastic. No one has ever problematized this transgression and the reason is clear. As long as it occurs within the confines of our own historical world, its legitimacy is obvious and no one notices the remarkable anomaly that it constitutes.

As soon as the same operation is performed outside our historical world, on a myth, its audacity becomes apparent and the same interpreters who routinely accept the reality of the victims in one domain refuse indignantly when I say that it must be there as well in the other. They no longer recognize an interpretive operation that they would perform almost unconsciously if it were presented to them in the usual domain.

If the operation is banal in one domain, it cannot be so inconceivable in the other that the very attempt to introduce it there should be regarded as a priori impossible, even reprehensible. To rule out the experiment I propose, which is what the critics of the mimetic theory are really doing, cannot be a sound attitude for researchers to take.

It is a false prudence that condemns the mimetic theory of myth. It is not always true that one rotten apple spoils a whole barrel. Far from being spoiled, the potentially sound apples in our myth are made paradoxically sounder by the proximity of the rotten apples.

The principle of the rotten apple should not be discarded lightly. All interpreters must assume that it applies until they can be sure that this very same principle governs the genesis of the text under examination or, in other words, that mimetic contagion must be responsible for the very existence of our text. In mythology, "scapegoating" is both the event (mis)represented and the source of its distorted representation.

The Venda people wanted the second wife to die because they feared that, if they did not get rid of her, the whole community might die. They were already thinking along the lines of the rotten apple, and if we ourselves follow their example and declare the text incredible because of the rotten apple in it, the incredible snake god, we will never discover its genesis. If we deal with the text just as the scapegoaters dealt with their scapegoat, we will never realize that our interpretive prudence is really one more scapegoating, a scapegoating outside the text that necessarily turns us into accomplices of the scapegoating inside the text.

One should not conclude from the above that I simply advocate abrogating the law of contamination by the unbelievable. This law is at the center of our insurance system against interpretive overconfidence. Contrary to what hasty critics believe, I do not minimize this threat.

Exceptions must be made only after careful investigation, when we are satisfied that scapegoating and scapegoating alone accounts for every feature in the text under examination, and for the arrangement of these features.

We must never relax our interpretive vigilance but we must not be so paralyzed by the fear of sounding naïvely realistic and referential that we turn the fantastic dimension of myths into a stumbling block. If we keep blindly applying the law of contamination by the unbelievable to myth, as we have done for centuries, if we disregard the converging clues of a scapegoat genesis, our understanding will never progress beyond a pure and simple reversal of the error that dominates mythology.

We will go on congratulating one another for our wise skepticism, never noticing that the key to foundational myths is within our reach and that it is the same generative scapegoating that we already know how to detect in many historical texts.

A blanket dismissal of all possible connections between myth and the outside world, indispensable though it was, no doubt, at an earlier stage of the interpretive process, makes us blind to the scapegoating mechanisms that obviously dominate the myths and therefore perpetuate their dominance.

The textual nihilism that now triumphs everywhere must be regarded as a last-ditch strategy of scapegoating itself, always supremely competent when it comes to preventing its own revelation.

The magical fear of magical contamination has been transferred from the existential to the textual level and it now dominates our relationship to the myth, so that the relationship of that myth to the reality it (mis)represents cannot be revealed. That this reversal still is a form of scapegoating can be seen from the continued inability of our culture to bring to light the reality of victimization behind even the most transparent myths, such as our Venda example.

As we discover the exact degree to which real magic, persecutional magic, influences our text, we become able to circumscribe its effects with precision, and far from embracing magical thinking, which is what the mimetic theory seems to be doing as long as we do not understand it, our reading moves farther away from magic than all previous readings.

The irrational thinker is not the mimetic interpreter but the narrow rationalist or the textual nihilist who resemble one another in their refusal to face the possibility that the law of contamination by the unbelievable might be just as irrelevant to foundational myths as it already is to all distorted accounts of scapegoating in our world.

When we apply the wrong law to our myth, we mimetically reproduce at the interpretive level the confusion that characterizes the myth. We keep placing believable and unbelievable features in the same category. We undifferentiate what should be differentiated.

The only real discrepancy between the anti-referential schools and mythical thinking *stricto sensu* is that mythical thinking trusts everything in a myth, whereas the anti-referential school trusts nothing. This is an advance, no doubt, but a very limited one that must give way to a more nuanced evaluation of the various themes.

The current interpretive nihilism is the twin brother of positivism and its misguided critical prudence. They both desire a second degree of mythical thinking that can and will be transcended by the selective referentiality of the mimetic theory.

The contamination by the fantastic and my metaphor of the rotten apple are two different names for a textual principle of interpretive guilt by association, if I may say so, an expulsion too encompassing that does not distinguish the wheat from the chaff. What this expulsion really expels is ... the expulsion that generates the text and that, being kept safely covered up, remains as virulently operative as it always was under the blanket of the anti-realistic, anti-referential principle, at a time when the real solution of the mythical enigma is at hand.

The mimetic theory provides an approach sophisticated enough to utilize all textual resources most effectively without surrendering to any referential fallacy, unless, of course, it is abused, and abuses are always possible. This is another subject, however, that cannot be discussed in the present essay.

At this time in our history, the only context in which academic researchers have learned to identify the scapegoat genesis of a text, the only context in which it is permissible to suspend the law of contamination by the unbelievable, insofar as evidence warrants, is still our own Western historical context. Within our own cultural realm, the lesson was learned centuries ago, I repeat, and so thoroughly that we can identify and interpret all relevant clues almost immediately and automatically.

In a historical context, we all perceive intuitively the tell-tale signs of scapegoating in any text structured like our Venda myth. We all perform the operation required by its elucidation so rapidly that they hardly reach our consciousness. Instead of appearing audacious to the point of temerity, my interpretive moves seem commonplace and their validity is taken for granted.

Gradually, I believe, the situation will change and at some time in the future, the *demythification* of myth will become as easy and banal as the *demystification* of a witchcraft trial record has been for centuries.

There are objective reasons, I said, why the interpretation of myth is lagging so far behind the interpretation of historical texts. The first reason is that the fantastic themes are often but not always more spectacular in a myth and the tell-tale signs of real scapegoating are harder to see. The second reason is the historical background and the historical experience that we have of our own society. Our society is the place where the battle against magical accusations was fought and where it was won. Mythology seems alien and forbiddingly majestic by comparison.

But there are also subjective reasons, the ideological prejudices of anthropologists and other students of myth. Our society as a whole is always biased in its own favor. But, precisely because they are so used to fighting this kind of prejudice, our professional interpreters are guilty of the reverse bias. They are biased in favor of myths and they prefer not to see in them the same collective violence that they are delighted to denounce in our own history.

Ever since the Renaissance, a quasi-religious respect for mythology has characterized and still characterizes academic research. Our ability to decipher scapegoat phenomena applies itself preferentially to the Judaic and Christian domains, for reasons which, at bottom, are anti-religious and anti-Christian.

The whole unfinished business of deciphering mythology and ritual belongs to the ongoing *history* of our ability to read scapegoat phenomena in all human relations as well as inside texts. Everything we are now poised to achieve will represent a new advance beyond the last great step, which was taken centuries ago, when the remnants of magical thinking in our world were finally liquidated. At that time, our culture reached a threshold beyond which the mythical and religious texts of all mankind become food for demystification or "deconstruction" in the same manner and for the same reasons as medieval witch-hunting and other forms of collective persecution. We have now been standing on that threshold for four or five centuries but we still hesitate to cross it. The mimetic-scapegoat theory is the crossing of that threshold.

Our willingness to cross the threshold depends on our constantly deepening ability to detect mimetic polarizations and scapegoating, and this deepening was long ago triggered by the influence on us of the Bible and above all of the Gospels. We can verify this, I believe, in the very form of the mimetic scapegoat interpretation.

All it takes to crack open our myth and all similar myths is the application to them of the principle of the innocent victim unjustly scapegoated. The model for this analysis is the story of the crucifixion and associated texts in the Christian Gospels. This is what we did in the case of our Venda myth. In order to identify the second wife as a "scapegoat," all we have to do is to slip under our text the text of the Christian Passion, the original revelation of the scapegoat mechanism.

The mimetic reading is scientific in the same sense as the demystification of witch-hunting achieved by the modern world. The two are scientific in opposition to the witch-hunters' and mythmakers' irrationality. Similarly, there is a *scientific* reading of the Nazi genocide in contrast with the mad theories of the "revisionists."

We must insist simultaneously on this scientific character of the mimetic interpretation and on its religious origin. The fact that the two words "scientific" and "religious" are used side by side cannot sit well with many people. It suggests that distinctions regarded as universally valid both by liberal rationalism and by religionists are being abolished. It suggests that the times we are living are truly revolutionary.

"The stone that the builders rejected has become the keystone." This is the principle which is being applied. It has applications in all possible fields, and it effectuates the most radical deconstruction. Our ability to read myth has little to do with the Greeks. It is inseparable from the intense concern for all victims that characterizes the modern world as a whole. It is not enough to dismiss this concern with a few desultory words about our Judaic and Christian "heritage." The word implies too much passivity. "Heritage" is an elegant version of a more recent and flat-footed attempt to put Christianity behind us by pompously labeling ourselves "post-Christian." We are about as "post-Christian" as we are "postnuclear" or "posttechnical" or "postmimetic." More than ever, the Gospels are the new wine that keeps bursting the old wine skins.

❧

One last word about a possible objection. Our Venda myth belongs to the rather small category of myths that have everything a myth can have that may help us uncover their scapegoat genesis: the scapegoat accusation, the crisis, the "guilt" and "punishment" of the victim, the beneficial consequences of her unanimous expulsion. Many myths lack one or more of these most revealing features that are all conveniently assembled in our myth.

The myths that lack one or more pieces of the puzzle are obviously less easy to decipher than our Venda myth. Until now, I have focused mostly on the basement level of mythical analysis, the easiest level.

In *The Scapegoat,* however, I tried to move beyond this stage in order to show that the absence of collective violence in a myth is due to normal development in the religious history of mankind. So are other transformations that make the detection of the scapegoat genesis more and more difficult but, as far as I have ascertained, never really impossible.

This essay is not the place for pursuing further this kind of exploration, but I would like to give some final indications on the road which, in my opinion, such investigation might take in the case of our Venda myth.

Some readers will have observed that this myth sounds like a variation on a famous mythical theme: feminine indiscretion, *mala curiositas.* Myths that emphasize that theme are found everywhere, it seems. In Greek mythology there are two famous examples, the myth of Psyche and the myth of Semele, two beloved mistresses of Zeus struck by his thunder for very much the same reason as the second wife in our Venda myth. Their lover has not said who he is and they are destroyed for pestering him about his divine identity very much in the manner of our Venda myth. Another closely related story is the Germanic Lohengrin.

Are we to believe that our Venda myth is influenced by these ancient myths, or is it the other way around? All such hypotheses are absurd, I believe. The only possible explanation for the similarities between them all is a common genesis of the mythical accusation, which must be the mimetic jealousy of two rival women, as I outlined in my reading.

Being more "primitive," or "archaic," or diachronically "younger," the Venda myth must have preserved what has completely or partially disappeared from the better known Greek and Germanic myths. At some point in the future, when the superiority of the mimetic theory is acknowledged, our Venda myth may turn out to constitute an important piece of evidence in the understanding of how all myths of the Psyche type were originally constituted.

The victimized heroine is always a favorite wife or mistress. In a polygamous world, she cannot be accused of adultery. She cannot be indicted simply for being intimate with the beloved "god." The only possible accusation is of the type we have in all these myths. The rival must be incriminated for abusing a privilege that was legitimately granted but must nevertheless be taken away from her, by the most violent means if necessary, because she keeps pestering the god. The pestering always has something to do with the superhuman status of the lover, or husband, whom the abandoned woman alone has the right to know.

The disgruntled ex-mistress manages to persuade herself that her more successful rival is usurping something she alone is entitled to have, a true awareness of who her husband really is, of how much he is worth.

Like all myths, our African myth hides its own victimization but less efficiently than the more elaborate Greek and Germanic myths, which must have been modified repeatedly before they reached us. Two themes are still present in the Venda version that must have originally belonged to the others as well but have subsequently been removed, the slanderous accusation by the jealous rival and the collective violence that this accusation triggers.

Whereas Zeus is supposed to punish the culprits directly with his own thunder, Python still needs human intermediaries. He acts through the assembled people and not he, but they, send the second wife to her death. The Venda version lets us see the crucial role of collective violence, its identity with sacred power.

Olympian mythology, as a rule, has been cleansed of its most sinister features, according to principles less drastic that those of Plato in *The Republic* but similar in their purpose. The Venda myth still preserves the crucial collective action for which the thunder of Zeus is really a metaphor. A careful comparison of African and Greek myths could reveal, I believe, what pieces of the mythical puzzle are removed, in what order, and for what reason, during the religious history of these myths. This is the process to which Freud so powerfully alluded in *Moses and Monotheism,* the multiple attempts at erasing the traces of the collective murder, and their ultimate failure. At a certain point in the evolution of mentalities, the themes most suggestive of what mythology really is become scandalous in the eyes of the faithful, and not without serious reasons. That is why they are suppressed along lines which seem to be always the same, more or less, in all observable traditions. Through a similar process, nowadays, the observations of anthropologists who still pay attention to the violence of mythology and ritual are being discredited in favor of nihilistic and anti-referential interpretations that are really much less significant.

The hypothesis of a scapegoat mechanism that turns the magical accusation in a text into the ostensible truth of that text enables us to circumscribe the unbelievable features and to distinguish them from the believable ones, the ones about the drought and the drowning of the victim that ends the drought, which become paradoxically more rather than less believable through their conjunction with the unbelievable accusation. The suspected presence of a scapegoat mechanism does more than merely suspend the application of the law of contamination by the fantastic. It literally reverses it. It turns a law of contamination by the unbelievable into a law of contamination by the believable. The idea that a text is never more reliable than the least reliable of its parts is replaced by its own opposite. If a text tells us about some violence inflicted on the victims of unbelievable accusations, the more unbelievable the accusation is and the more credulous the author is, the more likely it is that the violence really occurred.

The reasons for this opposition are clear. In our world, at the beginning of the modern age, there was a battle against the spirit of witchcraft, and the interpretation of texts inside our own culture was revolutionized by it. The benefits of this great victory have not yet been extended to the texts of other cultures.

To those who keep stubbornly repeating that an angry snake and his human wife cannot be the cause of a drought and that the myth is pure nonsense, I will answer that it is true, of course, but only in an absolute sense. In a relative sense, however, relative to the type of text to which our fantastic snake and its indiscreet wife belong, the story makes terrific sense, not as something "true" but as something "false," as the type of deception that happens in the real world, and when it happens it also usually happens that the other themes in a myth such as ours are real events as well. The referentiality of the snake not as a god but as a magical accusation commands the referentiality of the whole myth.

In the light of the magical accusation, the death of the woman makes complete sense as a panicked reaction of the community. So does the idea that this death put an end to the drought. And in the light of these two themes, of course, the story of the snake makes perfect sense as a magical accusation that reunites against and around the victim of a mimetically disturbed community. We are in such a circle of believability that the likelihood of a real social process behind our text is very high.

Our mimetic demythification is a purely interpretive operation, entirely self-contained and free from a priori assumptions. The claim that the victim is real is no a priori bias in favor of referentiality; it is demanded by a hypothesis that is simply too powerful to be rejected.

Part V

The Bible, the Gospels, and Christ

Chapter 10

The Bible's Distinctiveness and the Gospel

The truth of the human condition is twofold. It is both the truth of the mimetic predicament and the truth of the liberation that comes from revelation of this predicament in the Gospel witness to the crucifixion and resurrection of Christ, which both disclose and overcome the hidden founding murder. The victimary mechanism of human culture is rooted in this murder. It was first in ancient Israel that narrator-thinkers and prophets began to view their history from the standpoint of God's concern for victims rather than from the standpoint of the sacred social order.

The truth of the innocent victim is the power of God disclosed in the suffering of the one who uncovers our structures of desire and violence. This truth is expressed in the Servant of the Lord (Isa. 52:13-53:12), but is attested in its definitive and most sustained form in the Gospel witness to Jesus as Christ, Lord, Son of Man and Son of God. This selection from *Things Hidden*, 141-44, 146-49, 151-79, sketches the fundamentals of Girard's view of the Bible. The format of *Things Hidden* is that of a dialogue between Girard and two psychiatrist colleagues, Jean-Michel Oughourlian and Guy Lefort, indicated by the initials R.G., J.-M.O., and G.L., respectively.

— ❧ —

Similarities between the Biblical Myths and World Mythology

R.G.: We have now dealt with the hypothesis of the scapegoat as an exclusively scientific one. No doubt our discussions have been far too hasty, as well as too schematic. All the same, our readers now know our gist. We must turn to other subjects. Or rather, we must investigate other, even more spectacular ways in which the same truth has come to the fore.

From this point onward we shall take it for granted that the victimage mechanisms exist and that their role in the establishment of religion, culture, and humanity itself is an established fact, no longer open to doubt. Actually, I never lose sight of the point that this is only a hypothesis. I am hardly likely to forget it, for the very reason that the material remaining to be studied here will supply us with new proofs, and increasingly striking ones.

First of all, we shall look at Judeo-Christian Scripture. After that, we shall deal with psychopathology, and this will ultimately lead us to some conclusions about our own times. People will accuse us of playing at being Pico della Mirandola — the Renaissance Man — certainly a temptation to be resisted today, if we wish to be seen in a favorable light. But in fact a very different thing is in question here. We simply cannot confine our hypothesis to the area of hominization and primitive religion. As we shall see, this hypothesis will compel us to broaden our horizons, for it can acquire its fullest meaning only in universal terms.

If we turn to the Old Testament, and particularly to the books that come first or those that may contain the oldest materials, we find ourselves immediately in familiar territory. Immediately we come upon the three great moments we have defined:

1. Dissolution in conflict, removal of the differences and hierarchies which constitute the community in its wholeness;

2. the *all against one* of collective violence;

3. the development of interdictions and rituals.

To the first moment belong the very first lines of the text on the creation of the world, as well as the tale of the confusion of the Tower of Babel and that of the corruption of Sodom and Gomorrah. We also see immediately that in Exodus the ten plagues of Egypt form the equivalent of the plague at Thebes in Sophocles. The Flood, again, belongs with these metaphors of crisis. And in every case, from the first lines of Genesis, we have the theme of the warring brothers or twins: Cain and Abel, Jacob and Esau, Joseph and his eleven brothers, et al.

The second moment is no less easy to locate. It is always by violence, by the expulsion of one of the brothers, that the crisis is resolved, and differentiation returns once again.

In every one of the great scenes of Genesis and Exodus there exists a theme or quasi-theme of the founding murder of expulsion. Obviously, this is most striking in the expulsion from the Garden of Eden; there,

God takes the violence upon himself and founds humanity by driving Adam and Eve far away from him.

In the blessing that Isaac gives to Jacob rather than to his brother Esau, we are again dealing with the violent resolution of a conflict between warring brothers, and the surreptitious character of Jacob's act in substituting himself for his brother, when the act is discovered, does not compromise the outcome. It matters little, in effect, who is the victim, provided that there is one.

In Jacob's struggle with the angel, a conflict between *doubles* is in question — one that hangs in the balance for a long time because the contestants are perfectly matched. Jacob's adversary is first of all called a *man;* and it is with the defeat of this adversary and his expulsion at the hands of the victor that he becomes a God from whom Jacob demands and obtains a blessing. In other words, the combat of *doubles* results in the expulsion of one of the pair, and this is identified directly with the return to peace and order.

In every one of these scenes, the relationship between *brothers* or *doubles* has in the first instance a character of undecidability, resolved by expulsion through violence despite an arbitrary element involved, as in the case of Jacob and Esau.

Since the single victim brings reconciliation and safety by restoring life to the community, it is not difficult to appreciate that a sole survivor in a world where all others perish can, thematically, amount to the same thing as a single victim extracted from a group in which no one, save the victim, perishes. Noah's Ark, which alone is spared by the Flood, guarantees that the world will begin all over again. It is Lot and his family who are the sole survivors of the destruction of Sodom and Gomorrah. Lot's wife, who is changed into a pillar of salt, brings back into this story the motif of the single victim.

Let us now look at the third moment — at the establishment of interdictions and sacrifices, or circumcision, which comes to the same thing. Here references to this side of things can become confused with references to the founding mechanism. For instance, in the sacrifice of Isaac the necessity of sacrifice threatens the most precious being, only to be satisfied, at the last moment, with a substituted victim, the ram sent by God.

In the story of Isaac's blessing of Jacob, the theme of the kids offered to the father in a propitiatory meal represents a sacrificial institution — and one detail that reveals clearly, despite its link with the other themes of the story, the way in which the sacrifice operates. It is thanks to the hair of those kids that Isaac can mistake Jacob's hide-covered limbs for Esau, and so Jacob escapes his father's curse.

In all these mythic accounts, society and even nature appear as a whole being put in order, or in which order is being reestablished. In general, these belong to the end of the victimage account, the place where the logic of the hypothesis expects to be. But in the story of the creation of the world, the founding moment comes at the beginning and no victimage is involved. For Noah, the final reorganization is implied not only in the Covenant after the Flood, but also in the confinement of prototypes of all species within the Ark; here we have something like a floating system of classification, on the basis of which the world will repeople itself in conformity with the norms of God's will. We can also cite here God's promise to Abraham after the sacrifice of the ram substituted for Isaac, as well as the rules which are prescribed for Jacob after the expulsion of his divinized double. In both cases, the change of name points to the founding character of the process.

J.-M.O.: Up to now you have only shown us the similarities between the biblical myths and the myths which you spoke about earlier. Are you not concerned with stressing the differences between these mythologies and the Bible?

R.G.: I shall shortly be talking about these differences. If I insist first of all upon the similarities, it is to demonstrate clearly that I am not embarrassed by them, and that I am not trying to spirit them away. There can be no doubt that the first books of the Bible rest upon myths that are very close to those found all over the world. What I shall try to prove to you now is that these analogies are not the end of the matter. The biblical treatment of these myths offers something which is absolutely distinctive, and this is what I shall be trying to define.

The Distinctiveness of the Biblical Myths

Cain

R.G.: First let us take the story of Cain in Chapter 4 of Genesis.... The myth of Cain is presented in classic fashion. One of the two brothers kills the other, and the Cainite community is founded.

People have often asked why God, although he condemns the murder, responds to the appeal of the murderer. Cain says: "Whoever comes across me will kill me!" And God responds: "If anyone kills Cain, vengeance shall be taken on him sevenfold." God himself intervenes, and in response to the founding murder he enunciates the law against murder. This intervention makes it clear, in my view, that the decisive murder, here as elsewhere, has a founding character. And to talk in terms of "founding" is also to talk in terms of "differentiating," which is why we have, immediately afterward, these words: "And the Lord put a mark on Cain, to prevent anyone finding him from striking him down." I see in this the establishment of a differential system, which serves, as always, to discourage mimetic rivalry and generalized conflict.

G.L.: A great number of communities attribute their own foundation to a similar type of murder. Rome, for example. Romulus kills Remus and the city of Rome is founded. In both cases, the murder of one brother by another has the same founding and differentiating power. Discord between doubles is succeeded by the order of the new community.

R.G.: There is nonetheless a difference between the two myths that can easily be disregarded, within the normal context of statements about mythology. In our own particular context — that is, an anthropology entirely centered on victimage mechanisms and thus open to the proposition that to regard them as arbitrary is to misinterpret them — this difference can acquire a great significance.

In the Roman myth, the murder of Remus appears as an action that was perhaps to be regretted, but was justified by the victim's transgression. Remus did not respect the ideal limit traced by Romulus between the inside and the outside of the city. The motive for the killing is at once insignificant — since the city does not yet exist — and crucial, literally fundamental. In order for the city to exist, no one can be allowed to flout with impunity the rules it prescribes. So Romulus is justified. His status is that of a sacrificer and High Priest; he incarnates Roman power under all its forms at one and the same time. The legislative, the judiciary, and the military forms cannot yet be distinguished from the religious; everything is already present within the last.

By contrast, even if Cain is invested with what are basically the same powers, and even if he has the ear of the deity, he is nonetheless presented as a vulgar murderer. The fact that the first murder precipitates the first cultural development of the human race does not in any way excuse the murderer in the biblical text. The founding character of the murder is signaled just as clearly, and perhaps even more clearly, than in the nonbiblical myths. But there is something else, and that is moral judgment. The condemnation of the murder takes precedence over all other considerations. "Where is your brother Abel?"

The importance of this ethical dimension in the Bible is well-known. And yet few commentaries have sought to define it with rigor, particularly for texts which are not necessarily the most ancient, but which have to deal with archaic data. In my view, Max Weber has been the most successful in this regard. In his great but incomplete work *Ancient Judaism,* he comes to the conclusion at several stages that the biblical writers have an undeniable tendency to take the side of the victim on moral grounds, and to spring to the victim's defense.[1]

---

1. Max Weber, *Ancient Judaism,* trans. H. H. Garth and D. Martingale (Glencoe, Ill.: Free Press, 1952), 19–22, 86; 475–76; 492–95. Obviously Max Weber's theses must be compared with that of Nietzsche in *The Anti-Christ* and elsewhere.

Max Weber sees this observation as having a purely sociological and cultural significance. He takes the view that the propensity to favor the victim is characteristic of a particular cultural atmosphere peculiar to Judaism, and he looks for its explanation in the innumerable catastrophes of Jewish history and the fact that the Jewish people had not experienced any great historical success comparable to the successes of the empire-builders surrounding them: Egyptians, Assyrians, Babylonians, Persians, Greeks, Romans, et al.

He is therefore not at all interested in what might be derived on the level of mythic and religious texts from a factor that appears to him to be in the last analysis a form of prejudice comparable to so many others, a prejudice in favor of victims. Seen in the context of the victimary anthropology centered on victimage mechanisms that we have just sketched out, this attitude of indifference is unacceptable. Suppose that the texts of mythology are the reflection, at once faithful and deceptive, of the collective violence that founds a community; suppose that they bear witness of a real violence, that they do not lie even if in them the victimage mechanism is falsified and transfigured by its very efficacy; suppose, finally that myth is the persecutors' retrospective vision of their own persecution. If this is so, we can hardly regard as insignificant a change in perspective that consists in taking the side of the victim, proclaiming the victim's innocence and the culpability of his murderers.

Suppose that, far from being a gratuitous invention, myth is a text that has been falsified by the belief of the executioners in the guiltiness of their victim; suppose, in other words, that myths incorporate the point of view of the community that has been reconciled to itself by the collective murder and is unanimously convinced that this event was a legitimate and sacred action, desired by God himself, which could not conceivably be repudiated, criticized, or analyzed. If that is so, an attitude that involves rehabilitating the victim and denouncing the persecutors is not something that calls only for disillusioned and blasé commentaries. This attitude can hardly fail to have repercussions not merely on mythology itself, but on all that is involved in the hidden foundation of collective murder: forms of ritual, interdictions, and religious transcendence. One by one, the whole range of cultural forms and values, even those that appear to be furthest removed from the domain of myth, would be affected.

J.-M.O.: Isn't this happening already in the Cain myth, however primitive it may be?

R.G.: If we examine the story with care, we come to see that the lesson of the Bible is precisely that the culture born of violence must return to violence. In the initial stages, we observe a brilliant flowering of culture: techniques are invented; towns spring from the desert. But very soon, the violence that has been inadequately contained by the founding murder and the legal barriers deriving from it starts to escape and propagate. The borderline between legalized punishment, vengeance, and the blood feud is erased when Cain's seven victims become, for Lamech, seventy-seven.

G.L.: It is quite obvious that we have here a case of undifferentiated violence propagating contagiously...

R.G.: The Flood also results from an escalation that involves the monstrous dissolution of all differences: giants are born, the progeny of a promiscuous union between the sons of the gods and the daughters of men. This is the crisis in which the whole of culture is submerged, and its destruction is not only a punishment from God; to almost the same extent is the fatal conclusion of a process which brings back the violence from which it originally managed to get free, thanks to the temporary benefits of the founding murder.

With reference to the violence that both founds and differentiates, the story of Cain has, in addition to its unquestionable significance as myth, a much greater power of revelation than that of non-Judaic myths. Certainly there must be, behind the biblical account, myths in conformity with the universal norms of mythology; so the initiative of the Jewish authors and their critical reappraisal must undoubtedly be credited with the affirmation that the victim is innocent and that the culture founded on murder retains a thoroughly murderous character that in the end becomes self-destructive, once the ordering and sacrificial benefits of the original violence have dissipated.

Here we are not just making a vague conjecture. Abel is only the first in a long line of victims whom the Bible exhumes and exonerates: "The voice of your brother's blood cries to me from the ground."

Joseph

R.G.: Although it may be concealed in the Cain myth, the collective character of the persecution is fully visible in the story of Joseph.... [If we look at the chapters] that are most important for the purposes of our analysis [Genesis 37 and 39],... [we see that] once again, the hypothesis that best illuminates the biblical text is also the most common one. The authors of Genesis have recast a preexistent mythology, adapting it in the spirit of their special concerns. This involves inverting the relationship between the victim and the persecuting community. From the mythological perspective, the eleven brothers would appear first of all as the passive objects of the violence inflicted by a malevolent hero, then as the recipients of the benefits conferred by this same hero after he has been victimized and deified. Joseph would thus be at first a cause of disorder, and a remnant of this can be surmised from the dreams that he recounts, dreams of domination that excite the jealousy of his eleven brothers. The original myths would no doubt have sanctioned the charge of hubris. The kid that provided the blood in which Joseph's tunic was dipped in order to prove to his father that he was really dead would have played a directly sacrificial role in the prebiblical account.

In the first part of the account, two separate sources have been combined; each one seeks to rehabilitate the victim at the expense of his brothers, even if each is also concerned with partially exempting one of the brothers from blame. The first source, known as "Elohist," chooses Reuben and the second, known as "Yahwist," chooses Judah. Hence there are two different stories, juxtaposed with one another, that account for one and the same act of collective violence.

If we take into account that Joseph's Egyptian master behaved toward him as a father, then the accusation of the Egyptian's wife has an almost incestuous character. Instead of corroborating the accusation, as do so many myths (with the story of Oedipus at their head), the story of Joseph declares that it is false!

J.-M.O.: You are quite right. But surely the myth to compare with the story of Joseph is not the Oedipus myth but that of Phaedra and Hippolytus?

R.G.: Of course. But you will observe that in the Greek myth, as opposed to the Racinian version, Hippolytus is treated, if not as a guilty party in the modern sense, at least as being justly punished: his excessive chastity has an element of hubris that offends Venus. By contrast, in the story of Joseph the victim is simply an innocent party who is falsely accused.

Further on in the story, there is a second account of a victim who is falsely accused and in the end gets off free. This time, Joseph himself uses trickery to impugn his brother Benjamin — the other favorite son of Jacob and the only one younger than Joseph — with guilt. But on this occasion, one of the ten brothers is not willing to accept the expulsion of the victim. Judah puts himself forward in Benjamin's place, and Joseph is moved by pity to make himself known to his brothers and pardon them.

G.L.: The point that rehabilitating the victim has a desacralizing effect is well demonstrated by the story of Joseph, who ends up having no demoniac or divine aspects but simply being human....

J.-M.O.: Mythological culture and the cultural forms that have been grafted upon it, such as philosophy or in our own day ethnology, with a few exceptions tend first to justify the founding murder and then to eliminate the traces of this murder, convincing people that there is no such thing. These cultural forms have succeeded perfectly in convincing us that humanity is innocent of these murders. By contrast, in the Bible there is an inverse movement, an attempt to get back to origins and look once again at constitutive acts of transference so as to discredit and annul them — so as to contradict and demystify the myths....

R.G.: The proof that we are not entirely unaware of this inspired role played by the Bible lies in the fact that for centuries we have been accusing it of "laying blame" on humanity, which, of course, as the philosophers assure us, has never harmed a fly in its own right. Clearly the story of Cain lays blame on Cainite culture by showing that this culture is completely based upon the unjust murder of Abel. The story of Romulus and Remus does not lay blame upon the city of Rome since the murder of Remus is presented to us as being justified. No one asks if the Bible is not right to lay blame as it does, and if the city of man is not in fact founded on concealed victims.

G.L.: But your analysis has up to now been restricted to Genesis. Can you show that it remains valid for other great biblical texts?

J.-M.O.: In Exodus it is the whole of the chosen people which is identified with the scapegoat, vis-à-vis Egyptian society.

R.G.: Yes, indeed. When Moses complains that the Egyptians are not willing to let the Hebrews leave, Yahweh replies that soon the Egyptians will not only let them leave but will *expel* them.

As he himself causes the sacrificial crisis that ravages Egypt (the Ten Plagues), Moses is evidently playing the part of the scapegoat, and the Jewish community around him is associated with this role. So there is something absolutely unique in the foundation of Judaism.

In order to "function" normally, in the sense of the myths that we have already dealt with here, Exodus would have to be an Egyptian myth; this myth would show us a sacrificial crisis resolved by the expulsion of the trouble-makers, Moses and his companions. Thanks to their expulsion, the order that Moses disturbed would have been reestablished in the society of Egypt. We are indeed dealing with this kind of model, but it has been diverted toward the scapegoat, who is not only made human but goes on to form a community of a new type.

G.L.: I can certainly see that in this case there is a tendency once again to unearth the mechanism that is at the foundation of religion and to call it into question. But these great stories from Genesis and Exodus remain nonetheless inscribed within a mythic framework and retain the characteristics of myth. Are you going so far as to say that we are no longer dealing with myth at all?

R.G.: No. I believe we are dealing with mythic forms that have been subverted but still retain, as you rightly say, many of the characteristics of myth. If we had nothing but these particular texts, we would not be able to stress the radical singularity of the Bible vis-à-vis the mythological systems of the entire planet.

The Law and the Prophets

R.G.: Genesis and Exodus are only the beginning. In the other books of the Law and particularly in those of the Prophets, a reader who has been alerted to the role of the scapegoat cannot fail to note an increasing tendency for the victim to be brought to light. This tendency goes hand in hand with an increasing subversion of the three great pillars of primitive religion: first, mythology, then the sacrificial cult (explicitly rejected by the Prophets before the Exile), finally the primitive conception of the law as a form of obsessive differentiation, a refusal of mixed states that looks upon indifferentiation with horror.

There is no difficulty in discovering in the books of the law precepts that recall all codes of primitive law, and Mary Douglas in *Purity and Danger* has discussed at length the biblical fear of the dissolution of identities. In my opinion, she is wrong not to note the part played by fear of violence in this horrified reaction to forbidden mixtures.[2]

However this may be, in the biblical context these archaic legal

---

2. 54–72. Criticism of the cult of sacrifice by preexilic prophets is played down by the majority of commentators, whether they are religious or irreligious by persuasion, Jewish or Christian, Protestant or Catholic. People attempt to show that the prophets are only opposed to a "cultural syncretism" which they believe to be unorthodox and that their principal aim is to centralize worship at Jerusalem. But in fact the texts are too many in number and too explicit for there to be any room for doubt. See for example: Isaiah 1:10–17; Jeremiah 6:20; Hosea 5:6; 6:6; 9:11–13; Amos 5:21–25; Micah 6:6–8.

To combat sacrifices, these prophets have recourse to historical arguments. They draw a distinction between the profuse sacrifices of their own decadent times and the ideal period for the relationship between Yahweh and his people, which was that of the life in the desert when the absence of livestock made sacrifices impossible. And the deep-seated reason for their refusal comes to the surface in the link between animal sacrifice and the sacrifice of children, in Micah, for example — he perceives behind the increasing practice of sacrifice an escalation which, in the final analysis, always involves reciprocal violence and mimetic desire:

> With what shall I come before the Lord,
> and bow myself before God on high?
> Shall I come before him with burnt offerings,
> with calves a year old?
> Will the Lord be pleased with thousands of rams,
> with ten thousands of rivers of oil?
> Shall I give my first-born for my transgression,
> the fruit of my body for the sin of my soul?
> He has showed you, O man, what is good;
> and what does the Lord require of you
> but to do justice, and to love kindness,
> and to walk humbly with your God? (Micah 6:6–8).

The prophet contrasts the grotesque and threatening escalation of burnt offerings with the quintessence of the law, which is love of one's neighbor.

If Ezekiel takes a sacrificial position, once again, this is because in his period sacrifices quite clearly had nothing more than a ceremonial and archaeological value. The mimetic crisis stays "sacrificial" in the broader sense; but it is no longer sacrificial in the strict sense, it is no longer directly centered on the question of sacrificial rites properly speaking.

prescriptions are far less important than what comes after them. The inspiration of the prophets tends to eliminate all these obsessional prescriptions in favor of their true raison d'être, which is the maintenance of harmonious relationships within the community. What the prophets come down to saying is basically this: legal prescriptions are of little consequence so long as you keep from fighting one another, so long as you do not become enemy twins. This is the new inspiration, and it arrives, even in the books of the law such as Leviticus, at unambiguous formulations like: "Thou shalt love your neighbor as thyself" (Lev. 19:18).

J.-M.O.: So the three great pillars of primitive religion — myth, sacrifice, and prohibitions — are subverted by the thought of the Prophets, and this general activity of subversion is invariably governed by the bringing to light of the mechanisms that found religion: the unanimous violence against the scapegoat.

R.G.: In the prophetic books, we are no longer confronted with mythical or legendary accounts, but with exhortations, threats, and forecasts of the future of the chosen people. Our hypothesis highlights a common theme in the prophetic literature and the great myths of the Pentateuch. The phenomenon of the Prophets is an original response to a crisis of Hebraic society, one made worse by the great empires of Babylon and Assyria, which threatened the little kingdoms of Israel and Judah. Yet these political developments are invariably interpreted by the prophets as an exclusively religious and cultural crisis, in which the sacrificial system is exhausted and the traditional order of society dissolves into conflict. The way in which the Prophets define this crisis impels us to compare it with the definition required by our hypothesis. It is precisely because a common experience is involved that our crisis can be described using themes and metaphors taken from the mythical heritage of the chosen people.

If the crisis that we must suppose to be at the origin of these mythic texts is revealed directly by the Prophets, where it is spoken of as a religious and indeed a cultural and social reality, there is reason to ask whether the specific resolution of this type of crisis — the phenomenon of collective transference, which is the core of the mechanism that engenders religion — will not be more directly apparent in these exceptional religious texts than anywhere else.

That proves to be so. In the first books of the Bible, the founding mechanism shows through the texts here and there, sometimes strikingly but never completely and unambiguously. The mechanism never really gets described as such. By contrast, the prophetic books offer us a group of astonishing texts that are all integrally related, as well as being remarkably explicit. These are the four "Songs of the Servant of Yahweh" in the second part of Isaiah, perhaps the most grandiose of all the prophetic books. (They are located at Isaiah 42:1–4; 49:1–6; 50:4–11; 52:13–53:12.) Modern historical criticism has isolated these four "Songs," recognizing their unity and their relative degree of independence from the material surrounding them. This is all the more praiseworthy in that no one has ever been able to say what gives them this singular status. Speaking of the return from Babylon authorized by Cyrus, they develop as an enigmatic counterpoint the double theme of the triumphant Messiah, here identified with the liberating prince, and the suffering Messiah, the Servant of Yahweh.

To recognize the relevance of our hypothesis to the Servant, we need only quote one or two key passages. In the first place, the Servant appears within the context of the prophetic crisis for the purpose of resolving it. He becomes, as a result of God's own action, the receptacle for all violence; he takes the place of all the members of the community:

> All we like sheep have gone astray;
> we have turned every one to his own way;
> and the Lord has laid on him
> the iniquity of us all. (Isa. 53:6)

All the traits attributed to the Servant predispose him to the role of a veritable human scapegoat.

> For he grew up before him like a young plant,
> and like a root out of dry ground;
> he had no form or comeliness that we should look at him,
> and no beauty that we should desire him.
> He was despised and rejected by men;
> a man of sorrows, and acquainted with grief;
> and as one from whom men hide their faces
> he was despised, and we esteemed him not. (Isa. 53:2–3)

If these traits make him similar to a certain type of sacrificial victim within the pagan world — for example, the Greek *pharmakos* — and if the fate he undergoes, the fate reserved for the anathema, is similar to that of the *pharmakos*, it is nonetheless no ritual sacrifice that we are dealing with. It is a spontaneous historical event, which has at once a collective and a legal character, and is sanctioned by the authorities:

> By oppression and judgment he was taken away;
> and as for his generation, who considered
> that he was cut off from out of the land of the living,
> stricken for the transgression of my people?
> And they made his grave with the wicked
> and with a rich man in his death,
> although he had done no violence,
> and there was no deceit in his mouth. (Isa. 53:8–9)

This event therefore has the character not of a ritual but of the type of event from which, according to my hypothesis, rituals and all aspects of religion are derived. The most striking aspect here, the trait which is certainly unique, is the innocence of the Servant, the fact that he has no connection with violence and no affinity for it. A whole number of passages lay upon men the principal responsibility for his saving death. One of these even appears to attribute to men the exclusive responsibility for that death. "Yet we esteemed him stricken, smitten by God, and afflicted" (Isa. 53:4).

In other words, this was not so. It was not God who smote him; God's responsibility is implicitly denied.

Throughout the Old Testament, a work of exegesis is in progress, operating in precisely the opposite direction to the usual dynamics of mythology and culture. And yet it is impossible to say that this work is completed. Even in the most advanced texts, such as the fourth "Song of the Servant," there is still some ambiguity regarding the role of Yahweh. Even if the human community is, on several occasions, presented as being responsible for the death of the victim, God himself is presented as the principal instigator of the persecution. "Yet is was the will of the Lord to bruise him" (Isa. 53:10).

This ambiguity in the role of Yahweh corresponds to the general conception of the deity in the Old Testament. In the prophetic books, this conception tends to be increasingly divested of the violence characteristic of primitive deities. Although vengeance is still attributed to Yahweh, a number of expressions how that in reality mimetic and reciprocal violence is festering more and more as the old cultural forms tend to dissolve. Yet all the same, in the Old Testament we never arrive at a conception of the deity that is entirely foreign to violence.

J.-M.O.: So in your view there is an inconclusiveness in the Old Testament that affects all the still primitive aspects to the same degree: the myths are worked through with a form of inspiration that runs counter to them, but they continue to stand. The sacrifices are criticized, but they continue; the law is simplified and declared to be identical to the love of one's neighbor, but it continues. And even though he is presented in a less and less violent form, and becomes more and more benevolent, Yahweh is still the god to whom vengeance belongs. The notion of divine retribution is still alive.

R.G.: That is right. I think it is possible to show that only the texts of the Gospels manage to achieve what the Old Testament leaves incomplete. These texts therefore serve as an extension of the Judaic Bible, bringing to completion an enterprise that the Judaic Bible did not take far enough, as Christian tradition has always maintained. The truth of this whole account comes to the fore when we use the scapegoat in our reading. And it comes to the fore in a form that can immediately be verified against the texts themselves, albeit in an unforeseen form that will startle all traditions, not excepting the Christian tradition, which has never acknowledged the crucial importance in the anthropological domain of what I call the scapegoat.

The Gospel Revelation of the Founding Murder

The Curses against the Pharisees

G.L.: How do you intend to show that the truth of the scapegoat is written for all to see in the text of the Gospels?

R.G.: In the Gospels of Matthew and Luke, there is a group of texts that used to be entitled the "Curses against the Scribes and Pharisees." This title is no longer employed because of the embarrassment the reading of these texts usually provokes. In the literal sense, of course, such a title is perfectly valid. But it does tend to restrict unduly the vast implications of the way in which Jesus accuses his audience of Pharisees. Obviously he is directing his accusations at them, but a careful examination reveals that he is using the Pharisees as an intermediary for something very much larger, and indeed something of absolutely universal significance is at stake. But then this is always the case in the Gospels. Every reading that restricts itself to particulars — however legitimate it may seem on the historical level — is nonetheless a betrayal of the overall significance.

The most terrible and meaningful "curse" comes right at the end of the text in both Matthew and Luke. I quote first of all from Matthew:

> Therefore I send you prophets and wise men and scribes, some of whom you will kill and crucify, and some you will scourge in your synagogues and persecute from town to town, that upon you may come all the righteous blood shed on earth, from the blood of innocent Abel to the blood of Zechariah the son of Barachiah, whom you murdered between the sanctuary and the altar. Truly, I say to you, all this will come upon this generation.
>
> (Matt. 23:34–36)

The text gives us to believe that there have been many murders. It only mentions two of them, however: that of Abel, the first to occur in the Bible, and that of a certain Zechariah, the last person to be killed in the Second Book of the Chronicles, in other words the last in the whole Bible as Jesus knew it.

Evidently mention of the first and last murders takes the place of a more complete list. The victims who belong between Abel and Zechariah are implicitly included. The text has the character of a recapitulation, and it cannot be restricted to the Jewish religion alone, since the murder of Abel goes back to the origins of humanity and the foundation of the first cultural order. Cainite culture is not a Jewish culture. The text also makes explicit mention of "all the righteous blood shed on earth." It therefore looks as though the kind of murder for which Abel here forms the prototype is not limited to a single region of the world or to a single period of history. We are dealing with a universal phenomenon whose consequences are going to fall not only upon the Pharisees but upon this *generation,* that is, upon all those who are contemporary with the Gospels and the time of their diffusion, who remain deaf and blind to the news that is being proclaimed.

The text of Luke is similar, but it includes, before Abel is mentioned a further crucial detail. It identifies "the blood of all the prophets, shed from the foundation of the world, from the blood of Abel to the blood of Zechariah" (Luke 11:50–51). The Greek text has *apo kataboles kosmou.* The same expression comes up in Matthew when Jesus quotes from Psalm 78 in reference to himself:

> I will open my mouth in parables,
> I will utter what has been hidden
> since the foundation of the world.
> (Matt. 13:35)

On each occasion the Vulgate uses the translation *a constitutione mundi.* But *kataboles* really seems to imply the foundation of the world insofar as it results from a violent crisis; it denotes order insofar as it comes out of disorder. The term has a medical use to mean the onslaught of a disease, the attack that provokes a resolution.

We must certainly not lose sight of the fact that, for Jewish culture, the Bible formed the only ethnological encyclopedia available or even conceivable. In referring to the whole of the Bible, Jesus is pointing not only at the Pharisees but at the whole of humanity. Clearly the dreadful consequences of his revelation will weigh exclusively on those who have had the advantage of hearing — if they refuse to take its meaning, if they will not recognize that this is a revelation which concerns them in the same way as it concerns the rest of humanity. The Pharisees to whom Jesus is speaking are the first to put themselves in this difficult position, but they will not be the last. It cannot be deduced from the Gospel text that their innumerable successors will not fall under the same condemnation, even if they belong to a different religion named Christianity.

Jesus is very well aware that the Pharisees have not themselves killed the prophets, any more than the Christians themselves killed Jesus. It is said that the Pharisees were the "sons" of those who carried out the killings (Matt. 23:31). This is not to imply a hereditary transmission of guilt, but rather an intellectual and spiritual solidarity that is achieved by means of a resounding repudiation — not unlike the repudiation of Judaism by the "Christians." The *sons* believe they can express their independence of the *fathers* by condemning them, that is, by claiming to have no part in the murder. But by virtue of this very fact, they unconsciously imitate and repeat the acts of their fathers. They fail to understand that in the murder of the Prophets people refused to acknowledge their own violence and cast if off from themselves. The sons are therefore still governed by the mental structure engendered by the founding murder. In effect they are still saying:

> If we had lived in the days of our fathers, we would not have taken part with them in shedding the blood of the prophets.
> (Matt. 23:30)

Paradoxically, it is in the very wish to cause a break that the continuity between fathers and sons is maintained.

To understand what is decisive about the texts in the synoptic Gospels we have just been considering, we need to confront them with the text from the Gospel of John that is most directly equivalent:

> Why do you not understand what I say? It is because you cannot bear to hear my word. You are of your father the devil, and your will is to do your father's desires. He was a murderer from the beginning, and has nothing to do with the truth, because there is no truth in him. When he lies, he speaks according to his own nature, for he is a liar and the father of lies. (John 8:43–44)

Here the essential point is that a triple correspondence is set up between Satan, the original homicide, and the lie. To be a son of Satan is to inherit the lie. What lie? The lie that covers the homicide. This lie is a double homicide, since its consequence is always another new homicide to cover up the old one. To be a son of Satan is the same thing as being the son of those who have killed their prophets since the foundation of the world.

N. A. Dahl has demonstrated that calling Satan a homicide is a concealed reference to the murder of Abel by Cain.[3] It is undoubtedly true that Abel's murder in Genesis has an exceptional importance. But this importance is due to the fact that it is the first founding murder and the first biblical account to raise a corner of the curtain that always covers the frightful role played by homicide in the foundation of human communities. This murder is presented to us, we have seen, as the origin of the law that sanctions murder as a sevenfold reprisal, the origin of the rule against homicide within the Cainite culture, and in effect the origin of that culture.

3. N. A. Dahl, "Der Erstgeborene Satans und der Vater des Teufels," *Apophoreta* (Berlin: Töpelmann, 1964), 70–84.

So the synoptic Gospels refer to Abel's murder because it has an exceptional significance. But we should not wish to bring the Johannine text back at any price to the literal meaning of the synoptic text, which refers to a certain person called Abel or to a category of victims called "the prophets." In writing "he was a murderer from the beginning" John's text goes further than the others in disentangling the founding mechanisms; it excises all the definitions and specifications that might bring about a mythic interpretation. John goes to the full length in his reading of the text of the Bible, and what he comes up against is the hypothesis of the founding violence.

Biblical specialists are misled on this point in much the same way as ethnologists, and all other specialists in the human sciences, who move invariably from myth to myth and from institution to institution, from signifier to signifier in effect, or from signified to signified, without ever getting to the symbolic matrix of all these signifiers and signifieds — that is, to the scapegoat mechanism.

G.L.: It is indeed the same mistake. But there is something more paradoxical and exclusive about the blindness of the biblical experts compared with those in the human sciences, because they have right under noses, in the text which they claim to be able to decipher, the key to the correct interpretation — the key to every interpretation — and they refuse to make use of it. They do not even notice the unbelievable opportunities staring them in the face.

R.G.: Even with John's text, the danger of a mythical reading is still present, clearly so, if we do not see that Satan denotes the founding mechanism itself — the principle of all human community. All of the texts in the New Testament confirm this reading, in particular the "Temptation" made by Satan the prince and principle of this world, *princeps huius mundi.* It is no abstract metaphysical reduction, no descent into vulgar polemics or lapse into superstition that makes Satan the true adversary of Jesus. Satan is absolutely identified with the circular mechanisms of violence, with man's imprisonment in cultural or philosophical systems that maintain his *modus vivendi* with violence. That is why he promises Jesus domination provided that Jesus will worship him. But Satan is also the *skandalon,* the living obstacle that trips men up, the mimetic model insofar as it becomes a rival and lies across our path. We shall be considering the *skandalon* further in connection with desire.

Satan is the name of the mimetic process seen as a whole; that is why he is the source not merely of rivalry and disorder but of all the forms of lying order inside which humanity lives. That is the reason why he was a homicide from the beginning; Satan's order had no origin other than murder and this murder is a lie. Human beings are sons of Satan because they are sons of this murder. Murder is therefore not an act whose consequences could be eliminated without being brought to light and genuinely rejected by men. It is an inexhaustible fund, a transcendent source of falsehood that infiltrates every domain and structures everything in its own image, with such success that the truth cannot get in, and Jesus' listeners cannot even hear his words. From the original murder, men succeed in drawing new lies all the time, and these prevent the word of the Gospel from reaching them. Even the most explicit revelation remains a dead letter.

J.-M.O.: What you have shown, in short, is that despite differences in style and tone, the Gospel of John says exactly the same thing as the synoptic Gospels. For the majority of modern commentators, the work of exegesis consists almost exclusively in trying to find the *difference* between the texts. You, on the other hand, look for the convergence, since you believe that the Gospels represent four slightly different versions of one and the same form of thought. This form of thought necessarily escapes us if we start off from the principle that only the divergences are worthy of attention.

R.G.: These divergences do indeed exist, though they are minor ones. Yet they are not without interest. In a number of cases they allow us to discover what might perhaps be called particular minor defects in respect to the entirety of the message that they are obliged to transcribe.

The Metaphor of the Tomb

R.G.: I must now come back to the "Curses." They testify to a concealed relation of dependence on the founding murder; they demonstrate a paradoxical continuity between the violence of past generations and the denunciation of that violence in contemporaries. Here we are getting to the heart of the matter; in the light of this mechanism — the very one that has preoccupied us from the outset of these discussion — a great "metaphor" within the Gospel text becomes clear. This is the metaphor of the *tomb*. Tombs exist to honor the dead, but also to hide them insofar as they are dead, to conceal the corpse and ensure that death as such is no longer visible. This act of concealment is essential. The very murders in which the fathers directly took part already resemble tombs to the extent that, above all in collective and founding murders but also in individual murders, men kill in order to lie to others and to themselves on the subject of violence and death. They must kill and continue to kill, strange as it may seem, in order not to know that they are killing.

Now we can understand why Jesus reproaches the scribes and Pharisees for putting up tombs for the prophets who have been killed by their fathers. Not to recognize the founding character of the murder, whether by denying that the fathers have killed or by condemning the guilty in the interests of demonstrating their own innocence, is to perpetuate the foundation, which is an obscuring of the truth. People do not wish to know that the whole of human culture is based on the mythic process of conjuring away man's violence by endlessly projecting it upon new victims. All cultures and all religions are built on this foundation, which they then conceal, just as the tomb is built around the dead body that it conceals. Murder calls for the tomb and the tomb is but the prolongation and perpetuation of murder. The tomb-religion amounts to nothing more or less than the becoming visible of the foundations, of religion and culture, of their only reason for existence.

> Woe to you! for you build the tombs of the prophets whom your fathers killed. So you are witnesses and consent to the deeds of your fathers; for they killed them, and you build their tombs.
> (Luke 11:47–48)

"For they killed them, and you build their tombs": Jesus at once reveals and unambiguously *compromises* the history of all human culture. That is why he takes to himself the words of Psalm 78: "I will utter what has been hidden since the foundation of the world—*apo kataboles kosmou*" (Matt. 13:35).

If the metaphor of the tomb applies to all forms of human order taken in their entirety, it can also be applied to the individuals formed by that order. On the individual level, the Pharisees are absolutely identified with the system of misrecognition on which they rely as a community.

It would be foolhardy to call "metaphorical" our usage of the term "tomb," since we are so close to the heart of the matter. To speak of the metaphor is to speak of displacement, and yet no metaphorical displacement is involved here. On the contrary, it is the tomb that is the starting point of the constitutive displacements of culture. Quite a number of fine minds think that this is literally true on the level of human history as a whole; funerary rituals could well, as we have said, amount to the first actions of a strictly cultural type. There is reason to believe that these rituals took shape around the first of the reconciliatory victims, on the basis of the creative transference achieved by the first communities. This also brings to mind the sacrificial stones that mark the foundation of ancient cities, which are invariably associated with some story of a lynching, ineffectively camouflaged.

J.-M.O.: We must turn back at this point to what we said the other day on all these subjects. We must keep them continually in mind in order to grasp what is at once the simplicity of the hypothesis and the endless wealth of applications to be drawn from it.

R.G.: Archaeological discoveries seem to suggest that people were really building tombs for the Prophets in Jesus' period. That is a very interesting point, and it is quite possible that a practice of this kind suggested the "metaphor." However, it would be a pity to limit the significance generated in our text by the different uses of the term "tomb" to a mere evocation of this practice. The fact that the metaphor applies both to the group and to the individual clearly demonstrates that much more is involved than an allusion to specific tombs, just as much more is involved in the following passage than a mere "moral" indictment:

> Woe to you, scribes and Pharisees, hypocrites! for you are like white-washed tombs, which outwardly appear beautiful, but within they are full of dead men's bones and all uncleanness.
> (Matt. 23:27)

Deep within the individual, as within the religious and cultural systems that fashion the individual, something is hidden, and this is not merely the individual "sin" of modern religiosity or the "complexes" of psychoanalysis. It is invariably a corpse that as it rots spreads its "uncleanness" everywhere.

Luke compares the Pharisees not just to tombs but to underground tombs, that is to say, invisible tombs — tombs that are perfect in a double sense, if we can put it like that, since they conceal not only death, but also their own existence as tombs.

> Woe unto you! for you are like graves which are not seen, and men walk over them without knowing it. (Luke 11:44)

J.-M.O.: This double concealment reproduces the way in which cultural differentiation develops on the basis of the founding murder. This murder tends to efface itself behind the directly sacrificial rituals, but even these rituals risk being too revealing and so tend to be effaced behind postritual institutions, such as judicial and political systems or the forms of culture. These derived forms give away nothing of the fact that they are rooted in the original murder.

R.G.: So we have here a problem of *knowledge* which is always being lost, never to be rediscovered again. This knowledge certainly comes to the surface in the great biblical texts and above all in the prophetic books, but the organization of religion and law contrives to repress it. The Pharisees, who are satisfied with what seems to them to be their success in the religious life, are blind to the essentials and so they blind those whom they claim to be guiding:

> Woe to you lawyers! for you have taken away the key of knowledge; you did not enter yourselves and you hindered those who were entering. (Luke 11:52)

Michel Serres first made me see the importance of this reference to the "key of knowledge." Jesus has come in order to place men in possession of this key. Within the perspective of the Gospels, the Passion is first and foremost the consequence of an intolerable revelation, while being proof of that revelation. It is because they do not understand what he proclaims that Jesus' listeners agree to rid themselves of him, and in so doing, they confirm the accuracy and the prophetic nature of the "curses against the Pharisees."

They have recourse to violence, to expel the truth about violence:

> As he went away from there, the scribes and the Pharisees began to press him hard, and to provoke him to speak of many things, lying in wait for him, to catch at something he might say. (Luke 11:53)

Human culture is organized around a more or less violent disavowal of human violence. That is what the religion that comes from man amounts to, as opposed to the religion that comes from God. By affirming this point without the least equivocation, Jesus infringes upon the supreme prohibition that governs all human order, and he must be reduced to silence. Those who come together against Jesus do so in order to back up the arrogant assumption that consists in saying: "If we had lived in the days of our fathers, we would not have taken part with them in shedding the blood of the prophets."

The truth of the founding murder is expressed first of all in the words of Jesus, which connect the present conduct of men with the distant past, and with the near future (since they announce the Passion), and with the whole of human history. The same truth of the founding murder will also be expressed, with even greater force, in the Passion itself, which fulfills the prophecy and gives it its full weight. If centuries and indeed millennia have to pass before this truth is revived, it is of little consequence. The truth is registered and will finally accomplish its work. Everything that is hidden shall be revealed.

The Passion

R.G.: Jesus is presented to us as the innocent victim of a group in crisis, which, for a time at any rate, is united against him. All the subgroups and indeed all the individuals who are concerned with the life and trial of Jesus end up by giving their explicit or implicit assent to his death: the crowd in Jerusalem, the Jewish religious authorities, the Roman political authorities, and even the disciples, since those who do not betray or deny Jesus actively take flight or remain passive.

We must remember that this very crowd had welcomed Jesus with such enthusiasm only a few days earlier. The crowd turns around like a single man and insists on his death with a determination that springs at least in part from being carried away by the irrationality of the collective spirit. Certainly nothing has intervened to justify such a change of attitude.

It is necessary to have legal forms in a universe where there are legal institutions, to give unanimity to the decision to put a man to death. Nonetheless, the decision to put Jesus to death is first and foremost a decision of the crowd, one that identifies the crucifixion not so much with a ritual sacrifice but (as in the case of the servant) with the process that I claim to be at the basis of all rituals and all religious phenomena. Just as in the "Songs" from Isaiah, though even more directly this hypothesis confronts us in the four Gospel stories of the Passion.

Because it reproduces the founding event of all rituals, the Passion is connected with every ritual on the entire planet. There is not an incident in it that cannot be found in countless instances: the preliminary trial, the derisive crowd, the grotesque honors accorded to the victim, and the particular role played by chance, in the form of casting lots, which here affects not the choice of the victim but the way in which his clothing is disposed of. The final feature is the degrading punishment that takes place outside the holy city in order not to contaminate it.

Noticing these parallels with other rituals, certain ethnologists have attempted — in a spirit of hostile skepticism, as you can imagine, which does not diminish, paradoxically, their absolute faith in the historicity of the Gospel text — to attribute ritualistic motives to some of the actors in the Passion story. In their view, Jesus must have served as "scapegoat" to some of Pilate's legionaries, who were caught up in some sort of saturnalia. Frazer even debated with some German researchers the precise ritual that must have been involved.

In 1898, P. Wendland noted the striking analogies between "the treatment inflicted on Christ by the Roman soldiers and that which other Roman soldiers inflicted on the false king of the Saturnalia at Durostorum."[4] He took the view that the legionaries would have clothed Jesus with the traditional ornaments of King Saturn in order to make fun of his pretensions to a heavenly kingdom. In a long note added to the second edition of *The Golden Bough,* Frazer declared that he had also been struck by these similarities but had not been able to take them into account in the first edition because he was incapable of offering an explanation for them. Wendland's article did not seem satisfactory to him, in the first place for dating reasons — the Saturnalia took place in December whereas the crucifixion took place at Easter — but above all because he had by this time come up with a better explanation:

> But closely as the Passion of Christ resembles the treatment of the mock king of the Saturnalia, it resembles still more closely the treatment of the mock king of Sacaea. The description of the mockery by St. Matthew is the fullest. It runs thus: "Then released

4. P. Wendland, "Jesus als Saturnalien-König," *Hermes* 33 (1898): 175–79.

he Barabbas unto them: and when he had scourged Jesus, he delivered him to be crucified. Then the soldiers of the governor took Jesus into the common hall, and gathered unto him the whole band of soldiers. And they stripped him, and put on him a scarlet robe. And when they had platted a crown of thorns, they put it upon his head, and a reed in his right hand: and they bowed the knee before him, and mocked him, saying, Hail, King of the Jews! And they spit upon him, and took the reed, and smote him on the head. And after that they had mocked him, they took the robe off from him, and put his own raiment on him, and led him away to crucify him." Compare with this the treatment of the mock king of the Sacaea, as it is described by Dio Chrysostom: "They take one of the prisoners condemned to death and seat him upon the king's throne, and give him the king's raiment, and let him lord it and drink and run riot and use the king's concubines during these days, and no man prevents him from doing just what he likes. But afterwards they strip and scourge and crucify him."[5]

However suggestive it may be in certain respects, this type of hypothesis seems untenable to us because of the conception of the Gospel text it takes for granted. Frazer persists in making the Gospel no different from a historical account, or even a piece of on-the-spot reporting. It does not occur to him that the relationship between the rituals to which he refers and the Gospels could be based on anything but a chance coincidence between events; he does not take into account that there might be something much more profound on the level of the text itself — which could explain the way in which this religious and cultural document was internally organized. If this possibility is discounted, how could we account for the striking coincidence between the Saturnalia and the account that he gives to the "mock king of Sacaea"?

Here we are confronted with a kind of prejudice that flourished in the epoch of positivism. Although we are not going to succumb to the opposite prejudice, which is in the ascendant in our own period, we should nonetheless pay some attention to the internal organization of the text and, as a first stage, look at it independently of its potential reference.

Frazer's own thesis is not lacking in detailed observation. It is as ingenious as it is naïve. The analogies traced between religious forms are not by any means restricted to those which ethnologists parade because they believe that they can explain them consistently with their own views. These analogies extend to a whole group of religious phenomena — the servant of Yahweh, for example, not to mention a host of other Old Testament texts. An ethnological critic in the Frazer style will

5. Frazer, *The Golden Bough,* part 6, "The Scapegoat," one-volume ed. (New York: Macmillan, 1963), 413–14.

declare analogies of this kind to be ultimately inadmissable for the very reason that the Gospels themselves claim a kinship with such texts. He will proclaim them to be nonexistent, invented to serve the cause of religion, whereas in reality we are dealing with parallels very close to ones he congratulates himself about drawing to our attention. It is simply that his positivist spirit can tolerate only those analogies that he feels will discredit the claims of the Gospels, and jibes at those the Gospels themselves invoke in order to buttress those same claims.

For there to be an effective, sacralizing act of transference, it is necessary that the victim should inherit all of the violence from which the community has been exonerated. It is because the victim genuinely passes as guilty that the transference does not come to the fore as such. This piece of conjuring brings about the happy result for which the lynching mob is profoundly grateful: the victim bears the weight of the incompatible and contradictory meanings that, juxtaposed, create *sacredness*. For the Gospel text to be mythic in our sense, it would have to take no account of the arbitrary and unjust character of the violence which is done to Jesus. In fact the opposite is the case: the Passion is presented as a blatant piece of injustice. Far from taking the collective violence upon itself, the text places it squarely on those who are responsible for it. To use the expression from the "Curses," it lets the violence fall upon the heads of those to whom it belongs: "Verily I say unto you, All these things shall come upon this generation."

G.L.: You prove, I believe, that these words have nothing to do with the old primitive curses that are designed to draw the vengeance of a violent god upon the cursed individual. In this case, the effect is precisely the opposite. There is a complete "deconstruction" of the whole primitive system, which brings to light the founding mechanism and leaves men without the protection of sacrifice, prey to the old mimetic conflict, which from this point onward will acquire its typically Christian and modern form. Everyone will now seek to cast upon his neighbor the responsibility of persecution, and injustice will become more and more apparent; everyone will be reluctant to admit that they are involved.

R.G.: There has to be a close connection between the revelation in words of the founding murder and its revelation on the level of action; this murder is repeated, taking as its victim the person who has revealed it — whose message everyone refuses to understand. In the Gospels, the revelation in words immediately stirs up a collective will to *silence* the speaker, which is concretized as a collective murder. In other words, the founding mechanism is reproduced once again, and, by virtue of this, the speech it strives to stifle is confirmed as true. The revelation is one and the same as the violent opposition to any revelation, since it is this lying violence, the source of all lies, that must first of all be revealed.

The Martyrdom of Stephen

R.G.: The process that leads directly from the "curses" to the Passion can be found again in a form both compact and striking in a text which is not strictly speaking from the Gospels, but is as close as it could possibly be to at least one of the Gospel accounts in which the "curses" figure — that of Luke. I am talking about the Acts of the Apostles, which are presented, as you know, as the work of Luke himself, and may well be his.

The text I have in mind reconstitutes the sequence formed by the "curses" and the Passion, but does so in such a compact way, articulating its elements in so explicit a fashion, that we can really envisage it as a genuine interpretation of the Gospel text. I am referring to Stephen's speech and its consequences. The ending of this speech to the Sanhedrin is so disagreeable to its audience that it immediately causes the death of the person who made it.

Stephen's last words, the ones that trigger murderous rage in his public, are no more than the repetition, pure and simple, of the curses against the Pharisees. Obviously the murders already named by Jesus are joined, in Stephen's speech, by a reference to the murder of Jesus himself, which is by now an established fact and reenacts better than anything else the founding murder.

So it is the whole formed by the prophecy and its fulfillment that the words of Stephen isolate and underline. It is the relationship of cause and effect between the revelation that compromises the community's basis in violence and the new violence that casts out the revelation in order to reestablish that basis, to lay its foundation once again.

> "You stiff-necked people, uncircumcised in heart and ears, you always resist the Holy Spirit. As your fathers did, so do you. Which of the prophets did not your fathers persecute? And they killed those who announced beforehand the coming of the Righteous One, whom you have now betrayed and murdered, you who received the law as delivered by angels and did not keep it."
>
> Now when they heard these things they were enraged, and they ground their teeth against him. But he, full of the Holy Spirit, gazed into heaven and saw the glory of God, and Jesus standing at the right hand of God; and he said, "Behold, I see the heavens opened, and the Son of man standing at the right hand of God." But they cried out with a loud voice and stopped their ears and rushed together upon him. Then they cast him out of the city and stoned him. (Acts 7:51–58)

The words that throw the violence back upon those who are really guilty are so intolerable that it is necessary to shut once and for all the mouth of the one who speaks them. So as not to hear him while he remains capable of speaking, the audience "stop their ears." How can we miss the point that they kill in order to cast off an intolerable knowledge and that this knowledge is, strangely enough, the knowledge of the murder itself? The whole process of the Gospel revelation and the crucifixion is reproduced here in the clearest possible way.

It is worth pointing out that the Jews, like other peoples, reserve Stephen's method of execution — stoning — for the most impure of criminals, those guilty of the most serious crimes. It is the Jewish equivalent of the Greek *anathema*.

As with all forms of sacrifice, the execution must reproduce the founding murder in order to renew its beneficial effects, in this case wiping out the dangers to which the blasphemer exposes the community (cf. Deut. 17:7).

The repetition of this murder is a dangerous action that might bring about the return of the crisis which it is designed to avoid. One of the first precautions against the pollution of violence consists in forbidding any kind of ritual execution within the community. That is why the stoning of Stephen takes place — like the crucifixion — outside the city walls of Jerusalem.

But this initial precaution is not sufficient. Prudence dictates that there must be no contact with the victim who pollutes because he is polluted. How is it possible to combine this requirement with another important requirement, which is to reproduce as exactly as possible the original murder? To reproduce it exactly implies unanimous participation by the whole community, or at any rate by all those who are present. This unanimous participation is explicitly required by the text of Deuteronomy (17:7). How can it be arranged for everyone to strike the victim, while no one is soiled by contact with him? Obviously, stoning resolves this delicate problem. Like all methods of execution from a distance — the modern firing squad, or the community's driving Takarau from the top of a cliff in the Tikopia myth — stoning fulfills this twofold ritual requirement.

The only person taking part in this event whose name figures in the text is Saul of Tarsus, the future Paul. He is also, it would appear, the only person not to throw stones, although the text assures us that his heart is with the murderers. "And Saul was consenting to his death." Thus Saul's presence does not break the unanimity. The text makes it clear that the participants rushed upon Stephen "with one accord." This way of signaling the unanimity would have an almost technical ritual significance if we were not dealing with something quite different from a ritual. The unanimity that in ritual has a compulsory and premeditated character is here achieved quite spontaneously.

The hurried aspect of this stoning and the fact that the procedures listed in the text of Deuteronomy are not all observed have led a number of commentators to judge that the execution was more or less illegal and to define it as a kind of lynching. Johannes Munck, for example, writes as follows in his edition of the Acts of the Apostles:

> Was this examination before the Sanhedrin and the following stoning a real trial and a legal performed execution? We do not know. The improvised and passionate character of the events as related might suggest that it was illegal, a lynching.[6]

Munck compares Stephen's last words to "a spark that starts an explosion" (70). The fact that we are concerned here with a ritualized mode of execution and an irresistible discharge of collective fury is extremely significant. For this twofold status to be possible, it is necessary for the ritual mode of execution to coincide with a possible form of spontaneous violence. If the ritual gesture can be to a certain extent deritualized and become spontaneous without really altering in form, we can imagine that such a metamorphosis can also take place in the other direction; the form of the legal execution is nothing more than the ritualization of a spontaneous violence. If we look carefully at the martyrdom of Stephen, we inevitably come up against the hypothesis of the founding violence.

This scene from Acts is a reproduction that both reveals and underlines the relationship between the "curses" and the Passion. Stephen's death has the same twofold relationship to the "curses" as the Passion itself. It verifies them because Stephen, like Jesus, is killed to forestall this verification. Stephen is the first of those who are spoken of in the "curses." We have already quoted from Matthew (23:34–35). Here now is the text from Luke that also defines the precise function of this *martyrdom* which is indeed one of *witness*. Dying in the same way as Jesus dies, for the same reasons as he did, the martyrs multiply the revelation of the founding violence:

> Therefore also the Wisdom of God said, "I will send them prophets and apostles, some of whom they will kill and persecute," that the blood of all the prophets, shed from the foundation of the world, may be required of this generation.... (Luke 11:49–50)

This particular text must not be interpreted in a narrow fashion. It does not say that the only innocent victims, from now on, are to be the "confessors of the faith" in the dogmatic, theological sense used historically by the Christian church. It means that there will be no more victims from now on whose persecution will not eventually be recognized as unjust, for no further sacralization is possible. No more myths

6. *The Acts of the Apostles,* The Anchor Bible (New York: Doubleday, 1967), 69.

can be produced to cover up the fact of persecution. The Gospels make all forms of "mythologizing" impossible since, by revealing the founding mechanism, they stop it from functioning. That is why we have fewer and fewer myths all the time, in our universe dominated by the Gospels, and more and more texts bearing on persecution.

The Scapegoat Text

J.-M.O.: If I understand you rightly, the process of misunderstanding that is defined in the text must also be reproduced once again in the restrictive interpretations that have always been given of it — first and foremost, of course, in the interpretations that try to limit its application to those for whom it is immediately destined.

To read the material in this way is to take an attitude full of consequences. The reading will tend to reproduce, in circumstances which are historically and ideologically different but structurally invariant, a violent transference upon the scapegoat, the very form of transference that has been in force since the dawn of humanity. So it is by no means a fortuitous or innocent reading. It transforms the universal revelation of the founding murder into a polemical denunciation of the Jewish religion. So as not to have to recognize that they are themselves involved in the message, people will claim that it only involves the Jews.

R.G.: This kind of restrictive interpretation is indeed the only way out for a type of thought that is in principle made over to "Christianity" but is firmly resolved to divest itself of any form of violence, and so inevitably brings with it a new form of violence, directed against a new scapegoat — the Jew. In brief, what happens again is what Jesus reproached the Pharisees for doing, and since Jesus has been accepted, it can no longer be done directly to him. Once again, the truth and universality of the process revealed by the text is demonstrated as it is displaced toward the latest available victims. Now it is the Christians who say: "If we had lived in the days of our Jewish fathers, we would not have taken part with them in shedding the blood of Jesus." If the people whom Jesus addresses and who do not listen to him fulfill the measure of their fathers, then the Christians who believe themselves justified in denouncing these same people in order to exculpate themselves are fulfilling a measure that is already full to overflowing. They claim to be governed by the text that reveals the process of misunderstanding, and yet they repeat that misunderstanding. With their eyes fixed on the text, they do once again what the text condemns. The only way of transcending this blindness consists in repudiating — as is done today — not the process that is revealed in the text and can maintain itself, paradoxically, in its shade, but the text itself; the text is declared to be responsible for the acts of violence committed in its name and actually blamed for not, up to now, mastering the old violence except by diverting it to new victims. There is at present a general tendency among Christians to repudiate this text or an any rate never to take any account of it, concealing it as if it were something to be ashamed of. There is one last trick, one last victim, and this is the text itself, which is chained to a fallacious reading and dragged before the tribunal of public opinion. It is the ultimate irony that the Gospel text should be condemned by public opinion in the name of charity. Face to face with a world that is, as we well know, today overflowing with charity, the text appears to be disconcertingly harsh.

There is actually no contradiction between the choice of the Jews, as it is reaffirmed in the Gospels, and texts like those of the "curses." If anywhere in the world a religious or cultural form managed to evade the accusation made against the Pharisees — not excluding those that confess Jesus himself — then the Gospels would not be the truth about human culture. In order for the Gospels to have the universal significance Christians claim for them, it is necessary for there to be nothing on earth that is superior to the Jewish religion and the sect of the Pharisees. This absolute degree of representativeness is part and parcel of the status of the Jews as the chosen people, which is never disavowed by the New Testament.

Nor is there any contradiction between a revelation of violence made on the basis of biblical texts and the veneration that the New Testament never ceased to show for the Old. As we saw earlier, when we were considering the texts of Genesis and Exodus, the revelation of the founding murder and of its generative power in regard to myth become increasingly apparent in these texts. That implies that even at this early stage the inspiration of the Bible and the prophets is at work on the myths, undoing them in order to reveal their truth. Instead of invariably displacing the responsibility for the collective murder toward the victim, this form of inspiration takes a contrary path; it looks once again at the mythical elaborations and tends to deconstruct them, placing the responsibility for the violence upon those who are really responsible — the members of the community. In this way, it paves the way for the full and final revelation.

J.-M.O.: To understand that the Gospels really do reveal all this violence, we have to understand first of all that this violence engenders the mythic meanings. Now I can appreciate why you decided to place our initial discussions on Judeo-Christian texts after the section on basic anthropology. You wanted to show that we are now in a position to get to the truth about all non-Christian religious phenomena by means of purely scientific and hypothetical procedures. Then the shift to the Judeo-Christian texts confirms the analysis and makes it more compelling.

R.G.: What you say seems quite right to me. In fact, that is exactly why I wrote *Violence and the Sacred* in the way that I did. I am well aware of the blemishes in that work, as I am of the blemishes in what we have been saying here.

The thesis of the scapegoat owes nothing to any form of impressionistic or literary borrowing. I believe it to be fully demonstrated on the basis of the anthropological texts. That is why I have chosen not to listen to those who criticize my scientific claims and have determined to try to reinforce and sharpen the systematic character of my work, and to confirm the power of the scheme to reveal the genesis and structure of cultural phenomena.

In effect, all that I did in *Violence and the Sacred* was to retrace, with all its hesitations, my own intellectual journey, which eventually brought me to the Judeo-Christian writings, though long after I had become convinced of the importance of the victimage mechanism. In the course of this journey, I remained for a long period as hostile to the Judeo-Christian texts as modernist orthodoxy could wish. But I came to the conclusion that the best way of convincing my readers was not to cheat on my own experience and to reproduce its successive stages in two separate works, one of which would deal with the universe of sacred science, and the other with the Judeo-Christian aspect.

In the "modern" period, Judeo-Christian writings have become more and more alien to modern philosophy and all our "sciences of man." They now seem more foreign than the myths of the Ojibwa and the Tikopia. But our intellectual life is being influenced by forces that, far from taking Judeo-Christian Scriptures further and further away, in fact bring them closer by a process whose circularity the "sciences of man" still fail to grasp.

We can no longer believe that if it is we who are reading the Gospels in the light of an ethnological, modern revelation, which would really be the first thing of its kind. We have to reverse this order. It is still the great Judeo-Christian spirit that is doing the reading. All that appears in ethnology, appears in the light of a continuing revelation, an immense process of historical work that enables us little by little to catch up with texts that are, in effect, already quite explicit, though not for the kind of people that we are—who "have eyes and see not, ears and hear not."

Trusting ever more numerous and precise analogies, ethnological research has been trying for centuries to demonstrate that Christianity is just one more religion like the others and that Christianity's pretensions to absolute singularity are founded merely on the irrational attachment of Christians to the religion within which they chanced to be born. It might appear, at first sight, that the discovery of the mechanism that produces religion — the collective transference against a victim who is first reviled and then sacralized—would bring with it the final and most essential stone in the structure of "demystification" to which this present reading, quite obviously, presents a sequel. Yet the discovery contributes, not just one more analogy, but the source of all analogies, which is situated behind the myths, hidden within their infrastructure and finally revealed, in a perfectly explicit way, in the account of the Passion.

By an astonishing reversal, it is texts that are twenty or twenty-five centuries old — initially revered blindly but today rejected with contempt — that will reveal themselves to be the only means of furthering all that is good and true in the anti-Christian endeavors of modern times: the as-yet-ineffectual determination to rid the world of the sacred cult of violence. These texts supply such endeavors with exactly what is needed to give a radically sociological reading of the historical forms of transcendence, and at the same time they place their own transcendence in an area which is impervious to any critique by placing it in the area from which a critique would derive.

Of course the Gospels also speak tirelessly of this reversal of all interpretations. After telling the parable of the tenants of the vineyard who *all come together to drive out* the envoys of the Master and then finally to kill his son so that they would be the sole proprietors, Christ offers his audience a problem in Old Testament exegesis:

> But he looked at them and said, "What then is this that is written: 'The very stone which the builders rejected has become the head of the corner.' " (Luke 20:17)

The quotation comes from Psalm 118. People have always supposed that the question only invited "mystical" replies, replies that could not be taken seriously on the level of the only kind of knowledge that counts. In this respect as in many others, the anti-religious person is in complete accord with the weak-kneed, purely "idealist" religious person.

If we accept that all human religions and all human culture come down to the parable of the murderous tenants of the vineyard — that is, come down to the collective expulsion of the victim — and if this foundation can remain a foundation only to the extent that it does not become apparent, then it is clear that only those texts in which this foundation is made apparent will no longer be built upon it and so will be genuinely revealing. The words from Psalm 118 thus have a remarkable epistemological value; they require an interpretation for which Christ himself ironically calls, knowing very well that he alone is capable of giving it in the process of being rejected, of himself becoming the rejected stone, with the aim of showing that this stone has always formed a concealed foundation. And now the stone is revealed and can no longer form a foundation, or, rather, it will found something that is radically different.

The problem of exegesis Christ puts to his audience can be resolved, in short, only if we see in the words that he quotes the very formula for the reversal, at once an invisible and an obvious one, that I am putting forward. The rejected stone is the scapegoat, who is Christ. By submitting to violence, Christ reveals and uproots the structural matrix of all religion.

The text alerts us, in short, to its own functioning, which eludes the laws of ordinary textuality, and by virtue of this fact the warning itself eludes us, as it eluded Christ's audience. If such is indeed the movement of the text, then the claims of Christianity to make Christ the author of a universal revelation are far more securely founded than even its defenders would imagine. They fall back inevitably into ordinary textuality, blotting out once again the true point of origin, which is nonetheless clearly inscribed in Scripture; they reject all over again, in a final and paradoxical form of expulsion, the stone that is Christ, and they still fail to see that this selfsame stone continues to serve them as a concealed cornerstone.

If you read the commentaries customarily written about phrases of this kind, not only by Christians but also by so-called "scientific" exegetes, you will be amazed by the universal inability to recognize meanings that are for us by now so obvious that we are hesitant to repeat the train of reasoning which would make them explicit.

The exegetes are aware, obviously, that Christ identifies with the stone rejected by the builders, but they fail to see the formidable reverberations of this phrase on the anthropological level, and the reason why it is already present in the Old Testament.

Instead of reading myths in the light of the Gospels, people have always read the Gospels in light of myths. In comparison with the astonishing work of demystification effected by the Gospels, our own exercises in demystification are only slight sketches, though they may also be cunning obstacles that our minds erect against the Gospel revelation. But from now on the obstacles themselves must contribute to the invisible but ineluctable advance of revelation.

Chapter 11

The Nonsacrificial Death of Christ

The Gospels bring culture's scapegoat mechanisms to light in their account of Jesus' ministry, death, and resurrection. Paradoxically, the text itself is typically misunderstood. The founding mechanism that is exposed through Jesus' teachings and fate is misconstrued as the affirmation of the founding mechanism, i.e., of scapegoating and sacrifice. However, modern ignorance of the mechanism is not simply the work of fundamentalists and others who hold to a sacrificial religion. Modern agnosticism and atheism, skeptical about all religion, serve to perpetuate scapegoat mechanisms by effectively keeping them invisible.

The following discussion of the nonsacrificial death of Christ is taken from two parts of a chapter entitled "A Non-Sacrificial Reading of the Gospel Text" in *Things Hidden*, 180-82, 205-15. It should be noted once more that in recent years Girard has become more disposed to balance the violent, victimary side of sacrifice with an appreciation of its more positive effects and connotations. On this see the introduction to chapter 6. In the derived sense of the loving willingness to give of oneself, even one's very life, for the sake of the other, it has an appropriate usage in the language of Christian liturgy, fellowship, and theology. Likewise Jesus' willingness to give his life and to suffer an execution which was, historically considered, a kind of public or civic sacrifice, could appropriately be described as sacrifice. So from the standpoint of the historical background and context of Jesus' death, as well as the derived positive connotations of sacrifice, the language of sacrifice cannot be dismissed from the language of faith. But sacrifice, even if retained in these senses, must be redefined on the basis of faith in a God of love who does not make a secret pact with his Son that calls for his murder in order to satisfy God's wrath (see

Things Hidden, 184). The suffering and death of the Son, the Word, are inevitable because of the inability of the world to receive God or his Son, not because God's justice demands violence or the Son relishes the prospect of a horrible execution.

— ☙ —

R.G.: The Gospels speak of "sacrifices" only in order to reject them and deny them any validity. Jesus counters the ritualism of the Pharisees with an anti-sacrificial quotation from Hosea: "Go and learn what this means, 'I desire mercy, and not sacrifice' " (Matt. 9:13).

The following text amounts to a great deal more than ethical advice; it at once sets the cult of sacrifice at a distance and reveals its true function, which has now come full circle:

> So if you are offering your gift at the altar, and there remember that your brother has something against you, leave your gift there before the altar and go; first be reconciled to your brother, and then come and offer your gift. (Matt. 5:23–24)

G.L.: Surely the crucifixion is still the sacrifice of Christ?

R.G.: There is nothing in the Gospels to suggest that the death of Jesus is a sacrifice, whatever definition (expiation, substitution, etc.) we may give for that sacrifice. At no point in the Gospels is the death of Jesus defined as a sacrifice. The passages that are invoked to justify a sacrificial conception of the Passion both can and should be interpreted with no reference to sacrifice in any of the accepted meanings.

Certainly the Passion is presented to us in the Gospels as an act that brings salvation to humanity. But it is in no way presented as a sacrifice.

If you have really followed my argument up to this point, you will already realize that from our particular perspective the sacrificial interpretation of the Passion must be criticized and exposed as a most enormous and paradoxical misunderstanding — and at the same time as something necessary — and as the most revealing indication of mankind's radical incapacity to understand its own violence, even when that violence is conveyed in the most explicit fashion.

Of all the reappraisals we must make in the course of these interviews, none is more important. It is no mere consequence of the anthropological perspective we have adopted. Our perspective is rooted in the Gospels themselves, in their own subversion of sacrifice, which restores the original text, disengaging the hypothesis of the scapegoat and enabling it to be transmitted to the human sciences.

I am not speaking of my own personal experience here. I am referring to something very much larger, to the framework of all the intellectual experiences that we are capable of having. Thanks to the sacrificial reading it has been possible for what we call Christendom to exist for fifteen or twenty centuries; that is to say, a culture has existed that is based, like all cultures (at least up to a certain point) on the mythological forms engendered by the founding mechanism. Paradoxically, in the sacrificial reading the Christian text itself provides the basis. Mankind relies upon a misunderstanding of the text that explicitly reveals the founding mechanism to reestablish cultural forms which remain sacrificial and to engender a society that, by virtue of this misunderstanding, takes its place in the sequence of all other cultures, still clinging to the sacrificial vision that the Gospel rejects.

J.-M.O.: Any form of sacrificial vision would contradict, I suppose, the revelation of the founding murder that you have shown to be present in the Gospels. It is obvious that bringing to light the founding murder completely rules out any compromise with the principle of sacrifice, or indeed with any conception of the death of Jesus as a sacrifice. A conception of this kind can only succeed in concealing yet again the real meaning and function of the Passion: one of subverting sacrifice and barring it from working ever again by forcing the founding mechanism out into the open, writing it down in the text of all the Gospels.

G.L.: I can see very well that a nonsacrificial reading is necessary. But at first sight it looks as though the enterprise will come up against some formidable obstacles, ranging from the redemptive character of Jesus' death to the conception of a violent God, which seems to become indispensable when you take into account themes like the Apocalypse. Everything that you say here is bound to provoke in response the famous words that the Gospels have no qualms about putting in Jesus' own mouth: "I have come not to bring peace but a sword." People are going to tell you that the Christian Scriptures explicitly provide a reason for discord and dissension.

R.G.: None of what you say is incompatible with the nonsacrificial reading I am putting forward. It is only in the light of this reading that we can finally explain the Gospels' intrinsic conception of their action in history, in particular the elements that appear to be contrary to the "Gospel spirit." Once again, we must judge the interpretation that is being developed by the results it will offer. By rejecting the sacrificial definition of the Passion, we arrive at a simpler, more direct, and more coherent reading, enabling us to integrate all the Gospel themes into a seamless totality....

R.G.: If we can rid ourselves of the vestiges of the sacrificial mentality that soil and darken the recesses of our minds, we shall see that we now have all the elements to hand for understanding that the death of Jesus takes place for reasons that have nothing to do with sacrifice. All that remained unclear in the nonsacrificial reading should have been clarified in the most comprehensive way.

As we have seen, Jesus is the direct, though involuntary, cause of the division and dissension that is stirred up by his message, by virtue of the fact that it meets with almost universal incomprehension. But all of his actions are directed toward nonviolence, and no more effective form of action could be imagined.

As I have already pointed out, Jesus cannot be held responsible for the apocalyptic dimension that underlies Jewish history and ultimately all of human history. In the Jewish universe, the superiority of the Old Testament over all forms of mythology meant that the point of no return had already been reached. The Law and the Prophets, as we saw, constitute a genuine announcement of the Gospel, a *praefiguratio Christi,* as the Middle Ages testified, but could not show, unable as they were to recognize in the Old Testament a first step outside the sacrificial system, and the first gradual withering of sacrificial resources. At the very moment when this adventure approaches its resolution Jesus arrives on the scene — Jesus as he appears in the Gospels.

From now on, it becomes impossible to put the clock back. There is an end to cyclical history, for the very reason that its mechanisms are beginning to be uncovered.

G.L.: I think that the same thing [begins to happen in the pre-Socratics].... Empedocles gives us the splendid anti-sacrificial text that you quoted in *Violence and the Sacred,*[1] but the pre-Socratics are unable to see the ethical consequences of what they are saying in the domain of human relationships. No doubt that is why the pre-Socratics are *still* fashionable in the world of Western philosophy, while the Prophets *never* are.

R.G.: Let us come back to the attitude of Jesus himself. The decision to adopt nonviolence is not a commitment that he could revoke, a contract whose clauses need only be observed to the extent that the other contracting parties observe them. If that were so, the commitment to the Kingdom of God would be merely another farcical procedure, comparable to institutionalized revenge or the United Nations. Despite the fact that all the others fall away, Jesus continues to see himself as being bound by the promise of the Kingdom. For him, the word that comes from God, the word that enjoins us to imitate no one but God, the God who refrains from all forms of reprisal and makes his sun to shine upon the "just" and the "unjust" without distinction — this word remains, for him, absolutely valid. It is valid even to death, and quite clearly that is what makes him the Incarnation of that Word. To sum

1. *Violence and the Sacred,* trans. P. Gregory (Baltimore: Johns Hopkins University Press, 1977), 69.

up: the Christ can no longer continue to sojourn in a world in which the Word is either never mentioned or, even worse, derided and devalued by those who take it in vain — those who claim to be faithful to it but in reality are far from being so. Jesus' destiny in the world is inseparable from that of the Word of God. That is why Christ and the Word of God are, I reaffirm, simply one and the same thing.

Not only does Jesus remain faithful to this Word of Love, but he also does everything to enlighten men about what awaits them if they continue in the pathways they have always taken before. So urgent is the problem and so massive the stake that it justifies the remarkable vehemence, even brutality, that Jesus manifests in his dealings with "those who have ears and hear not, eyes and see not." That is indeed why — through a further paradox, which is outrageously unjust but could have been expected since we know that no mercy can be shown to the person who understands what all the world around him refuses to understand — Jesus himself stands accused of unnecessary violence, offensive language, immoderate use of polemics, and failure to respect the "freedom" of his interlocutors.

Within a process that has lasted for centuries — indeed, since the beginnings of human history — the preaching of the Kingdom, first in the Judaic world and later throughout the world, must intervene at the very point when the chances of success are maximized: that is to say, at the very point when everything is ready to slide into a limitless violence. Jesus lucidly perceives both the threat and the possibility of salvation. He therefore has the duty to warn mankind; by announcing to all the Kingdom of God, he is doing no more that observing in his own behavior the principles he proclaims. He would fail in his love for his brothers if he were to keep silent and abandon the human race to the destiny that it is unconsciously creating for itself. If Jesus has been called the Son of Man, this is principally, in my view, a response to a text in Ezekiel that accords to a "son of man" a mission to warn the people that is very similar to the one conferred on Jesus by the Gospels:

> So you, son of man, I have made a watchman for the house of Israel; whenever you hear a word from my mouth, you shall give them warning from me. If I say to the wicked, O wicked man, you shall surely die, and you do not speak to warn the wicked to turn from his way, that wicked man shall die in his iniquity, but his blood I will require at your hand. But if you warn the wicked to turn from his way, and he does not turn from his way; he shall die in his iniquity, but you will have saved your life.
>
> And you, son of man, say to the house of Israel, Thus have you said: "Our transgressions and our sins are upon us, and we waste away because of them; how then can we live? Say to them, As I

> live, says the Lord God, I have no pleasure in the death of the wicked, but that the wicked turn from his way and live; turn back, turn back from your evil ways; for why will you die, O house of Israel." (Ezek. 33:1–11)

Jesus does all in his power to warn mankind and turn them away from paths that will be fatal henceforth — the most terrifying texts, like the "Curses against the Pharisees," are just the most extreme and the most dangerous for the messenger of these warnings — but he also serves as the victim, once his audience has determined not to listen to him and to fall back into their old ways. He does not resist their blows, and it is at his expense that they would become reconciled and reestablish a ritualized community if that were still a possibility. On all conceivable fronts, he is always ready to take all risks upon himself; he is always ready to pay with his own person in order to spare men the terrible destiny that awaits them.

Refusing the Kingdom means refusing the knowledge that Jesus bears — refusing the knowledge of violence and all its works. In the eyes of those who reject it, this knowledge is ill-omened; it is the worst of all forms of violence. That is indeed how things must look from the perspective of the sacrificial community. Jesus appears as a destructive and subversive force, as a source of contamination that threatens the community. Indeed, to the extent that he is misunderstood he becomes just that. The way in which he preaches can only make him appear to be totally lacking in respect for the holiest of institutions, guilty of hubris and blasphemy, since he dares to rival God himself in the perfection of the Love that he never ceases to make manifest.

Certainly the preaching of the Kingdom of God reveals that there is an element of violence even in the most apparently holy of institutions, like the church hierarchy, the rites of the Temple, and even the family.

Faithful to the logic of sacrifice, those who have refused the invitation to the Kingdom are obliged to turn against Jesus. They can hardly fail to see in him the sworn enemy and corruptor of the very cultural order that they are vainly attempting to restore.

This means that violence will find in Jesus the most perfect victim that can be imagined, the victim that, for every conceivable reason, violence has the most reasons to pick on. Yet at the same time, this victim is also the most innocent.

J.-M.O.: What you mean, in other words, is that Jesus, of all the victims who have ever been, is the only one capable of revealing the true nature of violence to its utmost. Whichever way you look at it, his death is exemplary; in it the meaning of all the persecutions and expulsions in which mankind has ever engaged, as well as all the misconceptions that have sprung from them, stand revealed and represented for all time.

Jesus, in other words, provides the scapegoat par excellence — he is the most arbitrary of victims because he is also the least violent. At the same time he is the least arbitrary and the most meaningful, again because of being the least violent. We might say that the same reason always makes Jesus the victim par excellence, in whom the previous history of mankind is summed up, concluded, and transcended.

R.G.: Violence is unable to bear the presence of a being that owes it nothing — that pays it no homage and threatens its kingship in the only way possible. What violence does not and cannot comprehend is that, in getting rid of Jesus by the usual means, it falls into a trap that could be laid only by innocence of such a kind because it is not really a trap: there is nothing hidden. Violence reveals its own game in such a way that its workings are compromises at their very source; the more it tries to conceal its ridiculous secret from now on, by forcing itself into action, the more it will succeed in revealing itself.

We can see why the Passion is found between the preaching of the Kingdom and the Apocalypse. It is an event that is ignored by historians, who have much more serious topics, with their Tiberius and their Caligula; it is a phenomenon that has no importance in the eyes of the world — incapable, at least in principle, of setting up or reinstating a cultural order but very effective, in spite of those who know better, in carrying out subversion. In the long run, it is quite capable of undermining and overturning the whole cultural order and supplying the secret motive force of all subsequent history.

J.-M.O.: Let me cut in with two questions. First, are you not in fact hypostatizing violence by treating it like a kind of subjective agency, which is personally hostile to Jesus Christ? Second, how are you able to reconcile all you have been saying with the real history of historical Christianity, in other words, with the failure of the Gospel revelation to affect events? You are the first person to read the Gospels in the way that you do. However brilliant and rigorous the textual logic that you are unfolding for our benefit, it seems to have no hold on the real history of mankind, particularly on the history of the part of the world that claimed to be Christian.

R.G.: I would reply to your first question by reminding you that violence, in every cultural order, is always the true *subject* of every ritual or institutional structure. From the moment when the sacrificial order begins to come apart, this subject can no longer be anything but the *adversary par excellence,* which combats the installation of the Kingdom of God. This is the devil known to us from tradition — Satan himself, of whom some theologians tell us that he is both subject and not subject at once.

As for your second question, I cannot reply at the moment, but I shall do so presently. For the time being, it is only necessary to point out that we are searching for coherence in the text, and I believe that we are finding it. We cannot concern ourselves at this stage with its possible relationship to our history. The fact that this logic can seem abstract and foreign to history only serves to bring out more clearly its status as a logic, in relation to the text which we are reading—and nothing more is required at present.

First of all, it is important to insist that Christ's death was not a sacrificial one. To say that Jesus dies, not as a sacrifice, but in order that there may be no more sacrifices, is to recognize in him the Word of God: "I wish for mercy and not sacrifices." Where that word is not obeyed, Jesus can remain. There is nothing gratuitous about the utterance of that word and where it is not followed by any effect, where violence remains master, Jesus must die. Rather than become the slave of violence, as our own word necessarily does, the Word of God says no to violence.

J.-M.O.: That does not mean, if I have understood you rightly, that Jesus' death is a more or less disguised suicide. The maudlin and morbid element which is to be found in a certain type of Christianity makes common cause with the sacrificial reading.

R.G.: Yes, indeed. Since they do not see that human community is dominated by violence, people do not understand that the very one of them who is untainted by any violence and has no form of complicity with violence is bound to become the victim. All of them say that the world is evil and violent. But we must see that there is no possible compromise between killing and being killed. This is the dilemma brought out by tragic drama. But the majority of mankind do not accept that it is truly representative of the "human condition." Those who do gain a reputation for "exaggerating," for "taking things tragically." There are a thousand different ways, so it would seem, of escaping from such a dilemma, even in the darkest times of history. All well and good. But people fail to understand that they are indebted to violence for the degree of peace that they enjoy.

How can nonviolence become fatal? Clearly it is not so in itself; it is wholly directed toward life and not toward death! How can the rule of the Kingdom come to have mortal consequences? This becomes possible and even necessary because others refuse to accept it. For all violence to be destroyed, it would be sufficient for all of mankind to decide to abide by this rule. If all mankind offered the other cheek, no cheek would be struck. But for that to be possible, it would be necessary for each person separately and all people together to commit themselves irrevocably to the common purpose.

If all men loved their enemies, there would be no more enemies. But if they drop away at the decisive moment, what is going to happen to the one person who does not drop away? For him the word of life will be changed into the word of death. It can be shown, I believe, that there is not a single action or word attributed to Jesus — including those that seem harshest at first sight and including the revelation of the founding murder and the last efforts to turn mankind aside from a path that will henceforth be fatal — that is not consistent with the rule of the Kingdom. It is absolute fidelity to the principle defined in his own preaching that condemns Jesus. There is no other cause for his death than the love of one's neighbor lived to the very end, with an infinitely intelligent grasp of the constraints it imposes. "Greater love has no man than this, that a man lay down his life for his friends" (John 15:13).

If violence is genuinely the ruling factor in all cultural orders, and if circumstances at the time of the preaching of the Gospel are as the text proclaims them to be — involving, that is to say, the paroxysm of paroxysms within one single vast prophetic crisis experienced by Judaic society — then the refusal of the Kingdom by Jesus' listeners will logically impel them to turn against him. Moreover, this refusal will issue in the choice of him as a scapegoat, and in apocalyptic violence, by virtue of the fact that this last of victims, despite having been killed by unanimous consent, will not produce the beneficial effects that were produced before.

Once it has been possible to detect the operations of violence and the logic underlying them — or, if you prefer, the logic of violent men — confronted by the logic of Jesus, you will realize that Jesus never says a word that cannot be deduced from the events that have already taken place within the perspective of these two types of logic. Here and elsewhere, the "gift of prophecy" is nothing but the detection of these two logics.

So we can understand why it is that from the moment when the failure of the Kingdom becomes a certainty, the Gospels repeatedly announce through Jesus' mouth both the crucifixion and the Apocalypse. The old historical school interpreted these announcements as *ex post facto* prophecies destined to mask the impotence of the political leader in the face of an unexpected disaster.

The reason modern interpreters speak in this way is that they are unable to detect the two types of logic I have distinguished. Although the logic of violence provisionally has the last word, the logic of nonviolence is superior, since it comprehends the other logic in addition to itself — which the logic of violence is incapable of doing. This superior logic of nonviolence may be in the grip of illusions. But it exists and it must be detected and understood. Modern commentators fail to do so, and attribute to the Gospels objectives as futile as those of modern advertising or political propaganda because they do not even suspect the existence of such a logic.

This incomprehension can be identified with the attitudes stigmatized by the text. It simply reproduces and extends the reactions of Jesus' listeners, including the reactions of his disciples. There are those who believe that Jesus will kill himself, and there are those who believe in his wish for power. Not one of the positions taken up by modern criticism has not already been sketched within the Gospel text itself, so clearly that we might claim direct borrowing. Yet we must conclude that modern criticism is actually unable to see these positions in their original context. Interpreters never notice that they are themselves invariably understood and explained by the text that they pride themselves on understanding and explaining to us.

G.L.: So we can say that Jesus does nothing but obey, right up to the end, the promptings of the love that he declares has come from the Father and is directed toward all mankind. There is no reason to suppose that the Father has devised for him alone duties that he would not require of all mankind: "I say to you: Love your enemies, pray for your persecutors; so you will be sons of your Father which is in Heaven." All the world is called to become sons of God. The only distinction — though of course it is a crucial one — is that the Son hears the Word of the Father and himself conforms to it right to the end; he makes himself perfectly identical with the Word, while other people, even if they hear it, are incapable of conforming to it.

R.G.: So Jesus is the only man who achieves the goal God has set for all mankind, the only man who has nothing to do with violence and its works. The epithet "Son of Man" also corresponds, quite clearly, to the fact that Jesus alone has fulfilled a calling that belongs to all mankind.

If the fulfillment, on earth, passes inevitably through the death of Jesus, this is not because the Father demands this death, for strange sacrificial motives. Neither the son nor the Father should be questioned about the cause of this event, but all mankind, and mankind alone. The very fact that mankind has never really managed to understand what is involved reveals clearly that the misunderstanding of the founding murder is still being perpetuated, as is our inability to hear the Word of God.

That is indeed why people are constrained to invent an irrational requirement of sacrifice that absolves them of responsibility. According to this argument, the Father of Jesus is still a God of violence, despite what Jesus explicitly says. Indeed he comes to be the God of unequaled violence, since he not only requires the blood of the victim who is closest to him, most precious and dear to him, but he also envisages taking revenge upon the whole of mankind for a death that he both required and anticipated.

In effect, mankind is responsible for all of this. Men killed Jesus because they were not capable of becoming reconciled without killing. But by this stage, even the death of the just no longer had the power to reconcile them. Hence they are exposed to a limitless violence that they themselves have brought about and that has nothing to do with the anger or vengeance of any god.

When Jesus says: "Your will be done and not mine," it is really a question of dying. But it is not a question of showing obedience to an incomprehensible demand for sacrifice. Jesus has to die because continuing to live would mean a compromise with violence. I will be told that "it comes to the same thing." But it does not at all come to the same thing. In the usual writings on the subject, the death of Jesus derives, in the final analysis, from God and not from men — which is why the enemies of Christianity can use the argument that it belongs within the same schema as all the other primitive religions. Here we have the difference between the religions that remain subordinated to the powers and the act of destroying those powers through a form of transcendence that never acts by means of violence, is never responsible for any violence, and remains radically opposed to violence.

Presentations of Christ's Passion as obedience to an absurd sacrificial order disregard the texts that show it involves, of necessity, the love of one's neighbor, demonstrating that only death can bring this love to its fullest expression:

> We know that we have passed out of death into life, because we love the brethren. He who does not love abides in death. Any one who hates his brother is a murderer, and you know that no murderer has eternal life abiding in him. By this we know love, that he laid down his life for us; and we ought to lay down our lives for the brethren. (1 John 3:14–15)

Not to love one's brother and to kill him are the same thing. Every negation of the other leads, as we have shown, toward expulsion and murder. The basis for all of this lies in the fundamental human situation of a mimetic rivalry that leads to a destructive escalation. That is the reason why killing and dying are simply one and the same thing. To kill is to die, to die is to kill — for both stay within the circle of evil reciprocity, in which reprisals inevitably take place. Not to love is to die, therefore, since it is to kill. Cain — who is mentioned in the Epistle a few lines earlier — said: "Now that I have killed my brother, everyone can kill me." Everything that could be taken for a rupture in the text that we are following is in reality part and parcel of all the rest within the terms of the Gospel logic. There must be no hesitation about giving one's own life in order not to kill, so as to break out, by this action, from the circle of murder and death. It is quite literally true, when we are concerned with the confrontation of *doubles,* that he who wishes to save his life will lose it; he will be obliged, in effect, to kill his brother, and that means dying in a state of fatal misunderstanding of the other and of himself. He who agrees to lose his life will keep it for eternal life, for he alone is not a killer, he alone knows the fullness of love.

J.-M.O.: There is also a contradiction between what Jesus says about his relations with the Father, which do not involve any violence or any concealed element, and the assertion of a need for sacrifice that has its origin in the Father and requires the obedience of the Son. This economy of violence, which is not human but divine, can be rooted, from the standpoint of the Gospel, only in a projection of human violence on to God.

Chapter 12

The Divinity of Christ

The divinity of Christ is the full truth of the innocent victim. It is a truth which cannot abide in human culture, but must be inevitably expelled. The full disclosure of this truth can occur only in the moment it is being driven out. It is the Passion of Christ that is the key to revelation and it is the resurrection of Christ that confirms the work of God the Father rather than just another in the long line of victims transformed into gods by their lynchers.

If we human beings are entrapped in a mimetic predicament, then the revelatory act that saves us must be performed by the God-Man. As Girard says in the following excerpt from *Things Hidden*, 215-20, "Christ is the only agent who is capable of escaping from these structures and freeing us from their dominance" (219). This only agent must be human, because we are capable of comprehending only the human within the structures of existence. But this agent must also be God, for only God is able to subject himself to human desire and violence, overcome them, and show us the way to life.

R.G.: The Gospels tell us that to escape violence it is necessary to love one's brother completely — to abandon the violent mimesis involved in the relationship of doubles. There is no trace of it in the Father, and all that the Father asks is that we refrain from it likewise.

That is indeed why the Son promises men that if they manage to behave as the Father wishes, and to do his will, they will all become sons of God. It is not God who sets up the barriers between himself and mankind, but mankind itself.

G.L.: Does not that amount to eliminating any barrier between God and humanity — which would be the same as making humans godlike, in the same way as Feuerbach and the nineteenth-century humanists did?

R.G.: To hold that view you have to believe that love, in the Christian sense of the term — Nygren's *agape*[1] — is like common sense for

1. Anders Nygren, *Agape and Eros* (New York: Harper, 1969).

Descartes: the thing that is, of all others, most common among human beings. In effect, love of this kind has been lived to its end only by Jesus himself. On this earth, therefore, only the Christ has ever succeeded in equaling God in the perfection of his love. Theologians do not take note of the founding murder and the way in which everyone is trapped by violence, in complicity with violence; that is why they are fearful of compromising divine transcendence by taking the words of the Gospels at face value. They have no need to worry. Nothing in these words risks making the divine too accessible to humankind.

> You shall love the Lord your God with all your heart, and with all your soul, and with all your mind. This is the great and first commandment. *And a second is like it,* You shall love your neighbor as yourself. (Matt. 22:37–39; Mark 12:28–31; Luke 10:25–28)

The two commandments are like one another because love makes no distinctions between beings. Jesus himself says this. And we can repeat it after him with no fear of "humanizing" the Christian text overmuch. If the Son of Man and the Son of God are one and the same, it is because Jesus is the only person to achieve humanity in its perfect form, and so to be one with the deity.

The Gospel text, especially John but also to a certain extent the synoptic Gospels, establish beyond any doubt the fact that Jesus is both God and Man. The theology of the Incarnation is not just a fantastic and irrelevant invention of the theologians; it adheres rigorously to the logic implicit in the text. But it only succeeds in becoming intelligible if we read the text in nonsacrificial rather than sacrificial terms. This is, in effect, the only time that this notion of a fullness of humanity that is also a fullness of divinity makes sense in a context that is as "humanist" as it is "religious." If Jesus is the only one who can fully reveal the way in which the founding murder has broadened its hold upon mankind, this is because at no point did it take hold upon him. Jesus explains to us mankind's true vocation, which is to throw off the hold of the founding murder.

The nonsacrificial reading allows us to understand that the Son alone is united with the Father in the fullness of humanity and divinity. But it does not imply that this union is an exclusive one, or prevent us from envisaging the possibility of mankind becoming like God through the Son's mediation. Indeed, this process could only take place through him, since he is the only Mediator, the one bridge between the Kingdom of violence and the Kingdom of God. By remaining absolutely faithful to God's Word, in a world that had not received the Word, he succeeded in transmitting it all the same. He has managed to inscribe in the Gospel text the reception that mankind in its slavery to violence was obliged to offer him — a reception that amounted to driving him out. If we go beyond this point, we would become involved in questions of *faith* and *grace,* which our anthropological perspective is not competent to address.

The nonsacrificial reading is not to be equated with a humanist reading, in the ordinary sense, one which would try to cut the distinctively religious aspects out of the Gospel text. Although it brings to light the powerful demystificatory aspect of the Gospels, it has no difficulty in drawing attention to the religious aspects as well and in demonstrating their crucial importance, just as it draws attention to the great canonical statements about Jesus' divinity and his union with the Father.

Far from eliminating divine transcendence, the nonsacrificial reading shows it to be so far from us, in its very closeness, that we did not even suspect it to be there. Invariably, it has been concealed and covered up by transcendent violence — by all the powers and principalities that we have stupidly identified with it, to some extent at least. To rid ourselves of this confusion, to detect transcendent love — which remains invisible beyond the transcendent violence that stands between — we have to accept the idea that human violence is a deceptive worldview and recognize how the forms of misunderstanding that arise from it operate.

This differentiation between the two forms of transcendence appears negligible and absurd from the point of view of the violent mentality that possesses us — a mentality concerned with detecting the structural similarities between the Gospel enactment and the basic workings of all other religions: workings that we have ourselves been concerned to expose. These analogies are real ones, just as are analogies between the evil reciprocity of violence and the benevolent reciprocity of love. Since both surpass all cultural differences, the two structures, paradoxically, amount to very much the same thing, which is why it is possible to pass from one to the other by means of an almost instantaneous conversion. But at the same time, there is also a radical, an abysmal opposition between them, something that *no form of structural analysis can detect:* we see in a mirror, darkly, *en ainigmate.*

J.-M.O.: Precisely because the revelation of violence has always been greeted with incomprehension, it becomes easier to understand why the Christian text puts before us someone who triumphs over violence by not resisting it, and as the direct emissary of the God of nonviolence, shows his message emanating directly from him.

Within the human community, which is the prisoner of unanimous violence and of mythical meanings, there is no opportunity for this truth to be entertained, let alone to carry the day.

People are most open to the truth at the stage when false differences melt away, but this is also the point when they are most in the dark, since it is the point at which violence becomes even more intense.

Whenever violence starts to reveal itself as the basis of the community, it is accompanied by the manifestations one might expect at an acutely violent crisis, when mankind lacks the least vestige of lucidity. It almost seems as if violence is always able to conceal the truth about itself, whether by causing the mechanism of transference to operate and reestablish the regime of the sacred, or by pushing destruction as far as it will go.

R.G.: Either you are violently opposed to violence and inevitably play its game, or you are not opposed to it, and it shuts your mouth immediately. In other words, the regime of violence cannot possibly be brought out into the open. Since the truth about violence will not abide in the community, but must inevitably be driven out, its only chance of being heard is when it is in the process of being driven out, in the brief moment that precedes its destruction as the victim. The victim therefore has to reach out at the very moment when his mouth is being shut by violence. He has to say enough for the violence to be incited against him. But this must not take place in the dark, hallucinatory atmosphere that characterizes other religions and produces the intellectual confusion that helps conceal their founding mechanism. There must be witnesses who are clear-sighted enough to recount the event as it really happened, altering its significance as little as possible.

For this to happen, the witnesses must already have been influenced by this extraordinary person. They themselves will not escape the hold of the collective violence; but it will be temporary. Afterward, they will recover and write down in a form that is not transfigured the event that is primarily a transfiguration.

This unprecedented task of revealing the truth about violence requires a man who is not obliged to violence for anything and does not think in terms of violence—someone who is capable of talking back to violence while remaining entirely untouched by it.

It is impossible for such a human being to arise in a world completely ruled by violence and the myths based on violence. In order to understand that you cannot see and make visible the truth except by taking the place of the victim, you must already be occupying that place; yet to take that place, you must already be in possession of the truth. You cannot become aware of the truth unless you act in opposition to the laws of violence, and you cannot act in opposition to these laws unless you already grasp the truth. All mankind is caught within this vicious circle. For this reason the Gospels and the whole New Testament, together with the theologians of the first councils, proclaim that Christ is God not because he was crucified, but because he is God born of God from all eternity.

J.-M.O.: To sum up: the proclamation of Christ's divinity, in the sense of nonviolence and love, is not in any way a sudden disconnection or a break in the logic of the texts that we are elucidating. In fact, it forms the only possible conclusion to this logic.

R.G.: The authentic knowledge about violence and all its works to be found in the Gospels cannot be the result of human action alone. Our own inability to grasp knowledge that has been waiting there for two millennia confirms theological intuitions that are no less certain for being incapable of setting out explicitly their foundations in reason. These rational foundations can become intelligible only if we proceed beyond the sacrificial version of Christianity and are guided by the nonsacrificial reading which can emerge when the other one has fallen away.

G.L.: So theology is not being hyperbolic when it proclaims the divinity of Jesus. The belief is not just an excessive piece of praise, the product of a kind of rhetorical overkill. It is the only fit response to an inescapable constraint.

R.G.: To recognize Christ as God is to recognize him as the only being capable of rising above the violence that had, up to that point, absolutely transcended mankind. Violence is the controlling agent in every form of mythic or cultural structure, and Christ is the only agent who is capable of escaping from these structures and freeing us from their dominance. This is the only hypothesis that enables us to account for the revelation in the Gospel of what violence does to us and the accompanying power of that revelation to deconstruct the whole range of cultural texts, without exception. We do not have to adopt the hypothesis of Christ's divinity because it has always been accepted by orthodox Christians. Instead, this hypothesis is orthodox because in the first years of Christianity there existed a rigorous (though not yet explicit) intuition of the logic determining the Gospel text.

A nonviolent deity can signal his existence to mankind only by becoming driven out by violence — by demonstrating that he is not able to remain in the Kingdom of Violence.

But this very demonstration is bound to remain ambiguous for a long time, and it is not capable of achieving a decisive result, since it looks like total impotence to those who live under the regime of violence. That is why at first it can have some effect only under a guise, deceptive through the admixture of some sacrificial elements, through the surreptitious reinsertion of some violence into the conception of the divine.

Chapter 13

Satan

One of the important aspects of Girard's reading of the Gospels, which he approaches from the standpoint of his mimetic anthropology, is his concern with Satan. If this seems surprising, it should not be; it goes along with the illumination of mimetic rivalry, scandal, and collective violence that he undertakes in his work. He points out that Satan is a reality, expressing a source of transcendence. In his analyses of Satan he has bracketed and set aside the question of the "existence" or "reality" of Satan apart from human systems of order and the threat of disorder. Both order and disorder revolve around mimesis and mimetic rivalry. In this essay, published originally as "How Can Satan Cast out Satan?" in G. Braulik, W. Gross, and S. McEvenue, eds., *Biblische Theologie und gesellschaftlicher Wandel* (Freiburg: Herder, 1993), 125-41 (here slightly revised), Girard focuses on Satan anthropologically as the personification of the principles both of order and disorder: of order, because he embodies the self-organizing system that keeps mimesis within the bounds that will perpetuate the system; of disorder, because the order is based on a lie, a mode of representation as old as "the foundation of the world" which controls mimesis through victimage and scapegoating in order to maintain the "world" of which Satan is the *archē/archōn*, the "prince." The Christian revelation exposes Satan as "the father of lies" by disclosing not only the innocence of one victim, Jesus, but of all victims. Satan attempts to cast out Satan through murder, especially collective violence, but he is defeated in principle by the Cross. This defeat is accomplished because the disciples, with the aid of the Paraclete, the Spirit of God as defender of the falsely accused, break away from the mimetic consensus of the social order that is undergirded and constantly regenerated by the scapegoat mechanism.

— ☙ —

In Mark 3:23 Jesus asks a question that he does not answer: "How can Satan cast out Satan?" In the modern period we pride ourselves on our superior knowledge and rationality, so the question of Satan and expelling Satan is an embarrassing puzzle for us. But the solution to the puzzle may be found in the Gospels, and in the Gospels we must go to the center of all significance, the Passion. Jesus calls it the hour of Satan. Why? Because it is Satan's attempt to cast out Jesus, to expel him as if he were another Satan, a worse Satan than Satan himself.

This is the real answer to Jesus' question, but we do not really understand what it means. The reason for our puzzlement is that the Passion as a violent process, a demonic expulsion, has always been ignored. But theologians and modern critics have tacitly assumed that the Gospels intend to represent a violence so unique and incomparable that it can only be approached theologically or anti-theologically. It cannot be studied phenomenologically; it cannot be compared to any other violence.

I believe that it can. Far from presenting the Passion as an isolated event, the Gospels surround it with other acts of violence, collective or collectively inspired violence.

The Parable of the Vineyard is one example. After planting his vineyard, the owner entrusts it to tenants and departs for some distant land. From time to time, he sends messengers to collect his share of the crop but, each time, they are cast out of the vineyard, violently expelled by all the winemakers. And then, finally, acting collectively once again, the winemakers cast out and kill the last messenger, the owner's own son.

The last violence is unique in respect to the victim's identity, but it is not unique as violence; it is similar to all previous acts of violence.

When Jesus says that he will die like all prophets before him, it means that his death will repeat the ancient pattern of collective violence that we have in the Parable. The prophets are the same people as all the messengers sent by the owner of the vineyard before he sends his son. The same point is repeated time and again. "You have killed all the prophets," Jesus says to his listeners, "and now you are going to kill me."

The Gospel passages I just mentioned, and the others I am about to mention, are rarely quoted nowadays, except by those who want to show that the Gospels are anti-Semitic. Those who have no such intention find these texts embarrassing. They seem to single out the Jews as collective murderers not only of Jesus but of all holy men.

The emphasis is on the Jews in the immediate context, but the whole human race is always implicitly or even explicitly part of the picture.

This is the case in Matthew's phrase about the "righteous blood" of all the prophets that was shed *epi tēs gēs*. This expression means the entire earth, the whole human world. This is also the case in Luke's phrase about the prophets whose blood was shed "from the foundation of the world, the blood of Abel the just." At the time of Cain and Abel, the Jewish people did not exist.

Even when the wording seems to support the idea of an exclusively Jewish violence, the context makes this interpretation impossible. The collective murders are presented as worldwide since the dawn of history. The Gospels are really alluding to a specific phenomenon, an identifiable type of violence, with its own characteristic features. In order to achieve a correct understanding of the type as type, we must apprehend and gather all characteristic features.

Can we do this with the Passion alone? I am certain that we could but we do not have to. The Passion is not the only detailed account we have of a collective or collectively inspired murder in the Gospels. In two out of four we have a second murder, the beheading of John the Baptist. Our investigation must take this second murder into account.

The process behind John's death greatly resembles the process behind the Cross. In both instances it all begins with those people whose hostility to the two victims predates the actual event, in the case of Jesus the Jewish religious leaders, in the case of John a single individual, Herodias. The small beginning contrasts with the bigness of the phenomenon itself, the polarization of many people, a whole crowd, against a victim who, until then, had not been an object of hostility and even, in the case of Jesus, only a few days before, had been greeted with enthusiasm by the very same crowd. The polarization is the real event, the essential phenomenon, not the way in which it is triggered.

What is the force behind this hostile polarization? Is it God himself? Do the Gospels intend to portray a violence ordained and manipulated by God for the purpose of having an innocent victim sacrificed? If this were true, the God of the Gospels would greatly resemble the gods who incite the Greek and Trojan warriors against each other in the *Iliad.*

The hostile polarization against John the Baptist is facilitated by Salome's dancing. The Gospels certainly do not regard this dancing as divinely inspired. In pagan sacrifices the immolation is often preceded by ritual dances. Their purpose is to prepare the participants for this violent action. Salome's dancing has this kind of effect, which the Gospels regard as evil, as something satanic rather than divine.

The effects of dancing, traditionally, are defined as mimetic. Herod's guests are mimetically possessed by the dancer. There is no counterpart to Salome's dance in the Passion, but the two accounts relate the same mimetic effects of someone joining the hostile crowd. Peter's denial of association with Jesus is the most striking instance of this.

Peter is very much like us modern men. He wants to be religiously correct. He cannot stand the disapproval of his neighbors. When we want to make friends with a group of people, we first show them that we all have the same friends, but this is not enough; we must also show that we have the same enemies. That is why Peter mimics the crowd's contempt for Jesus. His vulnerability to mimetic pressure is not exceptional but typical. Peter, however, is not just any member of that crowd; he is the individual with the greatest spiritual investment in Jesus. If fidelity and steadfastness can be expected from anyone, they must be expected from Peter. The purpose of the scene is not to humiliate Peter but to reveal the immense power, the evil power of mimetic contagion.

The two collective murders portrayed in the Gospels are mimetic and so are the deaths of the biblical prophets that the Gospels explicitly associate with Jesus. There, too, a mimetic consensus is part of the picture. The Suffering Servant dies at the hands of a community mimetically united against him (Isaiah 53). Another example is Jonah, who does not die but, as we all know, is swallowed by a whale. This whale, however, would not swallow Jonah if he had not been cast into the sea by the unanimous crew of the ship on which he has embarked. This expulsion is a collective casting out similar to the Passion. The whale is an image of the violent crowd, and this is what Hobbes obviously understood when he entitled his famous work *Leviathan*.

❧

Instead of one collective murder, we now have many, and their mimetic nature is the reason for their similarities. What is the relevance of this mimetic violence to the idea of Satan casting out Satan?

Besides collective violence, there is also violence and conflict on a smaller scale in the Gospels, violence between two or a few individuals. This violence also has a mimetic dimension, like the collective violence, and Satan is also involved.

Not unlike Jesus, Satan says to us: "Imitate me" and he, himself, is an imitator. His ultimate model is God the Father, the same model that Jesus has.

Imitation is characteristic of both Jesus and Satan. We always imitate someone when we desire, either Jesus or Satan. In the Gospels, therefore, desire itself is mimetic. It is rooted not in the desiring subject, not in the desired object but in a third party, the model of our desire. If this model influences us through his own desire, we both desire the same object. We become rivals.

Since Jesus recommends imitation, mimetic desire is good. it is even very good, the best thing in the world, since it is the only road to the true God. But it is the same as human freedom, and it is also the road to Satan. What is the difference between the mimetic desire of Jesus and the mimetic desire of Satan? The difference is that Satan imitates God in a spirit of rivalry. Jesus imitates God in a spirit of childlike and innocent obedience and this is what he advises us to do as well. Since there is no acquisitive desire in God, the docile imitation of God cannot generate rivalry.

When mimetic rivalry is triggered, the two competing desires ceaselessly reinforce each other and violence is likely to erupt. But mimetic rivalry is not satanic to begin with, it is not sinful per se, it is only a permanent occasion of sin.

In order to designate the exasperation of mimetic rivalry, the Gospels have a marvelous word that, at times, seems almost synonymous with Satan, *skandalon.* The idea comes from the Bible and it means the obstacle against which one keeps stumbling. The Greek word appears first in the Greek Bible and it comes from a verb that signifies to limp. The more we stumble against an obstacle, the easier it should be to avoid further stumbling but, frequently, the opposite happens: we stumble so much that we seem to be limping.

The *skandalon* designates a very common inability to walk away from mimetic rivalry which turns it into an addiction. The *skandalon* is anything that attracts us in proportion to the suffering or irritation that it causes us. It is even the aching tooth that we cannot stop testing with our tongue, even though it hurts more and more. The *skandalon* is all kinds of destructive addiction, drugs, sex, power, and above all morbid competitiveness, professional, sexual, political, intellectual, and spiritual, especially spiritual.

The old translation, "stumbling block," made all this as clear as it can ever be. The disappearance from modern Bibles of the English expression "stumbling block" or, from the French Bibles, of its French equivalent, *pierre d'achoppement,* is a great and completely unnecessary loss. The new translations do not convey the idea of something that simultaneously attracts and repels. I do not know what has happened in German but, in English and in French, they are as deceptive as they are flat.

Like many contemporary Christians, the translators of the Bible are greatly intimidated by all the fashionable theories that would finally succeed in discrediting the Bible if they were not first discredited themselves. Christians are excessively impressed by all the incessant and crude propaganda against biblical ideas, notably against the *skandalon* which is often accused of being the child of Victorian puritanism, a remarkable accusation to say the least. Modern theories are secretly jealous because the *skandalon* easily achieves everything that our psychoanalyses and psychopathologies vainly try to achieve. This jealousy is the true reason for the rather ludicrous slander. The enormous range and power of *skandalon* makes it easy to refute these attacks. This is what we are now going to see.

❧

Scandals, Jesus says, must happen. When scandals start happening they proliferate to such an extent that the world seems to come to an end. But the world endures and some counter-force must be at work, not powerful enough to do away with scandals forever, which would prevent them from happening, powerful enough, though, to moderate their effects, to keep scandals under some form of control.

If Satan could indeed cast out Satan, it means that Satan himself and not God would be the policeman who keeps his own disorder in check. This necessarily means that, at some point in the crisis that scandals generate, they must turn, somehow, into a force for order. This idea sounds impossible and even crazy but a careful examination of the various uses of *skandalon* reveals that it is both possible and true.

Just before his Passion, Jesus warns his disciples that he is about to become a scandal to them. As a group, the disciples do not behave as badly as Peter but at the time of Jesus' arrest, they all scatter ingloriously and they do not reappear until after the resurrection. Whereas Peter, at least for a while, becomes an active persecutor, the other disciples are passive accomplices of the persecutors.

This passivity is a limited form of participation in the Passion, but it is participation nevertheless. It is fascinating that the word "scandal" would apply in this case. It truly applies to all degrees of participation in the Passion.

Scandals, we found, are permanently conflictual relationships in our individual lives. Now we see that the word also applies to the participation in the mimetic consensus against Jesus. This use is disconcerting. We tend to feel that our private rivalries, our intense conflicts, do express something genuinely personal and unique in us. The conflictual nature of scandals seems to guarantee that they are what the existentialists would call an authentic modality of human existence, that they cannot turn gregarious at the drop of a hat.

We feel this way because, as a rule, we are scandalized. Jesus is not and he feels differently. He knows that scandals are mimetic from the start and they become more so as they are exacerbated. They become more and more impersonal, anonymous, undifferentiated, and therefore interchangeable. Beyond a certain threshold of exasperation, scandals will substitute for one another, with no awareness on our part.

If we look carefully at the operation of scandals in the Gospels, we will have to conclude that they are very much the same thing as demonic and satanic possession, which is also characterized by a process of transference, as in the case of the Gerasa demons, for instance. Jesus, I believe, prefers to speak the language of scandals, whereas his disciples feel more at home in the language of Satan and his demons.

Once again, Peter is a good example. When Jesus first announces that he will suffer at the hands of the people, Peter is scandalized. His ideal is the same as ours, worldly success, and he tries to instill it into his master. He turns his own desire into a model that Jesus should imitate. This is how Satan operates, of course. Hence the famous words: "Move behind me Satan, because you are a scandal to me." If the scandalized disciple had succeeded in mimetically transmitting his own mimetic desire to his master, he would have scandalized Jesus straight out of his divine mission.

Peter's behavior is the combined effect of his preexisting scandal, which is mimetic, and the additional mimetic push provided by the crowd.

All those who join a belligerent crowd act more or less like Peter. They all transfer their private scandals to some public target. Men become so burdened with scandals that they desperately, if unconsciously, seek the public substitutes upon whom to unburden themselves. As they become more numerous, the target's attractiveness as a target increases, and the process becomes irresistible.

The notion of scandal bridges the gap between individual and collective violence. The mobility of scandals, their tendency to unite around a common victim, provides a mediation, a communication between the two levels.

The violent unanimity of the Passion results from a massive transference of scandals, a snowballing so powerful that its effects become inescapable.

When this unanimity is achieved, the guilt of the victim becomes an absolute certainty to the participants and the expulsion and destruction of that victim is experienced by each one as a destruction of his or her own scandal, a personal liberation. When this happens, peace immediately returns and the mob is no more.

These effects of the mimetic consensus are recorded in the account of the Passion. After Pilate submits to the crowd, all agitation subsides. The death of Jesus becomes a show at the end of which the mob peacefully disperses.

The unanimous violence produces a peace of its own, rooted in the mimetic consensus. In the specific case of the Cross, this violence, ultimately, is not unanimous. At first, the disciples are contaminated by it; they almost become a part of the consensus, but they finally break away from it. As a result, the Passion is not a perfect example of what it nevertheless illustrates, the unanimous collective murder. It comes close enough, however, to provide the readers with all the information required for a full understanding of the phenomenon.

Understandably, the Gospels pay more attention to the Christian communion around the resurrected Jesus than they do to the unholy communion of the persecutors, but they are not completely indifferent to this last phenomenon. Luke, in particular, mentions a most significant instance of this unholy communion.

When Herod turned Jesus over to Pilate, Luke informs us that "from this day, Herod and Pilate, who had been enemies, became friends" (Luke 23:12). From a historical viewpoint the information is insignificant but, in regard to the effects of the unanimous mimetic violence upon the participants, it is enormously significant.

The Christian communion is rooted in a passionate rejection and critique of what the other communion uncritically espouses, the guilt of the victim. It would be difficult to find two attitudes farther apart than these two.

The communion of mimetic rivalry is Satan's work. The word "Satan," originally, signifies the accuser, the one who brings a law suit against someone else. In the Gospels, Satan's power is his ability to make false accusations so convincing that they become the unassailable truth of entire communities. To call this process "Satan," which is what the Gospels really do, is highly appropriate.

The Christian communion is based on the rejection of the false accusation, on the understanding that it is false. According to John, this understanding must be ascribed not to men alone but to the Holy Spirit, whose name is highly appropriate, too, as appropriate as Satan for the other communion, since he is called the "Paraclete," a Greek word that simply means the lawyer for the defense, the defender of victims. Jesus is the first man who decisively disrupts the mimetic consensus against the most innocent of all victims, himself. That is why he is called the first Paraclete. After he is gone, a second Paraclete will continue his work.

Our understanding of the difference between the mimetic communion of the persecutors and the Christian communion depends upon the Paraclete. In the modern world, this understanding is either absent — and that explains why the modern world has never discovered the true difference between Christianity and the other religions — or it is present in forms that disguise its Christian origin. Instead of comparing innocent victims to the lamb of God, as we would do if we were willing to acknowledge the real source of our insight into social violence, we often say that these victims are "scapegoats." We use this word not in the ritual sense of Leviticus but in the everyday modern sense which is much more interesting, the sense of a victim unjustly persecuted by a semi-conscious or unconscious group of human beings.

❧

We can now go back to the question with which I began this presentation: "How can Satan cast out Satan?"

From the beginning, you will recall, my answer has been that Satan casts out Satan through the collective violence of the Passion and all similar murders. This answer, now, should be fully intelligible. When scandals proliferate too much at the local level they come together, they converge upon a necessarily irrelevant or totally innocent victim and a consensus is established at the expense of that victim. The order that is thus born, or reborn, in this fashion is less violent as a rule than the disorder it overcomes but it is violent and unjust nevertheless; it is never entirely free of arbitrary violence. When Jesus accepts to die on the Cross he accepts being one of the innumerable unknown victims upon which human order has always been based.

The idea that Satan is both the exorcised demon and the exorcist, the one cast out and the one who does the casting out is not a logical impossibility, a mythological absurdity unworthy of our scientific outlook.

In the twentieth century, some scientists have developed the theory of the so-called self-organizing systems, complex entities in which the principle of order and the principle of disorder are one and the same. As soon as disorder reaches a certain threshold in these systems, the forces of disruption turn into a force for reintegration and reordering.

The Satan of the Gospels is a self-organizing system. The words are not the same, of course, but the idea of Jesus is obviously the same. Jesus might very well have said: How can Satan cast out *himself?* but he chose to repeat the noun "Satan." All three synoptic Gospels repeat the word "Satan." This repetition is more pleasant to the ear, no doubt, but it is not for esthetic reasons that Jesus does it. Stylistic considerations are subordinate to his primary purpose, which is to emphasize the paradox implicit in his own question. This paradox is the oneness of order and disorder.

Far from being afraid of this paradox, as the now scientifically outmoded thinking of a Rudolf Bultmann would be, the thinking of Jesus focuses our attention upon this apparent scandal: *How can Satan expel Satan?* Who will be foolish enough to believe that such a thing is possible? According to the traditional conception of straight causality, it is impossible, but Jesus knows exactly what he is doing. He emphasizes what is the most original feature in his conception of Satan. Both the disorder and order of human culture are from the same source which is not directly divine and this, to my knowledge, is unique to the Gospels, so unique that, to my knowledge, it has never been really understood.

Satan, therefore, represents a source of transcendence. From the point of view of the Gospels, this transcendence is false in the sense that it is not really supernatural but it is real in the sense that the power of political and social institutions rooted in pagan religion is quite real. In order to designate these strange combinations of religious illusion and social reality, the Gospels have a number of labels such as "the powers of this world," "celestial powers," "thrones," "dominations," "principalities," "rulers of this world," "angels," and, of course, "Satan."

These powers are always presented as united in their decision to crucify Jesus. This is no propagandistic trick to inflate the historical importance of the Passion. The reference to the Cross is a definition of the powers in terms of the mimetic runaway and founding murder in which they are inevitably rooted even if they have not participated directly in the death of Jesus.

Even though theologians have not made this doctrine explicit, it upholds orthodox attitudes against what may be called the two great temptations of modern Christianity. The first consists in divinizing the social order, with the reactionary Christian thinkers of the nineteenth and early twentieth centuries such as Joseph de Maistre and Carl Schmitt. The second is still in full swing and it consists in divinizing the social disorder and revolution in the name of liberation.

These two currents oppose one another fiercely and continuously but they are very much alike at bottom. They are the two antithetical versions of *modernism,* a distortion and mutilation of Christianity which is the ransom of a real but still incomplete discovery of the founding role played by religion in human society. "Modernism" must be defined as the almost universal illusion in our world that society is everything and that religion ultimately boils down to political and social questions.

❧

The phrase concerning "the blood shed since the foundation of the world," shows the enormous scope of the idea I am trying to explore. It would be foolish to suppose that the coupling in the Gospels of the first collective murder and the first human culture suggests only a fortuitous conjunction of the two. The message is clear. From the beginning, human culture was rooted in the murders triggered and manipulated by Satan.

The story of Cain perfectly illustrates this vision. Cain has two titles to fame. The first is Abel's murder and the second is the foundation of the first civilization, or culture. A look at Genesis shows that the two events are one. The first law is promulgated as a result of the murder, and it is the first human law against murder. The word "Cain" stands not for a single murder but for the entire community unified by the first culture.

My thesis is really that the Gospels view Satan as the principle — if not the entire reality — of human culture since the foundation of the world. In order to clinch this thesis and to confirm the coherence of the Gospels, we need a text that would explicitly link Satan to the other two themes which are already linked by the texts we have already quoted, the collective murder and "the foundation of the world," the invention of human culture.

The synoptic Gospels have no such text, but John has one that seems somewhat obscure at first but is really the richest of all. It sums up and makes more complete a doctrine regarding Satan and the founding murder that is the same in all four Gospels, as is always the case with everything essential.

Like all our previous texts, this one must be read in the context not of Judaism alone but of mankind as a whole:

> You are of your father the devil, and your will is to do your father's desire. He was a murderer from the beginning, and has nothing to do with the truth, because there is no truth in him. When he lies, he speaks according to his own nature, for he is a liar and the father of lies. (John 8:44)

The "devil" means the same thing as "Satan." The "beginning" (*archē*) means the same thing as "the foundation of the world" (*katabolē tou kosmou*) i.e., the origin of human culture, not creation *ex nihilo*.

The devil is alien to all truth because he was a murderer from the beginning, a murderer of the collective type we are investigating. Satan's lie is his false accusation and the unanimous conviction of the human murderers that their victim is really guilty.

The foundation of the first culture was the moment when this lie began to envelop mankind in the sense not simply of some false information but of a "system of representation" that still permeates our thinking, long after primitive institutions are gone. This is an imprisonment that men do not passively inherit from their ancestors; they continuously revive it, even if only in attenuated and nonlethal, but fundamentally unaltered forms, as a result of their mimetic rivalries and scandals.

Men are forever rooted and rerooted in the foundational violence that makes a vicarious removal of scandals possible. To say that our human will is to do the desires of our father, the devil, is another way of saying that we cannot really cut loose from the primordial lie, from the effects of the primordial murder. We still cannot acknowledge our dependence on primordial violence. Satan is not merely "the father of lies" but, as some manuscripts have it, the "father of liars," which really means all men, insofar as men still do not understand what Jesus is talking about in the lines we are reading. Just as they did in the days of Jesus, they confidently assert that it must be sheer nonsense, some kind of magical belief in which modern man cannot share because he has become too "rational."

Let me reiterate my main point: when the disorder of scandals gets worse and worse, it automatically brings back the unanimous victimage that generates a new order or regenerates the old. If this is true, human history, before the Christian revelation, must be an endless alteration of order and disorder in all parts of the world. When one cycle is accomplished, everything returns to the crisis of scandals or, in mythical terms, to "primordial chaos," but then a new collective murder is triggered that initiates a new cycle.

From a Christian viewpoint, ancient theories of the Eternal Return contain some truth since they know about these cycles, which are the same thing as the "self-organizing system" of Satan, but they cannot discover the engine that powers the cycles, the foundational power of the mimetic consensus, or victimage mechanism, or generative scapegoating.

The end of this circular time, the shift from an eternally recurring world to a time which has a real beginning and a real end is inseparable from the revelation of the force that until the Judaic and Christian revelation had powered the cycles but now loses its effectiveness as a result of being revealed.

We must envisage this shift from a circular to a linear temporality in conjunction with the idea that the Cross is a decisive defeat for Satan, the end of his kingdom, which follows logically from the whole mimetic interpretation. This idea is part of the system of thought we are outlining, the total doctrine of Satan in the Gospels and the New Testament. It has nothing to do with a comforting illusion, an instance of wishful thinking that anti-Christian thinking could easily demystify.

This is the supreme theme regarding Satan, the most amazing and the most difficult to believe, the idea that the Cross is a decisive victory over Satan, the end of his power. Far from being absurd, this theme flows logically from everything we have learned so far. Once we realize that the power of Satan is dependent upon a lie, which will not remain effective unless it is firmly believed by all men, an untruth that is always mistaken for a sacred truth, everything else follows. In order to remain credible, this untruth, this satanic lie must remain hidden. It must be protected from human curiosity.

The founding murder is shrouded in darkness. Initially, this darkness springs from the collective madness and hallucination that characterize the transferential runaway and the unanimous violence. This is the darkness of myth and of mythical origins. The violence at the heart of myth resembles the violence of the Passion, but the victim is always guilty. Even when such mythical victims as Oedipus become gods, they are still guilty of whatever they were guilty to start with. They become gods of violence, gods of the violent sacred.

Only later, very much later, does the darkness of mythical origins give way to more decorous forms of befuddlement and self-deception, those of philosophies and ideologies. There is a sophisticated darkness of modern knowledge that is continuous with the darkness of mythology, and it is fitting that it would rely more and more on mythological expression, on the Oedipus myth, for instance, that may well be the myth par excellence of our post-Christian and neo-pagan confusion.

Satan would not be the prince of this world if he were not, first of all, the prince of darkness. The Christian revelation dissipates the darkness of the founding murder by showing the innocence not only of one victim, Jesus, wrongly accused by Satan, but of all such victims. The Christian revelation undermines the power of Satan, slowly at first but then faster and faster.

The texts on the subject all claim that mankind, thanks to the Cross, for the first time in its history, is no longer in bondage to Satan. Since Satan's power is revealed by the Passion, it has to be identical with the Passion in some essential respect and this identity can only related to the violent process we have uncovered, the mimetic polarization and unanimous murder which is the process of Satan casting out Satan. This is the secret that the Gospels force out of hiding merely by their faithful representation of one collective murder typical of them all, typical of the process that has dominated human culture since the foundation of the world.

The spotlight upon Satan makes it impossible for him to fool humanity any longer. Once the secret is revealed, it loses all its value. It even looks pathetic in comparison with its enormous historical effects. Paul never quite manages to define this secret, and the reason is not that he has doubts, or that he hesitates, or that his thinking is not up to the task, but the words he needs simply do not exist. There is no appropriate vocabulary for what he is saying. Here is how Colossians 2:13–15 articulates the whole question:

> And you ... God made alive together with Christ, having canceled the bond which stood against us with its legal demands; this he set aside, nailing it to the Cross. He disarmed the principalities and powers and made a public example of them, triumphing over them in him.

The metaphor of a legal document that would be the charter of our bondage is suggested to Paul, I suppose, by the legal tinge given to the whole question of victims by the very *names* of Satan and the Paraclete, one being the prosecutor, as I suggested before, and the other the lawyer for the defense. The nailing of this document to the Cross is a first attempt to say that the principalities and powers, in other words Satan, are defeated and even ridiculed by the Cross.

Let me repeat this essential point: once we understand that Satan's secret is the founding murder and the scapegoat mechanism, the idea that Satan's power is reduced to nothing by the Cross makes perfect sense. By providing us with an accurate portrayal of the mimetic process behind the death of Jesus, and secondarily the death of John the Baptist, the Gospels reveal something which, in the long run, is bound to discredit not one particular lie about one particular victim of collective persecution only but all lies rooted in the victimage mechanism, in the grotesquely deceptive scapegoat misunderstanding. Satan becomes a ludicrous nonentity.

The idea that the Cross was really a trap set by God himself in order to lure Satan flows logically from the preceding: Since Jesus, almost every time he opens his mouth, reveals the secret of Satan's power, he becomes, in the eyes of Satan, a most intolerable source of disorder; he must be silenced once and for all. In order to reach this goal, Satan only has to resort to his favorite trick, which is exactly what is needed in this case, the very trick about which Jesus is talking so much, the traditional trick of the mimetic murder and scapegoat mechanism. Since this trick has always succeeded in the past, Satan sees no reason why it would not succeed in the case of Jesus.

Everything turns out as anticipated by Satan except for one thing. With the help of the Paraclete, Jesus' disciples finally break away from the mimetic consensus and provide the world with a truthful account of what should remain hidden in this affair, at least from the perspective of Satan.

In the light of this reading, 1 Corinthians 2:7–8, which is the crucial text, becomes fully intelligible:

> But we impart a secret and hidden wisdom of God, which God decreed before the ages for our glorification. None of the rulers of this age understood this; for if they had, they would not have crucified the Lord of glory.

The rulers of this age are the same thing as the powers of this world and Satan himself. Had they foreseen that the crucifixion would deprive them of the powerful tool with which they had been operating all along, their first order of business would have been the protection of the scapegoat mechanism, and they would have refrained from crucifying Jesus. They would have become even before the Passion what they now have become, hypocritical lawyers for the defense; they would have imitated Jesus in a satanic way. They would have become the Antichrist much earlier than they have.

The idea that an ignominious death such as the Cross is really a victory, and a victory over Satan, seems so impossible to modern commentators that they see nothing but foolish triumphalism in the two texts I last quoted. They are inclined to ridicule the thinking of Paul and the entire New Testament. They reduce it to vulgar propaganda. They see the first Christians as a bunch of power-hungry narcissists, so depressed by their lack of worldly importance that they need some psychic compensation.

These commentators are typically modern for their brutality and bad taste, but they have illustrious Christian predecessors, at least up to a point. The theme of the Cross victorious over Satan has never been popular with the Western fathers. Being more rationalistic than their Greek counterparts, they were dissatisfied, I suppose, with what appeared to them as a magical handling of the theme by the Eastern fathers and they quietly dropped it. Their example has been widely followed in later centuries.

What Paul and the whole New Testament are really saying is that, once the Cross has revealed the mimetic violence at the root of human society, and the misunderstanding of this violence, the world can never be the same.

Paul and the New Testament were and are still right. The world at large has never been the same after the Cross. It has been enormously affected by the Christian revelation of the scapegoat mechanism, regardless of the inability of the wise and learned to understand what Jesus was really talking about.

The specific character of the modern world can be ascribed to the victory of the Cross over Satan in the sense of a growing concern for victims everywhere in the world. This concern remained feeble and highly tentative for a long time, but then it became stronger and more focused. We do not realize how anthropologically unique our modern attitude toward victims is. In no other culture has anything even remotely similar ever existed.

It is possible to read the history, first of the Christianized West, then of the Westernized planet, our modern history, as dominated by the consequences of the victory defined first by Jesus himself, then by Paul and others, a process of vindication and rehabilitation of more and more persecuted victims. New hidden victims of society are continuously being brought to light; the consensus against them always dissolves after a while. First it was slaves, then the lower classes, then people of different ethnic and religious backgrounds. Today the victimization of ethnic groups, of women, of handicapped people, of the very young and the very old, is coming to light. The unveiling of mimetic violence has had a more and more powerful influence on our history and on the entire modern world.

Injustice and arbitrariness are still with us, no doubt, and the greatest massacres in history, the most scandalous persecutions are just as characteristic of our world as the vindication of victims. There is no denying that immense forces have tried and are still trying to nullify our concern for victims, and these forces are not only outside of us but in all of us.

All such facts, however, do not contradict but confirm the paramount importance of victims in any serious definition of our world.

Another indirect testimony is the very perversion of that concern for victims which is highly visible in our world, the constant effort on the part of many groups and individuals to usurp the now privileged position of the most victimized victim, and thus to turn the concern for victims into an instrument of power and even into a paradoxical tool of persecution. All this reveals the infinite resourcefulness of man when it comes to transforming the best into the worst, but it does not provide us with an excuse for not acknowledging the best, in the world around us and in our own lives.

Far from promising peace on earth and presenting Christianity as a combination of welfare state and tourist paradise, the Gospels present the Christian future as full of division and strife. Far from announcing a peaceful world, Christ says that he brings a sword. All that he claims is that the truth of victims is out and that victimage patterns, systems of scapegoating will not provide the stable form of culture that they have had in the past. This is being verified every day. All of Western and then world history can be interpreted as a turbulent, chaotic, but constantly accelerating process of devictimization that is unique in all of world history and it can be traced only to Christianity.

The Satan who is defeated by the Cross is the prince of this world, Satan as a principle of order. We must remember that Satan is also the prince of disorder and this other Satan is still intact, and can even be said to be "unleashed," not by God, but by the greater and greater loss of scapegoat effectiveness that characterizes our world more and more with the passing of time. This world may well come to resemble the man in the Gospels from whom one demon was cast out but who failed to fill his life with divine things and the original demon came back with seven brothers, all more sinister than himself.

In order to make full sense out of eschatological and apocalyptic themes, we must never forget that whatever is happening to our world, coming as it does from the Gospels, must ultimately be good. Our being liberated from Satan's bondage means that the supernatural power of Satan and his demons is an illusion, that Satan does not exist.

The end of Satan is something we owe to the Gospels: it is part of what the Gospels call the victory of the Cross. The negation of Satan becomes bad only when it is accompanied by a minimization of mimetic contagion, by the illusion that, simply because, as a rule, we no longer believe in Satan, we are really independent thinkers, free from what Satan ultimately means, the enormous power of mimetic contagion and scandals, the inability of most of us to criticize the ideas that now rule the world.

After being afraid of Satan for many centuries, the Christians have become ashamed of him, and because of him, they often are ashamed of the Gospels themselves. Non-Christians point to Satan as proof that the Gospels are outmoded and the always timid Christians obediently try to censor Satan out of their own Scriptures. We must do the very reverse; we must focus on Satan and discover that the Gospels are their own best source of modernization.

We must focus on Satan to realize that far from being the archaic myth that we imagine, the defeated Satan of the Gospels in an enormously powerful critique of all archaic myths, a conception of culture and history so rich that its relevance to our own world is still unfathomable.

Chapter 14

The Question of Anti-Semitism in the Gospels

The accusation of anti-Jewishness in the New Testament Gospels is one of the favored attacks on the Gospels among many biblical critics, feminist critics, and other intellectuals. The agents of this hostile criticism range from certain members of the Jesus Seminar engaged in a renewed quest of the "historical" Jesus to practitioners of a more rarefied ideology criticism that appears in academic journals like *Semeia*. This now fashionable accusation was anticipated by Friedrich Nietzsche, who saw quite clearly that Christianity at its very core, stemming from the crucifixion of Christ, opposed the violent imposition of power and authority and held to a doctrine of divine concern for the weak and oppressed. He understood this morality, which took its Jewish legacy to a radical extreme, as the origin of *ressentiment* or the sublimated mimetic rivalry and desire for revenge stemming from envy of those who are powerful. In his view this resentment characterized the decadence of European culture. Nietzsche argued that Christianity, in its twofold inculcation of the desire for truth and for identification with the plight of the other, was in the process of destroying itself. His insights were prophetic if we view them in relation to recent postmodern theology and biblical criticism.

The following selection is an essay by Girard which appeared under the title "Is There Anti-Semitism in the Gospels?" in *Biblical Interpretation* 1 (1993): 339-52, with two pages deleted in order not to duplicate other material in this Reader. He points out that in the Gospels mimetic rivalry, scandal (the dead-end of the model-obstacle), crowd contagion, and the public need for order are set in a Jewish context, and involve primarily Jewish people (as well as the Roman government in some important instances), but the primary point is not to indict the Jews for the fate of Jesus;

it is rather to reveal things hidden since the foundation of the world, to expose all the murders since Cain and Abel, the beginning of human culture. If the significance of the founding murder is not understood in reading and interpreting the Gospels, many Christians will see their only options as an anti-Jewish Gospel or no Gospel at all. "What is needed," says Girard, "is a critique of the narrowly anti-Jewish reading of the texts, not an indictment of the Gospels."

— ❧ —

The possibility of an anti-Jewish or even "anti-Semitic" bias in the Gospels is often discussed nowadays. In order to be significant this discussion should not focus on matters of speech, such as the blanket substitution, in John, of the expression "the Jews" for the various religious groups mentioned under their specific names in the Synoptic Gospels. The real issue centers upon the large body of texts that seem to accuse the Jews, before the Passion, of preparing to kill Jesus in the same manner as they did many other victims. In the "Curses against the Pharisees," Jesus says: "You have killed all the prophets." The Jews are singled out, it seems, as a uniquely bloodthirsty nation that makes a habit of killing its holy men.

The parable of the murderous winemakers is an allegorized rendition of the same idea. After planting a vineyard on his own land, the owner entrusts it to tenants and departs for some distant land. From time to time, he sends messengers to collect his share of the crop, but, every time, all the winemakers get together and violently cast out these messengers, wounding or killing them in the process. The winemakers always act together and then, all together once again, they cast out and kill the last messenger, the owner's own son. This son is Jesus and the messengers are the prophets.

In the debate about the possible anti-Jewishness of the Gospels, the main evidence consists of this parable, plus the Curses against the Pharisees in the Synoptics, plus various texts in John, especially the one in which Jesus accuses his listeners of being the sons not of Abraham, as they claim, but of the devil "who was a murderer from the beginning."

Since I want to provide a global idea of my views, I must discuss all these texts; in the interest of space, however, I will greatly streamline my observations. In the texts mentioned above, the Jews are the foremost target of attack, but not the only one. In the statement about the murdered prophets, for example, Luke speaks of the blood "shed from the foundation of the world, the blood of Abel the just." There were no Jews at the time of Abel.

It can be objected that among both Jews and Christians, there is a tendency to regard the whole of Genesis as Jewish history. True enough, but then, in the statement about the murdered prophets, how are we to interpret the expression *epi tēs gēs* in both Matthew and Luke? It means on the earth, all over the earth. If the murders at issue were committed all over the earth, how could the Jews alone be responsible for them?

This idea of worldwide murders interests me not because it spreads the guilt thinner, so to speak, but because it makes us wonder why the Gospels should mention these murders at all. As long as they seem exclusively Jewish, we read them as a rhetorical amplification of Jewish ferocity. "No wonder these Jews killed Jesus; they indiscriminately massacre all their holy men." This reading is certainly wrong, but, incredibly, it is still the only reading available, and that is why the question of an anti-Jewish bias in the Gospels has some legitimacy.

If the Passion is only one example of a kind of murder that occurs all over the world, the Gospels are saying something about human culture as such, something we still do not understand. In order to discover what that is, we must ask: which features of the Passion are characteristic of all these murders?

The parable of the vineyard suggests one feature: the murders are never individual but collective, or collectively inspired. This is good to know but not yet enough. We need a comparative analysis. Fortunately the Passion is not the only portrayal we have of one of these murders. Two of the four Gospels, Mark and Matthew, contain an account of a second murder, the beheading of John the Baptist. Since John is regarded as a prophet, his violent death should conform to the principle formulated by Jesus. It should be *like* the Passion. And indeed it is. In both accounts the main phenomenon is a polarization, or mobilization, of many people against a victim who, until that moment, had not aroused the hostility of his future murderers. As a matter of fact, a few days before the Passion, the people of Jerusalem had greeted Jesus with enthusiasm.

In both instances, it all begins with a few instigators or even a single one: the religious leaders in the case of Jesus, Herodias in the case of John. They are the only people whose hostility to the victims predates the polarization that they do their best to trigger. They are not essential. The polarization alone is essential. What is its cause? In the case of John, the answer is disconcertingly obvious. Herod's guests and Herod himself are mimetically carried away, *possessed* by the famous dance of Herodias's daughter. In pagan sacrifices the immolation of the victim is often preceded by ritual dances. The effects of such dancing, traditionally, are defined as mimetic. The purpose is to unite the participants against the victim. This is what happens in the case of John.

The Passion contains no counterpart to Salome's dance, but all observable instances of someone joining the hostile crowd are also mimetic. The most spectacular is the text traditionally entitled Peter's denial. Like us moderns, Peter cannot stand the disapproval of his neighbors. In a Jerusalem crowd, he feels like an outsider and he wants to become an insider. He wants to show the people in the high priest's courtyard that he shares their feelings. He mimics what he presumes is the crowd's contempt for Jesus. He is the individual with the greatest spiritual investment in Jesus. If fidelity and steadfastness might be expected from anyone, they would be expected from him. The purpose of Peter's denial is not to indict a specific individual but to reveal how vulnerable even the best human beings are to mimetic polarizations such as we have in both murders.

Since we have reason to believe that all the violent murders mentioned in the Gospels are similar to the crucifixion and the beheading of John, we may also assume that they all result from mimetic polarizations. When Jesus says that he will die like all prophets before him, he means that his death will repeat a most ancient and worldwide pattern of mimetic violence. The common essence of these murders is something that modern observers vaguely identify as mob violence. Both the Passion and the death of John are sanctioned by a political authority, but this legal disguise does not really change the nature of the murders.

It has been suggested that Pilate's handling of Jesus reflects a pro-Roman bias or rather, once again, an anti-Jewish bias. The parallel handling of the Herod/John the Baptist relationship makes this interpretation most unlikely. There must be an intention common to both scenes, and it is readily intelligible. The sovereign, each time, must make his subservience to the crowd manifest. It will be manifest only if his personal desire differs from that of the crowd and yet, in the end, the crowd has its way. Herod and Pilate would like to save John and Jesus, but it cannot be done without antagonizing the crowd, and the two sovereigns yield to mimetic pressure; they become part of the crowd. The purpose is to show that a crowd in a lynching mood is the supreme power. For the Gospels, political power has been rooted in the crowd *since the foundation of the world.*

The coupling of the foundation of the world (*katabolē tou kosmou*) with the first murder is not a mere chronological coincidence. The importance of the idea is confirmed by the Gospel of John, which also has it, and in completely different words: "He [the devil] was a murderer from the beginning [*archē*]." Both statements refer not to divine creation, of course, but to the first human culture, which, in Genesis, is attributed to Cain. And Cain, indeed, has two titles to fame. The first is Abel's murder and the second is the creation of the first civilization or culture. A look at the text shows that the two events are one. The first law is the law against murder, and it is rooted in Abel's murder. The name Cain stands not for a single individual, but for the entire community cemented by the first collective murder analogous to the Passion.

Human society began and continued with mimetic murders similar to the Passion. In order to explore this amazing idea, I will summarize everything in the Gospels that pertains to mimetic contagion, mimicry, imitation.

Both Jesus and Satan are teachers of imitation and imitators themselves, imitators of God the Father. This means that human beings always imitate God, either through Jesus or through Satan. They seek God indirectly through the human models they imitate. When the model determines his imitator's desire through his own acquisitive desire, they both desire the same object. This is mimetic rivalry; once it is triggered, the two competing desires mutually keep reinforcing each other and violence is likely to erupt.

Imitation must be intrinsically good, nevertheless, since Jesus recommends it. It will never lead us into temptation as long as we imitate him, Jesus, who, in turn, imitates God in a spirit of childish and innocent obedience. Since there is no acquisitive desire in God, this imitation cannot cause mimetic rivalry. Mimetic rivalry is not sin but rather a permanent occasion of sin. The sin occurs when our relentlessness makes the rivalry obsessive. Its name is envy, jealousy, pride, anger, despair. For this satanic exasperation of mimetic rivalry, the Gospels have a marvelous word, *skandalon.* The idea is biblical, and it means an obstacle against which one keeps stumbling. The Greek word appears first in the Greek Bible and it comes from a verb that signifies "to limp." The more we stumble against an obstacle, the easier it should be to avoid further stumbling, but, most frequently, the opposite happens: we stumble so much that we seem to be limping.

Skandalon designates the intersubjective process that results from a very general but not universal human failure to walk away from mimetic rivalry. *Skandalon* is the process through which we are attracted to whatever or, rather, whoever treats us badly. *Skandalon* is destructive addiction of all kinds: drugs, sex, power, and, above all, morbid competitiveness — professional, political, intellectual, spiritual. *Skandalon* is the aching tooth that we cannot stop testing with our tongue, even though it hurts more.

Scandals, Jesus says, must happen. When scandals start happening, their contagiousness ensures their endless proliferation. The disorder becomes so pervasive that society, it seems, should disintegrate. Since society more often than not endures, some counter-force must be at work, not decisive enough to keep scandals from happening, which they must, but powerful enough to moderate their effects, to keep them under some form of control.

Scandalized people, meaning all of us, feel that their scandals, their personal problems, their most intense conflicts express something genuinely personal and unique in them, their innermost self. They are wrong. Being mimetic from the start, scandals become more so as they multiply and intensify. They become impersonal, anonymous, undifferentiated, and interchangeable. Beyond a certain threshold, they substitute for one another, with little or no awareness on our part. Scandals begin small, with two or three individuals, but, as they turn gregarious, they can grow very large.

People become so burdened with scandals that they desperately, if unconsciously, seek public substitutes, collective targets upon whom to unburden themselves. All those who join a belligerent crowd transfer their private scandals to some public target. As more and more people join in, the common victim's attractiveness as a victim increases, and the process becomes irresistible. This explains why Jesus uses the word scandal in connection with his Passion. When he warns his disciples that he is about to become a scandal to them, it really means that they will be affected by the mimetic tidal wave. In the case of Peter, we can follow this contamination in great detail, and what is true of him is true up to a point of the other disciples.

The violent unanimity of the Passion results from a snow-balling of scandals so powerful that even the disciples cannot escape it. The notion of scandal bridges the gap between individual and collective violence. When violence becomes unanimous, the victim has truly become the collective embodiment of all scandals and his or her destruction is experienced by individual participants as a destruction of his or her own scandal, a personal liberation. When this happens, peace immediately returns and the mob is no more. After Pilate surrenders to the crowd, all agitation subsides. The Cross becomes a spectacle at the end of which the mob peacefully disperses.

The crowd is appeased at the expense of an innocent victim. For this vicarious relief, the modern world has a word which, significantly, is borrowed from the Bible, "scapegoat." If scandals must keep happening, the survival and the very existence of human society may be dependent on periodical evacuations of scandals, on successful scapegoating.

We can understand now why, according to the Gospels, the foundation of the world should coincide with the first collective murder of the type exemplified by the Passion. Human culture and, no doubt, human religion are dependent on these murders. Jesus does not use the word "scapegoat," but he unquestionably refers to the process itself, and he identifies it as the founding mechanism of human society. He does this, I believe, when, right after the parable of the vineyard, he asks his puzzled listeners to interpret a quote from Psalm 118: "Do you understand what is said in this saying: The stone that the builders rejected has become the keystone?" The stone is rejected not by one builder, or by a few, but by all. Since nothing else is said about that stone, except that it is rejected, it can only be the rejection that transforms the stone into the keystone, and those who reject it into the builders that they might not be otherwise. The metaphor is transparent and made more so by the proximity of the violent winemakers. The idea of the rejected stone applies not merely to Jesus, as we are always told, but to all previous victims of the united winemakers. It applies not to Christianity alone, therefore, but to all religious and cultural institutions of humankind.

The Gospels clearly understand the key role of scapegoat expulsion in human society and in countless religious cults, as well as in Jesus' death. Traditional Christians have not really absorbed all implications of this teaching. We can well understand why. If Jesus is right, how can the Christian religion be as unique as it claims? Is it not fundamentally the same as other scapegoat religions?

At the end of the last century, comparative anthropologists showed that the overall scheme of Christianity is very similar to the overall scheme of archaic religion. The rationalist conception of Christianity as hardly less mythical than other religions seemed to be confirmed. This conception began to spread, even inside the Christian churches, the Protestant first and the Catholic later. It was the main cause of the *modernist* movement, which has now expanded into the greatest crisis in the history of Christianity, a disintegration of the faith more radical than the earlier rationalism since it incorporates the suspicion that the Gospels might be not only mythical but belligerently so because of their alleged anti-Semitism.

The resemblances are no doubt striking between the overall Christian scheme of collective death and resurrection, on the one hand, and, on the other hand, the sacred epiphany of many cults that may or may not be labeled a resurrection but that is also rooted, as a rule, in a collective murder. Primitive gods, primordial heroes, sacred kings, and founding ancestors are certainly keystones, each one in his or her territory, as a result of being the stones that the builders rejected.

The Gospel passages that I have discussed clearly confirm the structural similarities between the Christian revelation and countless other cults. By restricting their significance to the Jews, Christians have eluded this universal dimension, in an unconscious effort, perhaps, to postpone the crisis of faith that must have threatened Christianity almost from the beginning.

In order to bolster the uniqueness of their religion, Christians have always exaggerated the singularity of the Passion, its uniqueness as a violent event, and this tendency, inevitably, leads to an emphasis on the exceptional ferocity of the Jews. This trend contradicts the spirit and the letter of the Gospel texts discussed above. In the parable of the vineyard, the violence against the son is singled out because the victim is the son, but not because of the violence itself, which is the same as always. If Jesus himself says that the Passion is one example among many similar murders, Christians must resign themselves to this idea. They cannot be more Christian than Jesus Christ, more evangelical than the Gospels.

If there is something genuinely unique about the Christian revelation, it will become visible on the basis of the similarities between the Christian and non-Christian religions, on the basis of the total Gospel, and not of a slightly rearranged or incomplete Gospel.

The Christian fear is suicidal nonsense. Far from leading to the end of all distinction, the acknowledgment of the founding murder as something that all religions share, including Christianity, is the real prerequisite for reaching the plane upon which Christian uniqueness becomes a matter of immediate evidence, an incontrovertible fact. In order to reach this plane we must go back to the moment when, in the aftermath of the Passion, the people involved divide into two groups. On the one had, there is the large group of those united against Jesus: the religious and political leaders, as well as the bulk of the crowd. On the other hand, there is the small group of the first Christians.

Even though the Christian group is made up primarily of the original disciples, it is not some previous association with Jesus that determines its composition. For a while, during the Passion, it seemed that the mimetic consensus against Jesus was going to be unanimous. The Christians are the people who break away from the scapegoat consensus. Their communion is rooted in a passionate conviction that Jesus is innocent and was vindicated by God himself. This conviction is not an acceptance but a rejection of the founding murder that is uncritically espoused by the larger group.

Christianity, and prophetic Judaism, are the only examples of religions founded not on the blind acceptance of the founding murder but on a lucid rejection of it. The Gospels are the only example of a division of opinion regarding the founding murder. All other religions are continuous with this murder, which, as a result, does not appear as such. The people cannot distance themselves from it and challenge the justice of the victim's death. Everything we know about scapegoating comes from the Bible and, above all, from the New Testament.

The Gospels alone enable us to understand that religious epiphanies everywhere are rooted in scapegoat processes that must be spotted through indirect clues, such as the presumed guilt of the victim. We must question and demystify this guilt, just as the first Christians questioned and demystified the guilt of Jesus.

Whenever scapegoats truly function as scapegoats, they are seen as monsters of iniquity, whose expulsion is indispensable to the survival of the community. If the scapegoats were not unanimously feared and hated to start with, they could not sponge off the cesspool of scandals inside the community; they could not restore the peace. As a result of this process, these same scapegoats may arouse such gratitude and reverence that they are ultimately made divine. But their peace-making power is always dependent on a previous belief in their power as troublemakers.

Just as Jesus is guilty in the eyes of his persecutors, Oedipus is guilty in the eyes of his myth. Greek heroes are guilty; primitive gods are guilty; sacred kings are guilty. Archaic sacrifice runs parallel to myth. Before the immolation, the victims are regarded as malevolent and dangerous, and this is why they are often reviled before being killed. Only after the immolation do they become an object of reverence. This about-face reflects the effectiveness of unanimous scapegoating, which all rituals try to recapture in a spirit of religious piety, not of intersubjective manipulation.

Many myths and rituals conform to the pattern just outlined. Many others do not, and the reason is that religions keep evolving. After a while, the malevolence of the scapegoat is covered over by the benevolence of the god, which is retroactively extended to the preimmolation period. For a long time, however, many traces of scapegoating remain. Then, even these traces may disappear, except for two, I believe, that remain forever. The first is the innocence of the sacrificers; and the second, inseparable from the first, is the idea that the violence is necessary, justified by some higher good, even when it degenerates into political opportunism. This is exemplified in another great Gospel definition of scapegoating, Caiaphas's definition: "It is better that one man should die and that the whole nation not perish."

In non-Christian religions, scapegoat effectiveness is misinterpreted as something divine around which the people unite, but this "around" is necessarily preceded and determined by an "against." Only the Gospels do away with the initial "against." Only the Gospels denounce the founding violence as an evil that should be renounced. Only the Gospels put the blame not on the victim, but on the violent perpetrators. Only the Gospels do not regard the violence as sacred and do not transfigure it. Only the Gospels portray this violence as the vulgar scapegoat phenomenon that it is, the fruit of mimetic contagion. Only the Gospels reveal the founding murder as a fruit of humanity's fallen state, a sin that God alone can absolve.

The same scapegoating that myth misunderstands and therefore reveres as sacred truth, the Gospels understand and denounce as the lie that it really is. This denunciation is the alpha and omega of all genuine deconstruction and demythification.

When Jesus is called "the lamb of God," it means that he is an innocent scapegoat. But the expression is both more beautiful and more appropriate than scapegoat. The idea of vicarious immolation is retained, but the ugliness of the goat is eliminated. The injustice of the victim's death is made more obvious. Far from being the scapegoat religion par excellence, Christianity is the only religion that explicitly rejects scapegoating as a basis for a religious epiphany.

Many critics reject my views on the grounds that, being as visible as it is in the Gospels, the scapegoat mechanism must be operational in them, whereas myth and ritual are ambiguous about it and therefore one should wisely remain silent about their connection with scapegoating. These critics do not realize that the word "scapegoat," in the modern usage, which I make mine, defines a principle of collective self-deception, which, by definition, cannot be formulated in the texts that it structures. They always think in terms of a scapegoat "theme" or "motif." They find it extremely easy, therefore, to refute the mimetic theory, but the objections they brandish are misinterpreted evidence in its favor. They simply do not understand what I mean by generative scapegoating.

I can now return to my original question about the presumed anti-Jewishness of the Gospels. This accusation is false. The texts upon which it relies have a much vaster scope than New Testament exegetes have realized: they reveal the violent origin of all human societies. The anti-Jewish reading of these texts is the reason their real meaning is still generally misunderstood. All misunderstanding of the Gospels inevitably triggers a relapse into scapegoating, which occurs this time at the expense of the Jews. And another necessary consequence is that some of the violent sacred is reinjected into the text of the Gospels, in the violence of the Passion, which tends to be regarded as not quite human. In the Middle Ages, it seemed superhuman, in the sense of the Homeric gods intervening in the battles between the Greeks and the Trojans. With the waning of religious faith, this distortion turns into an indictment of the Jews. The disintegration of a Christianity somewhat contaminated with the spirit of scapegoating (sacrificial Christianity) is bound to generate Christian anti-Semitism.

The Gospels are not anti-Jewish, but as long as the significance of the founding murder in the texts that have nourished Christian anti-Semitism is not widely acknowledged, many Christians will believe that the only choice is between an anti-Semitic Gospel and no Gospel at all. What is needed is a critique of the narrowly anti-Jewish reading of the texts, not an indictment of the Gospels. The critics who indict the Gospels take for granted that the traditional reading is the good one, the only possible one. Their negative conservatism exonerates Christians from any feeling of guilt regarding their own anti-Semitism, which is quite real, of course, unlike the anti-Semitism of the Gospels.

The Christians can thus say to themselves: we are not responsible for scapegoating the Jews. We were misled by our religion. We sincerely believed what the Gospels taught us and they made anti-Semites out of us. It is probably inevitable that the relentless human effort to elude the substance of the Gospels should end up with this remarkable new twist: a scapegoating of the very text that made scapegoating intelligible to us by refusing it in all its forms.

Part VI

The Challenge of Freud and Nietzsche

Chapter 15

Freud and the Oedipus Complex

The three thinkers with whom Girard has been most engaged are Claude Lévi-Strauss, Sigmund Freud, and Friedrich Nietzsche. Lévi-Strauss has been important for Girard's structural reading of texts, and he shares with Lévi-Strauss the view that mythology, and by inference language and culture, represents the birth and development of differential thought. Girard criticizes Lévi-Strauss's dismissal of ritual, which preserves in a more archaic form than myth the traces of collective violence and transformation of violence into order. Girard holds, moreover, that the structural opposites of the anthropologist's differential thought, in and of themselves, can account for neither the expulsions recorded in mythology nor the sequence of negative and then positive connotations—in other words, the sacred character—of what or who is expelled. But Girard's engagement with the work of Freud and Nietzsche has been much more passionate and has made a much greater creative contribution to his mimetic theory. For Girard's critique of Lévi-Strauss, the two most convenient sources are "Lévi-Strauss, Structuralism, and Marriage Laws" in *Violence and the Sacred*, 223-49, and "Differentiation and Reciprocity in Lévi-Strauss and Contemporary Theory," chapter 8, in *"To Double Business Bound,"* 155-77. See also *Things Hidden*, 105-25.

Freud's speculation in *Totem and Taboo* about a primordial murder of the father-leader by the horde of brothers competing for the women of the band and greater power is well known, and it obviously influenced Girard—although it should be noted that Girard's ruminations on the execution of Jesus according to the Gospels and on the *pharmakon* of Plato as elucidated by Derrida were even more significant than the Freudian murder and incest prohibition (see under Scapegoat/Scapegoating)* for the further development of Girard's thinking. On the latter see "*Totem and Taboo* and the Incest Prohibition," chapter 8 of *Violence and the Sacred*,

193-222. Another important source on Girard's engagement with Freud is, "Interdividual" Psychology," book 3 of *Things Hidden*, especially pp. 352-92.

But the most important dimension of Girard's encounter with Freud's work is his critique of the Oedipus complex. Girard's dismantling of the Oedipus complex, including its ramifications in the concept of the superego, narcissism as distinct from object choice, and the death instinct, allowed him to account for all the phenomena in human reactions, relations, and origins in a much clearer, more elegant manner than Freud. As Girard summarizes in this selection, taken from chapter 7 of *Violence and the Sacred*, 169-85, Freud tried initially to develop the Oedipus complex from the basis of desire that is mimetic, yet he is inclined toward the desirability of objects (his *Besetzung* or cathexis); this attempt accounts for "the strange duality of the identification with the father and the libidinous attraction for the mother in the first [*Group Psychology and the Analysis of the Ego*], and even the second [*The Ego and the Id*], version of the complex. The failure of this attempt at compromise compelled Freud to base his complex on a purely cathectic desire [i.e., an object of desire invested with great emotion] and to reserve the mimetic effect for another psychic structure, the superego." Freud often started his analysis and theoretical constructions by taking mimesis very seriously, but he always abandoned it in favor of his sexual or libidinal theory. For Girard, however, the right path is the one intimated by Freud at the beginning of chapter 7 of *Group Psychology* where he focuses on identification, which is, practically speaking, mimesis or mimetic desire. The contradiction with which Freud ended, which he tried to resolve with the concepts of "ambivalence" and the "death instinct," was "a rivalry devoid of preliminary identification (the Oedipus complex) followed by an identification without subsequent rivalry (the superego)."

As can be seen from the following text, Girard's mimetic hypothesis is completely free of sexual bias in the sense of attaching mimesis to genetic heritage, anything biologically preordained, or a universal family structure or situation. The only thing that is universal and already given in the human condition is the mimetic structure and capacity of human beings, which require human others as models or mediators and objects to desire according to the model's desire—but *which* humans and *which* objects are not predetermined. This in spite of the frequent feminist charge that the mimetic theory is thoroughly "androcentric" or "patriarchal"! This conclusion is not based on thorough engagement with Girard's concept of mimesis in order to understand it, but a politically influenced version of "affirmative action," or, as the British aptly put it, "positive discrimination": instances of male and female examples are counted from the texts and other data cited and the totals indicate whether the thinker is "politically correct." But it misses the depth and implications of the generative mimetic scapegoat mechanism.

— ❧ —

We can observe both similarities and differences between mimetic desire and Freud's Oedipus complex. Mimetism is a source of continual conflict. By making one man's desire into a replica of another man's desire, it invariably leads to rivalry; and rivalry in turn transforms desire into violence. Although Freud may appear on first glance to have ignored this mechanism, he in fact came very close to apprehending it. A rigorous examination of this text will make it clear why he ultimately failed to do so.

The mimetic nature of desire plays an important role in Freud's work — not important enough, however, to dominate and revolutionize his thinking. His mimetic intuitions are incompletely formulated; they constitute a dimension of his text that is only half visible and tends to disappear in transmission. There is nothing surprising about the refusal of present-day psychoanalysts to turn their attention to this subject. Factions of psychoanalytic thought, bitterly opposed in other respects, are here at one. The mimetic aspect of desire has been ignored at once by those whose main concern is the elimination of inconsistencies in Freud's work in favor of a unified whole and by that other group who, while orthodox Freudians in name, quietly reject some of the most lucid and cogent of Freud's analyses on the grounds that they are tainted with "psychologism."

Although traces of the mimetic conception are scattered through Freud's work, this conception never assumes a dominant role. It runs counter to the Freudian insistence on a desire that is fundamentally directed toward an object, that is, sexual desire for the mother. When the tension between these opposing tendencies becomes too great, both Freud and his disciples seem to resolve it in favor of the object-desire.

The mimetic intuition of Freud gives rise to a series of concepts ambiguous in definition, obscure in status, and vague in function. Among the offshoots of this ill-defined mimetic desire are certain concepts that come under the heading *identification.* Among the categories of Freudian identification, one that nowadays receives little attention is the first one discussed in the chapter entitled "Identification," in *Group Psychology and the Analysis of the Ego*. This category has to do with the father:

> A little boy will exhibit a special interest in his father; he would like to grow like and be like him, and take his place everywhere. We may say simply that he takes his father as his ideal. This behavior has nothing to do with a passive or feminine attitude toward his father (and toward males in general); it is on the contrary typically masculine. It fits in very well with the Oedipus complex, for which it helps to prepare the way.[1]

There is a clear resemblance between identification with the father and mimetic desire; both involve the choice of a model. The choice is not really determined by parentage, for the child can select as model any man who happens to fill the role that our society normally assigns to the natural father.

As we have pointed out in the previous chapter, the mimetic model directs the disciple's desire to a particular object by desiring it himself. That is why we can say that mimetic desire is rooted neither in the subject nor in the object, but in a third party whose desire is imitated by the subject. Granted, the passage quoted above is hardly explicit on this point. But its implications are clear and conform to our definition of mimetic desire. Freud asserts that the identification has nothing passive or feminine about it; a passive or feminine identification would mean that the son wanted to become the object of his father's desire. How, then, will the active and "typically masculine" identification realize itself? Either it is wholly imaginary, or it finds concrete form in the desire for some particular object. The identification is a desire *to be* the model that seeks fulfillment, naturally enough, by means of appropriation, that is, by taking over the things that belong to his father. As Freud says, the son seeks to take the father's place everywhere; he thus seeks to assume his desires, to desire what the father desires. The proof that we are not distorting Freud's intention is supplied by the last sentence of the passage: "[The identification] fits in very well with the Oedipus complex, for which it helps to prepare the way."

What can this sentence mean, if not that identification directs desire toward those objects desired by the father? We have here an undeniable instance of filial desire undergoing the influence of mimesis. Consequently, there already exists in Freud's thought, at this stage, a latent conflict between this mimetic process of paternal identification and the autonomous establishment of a particular object as a basis for desire — the sexual cathexis toward the mother.

---

1. Sigmund Freud, *The Standard Edition of the Complete Psychological Works of Sigmund Freud*, ed. and trans. James Strachey, 24 vols. (London: Hogarth Press, 1953–66), vol. 18, *Group Psychology and the Analysis of the Ego*, 105.

This conflict is all the more apparent because identification with the father is presented as fundamental to the boy's development, *anterior to any choice of object.* Freud emphasizes this point in the opening sentences of an analysis that will eventually unfold into an overall description of the Oedipus complex and that is to be found in the chapter on identification previously referred to.[2] After identification with the father comes the sexual cathexis toward the mother, which, according to Freud, first appears and develops independently. The object-choice of the mother appears to have its origins in two factors: first, the identification with the father, the mimesis; second, the fixation of the libido on the mother. These two forces act together and reinforce one another, as Freud makes clear a few lines further on. After having subsisted "side by side for a time without any mutual influence or interference," the two "come together at last," and the libidinal drive is thereby strengthened. This is a wholly natural and logical turn of events if we choose to regard this identification as the mimesis of paternal desire. Indeed, once we have seen matters in this light all other explanations seem irrelevant.

I am not trying to put words in Freud's mouth. In fact, it is my contention that Freud saw the path of mimetic desire stretching out before him and deliberately turned aside. One need only examine his definition of the Oedipus complex, which follows a few lines further on, to see how he evades the issue:

> The little boy notices that his father stands in his way with his mother. His identification with his father takes on a hostile coloring and becomes identical with the wish to replace his father in regard to his mother as well. Identification, in fact, is ambivalent from the very first.[3]

The passage contains at least one point well worth noting. When, as Freud explains, the son discovers that his father is becoming an obstacle to him, his identification fuses with his desire "to replace his father in regard to his mother as well." That "as well" rivets the attention. Freud has earlier defined identification as the desire to replace the father, and he now repeats that formula. Must we therefore conclude that the mother was initially excluded, implicitly or explicitly, from the program? On examining the definition we see nothing that suggests such an exclusion; quite the contrary. As Freud has put it: "A little boy will exhibit a special interest in his father; he would like to grow like and be like him, and *take his place everywhere* [emphasis added]."

The casual reader may well assume that the "as well" in the phrase "in regard to the mother as well" is merely a slip of the pen; after all,

---

2. Ibid.
3. Ibid.

if the son wants to replace his father "everywhere," it follows that he would want to replace him in regard to the mother. But this apparent triviality in phrasing conceals an important point. As we have seen, it is impossible to elucidate Freud's theory of identification without encountering a mimetic mechanism that makes the father into the desire-model. It is the father who directs the son's attention to desirable objects by desiring them himself; thus, the boy's desires are inevitably directed toward his own mother. This much is clearly implied by Freud's text, yet these conclusions are never made explicit. Of course, it is possible that they never took shape in his mind, though they must surely have hovered there in some form when he was writing the opening passages of chapter 7, "Identification." Having first implied a mimetic interpretation, Freud then rejected it, also by implication, with the phrase "his mother as well." Such is the hidden meaning of that "as well." The two words retrospectively neutralize any mimetic interpretation of identification, at least in regard to the object of primary importance — the mother.

Freud's eagerness to dispel the mimetic elements that were impinging on his Oedipus theory can readily be discerned in his later work. Here, for instance, is his definition of the Oedipus complex as stated in *The Ego and the Id* (1923):

> At a very early age the little boy develops an object-cathexis for his mother...; the boy deals with his father by identifying himself with him. For a time these two relationships proceed side by side, until the boy's sexual wishes in regard to his mother become more intense and his father is perceived as an obstacle to them; from this the Oedipus complex originates. His identification with his father then takes on a hostile coloring and changes into a wish to get rid of his father in order to take his place with his mother. Henceforward his relation to his father is ambivalent; it seems as if the ambivalence inherent in the identification from the beginning had become manifest.[4]

At first glance this looks like a faithful resume of the concepts set forth in *Group Psychology and the Analysis of the Ego.* A further examination reveals certain differences that, though apparently minor, are in reality very important. My previous analysis dealt specifically with the mimetic elements to be found in the earlier text. It is precisely those elements, relegated to the shadows in that earlier description of the Oedipus complex, that are banished entirely from this later definition.

In the earlier text Freud insists on the anteriority of the identification with the father. In the later text he does not explicitly repudiate this

4. Freud, *Standard Edition,* vol. 19, *The Ego and the Id,* 31–32.

doctrine, but he gives first mention to the son's sexual attraction to the mother. In short, he discourages us from thinking that one and the same impulse — the wish to take the father's place *everywhere* — stimulates identification with the model and directs desire toward the mother.

That this inversion of the original order is not a matter of chance becomes abundantly clear when the process is repeated a little further on. In the second text, we find that the formulation of the "complex" is preceded by the reinforcement of the sexual wish; but instead of presenting this reinforcement as a consequence of the boy's first identification with the father, Freud inverts the order of the phenomena, thereby formally rejecting the cause-and-effect relationship suggested initially. This reinforcement of the libido is now totally lacking in motivation. The effect is retained, but because it now precedes the cause, neither cause nor effect seems to make much sense. As we can see, in *The Ego and the Id* Freud makes a clean sweep of all mimetic effects, but in so doing he sacrifices some of the most trenchant insights of *Group Psychology and the Analysis of the Ego* and some of his coherence as well.

Why did Freud banish mimesis from his later work? The best way to reply to this question is to continue along the path abandoned by him, to discover where he might have gone had he chosen to be guided by those mimetic effects that abounded in his earlier analyses but that were swept away as if by magic the instant they were found to cast doubt on his Oedipus complex. We must, in short, return to that phrase that is surreptitiously contradicted and canceled out by "the mother as well." To identify with the father, Freud informed us, is first of all to want to replace him: the little boy "would like to grow like and be like him, and *take his place everywhere* [italics added]."

In order to exclude the mother from this "everywhere," it is necessary to assume that the son is already conscious of the "law" and that he conforms to it without any prior instruction; for in principle it is the father who is supposed to teach him. But to exclude the mother is in actuality to assert that the Oedipus complex is already in operation; if that is not true the mother should be included, and that is what Freud has done — initially. The comprehensiveness of the statement that the son wishes to take his father's place "everywhere" is wholly appropriate, for the son cannot have a clear and distinct impression of his father's objects — including the mother — insofar as they are indeed his father's. In short, if the son turns toward his father's object, it is because he is following the example of his model, and this model necessarily turns toward his *own* objects — those that are already in his possession or that he hopes to acquire. The disciple's movement toward the objects of his model, including the mother, is already accounted for by the concept of identification as defined by Freud. Far from discouraging such an interpretation, Freud seems initially to have encouraged it.

Because disciple and model are converging on the same object, a clash between them is inevitable. The resulting rivalry appears "Oedipal," but it takes on a wholly different meaning. Because it is predetermined by the model's choice, there is nothing fortuitous about it; nor is it, strictly speaking, a question of one person's usurping what belongs to the other. The disciple's attraction to the model's object is wholly "innocent"; in seeking to take his father's place with his "mother as well," the son is simply responding in all candor to a command issued by the culture in which he lives and by the model himself. If we pause to consider closely the model-disciple relationship, it should become clear that the so-called Oedipal rivalry, reinterpreted in terms of a radically mimetic situation, must logically result in consequences that are at once similar to and quite different from those attributed by Freud to his "complex."

Earlier on I defined the effects of mimetic rivalry and affirmed that they invariably end in reciprocal violence. This reciprocity is the result of a process. If there is a stage in human existence at which reciprocity is not yet in operation and at which reprisals are impossible, that stage is surely early childhood. That is why children are so vulnerable. The adult is quick to sense a violent situation and answer violence with violence; the child, on the other hand, never having been exposed to violence, reaches out for his model's objects with unsuspecting innocence. Only an adult could interpret the child's actions in terms of usurpation. Such an interpretation comes from the depths of a cultural system to which the child does not yet belong, one that is based on cultural concepts of which the child has not the remotest notion.

The model-disciple relationship precludes by its very nature that sense of equality that would permit the disciple to see himself as a possible rival to the model. The disciple's position is like that of a worshiper before his god; he imitates the other's desires but is incapable of recognizing any connection between them and his own desires. In short, the disciple fails to grasp that he can indeed enter into competition with his model and even become a menace to him. If this is true for adults, how much truer it must be for the child experiencing his first encounter with mimetic desire!

The model's very first no — however softly spoken or cautiously phrased — can easily be mistaken by the disciple for an irrevocable act of excommunication, a banishment to the realms of outer darkness. Because the child is incapable of meeting violence with violence and has in fact had no real experience with violence, his first encounter with the mimetic double bind may well leave an indelible impression. The "father" projects into the future the first tentative movements of his son and sees that they lead straight to the mother or the throne. The incest wish, the patricide wish, do not belong to the child but spring from the mind of the adult, the model. In the Oedipus myth it is the oracle that puts such ideas into Laius's head, long before Oedipus himself was capable of entertaining any ideas at all. Freud reinvokes the same ideas, which are no more valid than Laius's. The son is always the last to learn that what he desires is incest and patricide, and it is the hypocritical adults who undertake to enlighten him in this matter.

The first intervention by the model between the disciple and the object is a traumatic experience, because the disciple is incapable of performing the intellectual operation assigned him by the adult, and in particular by Freud himself. He fails to see the model as a rival and therefore has no desire to usurp his place. Even the adult disciple is unable to grasp that conflict with the model is indeed rivalry, is unable to perceive the symmetry of their situation or acknowledge their basic equality. Faced with the model's anger, the disciple feels compelled to make some sort of choice between himself and the model; and it is perfectly clear that he will choose in favor of the model. The idol's wrath must be justified, and it can be justified only by some failure on the part of the disciple, some hidden weakness that obliges the god to forbid access to the holy of holies, to slam shut the gates of paradise. Far from reducing the divinity's prestige, this new attitude of vengeful spite serves to increase it. The disciple feels guilty — though of what, he cannot be sure — and unworthy of the object of his desire, which now appears more alluring than ever. Desire has now been redirected toward those particular objects protected by the *other's* violence. The link between desire and violence has been forged, and in all likelihood it will never be broken.

Freud, too, wants to show that an indelible impression is made on the child when he first discovers his own desires overlapping those of his parents. But because he eventually rejected the mimetic elements that had initially intrigued him, he takes a different approach. To appreciate this difference, let us look again at that crucial passage in *Group Psychology and the Analysis of the Ego:* "The little boy notices that his father stands in his way with his mother. His identification with his father then takes on a hostile coloring and becomes identical with the wish to replace his father in regard to his mother as well."

If we are to believe Freud, the little boy has no difficulty recognizing his father as a rival — a rival in the old-fashioned theatrical sense, a nuisance, a hindrance, a *terzo incomodo.* But even if this rivalry were provoked by something other than a desire to imitate the father's desires, a child would be unaware of this. We have only to look at the numerous everyday displays of envy and jealousy to realize that even adults never attribute their mutual antagonisms to that simple phenomenon. Freud is thus conferring on the child powers of discernment not equal but superior to those of most grown-ups.

Let me make myself clear. I am not objecting to certain basic Freudian assumptions, such as the attribution to the child of libidinal desires similar to those of adults, but rather to the bold and surely untenable assertion, which stands at the very center of his system, that the child is fully aware of the existing rivalry, of "the hostile coloring."

Undoubtedly I am flying in the face of psychoanalytical orthodoxy, denying the alleged evidence of "clinical findings"; and before the doctor's scientific mystique the layman can only bow. But the texts we have been examining are based on no specific "clinical findings." Their speculative character is obvious, and there is no more reason to treat them as holy writ (as some have done) than to try to sweep them under the carpet. In either case we would be depriving ourselves of some valuable insights (even if the object of these insights is not always what Freud takes it to be) and depriving ourselves as well of the fascinating spectacle of Freud's intellect at work, of the gradual and halting evolution of Freudian doctrine.

Undoubtedly "clinical findings" can be turned to almost any account, but we can hardly expect them to serve as evidence for a consciousness, no matter how transitory, of patricidal or incestuous desire. After all, it is precisely because this consciousness refuses to yield to clinical observation that Freud is obliged to devise such unwieldy and dubious concepts as those of the "unconscious" or "suppression."

And here we arrive at my principal complaint against Freud. The mythical element of Freudianism has nothing to do — despite traditional assertions to the contrary — with the nonconscious nature of those basic impulses that determine the individual's psychological make-up. If my complaint were a reiteration of that well-worn theme, it would undoubtedly be classified among the "reactionary" criticism of Freudianism. In the final analysis, what I object to most is Freud's obstinate attachment — despite all appearances — to a philosophy of consciousness. The mythical aspect of Freudianism is founded on the conscious knowledge of patricidal and incestuous desire; only a brief flash of consciousness, to be sure, a bright wedge of light between the darkness of the first identifications and the unconscious — but consciousness all the same. Freud's stubborn attachment to this consciousness compels him to abandon both logic and credibility. He first assumes this consciousness and then gets rid of it in a kind of safe-deposit box, the unconscious. In effect he is saying: ego can suppress all consciousness of a patricidal and incestuous desire only if at one time ego truly experienced it. *Ergo sum.*

The most remarkable aspect of this moment of unobstructed consciousness, which Freud posits as the basis for man's psychic existence, is its sheer uselessness. Only by stripping it away do we uncover Freud's essential point: the crucial and potentially catastrophic nature of the first contacts between child and parent or, in other terms, between the disciple's desire and the model's desire. This moment of consciousness not only offers us nothing of importance but also serves to obscure the mimetic process, which in both form and context possesses many advantages over the Freudian "complex."

Further discussion along these lines might distract us from our main subject of inquiry, so I shall only say in passing that I believe that a radically mimetic conception of desire offers a novel approach to psychiatric theory, one as far removed from the Freudian unconscious as it is from any philosophy of consciousness camouflaged as an existential psychoanalysis. Specifically, this new approach succeeds in circumventing the fetish of "adjustment" without plunging into the inverse fetish of "perversion" that is typical of so much of modern theory. The individual who "adjusts" has managed to relegate the two contradictory injunctions of the double bind — to imitate and not to imitate — to two different domains of application. That is, he divides reality in such a way as to neutralize the double bind. This is precisely the procedure of primitive cultures. At the origin of any individual or collective "adjustment" lies concealed a certain arbitrary violence. The well-adjusted person is thus one who conceals his violent impulses and condones the collective's concealment of them. The "maladjusted" individual cannot tolerate this concealment. "Mental illness"[5] and rebellion, like the sacrificial crisis they resemble, commit the individual to falsehoods and to forms of violence that are certainly more damaging *to him* than the disguised violence channeled through sacrificial rites but that bring him closer to the heart of the enigma. Many psychic catastrophes misunderstood by the psychoanalyst result from an inchoate, obstinate reaction against the violence and falsehood found in any human society.

A psychoanalytic system that no longer oscillated between the rigid conformism of social adjustment and the false scandal arising from the assumption of a mythical patricide-incest drive in the child would not result in mere tepid idealism. Rather, such a system would bring us face to face with some traditional concepts that are troubling, to say the least. For example, in Greek tragedy, as in the Old Testament, the "good" son cannot generally be distinguished from the "bad" son; the "good" son is Jacob rather than Esau, the prodigal son rather than the faithful son, Oedipus.... For the good son imitates the father with such passion that father and son become each other's chief stumbling block — a situation the indifferent son more easily avoids.

It may appear, at this point, that all these concerns are foreign to the Freudian mode of thought and that the mimetic double bind has nothing

5. Because the very notion of "mental illness" has been, up to a point, correctly challenged in the writings of some contemporary physicians, I put the term in quotation marks.

to do with Freudian theory. "Act like your model / do not act like your model" — the contradictory double imperative we see as fundamental — may be thought to lead us far from the realms of psychoanalysis.

In reality it does not, and this shows that Freud's work is too precious to be left to the psychoanalysts. The mimetic approach preserves and enhances Freud's most acute insights. In *The Ego and the Id* Freud explains that the relation between the ego and the superego "is not exhausted by the precept: 'You ought to be like this (like your father).' It also comprises the prohibition: 'You *may not be* like this (like your father) — that is, you may not do all that he does; some things are his prerogative.' "[6]

Who, after reading this passage, can deny Freud's proximity to my mimetic double bind? Not only was he familiar with its operation, but the context in which he placed it can help us realize its full potential. Freud's definition of the superego presupposes something quite different from a mythical consciousness of rivalry; he seems to have based it on the model's identification with the obstacle, an identification unperceived by the disciple. The superego is in fact nothing more than a resumption of identification with the father, now appearing chronologically *after* the Oedipus complex rather than *before* it. As we have seen, Freud did not actually suppress this previous identification, perhaps because he balked at contradicting himself; but he cunningly relegated it to secondary status by eliminating its primordial character. In any case, the identification with the father now operates chiefly after the complex has taken hold; it has become the superego.

If we reflect on the definition of the superego offered by Freud two facts become clear. In the first place, the definition accords with the concept of the double bind. In the second place, it fails to harmonize with Freud's picture of a "sublimated" Oedipus complex, that is, a patricide-incest desire that has been transposed from the conscious to the unconscious.

To appreciate in full the predicament brought about by the superego's contradictory commands, issued as they are in the atmosphere of ignorance and uncertainty implied by Freud's definition, we must try to imagine the son's initial act of imitation. It is performed with fervor and devotion and rewarded by sudden, stupefying disgrace. The positive injunction, "Be like your father," had seemed to cover the entire range of paternal activities. Nothing in this first command anticipates, much less helps the son to understand, the contradictory command that follows: "You may not be like your father." And this command too seems to brook no exceptions.

All the son's efforts to differentiate between the commands and to

6. Freud, *The Ego and the Id,* 32.

formulate distinctions end in failure, and his bewilderment gives rise to terror. He wonders what he has done wrong and struggles to find separate areas of application for the two commands. He finds it difficult to see where he is at fault—certainly he has broken no law yet known to him—so he applies himself to discovering some new law that will allow him to define his conduct as illegal.

What conclusions must be drawn from this definition of the superego? Why did Freud again toy with the mimetic effects that he had rejected at the Oedipal stage? There seems only one possible answer: he had no intention of renouncing the mimetic effects resulting from identification. For he reverts to them when he takes up the concept of the superego. Yet the definition of the superego follows almost immediately on the definition of the Oedipus complex previously quoted, a definition purged of the mimetic elements that had characterized Freud's earlier definition in *Group Psychology and the Analysis of the Ego*.

It seems possible, then, to follow the evolution of Freud's thought from *Group Psychology* in 1921 to *The Ego and the Id* in 1923. In the earlier work Freud believed it possible to reconcile the mimetic effect with his main thesis, the Oedipus complex; that is why observations on the mimetic phenomenon are sprinkled throughout his work. But in the very course of composition, it seems, Freud began to sense the incompatibility of the two themes. And this incompatibility quickly becomes all too clear. The mimetic process detaches desire from any predetermined object, whereas the Oedipus complex fixes desire on the maternal object. The mimetic concept eliminates all conscious knowledge of patricide-incest, and even all desire for it as such; the Freudian proposition, by contrast, is based entirely on a consciousness of this desire.

Freud evidently decided to permit himself the luxury of his Oedipus complex. When he had to choose between the mimetic concept and a full-blown patricide-incest drive, he opted firmly for the latter. This is not to say that he renounced exploring the promising possibilities of mimesis; the admirable thing about Freud is his refusal ever to renounce anything. In suppressing the effects of mimesis he was simply trying to prevent mimesis from subverting his own cherished version of the Oedipus myth. He wanted to get hold of the "Oedipus complex" once and for all so as to be free to return to the mimesis question. Once he had the complex behind him, he could take mimesis up where he had left it before the burgeoning of the idea of the complex.

In short, Freud attempted initially to develop the Oedipus complex on the basis of a desire that is both object-oriented (cathectic) and yet originates in mimesis—whence comes the strange duality of the identification with the father and the libidinous attraction for the mother in the first, and even the second, version of the complex. The failure of this attempt at compromise compelled Freud to base his complex on a purely cathectic desire and to reserve the mimetic effect for another psychic structure, the superego.

The duality of Freud's position stems from his effort to separate two poles of his thinking on desire: cathectic and Oedipal at one extreme, mimetic at the other. But any attempt to sever the link between the two will end in failure, as did the attempt at synthesis that preceded it.

It is hopeless to attempt to isolate the three elements of mimetic desire: identification, choice of object, and rivalry. That Freud's thought was never free of the influence of mimetic preoccupations can be proved by the irresistible conjunction of these three elements; whenever any one of them appears, the other two are sure to follow. It was only with the greatest effort and at the expense of much of his credibility that Freud managed to rid his Oedipus complex of all traces of mimesis. Conversely, in the case of the superego, where in principle nothing interferes with the son's paternal identification, we witness once again an upsurge of rivalry for the mother object. When the superego proclaims, "You may not be like this (your father)...some things are his prerogative," Freud is clearly referring to the mother. That is why he adds: "This double aspect of the ego ideal derives from the fact that the ego ideal had the task of repressing the Oedipus complex; indeed it is to that revolutionary event that it owes its existence."[7]

This superego, simultaneously repressing and repressed, which exists only thanks to "that revolutionary event," poses a formidable problem. It knows too much, even in a negative sense. The truth is that the reactivating of the father-identification, which gives the superego its meaning, automatically reactivates the Oedipal triangle. As I have remarked, Freud cannot evoke one of the three elements of the mimetic configuration without the other two's putting in an appearance. The reappearance of the Oedipal triangle was not in his program. The Oedipus complex, the capital that served to launch the entire psychoanalytic enterprise, is supposed to be firmly locked away in the unconscious, deposited deep in the vaults of the psyche.

This inopportune reappearance of the Oedipal triangle compelled Freud to admit that the son might experience certain difficulties in repressing his Oedipus complex! In fact, it is Freud himself who was having trouble disposing of the mimetic triangle. Haunted by the mimetic rivalry, he repeatedly sketched out triangular formations he believed to represent his complex, whereas in fact they depict a constantly thwarted mimesis — an interplay of model and obstacle that lingers at the edge of his thought but that he never succeeds in articulating fully.

I limited myself to examining two or three passages whose comparison seems particularly revealing; other passages could have been chosen

7. Ibid.

that would have suited my purposes equally well, including some from the so-called clinical cases. In my chosen passages a term fundamental to Freudian speculation — "ambivalence" — reappears at frequent intervals. It seems to me that this term testifies to the existence of the mimetic pattern in Freud's mind and to his inability to express correctly the relationship among the three elements of the structure: the model, the disciple, and the object that is disputed by both because the model's desire has made the object desirable to the disciple. The object represents a desire shared by both, and such sharing leads not to harmony, as one might suppose, but to bitter conflict.

The term "ambivalence" appears toward the close of the two definitions of the Oedipus complex previously quoted. Here are the passages again:

> His [the boy's] identification with the father takes on a hostile coloring and becomes identical with the wish to replace the father in regard to his mother as well. Identification, in fact, is ambivalent from the very first.
>
> His identification with his father takes on a hostile coloring and changes into a wish to get rid of his father in order to take his place with his mother. Henceforward his relation to his father is ambivalent; it seems as if the ambivalence inherent in the identification from the beginning had become manifest.

When we recall how the identification with the father is initially presented — "This behavior has nothing to do with a passive or feminine attitude toward his father ... " — we seem to be dealing with a unified relationship, free of ambiguity. Why then does Freud, a few lines later and seemingly as an afterthought, attribute an underlying ambiguity to this identification? Simply because he now senses (and his intuition does not betray him) that the positive feelings resulting from the first identification — imitation, admiration, veneration — are fated to change into negative sentiments: despair, guilt, resentment. But Freud does not realize *why* such things must happen. He does not realize because he cannot accept a concept of desire based on mimesis; he cannot openly acknowledge the model in the identification to be a model of the desire itself, and thus a powerful force of opposition.

Whenever he encounters the effects inherent in mimetic desire and finds himself struggling vainly to formulate its mechanism of rivalry, Freud takes refuge in the idea of ambivalence. To label these effects as ambivalent is to confine them to a solipsistic context, a traditional philosophic subject, instead of identifying them as a fundamental trait of all human relations, the universal double bind of imitated desires. If we try to grasp these effects of mimetic desire as individual pathology or psychology, they become utterly incomprehensible; in consequence, we ascribe them to "physical" causes. Freud himself conveys this impression and managed to persuade himself that in using the term "ambivalence" he had made a daring plunge into the dark regions where the psychic and the somatic meet. In reality, he was simply refusing to decipher a perfectly decipherable message. And because the "physical" is by nature mute, no rebuttal is possible. Today everyone imagines himself tuned in to the "physical," able to decode the body's messages after the example of Freud. Yet in all Freud's work there is not a single example of "ambivalence" that does not have its origins in the obstacle-model.

To attribute the conflict to the "body" is to give up on the logic of mimetic desire that can account most intelligibly and economically for all phenomena. With Freud, the "physical" aspect of the subject, the corporeal regions of the psyche, are endowed with a more or less organic propensity to run head on into the obstacle of the model-desire. Ambivalence becomes the main virtue of the physical insofar as it nourishes the psyche; it becomes the *virtus dormitiva* of modern scholasticism in the face of desire. Thanks to this idea and a number of others, psychoanalysis has been able to grant a reprieve — even apparently to grant new life — to the myth of the individual, by reasserting the claims of the physical. Yet this is the very myth it should be trying to demolish.

Freud's use of the term "ambivalence" reveals a genuine, if very limited, recognition of mimetic desire — which is more than can be said for many of his followers. The interesting question is how Freud managed repeatedly to misconstrue such a simple mechanism. In a sense its very simplicity served to camouflage its presence; but there is something else at work here as well.

That something else is not difficult to identify; we have encountered it at every turn in the course of our inquiry. It is, of course, the hard core of the Oedipus complex: that brief interval of consciousness when the patricide-incest desire is felt to become a formal expression of the child's intentions. It is clear that this Freudian view makes Freud's full discovery of mimetic desire impossible. To persuade himself that the patricide-incest desire actually exists, Freud was obliged to disregard the model, insofar as it is responsible for awakening the desire and designating the object. Freud was forced to perpetuate a traditional, retrogressive concept of the desire. The drift of his thought in the direction of mimesis was perpetually checked by his strange loyalty to the patricide-incest motif.

As an interpretative tool the concept of mimetic rivalry is far more serviceable than the Freudian complex. By eliminating the conscious patricide-incest desire it does away with the cumbersome necessity of the desire's subsequent repression. In fact, it does away with the unconscious. The concept explains the Oedipus myth and does so with an economy and precision lacking in the Freudian approach. Why then, we may well ask, did Freud renounce the superior utility of mimetic desire to lavish his attention on the poor substitute of patricide-incest?

Even if I am mistaken — even if I am blind to the virtues of the Oedipus myth as a universal model for the human psyche — still my question remains valid. It seems unlikely that Freud ever formally rejected the interpretation I am proposing here as a substitute for his complex; in all likelihood, it never came to his attention. Had it done so, Freud would surely have taken it under consideration, if only to reject it. My reading brings together a number of clues that seem to play little part in Freud's texts; the obstacle of the patricide-incest motif once removed, we can bring together elements that remain disconnected in Freud's own work. Freud was dazzled by what he took to be his crucial discovery. Loyalty to this discovery kept him from forging ahead on the path of mimesis. Had he done so he would have come to realize the mythic nature of the patricide-incest motif, as it appears in the Oedipus myth and in psychoanalysis as well.

The whole of psychoanalysis seems to be summed up in the patricide-incest theme. It is this theme that has won psychoanalysis its glory and its notoriety, that has provoked the incomprehension, hostility, and extraordinary devotion we have come to associate with the discipline. It is this theme that is invariably invoked whenever any rebellious spirit dares to cast doubt on the efficacy of psychoanalytic doctrine.

Freud's intimations of mimetic desire never crystallized into a theory. The founder of psychoanalysis brooded over the same themes throughout his lifetime, and his unending struggle to reorganize the elements of desire never produced truly satisfactory results, because he refused to abandon his object desire, his "cathectic" viewpoint. The various structures and examples of Freudianism, theoretical concepts such as the castration complex, the Oedipus complex, the superego, the unconscious, repression, ambivalence — all these are nothing more than defensive positions in his eternal battle to resolve the problem of desire.

Freudian analysis should not be regarded as a fully articulated system, but as a series of experiments dealing almost invariably with the same subject. The superego, for instance, is only a recasting of the Oedipus complex; the more I examine the origins of the two concepts, the more convinced I become that their differences are purely illusory.

Freud at his best is no more "Freudian" than Marx at his best is "Marxist." Nevertheless, uncomprehending critics did on occasion provoke him to adopt a dogmatic line of argument that his followers blindly accepted and his opponents as blindly rejected, therefore making it difficult for any of us to approach these texts with an open mind.

Post-Freudian psychoanalysis has clearly perceived what must be done to systematize Freudianism — or rather, to sever it from its living roots. To assure the autonomy of desire it is only necessary to erase the last traces of mimesis from the Oedipus complex. Thus, the identification with the father must be dropped. Freud had already pointed the way, after all, in *The Ego and the Id.* Inversely, to establish the supremacy of the superego on a firm basis, one need only eliminate all those elements that tend to implicate the object and the subject of rivalry in its definition. In short, the post-Freudian psychoanalyst reasserts a system, an order of things based on "common sense," such as only Freud himself ever challenged. In the case of the Oedipus complex the father becomes a disgraced rival; thus there is no question of his being a venerated model. Reciprocally, in the case of the superego, the father is the venerated model, with no trace of the disgraced rival about him. Ambivalence, it would appear, is good for patients, but of no use to psychoanalysts.

We are presented, therefore, with a rivalry devoid of preliminary identification (the Oedipus complex) followed by an identification without rivalry (the superego). In one of his earliest articles, "Aggression in Psychoanalysis," Jacques Lacan noted the bewildering character of this sequence: "The structural effect of the identification with the rival does not follow naturally, except perhaps in mythic thinking."[8] But let us leave the myth aside; we will presently see that it can take care of itself. Moreover, the effect noted by Lacan makes perfect sense in terms of the mimetic nature of desire, which Lacan, too, failed to discover, forced as he was by his linguistic fetishism to reinforce the more rigid and "structural" aspects of Freudian thinking.

The interest of Freudian analysis does not lie in its results, in its pretentious accumulation of psychic agencies; nor does it lie in the spectacle of Freudian apprentices clambering up and down the precarious scaffolding of Freudian doctrine with an agility as remarkable as it is futile. It lies, paradoxically enough, in the ultimate inadequacies of the whole system. Freud never succeeded in establishing the precise relationship of the model, the disciple, and their common object, although he never entirely abandoned the effort. Whenever he attempted to manipulate any two of the terms, the third raised its head like a mocking jack-in-the-box, which his disciples made haste to cram back in its box in the belief that they were doing something useful. In fact, it is hard to imagine a more effective method of "castrating" the Master!

8. Jacques Lacan, *Ecrits* (Paris: Seuil, 1966), 117.

Chapter 16

Nietzsche versus the Crucified

Both Nietzsche and Girard are "christocentric." That is, the real point of departure for both is the Crucified as the center of history. For Nietzsche, the Crucified is the center of *past* history but his reign over morality must end with the murder of God (*The Gay Science*, no. 125) and the beginning of a new era. For Girard, the Crucified is the Innocent Victim who reveals the scapegoat mechanism of human culture and the love that overcomes it.

From some point in the development of his thinking, perhaps in the late 1960s or early 1970s in conjunction with his discovery of Dionysus* and *The Bacchae* of Euripides, Girard began to see Nietzsche not only as the greatest thinker of the nineteenth century, but also as a negative guide to the meaning of the Christian revelation. What Nietzsche intuited and understood in Christianity he tried to exorcise from himself and his radical visions of a new humanity as though it were the worst of plagues. Nietzsche understood the religion* of the crucified Christ as the historical culmination of the Jewish "slave morality" that is rooted in *ressentiment*. *Ressentiment* is the sublimated desire for revenge against the masters of history on the part of those who view themselves as their victims. Or, as Girard says in the following essay, it "is the interiorization of weakened vengeance," whose "ultimate target is always *ressentiment* itself, its own mirror image, under a slightly different mask that makes it unrecognizable."

Nietzsche held that Christian morality became not only the most powerful but also the most baneful combination of conviction and lifestyle to emerge in history. He envisioned the appearance of the superior human being, *der Übermensch*, whose god is Dionysus and whose will to power transcends *ressentiment*. In the following piece, published originally as "Dionysus versus the Crucified" in *Modern Language Notes* 99 (1984): 816-35, Girard analyzes the real differences between the Christ of the Gospels and Nietzsche's Dionysus, differences which Nietzsche himself understood only too well. He knew that Jesus brought a sword which was "the order of charity" or love, as Pascal put it. But in the antithesis of Dionysus versus the Crucified, he willed and tried to affirm an order he understood as "life itself, its eternal fruitfulness and recurrence," which "creates torment, destruction, the will to annihilate. . . ." (*Will to Power*, no. 1052).

Girard has written a number of other essays on Nietzsche. On Nietzsche's work as a strategy of madness stemming in great part from his rivalry with Wagner, see "Strategies of Madness — Nietzsche, Wagner, and Dostoevski" in *"To Double Business Bound,"* 61-83. On Nietzsche's proclamation of the murder of God through his madman, see "The Founding Murder in the Philosophy of Nietzsche," in *Violence and Truth*, ed. P. Dumouchel (Stanford, Calif.: Stanford University Press, 1988), 227-46.

— ❧ —

For a while, after the war, a great debate raged about Nietzsche's own responsibility in the Nazi exploitation of his writing for anti-Semitic purposes. There was mostly silence, however, regarding his anti-Christian stance; it is too explicit and consistent to be denied.

To those who felt that Nietzsche's work should not fall into neglect, the point was irrelevant anyway. Why should Nietzsche be exonerated from an attitude that a majority of intellectuals regarded as sound? No apology needed to be made.

No apology was made. Nietzsche was in the clear. But the anti-Christian polemics of Nietzsche have received scant attention since World War II. Why? If they were asked — they never are — contemporary Nietzscheans would probably answer that their thinker's passionate attitude toward religion has lost its relevance.

Nietzsche remains "important" because of some avatars of his that came to light in recent years, mostly through the ingenuity of French critics. Nietzsche the genealogist, Nietzsche the advocate of "free play," Nietzsche the exponent of counter-culture....

Different as they are from one another, at least in some respects, these avatars are all alike in their indifference to the great struggle that obsessed the last lucid years of Nietzsche. Is there some obscure reason why this should be? Is there something inopportune or embarrassing about the theme; is it strategically advisable not to insist upon it?

Whatever the case may be, Nietzsche's religious problematic was already marginalized when the French critics began their work. The real job was performed by Martin Heidegger. Even those who reject the interpretation of Nietzsche as the last great metaphysician of the West are dependent on Heidegger for their evacuation of "Dionysus versus the Crucified." Just as existentialism in the French style was an offshoot of German philosophy and above all Heidegger, the new "French Nietzsche" is another lively mouse, or rather a whole litter, brought forth by the Heideggerian mountain.

Nietzsche's forced conversion to inverted platonism is rooted in one essential Heideggerian tenet, which is the mutual incompatibility of religion and thought in the highest sense, the postphilosophical and Heideggerian sense.

Everything in Nietzsche that comes under the heading "Dionysus versus the Crucified" must be alien to "thought" and is therefore harshly condemned as a pure and simple "return to monotheism," the very reverse in other words of what Nietzsche himself imagined he was doing. This condemnation is also an allusion to the fact that someone fighting Christianity with the passionate intensity of Nietzsche must still have been under its influence. Even though brief flashes of hatred appear here and there in his writings, Heidegger on the whole gives an impression of radical indifference to religion, an attitude that has become a model for quite a few people. The subject is of little or no interest. Period.

Heidegger interpreted monotheism as a monopolistic claim on the divine that constituted, in his eyes, the height of *ressentiment.* I will be the last to disagree with Heidegger regarding the importance of *ressentiment* in Nietzsche's work. I do not believe, however, that Heidegger or anyone else can disentangle the strands that belong to *ressentiment* and therefore to religious nonthought from the strands that do not and belong therefore to the philosophical thought that deserves to be considered and interpreted.

To Heidegger, "Dionysus versus the Crucified" was merely the Nietzschean reversal of a previous Christian formula: "The Crucified versus Dionysus," and therefore the same empty struggle for power between two rival religions. As institutional Christianity weakens, the philosophical hostility to it turns to silence but it does not decrease.

To Heidegger, the essential history of our world is postphilosophical and religion is irrelevant. The Nietzsche of "Dionysus versus the Crucified" is more alien to the real issues of our times than the "withdrawal of being" and its comet tail of postphilosophical discourse. Is this view going to prevail?

Even from the standpoint of Nietzschean studies in the narrowest sense, this negative attitude is a mutilation. It deprives us of what is really exciting and novel in the Nietzschean corpus. Now that we are no longer limited to the excerpts carefully selected and organized by Nietzsche's sister, and we can read all of the formerly unpublished writing, we cannot doubt that the closer we get to the end the more obsessive the Christian theme becomes with Nietzsche. The number and importance of the fragments dealing with the subject increase.... We are reminded of a volcano pouring greater and greater torrents of murky lava with, here and there, the sparkle of a jewel still untouched by human hands...; for these some of us at least would gladly burn one finger or two.

Here, the most daring material becomes inseparable from the grotesque. Genius and insanity lend each other a hand until the last instant, giving the lie to the orthodox thesis that disconnects the two. If we receive the evidence of their mutual contamination, we commit the one unforgivable sin, punishable by immediate exclusion from the club of the respectable Nietzscheans.

These later fragments are the height of *ressentiment* in the sense that the final breakdown also is. Nietzsche's superiority over his century and ours may well be that he alone pushed the *ressentiment* that he shares with quite a few lesser mortals to such a height that it yielded its most virulent and significant fruit. None of Nietzsche's achievements as a thinker can be divorced from *ressentiment,* whether the subject is Wagner, the divine, or Nietzsche himself in *Ecce Homo.*

Unlike Heidegger, unlike most of his contemporaries and ours, Nietzsche strongly believed in the unique specificity of the biblical and Christian perspective. His reasons cannot be dismissed as summarily as they would if he were a Christian. The ethnocentric fallacy will not do.

The uniqueness of the Bible and the New Testament is affirmed by Nietzsche in a context directly opposed to Christian apologetics. Nietzsche tried to put his critique of Christianity on a basis less shaky than the one that was already standardized in his time, the great positivistic equivalence of all religious traditions. He knew too much about pagan mythology not to be revolted by the shallow assimilation of the Judeo-Christian with the pagan.

He maintained that the Christian spirit tries to stifle "life" by repressing the most dynamic individuals of a culture. This is the famous "morality of the slaves" versus "the morality of the masters," the one thing everybody knows about the Nietzschean distinction between paganism and Judeo-Christianity.

A culture has to pay a price in order to breed a class of higher men. It has to assume even the worst forms of violence. Time and time again, Nietzsche tells us that Dionysus accommodates all human passions, including the lust to annihilate, the most ferocious appetite for destruction. Dionysus says yes to the sacrifice of many human lives, including, not so paradoxically, those of the highest type that is being bred in the process.

Already in *The Birth of Tragedy,* Nietzsche mentioned the violence that accompanies and often precedes Dionysus everywhere. All epiphanies of the god leave ruins in their wake. "Mania," after all, mean homicidal fury. Unlike many of his followers, Nietzsche did not turn the Dionysian into something idyllic and inconsequential. He was too honest to dissimulate the disturbing sides, the ugly sides of the Dionysian.

With the years, his references to that frenzied and seemingly haphazard violence that marks all the episodes of the Dionysian saga became even more frequent and insistent than in the past, but Nietzsche often repeated them almost verbatim, and they became stereotyped.

Nietzsche never went into an analysis in depth of *The Bacchae,* for instance, but he always dutifully mentioned the Dionysian violence. The reason for this is not that Nietzsche particularly relished that violence; the opposite is true, but this violence plays an essential role and it should not be suppressed.

Nietzsche clearly saw that pagan mythology, like pagan ritual, centers on the killing of victims or on their expulsion, which can seem perfectly wanton. He realized that this type of killing, which is reflected in many rituals as well as represented in myths, is often executed by a large number of murderers; it is a collective deed in which an entire human group is involved. Only exceptionally, but then most strikingly, as we will see later, did Nietzsche focus his attention directly on the collective aspect of the god's murder, but his entire problematic depends on this and his most interesting fragments clearly demonstrate that need. This is the case, especially, of a well-known text that figures in *The Will to Power* under the number 1052.

Nietzsche himself gave that important text a title: "The Two Types: Dionysus and the Crucified." The second paragraph formulates most clearly the attitude of Nietzsche:

> Dionysus versus the "Crucified": there you have the antithesis. It is *not* a difference in regard to their martyrdom — it is a difference in the meaning of it. Life itself, its eternal fruitfulness and recurrence, creates torment, destruction, the will to annihilation. In the other case, suffering — the "Crucified as the innocent one" — counts as an objection to this life, as a formula for its condemnation. — One will see that the problem is that of the meaning of suffering: whether a Christian meaning or a tragic meaning. In the former case, it is supposed to be the path to a holy existence; in the latter case, being is counted as *holy enough* to justify even a monstrous amount of suffering. The tragic man affirms even the

> harshest suffering.... Dionysus cut to pieces is a *promise* of life: it will be eternally reborn and return again from destruction.

Nietzsche obviously felt that the collective murder of Dionysus, in the episode of the Titans, is analogous enough to the Passion of Jesus to be regarded as equivalent. There is a difference between the two but "it is *not* a difference in regard to their martyrdom." The italics are Nietzsche's.

The insight regarding the similarity of the two collective deaths is not uncommon among thinkers and anthropologists of the period. It is the insight of Freud's *Totem and Taboo* as well. It has disappeared from modern anthropology, lost and buried beneath the fast accumulating rubble of scholarly fashion. The structuralist analyst, for instance, is still concerned with the episode of the Titans in the Dionysus saga but his interest has shifted from the murder of the god and the cannibalistic feast to the culinary preparation that took place in between, an interesting question no doubt but one that diverts us from the tragic apprehension of Nietzsche.

When the anthropologists first observed the great abundance of gods collectively murdered in religious cults everywhere, they felt they had discovered something important and so did Nietzsche, obviously. This insight provided students of religion with a powerful focus for comparative analysis. There is no sacrificial religion without a drama at the center, and the more closely you observe it, the more you discover that the features common to the *martyrdom* of Dionysus and Jesus are also common to an immeasurable number of other cults not only in Greek or Indo-European religions but in the entire world.

This remarkable similarity is one important reason why the later Nietzsche can resort to a single symbol, Dionysus, for countless mythological cults. To say that Dionysus stands for some kind of nonbiblical monotheism is a little ludicrous really and unworthy of Heidegger.

Even though anthropologists never discovered why all these cults had that collective drama as a center, they felt entitled to draw some preliminary conclusions from its constant presence. They were positivists, of course, men who believed in facts and nothing but hard facts.

If the facts are the same in all these cults, it can be safely assumed, or so they thought, that these religions must be the same. And this element of sameness is obviously present in the Judaic religion with its ritual sacrifices, and even more spectacularly in the Christian religion. The Passion of Jesus certainly constitutes the heart of the Gospels, and what is it if not one more instance of these collective murders that are the daily bread of religions all over the world?

This point was made in almost all great works of religious anthropology between 1850 and World War I. Even today, it remains the hidden basis and principal argument, at least potentially, for what has become a popular cliché regarding the many religions of mankind. All of them are "more or less alike."

Although, or rather because Nietzsche shared this comparative insight regarding collective murder and sacrifice, he refrained from the habitual conclusion. The only other thinker who also did, at least up to a point, was Freud.

Nietzsche rejected that conclusion because he was no positivist. He knew that the "facts" mean nothing unless and until they are interpreted. The martyrdom of Dionysus is interpreted by the adepts of his cult in a manner quite different from the Christian interpretation of Jesus' Passion.

In the case of Jesus, the emphasis lies on the *innocence* of the victim and, as a consequence, on the guilt of his murderers. One could object that Dionysus, too, was martyred wrongly and that the Titans were just as guilty from the standpoint of the myth as the murderers of Jesus, and they must have been indeed, since they were destroyed by the thunder of Zeus.

Nietzsche did not even mention this objection because he saw its superficiality. In all the other episodes of the Dionysus cycle, there is a collective *diasparagmos,* a martyrdom similar to the martyrdom of Dionysus at the hands of the Titans. In all of these, however, the god is not the victim but the instigator of mob lynching.

Every time Dionysus appears, a victim is dismembered and often devoured by his or her many murderers. The god can be the victim and he can also be the chief murderer. He can be victimized and he can be a victimizer. This change of roles, which also occurs in most primitive religions, clearly confirms what Nietzsche thought regarding the indifference of mythology toward biblical morality.

From the one episode in which Dionysus himself is the victim, one cannot conclude that the Dionysian as such condemns violence in the sense that the Gospels do. It is inconceivable that Jesus could become the instigator of some "holy lynching." When the possibility of lynching occurs in the Gospels, as in the case of the adulterous woman about to be stoned (John 8:2–11), Jesus forestalls the violence and disperses the mob.

At some point, no doubt, with the orphic tradition, the murder of the little Dionysus became a symbol of the human propensity to evil, in a manner that could be said to approximate somewhat the Christian view of the Passion, but this view was completely alien to the Dionysus that Nietzsche opposed to "the Crucified": It is a reinterpretation of the old myth that must have occurred under the influence of the Bible.

There are two types of religion, according to Nietzsche. The first one, the pagan, understands that "life itself, its eternal fruitfulness and recurrence, creates torment, destruction, the will to annihilate," and it says yes to all this; it assumes willingly the worst together with the best. It is beyond good and evil. "It affirms event he harshest suffering," as Nietzsche puts it.

The second type of religion rejects this same suffering, Nietzsche thought. It is interesting that Nietzsche would have condemned Christianity for rejecting suffering. The habitual criticism is that Christianity encourages suffering. Nietzsche saw clearly that Jesus died not as a sacrificial victim of the Dionysian type, but against all such sacrifices. Nietzsche accused this death of being a hidden act of *ressentiment* because it reveals the injustice of all such deaths and the "absurdity" not of one specific mob only but of all "Dionysian" mobs the world over. The word "absurdity" is Nietzsche's own.

When Nietzsche keeps repeating that the Passion of Jesus is "an objection to life," or "a formula for its condemnation," he understands that the Christian Passion is a rejection and an indictment of everything upon which the old pagan religions were founded and with them all human societies worth their salt, in Nietzsche's estimation, the societies in which "the strong and the victorious" were not prevented by the downtrodden masses from enjoying the fruits of their superiority.

Nietzsche, in short, espoused the common ethnological understanding of his time regarding the presence of violence at the heart of most religious cults but he rejected the positivistic conclusion that puts all these cults in the same bag. He singled out the biblical and the Christian not because Jesus' martyrdom is different but because it is not. It has to be the same for that martyrdom of Jesus to be an explicit allusion to the genesis of all pagan religions and a silent but definitive condemnation of pagan order, of all human order really.

The Christian Passion is not anti-Jewish as the vulgar anti-Semites believe; it is anti-pagan; it reinterprets religious violence in such a negative fashion as to make its perpetrators feel guilty for committing it, even for silently accepting it. Since all human culture is grounded in this collective violence, the whole human race is declared guilty from the standpoint of the Gospels. Life itself is slandered because life cannot continue and organize itself without this type of violence.

The Jewish Bible, the Old Testament of the Christians, is similar to the New in respect to the issue discussed in fragment 1052. A positivistic anthropologist sees no real difference between the Romulus story and the Cain story. In both stories, a brother kills his brother and a human community is founded. The data of the stories are the same but in the Bible, the interpretation is unique. It is not the same thing to interpret the same murder as a glorious deed with the Romans and to interpret it as a crime with the Bible.

In the Bible, the story of Cain is symbolical not of one human society only but of many. It is a statement about human culture in general. And it may be more pertinent than all other discussions of anthropological origins. Either the vast number of brothers killing brothers and other similar crimes in innumerable founding myths signifies nothing at all, or it points to a violent origin of human society passively reflected and assumed by mythological cultures whereas it is denounced and rejected by the Bible and the Christian Gospels.

All mythological heroes are fundamentally the same. If you call them Cain, however, your interpretation of mythology is not the same as if you call them Dionysus. Nietzsche is not satisfied with ignoring the Bible in the sense that his time is beginning to do; he is trying to reverse it and to rehabilitate the violence of Cain.

Cain, Romulus, and Dionysus commit the same deed and, from the standpoint of the Gospels, they must be given the same name. It is not the name of a monotheistic god but the name of the one "who was a murderer from the beginning" (John 8:44), Satan, a word that really means the false accuser, whereas the Paraclete, the Holy Spirit of the Christians, really means the lawyer for the defense, the one who turns all martyrs into witnesses to the truth of the Gospels, therefore to the untruth of their own violent deaths.

All four Gospels explicitly link the innocent death of Jesus to the death of all previous collective victims beginning with "Abel the Just." The violence of Cain is part of a long chain of murders that leads to the Passion conceived as a return of the same reenacted, this time, in the full light of a revelation that spells the doom of "the prince of this world," or "the powers of this world," or "the celestial powers." All this refers to the end of the type of society grounded in the Dionysian attitude, in the docile acceptance of the scapegoat process and of its violence.

We do not have to share Nietzsche's value judgment to appreciate his understanding of the irreconcilable opposition between the Bible and mythology, his disgust with the bland eclecticism that dissolves all sharp issues and dominates the atheism of our time, as well as its vague and shapeless religiosity.

Nietzsche is a marvelous antidote to all fundamentally anti-biblical efforts to turn mythology into a kind of Bible, and that is the enterprise of all the Jungians of this world, or to dissolve the Bible into mythology, and that is the enterprise of more or less everybody else.

You find nothing in Nietzsche that recalls the saccharine idealization of primitive culture that began at the end of the eighteenth century and that we have so successfully revived. At the very height of the great syncretic mishmash of modernity, Nietzsche drew attention to the irreconcilable opposition between a mythological vision grounded in the perspective of the victimizers and a biblical inspiration that from the beginning tends to side with the victims and produces not only very different results from the ethical but also from the intellectual standpoint.

Nietzsche's value judgment is untenable. Pious efforts to exonerate the thinker from the consequences of his own thinking are misguided. It is undeniable that he himself extended the scope of this judgment to political and ethical questions in a manner that can only provide encouragement to the worst ideological aberrations.

Hundreds of texts can be quoted that show beyond all doubt that Nietzsche's fierce stubbornness in opposing the inspiration of the Bible in favor of victims logically and inexorably led him toward the more and more inhuman attitudes of his later years which he espoused, in words of course rather than in deeds, with a fortitude worthy of a better cause.

There is a tendency for critics to play hide and seek with the later writings of Nietzsche. It would be more interesting to investigate the inner compulsion that has led so many intellectuals to adopt inhuman standards in the last two centuries. No one exemplifies this tendency with the perfection that Nietzsche does. *Ressentiment* has to be part of the picture of course. One essential thing about *ressentiment* is that its ultimate target is always *ressentiment* itself, its own mirror image, under a slightly different mask that makes it unrecognizable.

Ressentiment is the interiorization of weakened vengeance. Nietzsche suffers so much from it that he mistakes it for the original and primary form of vengeance. He sees *ressentiment* not merely as the child of Christianity, which it certainly is, but also as its father which it certainly is not.

Ressentiment flourishes in a world where real vengeance (Dionysus) has been weakened. The Bible and the Gospels have diminished the violence of vengeance and turned it to *ressentiment* not because they originate in the latter but because their real target is vengeance it all its forms, and they have succeeded only in wounding vengeance, not in eliminating it. The Gospels are indirectly responsible; we alone are directly responsible. *Ressentiment* is the manner in which the spirit of vengeance survives the impact of Christianity and turns the Gospels to its own use.

Nietzsche was less blind to the role of vengeance in human culture than most people of his time, but nevertheless there was blindness in him. He analyzed *ressentiment* and all its works with enormous power. He did not see that the evil he was fighting was a relatively minor evil compared to the more violent forms of vengeance.

His insight was partly blunted by the deceptive quiet of his post-Christian society. He could afford the luxury of resenting *ressentiment* so much that it appeared as a fate worse than real vengeance. Being absent from the scene, real vengeance was never seriously apprehended. Unthinkingly, like so many thinkers of his age and ours, Nietzsche called on Dionysus, begging him to bring back real vengeance as a cure for what seemed to him the worst of all possible fates, *ressentiment.*

Such frivolity could flourish only in our privileged centuries, in privileged parts of the world where real vengeance had retreated so much that its terror had become unintelligible. But sincere prayers are never in vain, and the prayers of those who desired the return of vengeance have finally been heard.

Real vengeance is back among us in the shape of nuclear and other absolute weapons, reducing our planet to the size of a global primitive village, terrified one again by the possibility of unlimited blood feud. Real vengeance is so awesome that even the most vengeful men do not dare to unleash it, knowing perfectly well that all the dreadful things they can do unto their enemies, their enemies can also do unto them.

Compared to this, *ressentiment* and other nineteenth-century annoyances pale to insignificance, or rather their only significance is the increasing rage everywhere that turns *ressentiment* back into irrepressible vengeance and can unleash the unspeakable.

At more and more levels of reality, the urgency of the Gospel message can no longer be disregarded with impunity. Those thinkers who, like Nietzsche, unthinkingly appealed to real vengeance in their itch to get rid of *ressentiment* resemble these foolish characters in fairy tales who make the wrong wish and come to grief when it comes true.

This can be interpreted as a warning of sorts. But this warning can and is disregarded with impunity by almost everybody. Most people go on spouting nineteenth-century ideas as if the return of real vengeance in our world were not an accomplished fact. The truth is that, for the time being at least, real vengeance has a power of dissuasion such that, concretely, nothing has changed. The very enormity of the threat protects us from the threatened violence. *Ressentiment* is intense enough to generate more and more intellectual nihilism but not intense enough so far to annihilate real being.

Real vengeance has not yet concretely demonstrated its power upon our lives and it never will, in a sense, because if it did, there would be no more lives to be affected by anything. There would be no one left to acknowledge the return of absolute vengeance as the real event of our time.

As a result one can go on thinking frivolously and pretending today that Nietzsche makes sense as a teacher of ethics, or of history, or as a philosopher, or as a guide for some kind of "lifestyle," or whatever. This cannot fail to sound more futile and unreal with each passing year. The price to be paid for this is the price any historical era must pay for avoiding its real issues, a certain barrenness of the spirit and a growing sterility in all its "cultural activities."

Our military men love to give mythological names to their nuclear missiles, Pluto, Poseidon, Ariadne, and the like. Too bad they never resorted to Dionysus himself, but it really does not matter. Those who understand do not need such literalness and it would not make any impression on those who do not understand. The contemporary use of mythology is more profound that all the mythological games of our philosophers since the Renaissance.

Even though Nietzsche had ceased writing long before his espousal of mythological violence began to reveal its frivolous side, there was something in him that fiercely resisted his own wager. When studying "Dionysus *versus* the Crucified," we should place the emphasis on that "versus." We can hear in it an echo of the fierce battle Nietzsche fought and finally lost in his effort to insure the revenge of Dionysus over the Crucified. We can also hear these echoes in the inhuman aspects of Nietzsche's writing at the time, in the obligation he imposed upon himself to justify even the worst forms of oppression and persecution.

There is a universal wager nowadays against the biblical principle regarded as intrinsically perverse rather than as perverted by the enormous human ingenuity in the service of this perversion. This wager cannot be sustained without some form of the sacred, and it has to be that violent sacred which Nietzsche calls Dionysus. Even though Heidegger also detected the presence of violence in it, he too glorified the primitive *sacred.* He looked forward to future epiphanies of it and did not anticipate any particular problems with this violence even though he was writing about this after the end of World War II.

In his later years, Nietzsche kept reviving, glorifying, and modernizing more and more sinister aspects of the primitive sacred. I am convinced that this process became more intolerable as it became more radical and led to his final breakdown.

The greatness of Nietzsche is that he committed himself totally to that process and he paid for his commitment literally with his life. For things to come to such a pass, the forces on both sides had to be almost evenly balanced. As the prophets would say: "It is a dreadful fate to fall into the hands of the living God."

Paradoxically, Nietzsche is the one thinker in the modern world whose work did achieve something that the Christian thinkers have always failed to achieve. They have never dared. He put his finger on that "sword" that Jesus said he brought, the sword destructive of human culture, that sword no human being can fail to dread and resent even though — or is it because? — it belongs to what Pascal calls *l'ordre de la charité.*

This force destroys the old sacred through the revelation of its violent nature, but so far, it has only managed to wound it, turning it into a fierce monster that now threatens to devour us all. Mimetic doubles are everywhere in that cosmic battle and it is tempting to see nothing else, nothing but empty mimetic rivalry in the opposition between Dionysus and the Crucified.

This is what Heidegger did. Heidegger, here, was still the voice of a modern demystification that exposes so many false differences that in the end it misses the one and only difference that is real.

Heidegger fought on the same side as Nietzsche, no doubt, the side of the old sacred, but on positions less exposed, less forward, less dangerous and revealing than Nietzsche's. He has succeeded, at least for a while, in neutralizing the "imprudence" of Nietzsche in the domain of religion. With time, it will become easier and easier to realize that, before exploding into the hands of its maker, this machine was producing the opposite of what it was built for, the glorification of what is was supposed to vilify, the vilification of what it was supposed to celebrate.

For quite a few years, I have emphasized the role of collective violence in the genesis of the primitive sacred and the role of the Bible in the increasing intelligibility of that genesis. My purpose in the present essay is to show that Nietzsche is deeply but paradoxically involved in that process.

The present effort will probably meet with skepticism. Many readers will suspect that I am projecting upon Nietzsche a preoccupation too idiosyncratic to yield significant results. This attempt has to result not in a mutilation of what Nietzsche "really thought" (which does not seem to matter anymore and cannot be reached in any case), but in a revelation of the real fecundity of Nietzsche's work, his possible contribution to the critical formulae currently fashionable.

The general reaction to the theme of *the collective murder of God* resembles the bewilderment and amused condescension that greeted the Nietzschean madman when he addressed his contemporaries in the market place. This anonymous lunatic

> lit a lantern in the bright morning hours, ran to the market and cried incessantly, "I seek God, I seek God!" As many of those who do not believe in God were standing around just then, he provoked much laughter. Why, did he get lost? said one. Did he lose his way like a child? said another. Or is he hiding? Is he afraid of us? Has he gone on a voyage? or emigrated? Thus they yelled and laughed.

This is the beginning of the most famous text in *The Gay Science,* aphorism 125. Even today, especially today perhaps, whoever touches upon this untouchable subject, *the collective murder of God,* finds himself in a position curiously reminiscent of the one described here. After more than a century, nothing has really changed, especially in those academic circles that did not appreciate Nietzsche at the time any more than he appreciated them.

My readers are too careful with texts, too erudite, attentive, deliberate, thorough, and above all too shrewd, too good as readers of texts to be scandalized, or ever surprised when they see me appropriate this text in the informal fashion that I just did. They certainly would not dispute my right to do this. They have kept in mind the extraordinary similarity of content if not of form between my somewhat tiresome insistence on the religious significance of the collective murder and the parallel insistence of this enigmatic text.

Here is the first proclamation of the madman:

> "Whither is God," he cried. "I shall tell you. We have killed him—you and I. All of us are his murderers. But how have we done this? How were we able to drink up the sea . . . ?

Since the late eighteenth century, from Jean Paul to Victor Hugo and beyond, pronouncements regarding the death of God have multiplied with each passing year, and belated prophets are now forming what is probably the largest crowd ever gathered in our intellectual history. What everybody has been announcing, of course, is that the biblical god is dying of old age. It is a more or less natural death in other words.

Most people believe that Nietzsche's text refers exclusively to modern atheism. This is part of the story, no doubt, but only a part, and an enigmatic part already because it rejects very pointedly the very notion everybody is trying to find there, the notion of God as something childish and meaningless really that men gradually learned to do without in the modern age, as they became more "mature" and learned about electricity, and now computers.

Instead of that gradual fading away of God, with no particular violence or drama, Nietzsche sees the disappearance of God as a horrible murder in which every man is involved: "*We have killed him*—you and I. All of us are his murderers."

"If God never existed, if there is no such thing as God, how could he be killed?" That is the question only the uninformed reader dares to ask and, as usual with great texts, it is a much smarter one than all the "informed" philosophical questions.

Gods do not have to exist really in order to be murdered. As a matter of fact, unless they are first murdered they will never exist. Unlike ordinary beings who can exist only if they are not murdered, gods begin to exist as gods, at least in the eyes of men, only after they have been murdered.

In the entire text, the hackneyed expression "God is dead" appears in one passage only, and it is followed by an insistent return upon the theme of the collective murder of God, as if Nietzsche suddenly realized the difference between the hackneyed conception of God's "death" as a spectacle passively watched and the active deed he had in mind, the collective crime that seems to come from nowhere.

And he seems to have felt that the collective crime was the more powerful idea but harder to communicate, an idea indeed that would be resisted and eluded with the utmost energy. More emphasis was needed, therefore, and Nietzsche provided it, including even a gory description of the collective murder of God:

> God is dead. God remains dead. And we have killed him. How shall we, the murderers of all murderers, comfort ourselves? What was holiest and most powerful of all that the world has yet owned has bled to death under our knives. Who will wipe this blood off us? What water is there for us to clean ourselves? What festivals of atonement, what sacred games shall we have to invent?

The first two sentences are all we have in that text that resembles the old "God is dead" theme. But this is enough of an excuse for all the commentators to seize upon it and substitute once more the harmless cliché for what Nietzsche is really saying. The references to the blood, and to the knife, and to the wiping of the blood, forcefully take us back to the first announcement of the madman. God did not die a natural death; he was collectively killed.

And the crime is so great that new festivals of atonement, new sacred games will have to be invented. New rituals will undoubtedly appear. The consequences of God's murder are religious, therefore, purely religious. The very deed that seems to put an end to the religious process is really the origin of that process, the sum total of it, really, the religious process par excellence. These new festivals and sacred games will certainly reenact the collective murder of God. They will be sacrificial rites. The death of God is also his birth.

If God is always the product of his own collective murder, does not this text really say that the death of the gods is their life and that the life of the gods is their death? What kind of eternal return of religion is this? Can Nietzsche himself account for all this?

When it comes to what everybody improperly calls the death of God, the only text that is ever quoted is this one, but no reference is ever made to the substitution of God's murder for the earlier peaceful death. Is it not strange?

On "the death of God" this is only one text among many, but it is the most memorable. Unquestionably, the element of novelty in it stems from the replacement of death by murder. And yet, when the admirers of that text refer to it, they always label it as the greatest text on the death of God. They always substitute their own concept of God's death for the more mysterious murder of Nietzsche.

The aura of this text is inseparable from its dramatic power, and here as in Greek tragedy and everywhere else, dramatic power is rooted in the collective murder of God. The genius of Nietzsche takes him to the real beginning.

Perfectly respectable scholars, men who would not touch my own collective murder with a ten-foot pole, quote Nietzsche's text in preference to any other, but their comments betray no awareness of the murder theme. They never seem to notice the strange little twist that makes this text different from all others, *even though it is this difference that determines their preference.*

They see this difference as a purely *esthetic* difference, of course. The esthetic difference par excellence, I would add. When Nietzsche is quoted, a certain excitement is generated, even today. Quite innocently and unconsciously, of course, the collective murder of God becomes our own deed too. We are invited to partake in it. It is a kind of avant-garde version of the Eucharist, a symbolic sacrifice that has not yet completely exhausted its ritual efficacy *because its significance is not perceived.* Some people have tried to transfer the efficacy of Nietzsche's text to the "death of man" and now the death of science, of truth, of almost everything, but they do not see that, each time, they should say murder and anyway, the sacred *pharmakon* has already evaporated.

Aphorism 125 functions in the same manner as the collective murder itself, which is now hidden behind the theme of an entirely "natural" and peaceful death, a radically undramatic death, a death *sans histoire.* The text on the death of God functions as one more murder of God as long as the theme of the murder remains unacknowledged. Even this textual epiphany of the divine is the product of a collective murder that the murderers are not aware of having committed. "This deed is still more distant from them than the most distant stars—*and yet they have done it themselves.*"

Heidegger gave what is regarded by many as the "definitive" comment about that text. This essay is separate from his two-volume *Nietzsche,* and its title already spells out the effort to reinsert Nietzsche into a tradition from which this text secedes, a tradition to which Heidegger had really returned. The title is, of course, "Nietzsche's Word, God Is Dead."

It is relevant to observe at this point that, except for his vocabulary, Heidegger's pronouncements on the future of the religious in general are a continuation of nineteenth-century historicism. Like Victor Hugo or any nineteenth-century idealist, Heidegger felt that the death of an exhausted religion, the biblical religion, would leave room for the *independent* birth of some new god, a birth that would not be rooted in the death of the hated biblical God.

Heidegger often spoke mysteriously of some god that should appear at some point in the future. When he was in the right mood, he would graciously extend the wondrous promise of some brand new divinity to his theologically minded admirers — he had quite a few — eagerly but respectfully waiting for the latest word from high above, regarding a possible future for that lesser authority, God.

Even if we had not read it we could have predicted that Heidegger's essay could only bury the dramatic force of Nietzsche's madman under the crushing weight of its philosophical pedantry. And indeed it does. According to Heidegger the madman's announcement really means: "the end of the supra-sensible in the platonic sense."

After this breathtaking announcement you cannot expect from someone like Heidegger that he would take notice of something as insignificant as the collective murder of God. Obviously this is the type of rhetorical ornament that a thinker still superior to Nietzsche, one that has really gone beyond the supra-sensible in the platonic sense, should do well to avoid.

Heidegger wrote that, even though no specific god is mentioned, the only god to whom Nietzsche can and must allude is the Christian God. That last precision fits well with the rest of his essay. Even though Heidegger haughtily protests that his interpretation has nothing to do with the "vulgar atheism" that is so often read into this text, the difference is not always visible to me.

To speak primarily of "the death of God," apropos of this text, as Heidegger does, is to fall into the same trap as everybody before. All gods are "beings" (*Seiende*) with a certain historical lifespan, and then they must die, unlike Being itself (*Sein*). Now that the twilight of the biblical God has finally come, similar to the twilight and death of the pagan gods before, Dionysus for instance, some entirely new gods may well show up in the future. Heidegger thought he could recognize his own thought in the text of *The Gay Science* but he was wrong. He would have been well advised, from his own standpoint, if he had distrusted that text to the same extent that he did *Dionysus versus the Crucified*. From the standpoint of modernistic orthodoxy, the one is as treacherous as the other.

But was Nietzsche's own thought really that different from Heidegger's, especially in 1882? Explicitly perhaps, it was not, but in the writing of that text, when Nietzsche shifted from the death of God to his murder, he must have felt, as we all feel, the sudden enormous increase in the symbolical power at his disposal. It was like an unexpected gift from the gods, and Nietzsche was not the sort of writer who would refuse such a gift.

The fact that he made that shift from death to murder suggests that the real basis, the ultimate foundation for the later parallel and opposition between Dionysus and the Crucified was already a preoccupation of his, a preoccupation that rarely comes to the fore, it seems — a careful analysis might still show otherwise — but one that must have been quite pregnant with significance in order to generate such a great and enigmatic text as this collective murder of God.

The ultimate foundation of the collective murder of God is identical, of course, with that *martyrdom* of Dionysus which is recognized as identical to the *martyrdom* of Jesus in fragment 1052 of *The Will to Power.* There is no difference between this dual insight and the definition of God's disappearance in our world as one more instance of that martyrdom. This does not mean that all these murders can really be equated to each other, of course.

The same insight dominates the two texts we have read. And this insight is never more prominent in Nietzsche's mind than at the very instant before the final breakdown, when the formula "Dionysus *versus* the Crucified" is changed to "Dionysus *and* the Crucified."

It cannot mean at this late stage that Nietzsche is turning into a positivist and that he gives up the difference that interpretation makes. But it certainly means that the difference for which he has been fighting is breaking down and collapsing back into the undifferentiation from which it had earlier emerged.

Aphorism 125 expresses the first undifferentiation, enormously creative and symbolically polyvalent in its reaching for the essential significance of the murder of God. If we believe, with Heidegger, that the Christian God alone is present in this text, we will never apprehend its enormous polyvalence. The text plays with the murder of God on several primary levels that tend to contaminate each other but can nevertheless be logically distinguished from one another.

The most obvious level is the modern disappearance of god as collective murder; a little behind comes the collective murder of the pagan gods as the generative power behind their existence, and way behind, the most difficult level of all, is the Passion of Jesus that cannot be the death of the Christian God if the murders of the gods are always their birth but that could well be the death of all other gods in the banal sense we have in mind when we talk of "the death of god." It is not quite true, however, and these pagan gods "die hard," or rather they are perpetually reborn in works like Nietzsche's own.

What are we to do with such a maelstrom of collective murders? In order to make sure that the madman makes sense on more than one level, let us listen to someone who certainly is not mad, at least not in our current theoretical Gospel, the great Sigmund Freud.

A few years after Nietzsche wrote *The Gay Science,* Freud discovered, he thought, that all "festivals of purification and atonement, all sacred games," all the religious rituals of mankind, are rooted in the collective murder of some real victim men call God. . . .

My readers are frowning. Yes, I know; that is not a text of Freud that should be quoted. Our great thinkers do not think much of it. It is an exception. They really think that Freud was temporarily out of his mind when he wrote it, madly estranged from his own best work. And indeed he was like the madman of *The Gay Science*. He dared talk about that taboo subject, the collective murder of God. That is the only reason *Totem and Taboo* has been excommunicated and declared anathema. Just as there are nonpersons nowadays, there are also nonbooks, which should never be mentioned, even when they seem to belong to the work of sacred authorities.

Aphorism 125 of *The Gay Science* has been treated very differently from *Totem and Taboo*. It has been enshrined and declared sacred. But this idolatry is really the other side of an excommunication and the result shows it. Nietzsche's statement on the collective murder of God is just as ignored as Freud's. The excommunication and enshrinement are two opposite means to achieve the same end, which is to prevent any perception of a most enigmatic similarity between Freud and Nietzsche on the question of God. On everything else, these two texts are extremely distant from each other and their overlapping in respect to the fundamental theme of the collective murder of God should provide food for thought, but it does not. Why?

Let us ask Nietzsche for the answer to that question. He knows the answer very well. We are not yet ready, we are never ready for a real investigation of the subject:

> "I come too early," [the madman] said then; "my time has not come yet. This tremendous event is still on its way, still wandering — it has not yet reached the ears of man. Lightning and thunder require time, the light of the stars requires time, deeds require time even after they are done, before they can be seen and heard. This deed is still more distant from them than the most distant stars — *and yet they have done it themselves.*"

Epilogue

The Anthropology of the Cross: A Conversation with René Girard

James Williams: As you look back over your career, what has been the most satisfying thing to you in your work?

René Girard: The most satisfying thing has been the actual experience of discovery. I would say that there have been three great moments in the process of my thinking and writing.

First was mimetic desire and rivalry, when I realized that it accounted for so much. The second was the discovery of the scapegoat mechanism. This basically completed the mimetic theory. I felt it gave a highly plausible interpretation of myth and ritual in archaic cultures. From that time on I was convinced that archaic cultures, far from being simply lost in superstition or having no constancy or stability, represented a great human achievement.

The third great moment of discovery for me was when I began to see the uniqueness of the Bible, especially the Christian text, from the standpoint of the scapegoat theory. The mimetic representation of scapegoating in the Passion was the solution to the relationship of the Gospels and archaic cultures. In the Gospels we have the revelation of the mechanism that dominates culture unconsciously.

It seemed to me, as I experienced these moments, that a great deal of evidence was piling up, an avalanche, to support them. I naively thought that everyone would agree with my theory immediately, because I saw it as so obvious and overpowering.

J.W.: Concerning the relation of the New Testament to the full development of the mimetic scapegoat theory, already in your first book, *Deceit, Desire, and the Novel,* you recognize the importance of the Gospels. But are you saying it took a number of years for the full extent of the Passion as revelation of the scapegoat mechanism to occur to you?

R.G.: Sure. I recognized the importance of the Gospels in the individual experiences of the novelists who came to grips with mimetic desire and came to a knowledge of mimetic desire. In fact, they have a kind of conversion experience, and this conversion is of the same nature as the shift from mythology to the Gospels. Of course, I didn't fully understand that at the time.

This is the most difficult thing for people to understand about my theory — that scapegoating does not play an essential role in the Gospels, whereas it has an enormous role in myths since it generates them. Many observers think that because scapegoating becomes more and more visible in them, the Gospels must approve of it, they must advocate some kind of scapegoat religion. But to use a modern analogy from the history of France, this would be like saying the pro-Dreyfus people were really the scapegoaters of Dreyfus. This is the mistake so many theologians and biblical scholars have made regarding the mimetic scapegoat theory. They simply do not understand the enormous difference that the representation of scapegoating makes. They think only in terms of themes rather than a hidden, generative mechanism which cannot appear in what it generates.

J.W.: If the Gospels could be understood by analogy to the pro-Dreyfus party, give another similar historical instance of scapegoating.

R.G.: An example which I have been working on a little bit is Joan of Arc. The people who put her on trial divinized her, or "demonized" her, in the sense of regarding her as a witch. She was avowed to have supernatural powers and turned into a witch, whereas her canonization by the church acknowledges another form of relationship to the supernatural which is different from the demonized-divinized scapegoat. Now there is a form of divinization reported in the Gospels, which is magical and mythical, for instance Herod Antipas's belief in the resurrection of John the Baptist, and the divinization of Christ, which is just the opposite. The Gospels seem so close to myth in a way, and yet they are poles apart.

This is a difficult problem because certain forms of monotheism move God so far away from any involvement in the scapegoat mechanism that they view with suspicion any contact with it in religious thought and symbolism. But I think the power and truth of Christianity is that it completes the great forms of monotheism, as in Judaism and Islam, by witnessing to the God who reveals himself to be the *arch*-scapegoat in order to liberate humankind.

J.W.: Does the analogy of Joan of Arc imply that the scapegoating of Jesus may have occurred even among his own followers?

R.G.: Yes, and the conception of Jesus as some kind of primitive God.

You find a recognition of that in Mark and Matthew especially. Peter, James, and John expect him to be a kind of divine potentate when he comes into his full honor and glory. Herod Antipas believes that Jesus is John the Baptist resurrected. This divinizing of John is a kind of mythical genesis. I think this is why there is a fairly long description of the murder, which is an analog of the Passion. But not only an analog of the Passion, for there were many such murders — mythical, nonmythical, prophetic — in which a crowd united against a victim.

In the Herod story the dancing of Herod's stepdaughter was important in the ritual aspects of the action of the crowd.

J.W.: The dancing is a textual signal of scapegoating?

R.G.: Yes. The story of the beheading of John is one of the reasons why the synoptic Gospels are so incredibly valuable for understanding the anthropology of revelation.

J.W.: The Gospel of Luke omits the banquet and dancing episode.

R.G.: Yes, but Luke has another scene in which Herod and Pilate become friends when Pilate sends Jesus to Herod for questioning after he is arrested. This shows that Luke is aware of the pacifying effect of scapegoating. This is the communion of the scapegoaters as opposed to the Christian communion. So if you put this scene with the beheading of John in Mark and Matthew, you can see how the Gospels complement each other in dealing with the mythical tendencies of scapegoating.

J.W.: What is the most disappointing aspect of your career?

R.G.: I think that I have not expressed the relation of the Gospel to mythology in a way that makes it clear to everybody. It should be possible to find more metaphors from different areas of experience which are familiar to everyone. Also, I would like to do a better job of showing that the Gospels enable one to read and decipher myth.

Until now the order of discovery for me has been mimetic desire, archaic religion and culture, and finally the Christian text. It should be possible, especially for a Christian scholar, to reverse this order and analyze myth and culture from the standpoint of the Gospels.

J.W.: The Gospels themselves have come under attack as sources of scapegoating and demonization. To take the Gospels seriously in the way you do is extremely difficult.

R.G.: It is difficult because it is also too simple. Everything that happened to Jesus is happening to the texts of revelation themselves. This scapegoating of the Gospel texts is probably a necessary — but not excusable — phase that we are going through. It is a form of ingratitude toward God, and one should say so, boldly.

J.W.: So to discern the relation of the Gospels to myth and misunderstanding in our culture, where do you look? Do you find signs in our time?

R.G.: Well, I look first to the Gospels themselves, and particularly to certain key passages. Of course, the Gospels must look not like a *tour de force* but another myth to many readers now because they are centered on Jesus, and how could this reveal mythology? But in my view the whole theory of Satan, for example, is completely rational; the Gospels unveil Satan as the principle of destructive mimesis in the world. Or to take another example, Herod murders John, divinizes him, but he never repents. Peter denies his association with Jesus and later recognizes him as his risen lord, and Paul persecutes the followers of Christ before his own revelatory experience. But both Peter and Paul repent. This is the main difference made by the resurrection, as contrasted to human divinization or apotheosis: repentance.

J.W.: Do you want to say any more about the use of metaphor and analogy to understand the Gospel texts?

R.G.: Well, I was talking about Joan of Arc. The sources about her are pretty reliable. This is a perfect example of persecution and ascription of supernatural powers to someone considered a witch and disrupter of public order. An instance like this should be of great interest to the Jews because of what they have suffered in history.

J.W.: Aren't all these topics, such as the fate of Joan of Arc, encumbered with the "political correctness" and obsession with victims of those who study them?

R.G.: Political correctness is good to the degree that we now have an awareness of victimization and victimary mechanisms. But now this awareness supports attacks on Christianity and its texts, which are the very inspiration of our modern concern for the victim.

J.W.: This brings me back to what has been disappointing for you in your career. When you speak of attacks on the Bible, particularly the Gospel texts, I take it you are talking about your critics, at least in part.

R.G.: Yes, I am talking about my critics in part. But you know, I think the attacks on the Gospel are necessary; they are part of an apocalyptic situation.

J.W.: You mean these attacks are part of a sorting or refining process in history?

R.G.: It's part of a process that is revealing the truth of the Gospel.

But I know I am primarily responsible for what I write and how I bring my subject to expression. Anthropologists and theologians, many of them, have not understood what I was about, and I should be able to say it better. I would like to begin at the stage of *Things Hidden,* where the Gospels seem to be explained by the mimetic theory rather than explaining it. It should be possible to move in reverse to myth and mimetic desire. The sequence leading up to *Things Hidden,* which is true, in part, to my own creative experience, gives the erroneous view of a theoretical movement from mimesis to myth, then to the Gospels, whereas in fact, a more fundamental understanding goes in the opposite direction.

J.W.: Do you see signs that reception of your work is beginning to occur?

R.G.: There are some signs, but I'm not sure that at this time there could be a really good reception, especially among academics. It would be such a change in regard to Christianity that it is most unlikely. One can always hope for a good reception of the Gospels which would be closer and truer to them as they really are. If the mimetic theory became fashionable, I would be really worried.

But it is difficult; there are so many tendencies toward politicization, or toward wandering off into irrelevant individualistic spiritualities. Of course, one could go back and see politicization throughout the whole history of Christianity. These attempts at politicization, which take various forms, are part of the progress and regress of revelation in history.

J.W.: What would you say is the most important aspect of your thinking to grasp? If the most important is the most difficult, please comment on that.

R.G.: The most important thing is too simple, I repeat, not to be difficult. It is the reversal of scapegoating, or the shift that shows that scapegoating comes from a cultural mechanism and is not approved by God. We ordinarily like to believe that scapegoating stems from rulers or leaders hatching a plot, but it is much more complex than that. When I use the term "mechanism," as in "scapegoat mechanism," I mean basically and simply a generative principle which works unconsciously in culture and society. As Peter says in Acts, "And now, brothers, I know that you acted in ignorance, as did also your rulers. But what God announced beforehand by the mouth of all the prophets, that his Christ should suffer, he thus fulfilled. So repent, and turn again . . . " (Acts 3:17–19a). Everyone is guilty, yet not completely responsible. I find the mention of the rulers especially interesting. One of our favorite ways of dealing with scapegoating is to see it as a plot of government leaders, whereas the rest of us have not participated in it. But scapegoating is a collective phenomenon. It would not work if it were not. Of course, leaders can manipulate it, but there must be something to manipulate, which is the belief of the crowd, our own belief.

In the Gospels, for example, the priests plot to scapegoat Jesus, but they cannot accomplish this without stirring up the crowd. The crowd takes over the most significant role in the narrative. Mark, above all, makes this clear. Aside from any other details about Pilate, his main fear is that a riot will occur. Pilate is presented as knowing it is a scapegoat situation. If the situation is still fluid, a substitute for the designated scapegoat could be offered (Barabbas). But things have gone too far, so Jesus is put to death. It is a crowd that has called for his death, it was a crowd that welcomed him as he entered Jerusalem. There is nothing, by the way, anti-Semitic about this; it is the Gospels' comment on the mimetic behavior of crowds. Another excellent example of such behavior is found in the book of Job. The people treated him as an idol one day, but turned against him the next.

J.W.: I wonder whether the crowd behavior is even clearer in the book of Job (Job 29:1–30:15).

R.G.: Yes, this is made clear by the metaphor of the mountain torrent (6:15). It does not have a drop of water when you need it, but turns into a deluge when you don't need it. It is a wonderful, mimetic metaphor of the crowd.

J.W.: But back to the reversal of the scapegoating phenomenon in the Gospel texts — do you really think this is the most difficult aspect of your model? Conceptually it is not so difficult, but perhaps psychologically...

R.G.: Let's face it, readers, including academic ones, usually read texts pretty simplistically. They look for *themes,* and since they find a scapegoat theme in the Gospels, for instance, they conclude that the Gospels are built on scapegoating. Myths, they would say, are not about scapegoating because they don't talk about it. But that's just the point: they don't talk about it; they disguise their generative center. It is the most difficult thing to make people conscious of this generative center. It is the sort of thing you either see or do not see. It's like a flash of lightning; you either get it or you don't get it. Ordinary reasoning just loops back on to its own premises.

But there should be a way of expressing this insight which is better than I have done so far. I keep trying and trying. That is why I turn to such historical scapegoats as Joan of Arc or Dreyfus. The people who condemned Dreyfus are the ones who never called him a scapegoat because they turned him into one. To me the Oedipus myth is a still undeciphered Dreyfus case.

J.W.: Let's turn to a part of your theory that may be conceptually difficult for many people who encounter your work: mimetic desire. Don't you think many people have misunderstood mimetic desire or mimesis? Also, it would be helpful if you would say something about its prerepresentational character.

R.G.: There are many who would prefer to say that the real problem is the wish to kill one's own father or mother, and they ignore or resist the possibility that the most common problem — our predicament — is that of trying to beat one's rival at his own game. So there is a resistance to shedding light on the role of rivalry in our own lives.

J.W.: So the difficulty with the concept of mimesis is practically the same as the resistance to the recognition of scapegoating. Just as we ignore or evade knowing ourselves as scapegoaters, so also we ignore or evade our penchant for mimetic rivalry.

R.G.: Yes, a deeper knowledge and self-examination are required. The knowledge of mimesis is really tied to conversion. That is why the matter of *fides quaerens intellectum* (faith seeking understanding) is so important. A personal knowledge, fully rational and yet not always accessible to reason, is needed.

J.W.: René, isn't part of the problem just what you are touching on, that mimesis is really prerational and prerepresentational? This is important, and is not included in any of the selections for the Reader. You seem to be saying at times that to break away from the mimetic predicament...

R.G.: You must change your personality.

J.W.: But that also requires mimesis, does it not? A mimesis that is good, a mimesis of love.

R.G.: Sure. Part of the problem is with the phrase "mimetic desire." And because of Freud the word "desire" connotes the sexual or erotic. I said recently that we should be able to substitute some other term — I don't know, perhaps "drive," or *élan vital,* or even Sartre's "project." Almost any word that could express the dynamism, the dynamics of the entire personality.

J.W.: Here you seem to be distinguishing different kinds of mimesis. But you don't want to say that, do you? In other words, mimesis is always along a continuum.

R.G.: That's right. It is something that involves the whole personality. Sartre's idea of the "project" is appropriate in a way, although resorting to Sartre too exclusively would be misleading. Maybe the idea of Kierkegaard, the idea of subjectivity as passionate inwardness and choice, would be helpful.... I don't know; whatever the term, something bigger and other than "desire" should be used. "Desire" has, necessarily, that narrow libidinal connotation.

J.W.: Okay, let's move on to another part of the question, the relation of mimesis and representation.

R.G.: Well, mimesis is rooted deep in our biology, I'm sure of that. I agree with those who hold that there is a biological basis for holding that the human brain is a kind of mimetic machine. Even ritual, in its earliest stages, is more like a reflexive mimetic repetition than anything that could be called precisely an institution founded on a correct representation of a founding murder. Much like a child's earliest reactions as it begins to learn...

J.W.: You're referring specifically to an originary murder...

R.G.: Yes. Then at a certain stage, the scapegoat phenomenon and its ritual repetition create the possibility of representation, which requires some degree of reflection, and not simply reflexive imitation. So it is that mimesis is "undecidable," in the sense that it is decided in common with the model. Continuity ultimately produced discontinuity. A good model will make our mimesis good (Christ); a bad model will make our mimesis rivalrous.

J.W.: So in beginning stages of what we know as human there was basically reflexive imitation.

R.G.: Yes, that was the primary thing. Representation as such is a late development. It may have taken hundreds of thousands of years, or longer, to reach the representational capacity of "humanity."

From a theological point of view which is compatible, I hope, with my mimetic anthropology, I would say that the Word or Christ is at work in this whole long process toward humanity and representation. Representation is still distorted, of course, in that it distorts or disguises the violence stemming from originary mimesis. This is what I have called *méconnaissance,* misrecognition, or even "misprision," as Shakespeare and Harold Bloom would say. I think Gil Bailie has expressed this well in his recent paper on the vine and the branches: the Word was the light accompanying the "mythic darkness of the sacred violence that accompanied hominization.... Humanity generated its own crude forms of illumination precisely by periodically expelling this light."[1]

J.W.: Another topic not included in the Reader is your hypothesis about the origin of kings and gods. Would you briefly review it now?

R.G.: It is very simple. Scapegoating, when it becomes unanimous, affects the whole community. The crisis has been long; it seems the community is splitting or disintegrating. Then all of a sudden it's over, and it's over because of the scapegoat. Who or what is responsible for ending this crisis? Who or what provoked the crisis? Here arises a problem that is the basis of what must eventually become interpretation and representation, though in primitive or originary situations the crisis and its resolution are still prerepresentational.

Now since the community is not aware of the mimetic nature of its scapegoating, it must look for a cause outside of the community. At this

1. Gil Bailie, "The Vine and Branches Discourse: The Gospel's Psychological Apocalypse," paper written for the annual conference of the Colloquium on Violence and Religion, Stanford University, June 27–29, 1996.

stage the community is humble. It does know its own violence, although it does not understand its source. Indeed, the conflict and violence are so overwhelming — so seemingly "interminable" — that the community does not believe its powers alone could have ended it, just as it does not know how it began. The only convincing answer in this situation is the victim: the victim brought the violence about; the victim ended it. The victim is bad, but the victim is also good. Bad because he or she is blamed for the crisis, but very good because her or his death ends the crisis. This is experienced as so effective that the whole chain of events becomes a mechanism repeated in ritual. In order to repeat the scenario, it is necessary to have a new victim, a substitute, to whom is imputed the behavior that caused the original crisis. The killing of this victim we call sacrifice. But let us imagine what could happen. The repetition of sacrifice is going to evolve, evolve I think in two possible directions. Either the victim will be sacrificed immediately or there will be a waiting period, the victim being already earmarked and present in the community. In the latter instance the victim is alive in the community and already sacred in anticipation of his death. Rather than becoming a god, which I think is what happens when the victim is killed promptly, the victim whose execution is postponed, for any reason whatever, has the opportunity to gain power over people, due to his sacrality. I think the victim in this case eventually becomes what we call a "king." This, by the way, would be a model for how representation evolves out of ritual. You have first the spontaneous unanimity through the victim, then many sacrificial repetitions of this model, and then, eventually, representation in the form of new offices, institutions, etc. So here you have two types of representation: one in which the victim becomes what we call a "god"; another in which the victim's execution is delayed and, in many instances, the victim may be smart enough to capitalize on the sacred powers ascribed to him. The latter is what we call a "king," the origin of political power.

J.W.: What sort of evidence do you think would support this hypothesis? In the case of monarchs we see, of course, that they have been ritually killed, sometimes regularly, sometimes occasionally, and that has occurred even until very recent days...

R.G.: Sure, and it may still be happening. The main evidence is the structural homologies of kingship ritual and sacrificial ritual.

J.W.: So that would be one kind of test of your proposal. But what would you say to someone who replied, in effect, "Is it realistic to think that someone in this archaic or prearchaic situation who is the designated victim could gain that kind of power over others?"

R.G.: Well, for one thing there is evidence from Native American peoples of the not too distant past that an animal captured or a prisoner taken in battle was treated "royally," or "divinely," for a period of time, then executed. If it is true to say that a king is a "living god," it is just as true to say that a god is a dead king. So the question is whether we can understand the death of the victim in these situations as shedding light on the beginnings of human culture and as potentially meaningful in a number of directions, one of them being kingship.

J.W.: Do you think it's possible that in a situation of originary violence, or of the fear of imminent violence, a person could come forward as leader, become designated as you say, but take over due to the force of a powerful personality without being placed in the predicament of the victim who is to be executed? The leader, of course, is always a potential victim.

R.G.: That's true, one can imagine that, but I would prefer not to take the matter outside of my scapegoat hypothesis. You see, becoming a "leader" is not a natural thing among human beings. I don't think one can simply appeal to dominant animals in packs and herds, for example; all the symbols of human leadership are associated with victimage. Now, of course, there is some evidence, for example, in all the data collected by Frazer, that there are all sorts of intermediary variations on the spectrum from crisis to kingship. But what appears first is the victimage.

J.W.: That's very reminiscent of the story of the selection of Saul as king in 1 Samuel. He bears various signs of the victim according to 1 Samuel 10:20–24: he was different from all the others in being much taller than any of them; he was from the smallest tribe, Benjamin, which had a bad reputation in the biblical traditions and eventually disappeared; and of course he was "taken by lot." In the three other narratives of someone taken (really captured) by lot — Achan in Joshua 7, Saul and Jonathan in 1 Samuel 14, and Jonah in the book of Jonah — it's an obvious victimage situation.

R.G.: Yes, that is very important, the practice of taking by lot. It reflects some awareness of scapegoating, its randomness.

J.W.: Would you clarify "randomness"?

R.G.: Well, there are preferential signs of victimization which I delineated in *The Scapegoat.* In a crisis communities look for someone to blame for the worst crimes imaginable, and we see a common pattern of picking on those people who are marginal or different in some way that doesn't fit the system of differences in the community; perhaps they are foreigners. Perhaps they have lost an eye like Wotan; perhaps they smell bad like Philoctetes. But these preferential signs don't absolutely have to exist. In a crisis there will be an inexorable movement toward finding a scapegoat.

J.W.: So the one necessary condition is vulnerability?

R.G.: Sure, you can say that as a generalization, but vulnerability is relative; it depends on the situation in the community. If the crisis is moving toward a frenzy, a turbulence of Dionysiac proportions, there is less and less need for preferential signs. When a mob is really frantic, the slightest incident will be interpreted as a sign of someone's guilt. Our approach to collective crises should be extremely fluid, in keeping with the fluidity of mimesis itself.

Now of course there are clearly features of disability or abnormality that tend to play a role in the designation of the victim — Oedipus's limp, for example. This is what I mean by preferential signs.

On the matter of preferential signs, take the Venda myth of the snake god and his two wives.[2] It is the second, younger wife who is accused of witchcraft. So I speculate that it is her second wife status that makes her vulnerable to the witchcraft accusation. The second wife status is a preferential sign of victimage in this particular myth, but not necessarily everywhere.

So if some sort of marginality or vulnerability is present in the myth, so much the better. The evidence of such signs piles up. But it is not absolutely necessary to the identification of a "scapegoat."

J.W.: Let's move on to questions arising from currents of suspicion and opposition. First, some people ask, in effect, "How could a sacrificial reading be dominant for two thousand years — if it has been dominant — and then all of a sudden Girard discovers the true nonsacrificial reading." How do you reply to this implied accusation of *hubris?*

R.G.: I have come to be more positive about the word "sacrificial," so I would like first of all to make a distinction between sacrifice as murder and sacrifice as renunciation. The latter is a movement toward freedom from mimesis as potentially rivalrous acquisition and rivalry.

Well, I think a nonsacrificial reading, or a sacrificial one expressing genuine renunciation, is found in many passages in the writings of the church fathers. It is not the only one, to be sure. And then this reading is not mine first of all, it is Nietzsche's. Nietzsche was the first thinker to see clearly that the singularity of Judeo-Christianity was that it rehabilitates victims that myths would regard as justly immolated. Of course for Nietzsche this was a dreadful mistake that first Judaism, then Christianity had inflicted on the world. Nietzsche chose violence rather than peace, he chose the texts that mistook the victim for a culprit. What he could not see was the scapegoat mechanism.

J.W.: Is there any indication in any of Nietzsche's writings that he understands Jesus as culpable in some way, thus responsible for his fate?

R.G.: No. In his book entitled *The Antichrist* it is clear that he considered Jesus honest and sincere. Nietzsche thought it was wrong for

2. Girard's essay on this myth is included as chapter 9 of the Reader.

Christianity to speak of the innocence of the victim, not because sacrificial victims are really guilty, but because societies need sacrifice. He saw the central religious issue as no one else did. He understood that the gods and heroes immolated in pagan mythology were similar in form to the killing of Christ. But he thought Christianity's witness to the innocence of Christ was socially harmful and that the world needs the sacrifice of the victim as part of life's eternal return, which includes destruction.

Nietzsche was the first to see this problem clearly, but he was perverse in choosing the violent lie instead of the peaceful truth of the victim.

J.W.: Isn't it ironic that he is a real scriptural source for many academics upholding "political correctness"?

R.G.: Yes, the upholders of PC can find a strange kind of support in his writings. He was entranced with violent differentiation. You know, in his own time he lashed out at those who were among the first to embrace PC. He confused PC with authentic Christianity.

J.W.: Back to the question about the nonsacrificial reading of Christianity: to what other evidence do you point? Are there other persons and texts between the fathers and Nietzsche who understand the nonsacrificial approach?

R.G.: All those who have tried to follow the way of Christ and the Kingdom of God, living as nonviolently as possible, have understood, though not necessarily intellectually.

J.W.: But on the other hand, you have stated a number of times and in a number of ways that institutional Christianity and the majority of Christians have turned the Cross into a sacrificial instrument used to punish and eliminate minorities and enemies. It has been turned against the Jews, which has become a crucial matter since the Holocaust.

R.G.: This is true, but I do not single out historical Christianity as the sole culprit, as many Christians seem to believe. I am just repeating what Paul says about all of us being guilty so that God can save us all. Concerning the Jews, the complexity of the New Testament texts is never recognized either by hatemongers and persecutors or by critics and theologians caught up in the cult of PC. We have already noted that Peter says to the Jewish crowd in Jerusalem, "And now, brothers, I know that you acted in ignorance, as did also your rulers." The Jews are implicated no more than the minions of Caesar or lynchers all over the world. Therefore one cannot say that all the Jews in Jerusalem were innocent of Jesus' death while the Romans were guilty. If to implicate some of the Jews also in Jesus' death makes the New Testament anti-Semitic, well it would make just as much sense to hold that it is anti-British to condemn the burning of Joan of Arc. Because no one, no, not one, can escape implication in the death of the one who died for all. And then all lynchings are alike as well, whether they take place in

Palestine during the Roman Empire or in the American South after the Civil War.

Even Euripides will tell you in *The Bacchae* that Dionysus was right and Pentheus the victim was wrong to rebel against the god.

Or take the myth of Purusha in the Vedas: he was killed by a great crowd of sacrificers, and out of this sacrifice the three great castes of India appeared. The parts of the body were divided, with the head as the higher caste, then the chest as the middle, warrior caste, and finally the legs as the lowest caste. Now the myth does not tell you Purusha was guilty, but it doesn't tell you he was innocent either — and this is what the Gospels alone tell you, that Jesus was innocent. "We were wrong," says the New Testament community, "to the extent that we were involved in that."

J.W.: The picture of the Servant in Isaiah 53 also includes the confession of the people. Those speaking confess they were wrong about the Servant, and that he was innocent.

R.G.: Yes, you are right. Isaiah 53 is a key revelatory text. There is already a foreshadowing of the Servant in the story of Joseph and his brothers when Judah offers himself in place of his younger brother.

J.W.: Is this the Gospel?

R.G.: Yes, this is already the Gospel.

❧

J.W.: To shift to another question, one pertaining to the events of history and ethics, do you think the Holocaust sensitized the Western world to the plight of the victim? Someone like you comes along with your idea or set of ideas only after World War II. Of course, other momentous events have occurred. One thinks immediately of the civil rights movement in this country during the 1950s and 1960s. Is there something peculiar about the period from World War II to the present?

R.G.: The revelation of the sacrificial mechanism continues to penetrate deeper and it deprives human culture of a certain protection, the protection of ritual, rules, mediating institutions. More and more freedom is given to individuals and communities. Therefore there is more and more that is good and at the same time more and more that is bad in culture and social life. Indeed, our situation is increasingly apocalyptic as freedom increases. The Gospels have brought about this freedom, but you cannot blame them for it; you cannot ask human beings to become enslaved again to the scapegoat mechanism. Of course people can try to go back to Dionysus. The Gospels cannot guarantee that people will act the right way; they are not some kind of recipe for the good society. What the Gospels do is to offer more freedom and to set the example, above all through witness to the message, death, and resurrection of Christ, about how to use this freedom wisely.

You could say that the Gospels may increase violence, in the sense of Jesus' saying, "I have come not to bring peace but a sword" (Matt. 10:34). So the Gospels do not promise eternal peace; they don't lend themselves to an election campaign. The Holocaust is a radical example of how a cultural crisis is used for evil; it is used to destroy the effect of the Gospels.

You know, there are two forms of totalitarianism. One tries to destroy the concern for victims openly and directly. Its proponents basically attempt to kill as many victims for as little reason as possible. Then there is the insidious totalitarianism. Communism in many of its forms was insidious, but it will probably be replaced by ideologies still more insidious which outflank the Gospel on the left, presenting themselves as better than the Gospel, trying to show that the Gospels do not side with the victims, but demonize them. Some of these people see themselves as super-Christians, but they are heirs of the predecessors of Marx who thought they could achieve a new humanism. Feuerbach, for example. But they laid the groundwork for a disrespect of truth. I think it would be helpful to study Feuerbach, who was a primary agent of the transformation of Christianity into Marxism.

J.W.: Could we talk for a few minutes about feminist critics? They argue that your mimetic model is only for males or that you are gynophobic because you use only male examples in the texts and other data you cite. What is your response to these accusations?

R.G.: I find it strange that women so badly want participation in the male power of archaic societies, for it is precisely their real superiority that women don't appear, for the most part, as the primary agents of violence. If they want now to join the power games of the males, and that is understandable, are they not losing their real moral superiority?

As important as the apostles are in the Gospels, the women around Jesus are just as important but in a different way: they are that part of humanity which has nothing to do with scapegoating him. They are the ones who stick with him through the crucifixion. Or in *The Bacchae* of Euripides, there may be a slander of women as the perpetrators of the paroxysmic violence.

J.W.: You mean there is a misrepresentation of the Bacchic ritual?

R.G.: No, there is a misrepresentation of the events that precede and justify *The Bacchae*. In *Violence and the Sacred* I suggested that there could be a similarity to what used to happen among the Amazonian Yanomamö. When the tribes visited each other games of rivalry were usually followed by violence. When it began the women fled the village. This is perhaps what happened in the real event behind *The Bacchae*. Just as the Yanomamö women fled when violence began, so the mass migration of women to Mount Cithaeron in Dionysian lore may originally have been in order to escape the violence precipitated by a mimetic crisis, which was essentially a *masculine* phenomenon.

In *Violence and the Sacred* I also mentioned something else, the structure of the Bororo villages in Brazil. The men's house was in the center, and there they stuck feathers on themselves and played war games. The houses of the women were separate, on the periphery. The married men went back and forth to these houses on the periphery several times a day, but the women were forbidden to enter the men's house located in the center of the village. So the plan of a Bororo village symbolized the status of women: they were on the outside, or as marginal as could be and still belong to the social structure. They played no role in the games of violence and the sacred, which is their superiority. Their marginality was inseparable from their nonparticipation in male violence.

If anything my hypothesis is pro-woman. It is peculiar how people moved by new ideologies want to be part of the power structure even retrospectively, and to be seen as responsible for some of the horrors that have left their mark on us. This greed to participate in the violence of men is incomprehensible to me.

J.W.: Some feminists and others argue that women were often — perhaps even the most frequent — sacrificial victims, but you ignore this in the examples you discuss.

R.G.: I do not. There were female victims since there were female gods. It is simply not true that I don't talk about female victims. There is the Venda myth of the snake god and his two wives [see chapter 9]. There is also the Dogrib myth of the women who is a mother of dogs.[3] She is a great goddess. When she has puppies the community banishes her. But the puppies turn out to be children. When they are undressed she takes their skins away, and so they are forced to keep their human identity. Here the woman god was a scapegoat whose victimization generates the human community, according to the myth.

I think the objection that I leave women out of the mimetic scapegoat theory is a red herring. It's based on a reading not of my books, but of some hostile reviews which are mimetically repeated by fellow-travelers.

J.W.: There are some male thinkers whom feminists gravitate toward, Foucault for example.

R.G.: His systematic anti-Western stance fits the ideological temper of our intellectual elites.

J.W.: ...and there are those who are anti-Christian, who attract large followings, Freud and Derrida for instance, also Heidegger.

R.G.: Yes, if we are anti-Christian, we are bound to attract many eager intellectuals, not least the feminists. Another is Nietzsche, the patron

3. Discussed in *The Scapegoat,* 49.

saint of postmodernism. Although I have a great admiration for his real insights and I think he has not been well understood by most of his devotees, he is also a madman. The blind worship of him is not merely foolish but destructive.

❧

J.W.: Here is a different kind of question for you. I have recently encountered the criticism that Girardians wish to point to a historical or empirical basis not only for religion and culture but also for the dynamics of human relations. Yet so far Girardians have not used or engaged in empirical testing.

R.G.: I have observed a lot of mimetic rivalry lately with my grandchildren. It is very easy to verify rivalry in infants. It is true, however, that people interested in the mimetic theory, and I myself, do not feel attracted to the type of experimentation that keeps enormous armies of psychologists busy.

J.W.: It occurs to me that it would be really interesting to delve into infant and child development.

R.G.: I have received a lot of material from experimental psychologists on imitation, and it verifies that imitation precedes consciousness and language. It would be interesting to experiment with more complex aspects of the mimetic theory. Unfortunately, experimental psychologists are not yet aware of its existence, it seems. Furthermore, it is not easy to test. You need parameters and controls for long periods of time and a way of analyzing the social order of the subjects, of which the experimenter is also a part. The experimenter too is involved in mimesis. So it's very difficult to test in a way that truly meets scientific requirements. It is always nice to verify the obvious scientifically.

It would probably be a good thing if some investigators holding to the mimetic theory did that kind of testing. It would be a sort of validation, but it would be of limited value. It would not be at the intellectual level of the theory as a whole, most of which cannot be subjected to empirical verification or falsification through empirical testing or the canons of contemporary science, especially the principle of falsifiability. The complexity of what we are talking about is too great for that.

J.W.: Some followers of Ernest Becker are doing testing on "mortality salience." This means that subjects are given questions about their own mortality; then when they complete that part of the testing they are given questions about social and legal issues which involve people who have gone over the boundaries of culturally accepted behavior. When asked to impose penalties, those who have been asked to reflect on, or react to, their own death tend to be much more severe than those in the control group. Those who are rigid or conservative in their religious or cultural values are the most punitive of all. What do you think of that kind of test? And how do you unravel rivalry from mortality, from abandonment and isolation — all the states or conditions symbolically associated with death?

R.G.: I do not see why "subjects" who are asked questions in laboratories should be regarded as more reliable than the rest of us. The preoccupation with death in a subjective sense is peculiar to modern Western societies. In archaic societies death did not mean the same thing. Most of the time, death was interpreted as a consequence of violence, human and/or supernatural. So the kind of focus to which you refer reflects a new freedom and is a kind of luxury, really. It is no accident, from a religious point of view, that so many aspects of life are getting easier and easier. As they do, we have plenty of time to think about old age and death.

The experience of death is going to get more and more painful, contrary to what many people believe. The forthcoming euthanasia will make it more rather than less painful because it will put the emphasis on personal decision in a way which was blissfully alien to the whole problem of dying in former times. It will make death even more subjectively intolerable, for people will feel responsible for their own deaths and morally obligated to rid their relatives of their unwanted presence. Euthanasia will further intensify all the problems its advocates think it will solve.

J.W.: Surveys I have seen indicate that the general populace supports assisted suicide, at least in Michigan, where the state's cases against Dr. Kevorkian have been in the news.

R.G.: The increasing subjective power of death converges with the fact that people are living longer lives. It is an enormous religious and ethical issue, to my mind. In the Netherlands, where I gather assisted suicides have become commonplace, there are claims that some of the assisted suicides are not suicides at all. Even if they are, the suspicion will linger that they are not, and the fear of being murdered is going to merge once again with the fear of dying. Our supermodern utopia looks very much at times like a regression to archaic terror.

J.W.: You just touched on the question of ethics. There is a sense or intuition that the mimetic scapegoating theory is driven by ethical concerns. Certainly it should have important ethical implications, don't you agree?

R.G.: It certainly does, and one should always look to the Gospels. What are the prescriptions of the Kingdom of God? Basically, give up a dispute when mimetic rivalry is taking over. Provide help to victims and refuse all violence. I find the allegory of the sheep and goats in Matthew 25 to be a key text; it's all there. When we identify with the person in need or who has been victimized, we encounter the Son of Man, Jesus Christ.

What the mimetic theory as such facilitates is the understanding that these ethical prescriptions or principles are against the mimetic spirit of the mob. The Gospels show that faith emerges when individuals come out of the mob.

J.W.: It seems at first blush ironic and even contradictory that here you should put such emphasis on the importance of the individual separating from the mob. You undoubtedly don't understand it as contradictory, but how do you relate the individual coming out of the crowd or mob to the critique of modern exaltation of the self, which becomes even a sort of divinization of the self?

R.G.: I don't think there is any contradiction. All the excesses of the modern world are distortions of Christian truth. The fact that there is a new type of individual in Christianity is the most important thing in the world. The Christian person is new and would have been viewed by traditional cultures as subversive. The only difference is that our narcissistic culture, which is really intensely mimetic and other-centered, is a deviation and a caricature of the Christian person, not its fulfillment. Jesus is a real person in the Christian sense. So were the prophets. There is great continuity between the prophets and Jesus.

The Servant of Yahweh in Isaiah is at the same level as Christ in the Gospels. But Christian faith emerged because Christians saw Jesus as the real fulfillment of what had merely been professed before. He is so close to God that we affirm that he is God.

J.W.: You are now approaching the Christian doctrine of incarnation. So far you have talked about Jesus the man as God. But you could go the other way, could you not, and talk about God as becoming a human being?

R.G.: Yes, no human is able to reveal the scapegoat mechanism. The number one proof of this is the denial of Peter. It could be interpreted psychologically as the weakness of Peter. The number one disciple should be able to imitate Christ and stand up for him. But as soon as he is immersed in a mob of scapegoaters, he surrenders to the mimetic pressure and joins them. This is the true revelation of a weakness which is ours as well as Peter's.

And by all accounts, in myths from all societies, the embodiment of mimetic rivalry and accusation, Satan, should so distort Jesus' mission and message that he is viewed as the guilty hero or god. In fact, Jesus has already called Peter "Satan" because Peter did not understand nonrivalrous love and innocent suffering, and so tried to obstruct Jesus.

So the question becomes one of the transformation of the disciples, how they become able to advocate the truth of Christ and the Kingdom of God. This has to occur through the power of grace alone. So Jesus says "it is better that I go," because then the Spirit will be sent. Because Christ did what he did, grace filled the hearts of the disciples. One person did something for all the others, like Judah to save Benjamin in the Joseph story. Jesus alone acts as God would like all human beings to act. Jesus never yields an inch to mimetic pressure.

I now accept calling this "sacrifice" in a special sense. Because one person did it, God the Father pardons all, in effect. I had avoided the word "scapegoat" for Jesus, but now I agree with Raymund Schwager that he is scapegoat for all — except now in reverse fashion, for theologically considered the initiative comes from God rather than simply from the human beings with their scapegoat mechanism. I think the Gospels understand Jesus basically that way, and also Paul, when he speaks of God making Christ to be sin, but also our wisdom and righteousness. He is the scapegoat for all.

In the common human pattern Jesus' death should have been transfigured in a mythical way, but it was not. So the Suffering Servant of Isaiah 53 is revelation, to be sure, but in the Gospels the revelation is more complete.

J.W.: This is a good point to ask you about the resurrection. In a recent article in *First Things* you made comments about the disciples and the resurrection similar to what you have just said in our conversation.[4] How does your position differ from that of Rudolf Bultmann, who spoke of the resurrection as Christ's rising into the kerygma or proclamation of the church through the disciples? For him it was not an objective event, but an interpretive event in the minds and hearts of the disciples.

R.G.: For me the resurrection is an objective fact. Even though it is visible or comprehensible only to those converted or in the process of converting, like Thomas, it does not mean, in my view, that it is not an objective fact. The mimetically blind cannot see the truth. In the story of the two disciples on the way to Emmaus (Luke 24:13–35) you have both the "rising into the kerygma" and the real presence of a real human being who breaks the bread and eats it. Bultmann found it impossible to believe in the resurrection in the age of the automobile and electricity. He gives the impression of conforming to the contemporary mob that believes only in technology, the real visible power in our world. I do not. I find electricity very usefully and impressive, but I do not worship it.

J.W.: You don't care to speculate about the content of the experience, I gather. As you mention, there are a variety of ways of reporting the resurrection.

R.G.: Yes, and these modern historians usually read them in such a way as to deny the reality of the resurrection. When accounts are too

4. "Are the Gospels Mythical?," *First Things* 62 (April 1996): 31.

neat, this is held against their veracity. When they are not neat, this is held against their veracity as well. But to me the variety is fascinating. In Matthew the disciples encounter Jesus back in Galilee; in John it occurs both in Jerusalem and Galilee; in Luke only in Jerusalem; and in Mark the disciples are supposed to meet Jesus in Galilee, but the ending is aborted, and that is problematic because there may have been a longer original ending that we don't have. Now many of the historical critics practically tell us that the Gospels try to hoodwink us. If they do, they certainly botched the job very badly. So badly that the pseudo-scientific skepticism leaves me skeptical. Don't we find such a variety of narrative portrayals of the experience of the resurrection that this lends itself to credence rather than disbelief? I don't think the Gospels are hoodwinking us at all.

This, by the way, is one of the reasons why I think the final composition of the Gospels was probably earlier than New Testament criticism generally holds. There are signs of disarray which come across as very close to the experiences themselves, and which contradict, in my opinion, the thesis that turns the Gospels into clever propaganda for Christian missionaries. As propagandists, the evangelists are either dreadful, or so sophisticated (if their disarray is a clever trick) that our historians have not yet caught up with them.

J.W.: There is even a touch of disarray in the depiction of Jesus, for example, his anguish in the Garden of Gethsemane as he prayed, or his cry of abandonment from the Cross according to Matthew and Mark.

R.G.: Who are very different from Luke and John. That is why I say Christianity is dynamic and must be interpreted. It is not a matter of crafty priests coming and taking over in order to oppress people, an impression one might get from certain modern theologians and critics. To put it simply, the multiplicity of the Gospels is a call to interpretation.

J.W.: That's what your work is about, isn't it? Especially now. The multiplicity of the Gospels is a call to interpretation.

R.G.: Yes. There are contradictions, no doubt, but these are minor. The fallibility of the disciples, the multiple experiences represented, the clear differences in style and focus among the evangelists—these for me are all signs of authenticity.

J.W.: Allow me to review one thing before we leave this topic. You said that for you the resurrection is an objective event. Do you distinguish between "objective" as you use it here and "historical."

R.G.: I am not certain I understand the difference. You see, the thing about the Gospels is that there may be tiny mythical infiltrations in them, but their basis is not mythical. The mythical mentality can take them and construe them mythically, but quintessentially they are the destruction of myth. Early Christian faith intuits or understands the nonmythical element and discerns, one way or the other, the mimetic phenomena that are unraveled. The structure of mythology is repeated in the Gospels, but in such a truthful way that the mythological structure is unmasked. The fathers of the church saw this, but were not able to express it in terms of generative scapegoating and the liberating representation thereof. Our mimetic interpretation is less important than their faith but, if it can help our own vacillating faith a little, it is useful.

Part of the problem in the history of Christian interpretation, beginning already with the fathers, was that the Passion was for them a unique event. That is understandable of course. They saw it as a unique event, a single, unique event in worldly history. It is indeed unique as revelation but not as a violent event. The earliest followers of Jesus did not make that mistake. They knew, or intuited, that in one sense it was like all other events of victimization "since the foundation of the world." But it was different in that it revealed the meaning of these events going back to the beginnings of humanity: the victimization occurs because of mimetic rivalry, the victim is innocent, and God stands with the victim and restores him or her. If the Passion is regarded not as revelation but as only a violent event brought about by God, it is misunderstood and turned into an idol. In the Gospels Jesus says that he suffers the fate of all the other prophets going back to Abel the just and the foundation of the world (Matt. 23:35; Luke 11:50).

So what theology needs is a corroborating anthropology. This anthropology will open up the Gospels again to their own generative center and witness.

J.W.: You have already presented an atonement theory, in effect. Would you care to say more about it?

R.G.: The word "atonement" is unique to English as far as I know. Atonement is what the French, I believe, would call *expiation.* Atonement is "at-one-ment," becoming reconciled with God, and this is the work of Christ.

J.W.: The doctrine that has dominated Christian thought, certainly since Anselm, is the satisfaction theory. According to it, the justice of God and God's honor are satisfied by the one who dies, who is allowed to be scapegoated for the sake of all.

R.G.: What you can say, in my view, is that the Father is working on a sort of historical schedule. Christ comes at the right time, at the right hour. I think Gil Bailie's paper (already cited) is very important because it suggests that *kenosis,* emptying, here the emptying of the personality, is crucial. Bailie refers to Jean-Luc Marion, *God without Being,* and helps me understand it. I had struggled with the book. I think the title "God without being" could be translated as "God without the sacred"—God without sacred violence, God without scapegoating.

J.W.: This reminds me of Levinas, one of whose books is *Autrement* *qu'être* (Otherwise than being). Levinas's main target, of course, is Heidegger, whom he associates with the concept of being.

R.G.: I would say that "being" in this case is the wrong being. One should not prescribe a general elimination of the word "being" or any concept of being from our vocabulary, although I acknowledge that Levinas's and Marion's concerns are commendable.

Perhaps people like Thomas Aquinas, who live in a Christian period, tend to minimize evil. But the danger now is probably the opposite, that is, minimizing the idea of God as a source of peace and being, due to the sway of Heidegger's thought and our general ontological impoverishment. We must not retrospectively foist this alien idea of God upon Thomas and Augustine. Both Levinas and Marion are too unconditionally Heideggerian in their conception of being. Heidegger's conception of being is insightful with regard to our age, but should not be indiscriminately projected back onto the past, even if we do not necessarily agree with Thomas and Augustine on everything. Heidegger's being, I think, is the sacred, the violent sacred. His *Introduction to Metaphysics* shows this clearly, but that set of lectures in 1935 was not simply an anomaly. You can find similar things in *Being and Time* and in the "later," mythopoetic Heidegger.

Some novelists reveal Heidegger's being as idolatrous desire. All the desire of Proust is disclosed retrospectively as mimesis of the violent sacred. In Proust, desire is redeemed by the fact that it is no longer desire; it has become a serene recollection. This transformation is insufficient to make Proust into a Christian, but as pure recollection, his former desire is emptied of mimetic rivalry and it is represented more truthfully than it can be when still transfigured through mimetic rivalry. This peaceful representation gives us a glimpse of true being, formerly pushed aside by the sacred transfiguration of mimetic desire. Sacred transfiguration of desire is why time has been *perdu,* wasted away.

J.W.: You have only recently made a published statement about your experience of Christian conversion.[5] Would you recount this experience and indicate its importance for your life and research?

R.G.: It was intimately connected with my work on my first book, *Deceit, Desire, and the Novel.* I started working on that book very much in the pure demystification mode: cynical, destructive, very much in the spirit of the atheistic intellectuals of the time.[6] I was engaged in debunking, and of course recognizing mimesis is a great debunking tool because

5. *Quand ces choses commenceront... entretiens avec Michel Treguer,* 190–95.

6. Girard's first book was published in French in 1961, but here he refers to a period somewhat earlier than his conversion in 1959.

it deprives us moderns of the one thing we think we still have left, our individual desire. This debunking is the ultimate deprivation, the dispossession, of modern man. The debunking that actually occurs in this first book is probably one of the reasons why my concept of mimesis is still viewed as destructive. Yet I like to think that if you take this notion as far as you possibly can, you go through the ceiling, as it were, and discover what amounts to original sin.

An experience of demystification, if radical enough, is very close to an experience of conversion. I think this has been the case with a number of great writers. Their first conception of their novels was very different from what it became ultimately. The author's first draft is an attempt at self-justification, which can assume two main forms. It may focus on a wicked hero, who is really the writer's scapegoat, his mimetic rival, whose wickedness will be demonstrated by the end of the novel. It may also focus on a "good" hero, a knight in shining armor, with whom the writer identifies, and this hero will be vindicated by the end of the novel. If the writer has a potential for greatness, after writing his first draft, as he rereads it, he sees the trashiness of it all. His project fails. The self-justification the novelist had intended in his distinction between good and evil will not stand self-examination. The novelist comes to realize that he has been the puppet of his own devil. He and his enemy are truly indistinguishable. The novelist of genius thus becomes able to describe the wickedness of the other from within himself, whereas before it was some sort of put-up job, completely artificial. This experience is shattering to the vanity and pride of the writer. It is an existential downfall. Very often this downfall is written symbolically, as illness or death, in the conclusion. In the case of Proust and Dostoyevsky it is explicitly presented as a change in outlook. Or to take Don Quixote, on his deathbed he sees finally his own mimetic madness, which is also illness and death. And this existential downfall is the event that makes a great work of art possible.

Once the writer experiences this collapse and new perspective, he can go back to the beginning and rewrite the work from the point of view of this downfall. It is no longer self-justification. It is not necessarily self-indictment, but the characters he creates are no longer "Manichean" good guys or bad guys.

So the career of the great novelist is dependent upon a conversion, and even if it is not made completely explicit, there are symbolic allusions to it at the end of the novel. These allusions are at least implicitly religious. When I realized this, I had reached a decisive point in the writing of my first book, above all in my engagement with Dostoyevsky. Dostoyevsky's Christian symbolism was important for me. *Demons* presents Stepan Verkhovensky, whose deathbed conversion is particularly moving, but there is also the end of *Crime and Punishment* and

The Brothers Karamazov. The old Verkhovensky discovers that he was a fool all the time and turns to the Gospel of Christ. This is the existential conversion that is demanded by a great work of art.

When I wrote the last chapter of my first book,[7] I had had a vague idea of what I would do, but as the chapter took form I realized I was undergoing my own version of the experience I was describing. I was particularly attracted to the Christian elements, for example, Stepan Verkhovensky's final journey and turn to the Gospel before his death. So I began to read the Gospels and the rest of the Bible. And I turned into a Christian.

Now this experience of an intellectual-literary conversion, as you might call it, was an enjoyable one. I was teaching at Johns Hopkins at the time, and I had been invited to teach a course every week at Bryn Mawr. So I traveled there and back every week by train. I remember quasi-mystical experiences on the train as I read, contemplated the scenery, and so on. But this initial conversion did not imply any change of life... up till the day I found out that I had a cancerous spot in the middle of my forehead. I went to a medical doctor, a dermatologist, who was — how shall I say? — remote, unsympathetic, distrustful of me. Perhaps he feared he wouldn't be paid. He removed the bit of tissue which turned out to be cancerous. From that time on I was pretty scared, because he never told me that this type of cancer was eminently curable and usually did not return after it was removed. So to me it was as though I was under a death sentence. For all I knew, I had melanoma, the worst form of skin cancer. A complication was that I had some swelling of that area of the forehead, which turned out to be due to acne.

So my intellectual conversion, which was a very comfortable experience, self-indulgent even, was totally changed. I could not but view the cancer and the period of intense anxiety as a warning and a kind of expiation, and now this conversion was transformed into something really serious in which the aesthetic gave way to the religious.

So I had an extremely bad period, and this period coincided with the liturgical period of Lent in 1959. I was thirty-five years old. I was aware of the liturgical period, though I had never been a practicing Catholic. The doctor himself had been somewhat concerned about the swelling, so he evacuated it. I will never forget that day. It was Holy Wednesday, the Wednesday before Easter. Everything was fine, completely benign, no return of the cancer.

Immediately after that experience, I went to confession and I had my children baptized. My wife and I were remarried by a priest. The priest to whom I went for confession was an Irishman, whose religious

7. "The Unity of Novelistic Conclusions," which is included in its entirety as chapter 4 of the Reader.

and cultural background was a little alien to me. He had a hard time understanding my experience.

J.W.: You noted in the interview with Treguer[8] that Holy Wednesday is the traditional end of the period of penance.

R.G.: It is the beginning of the holiest part of Holy Week. So on Holy Thursday I went to Mass after going to confession. I took the Eucharist. I felt that God liberated me just in time for me to have a real Easter experience, a death and resurrection experience.

J.W.: So resurrection and conversion are very difficult to distinguish...

R.G.: Conversion *is* resurrection. But conversion is a more objective reality than what we call objective the rest of the time. Awareness of guilt is forgiveness in the Christian sense. Since I tend to analyze everything to death, I might not have believed in my own experience of conversion if I had converted as a result of fear rather than before I had experienced the fear. The prior conversion was too easy; it entailed no demands or commitments which I perceived at the time, but it prepared the way. So with the definitive conversion I was both emotionally and mentally prepared to accept God's grace and believe.

J.W.: Your experience is similar to the Gospel pattern of discipleship. Recently, in preparation for writing a paper on discipleship, I conferred with scholars in Judaism, Hinduism, etc., and I found that the Gospel pattern is evidently unique: the disciples are initially called, but they fall away and then return through a kind of second conversion, which is associated with the resurrection.

R.G.: That's true... true of all the martyrs in fact.

J.W.: I think you have already begun responding to a question in which many readers will be interested: what is important for you in the practice of faith?

R.G.: I am not really ritualistic. I pray, but I don't really enjoy ritual that much. I do enjoy the Gregorian Mass. We are lucky to have the Gregorian Mass at Stanford, thanks to William Mahrt, who has been devoted to it since 1963. I attend Mass every Sunday of course, as well as on the obligatory holy days. I am an ordinary Christian.

J.W.: What about non-Christians and a pluralistic society? Do you favor converting all non-Christians to Christianity?

R.G.: Jesus said, "I am the way, the truth, and the life," and he told his disciples to go into the world and make converts. If we give that up, are we still Christian? The idea that if we respect other religions more than our own and act only according to PC peace will break out all over the world is fantasy and delusion. The Christians should certainly enjoy the freedom to spread their faith as much as the other religions.

---

8. *Quand ces choses commenceront,* 194.

You see, is Christianity really so powerful that it should be forbidden to spread its ideas, whereas other religions should be allowed that same right?

J.W.: You are advocating freedom of religious expression....

R.G.: Of course. I think the Christians who do not want to share their faith do not really believe. The fear of religious tyranny is an anachronism, a false issue which puts political correctness ahead of the truth. I believe there is a truth, and the only way of telling it is by connecting with people.

J.W.: A question related to the conversion of others, yet distinct from it, is whether one's Christian faith should enter into one's approach to other religions and cultures? Or is it necessary to "bracket out" one's faith in order to do scholarly work or to be a thinker?

R.G.: I don't think you can bracket out a faith which is responsible for the best in the modern world. That is totally artificial. I don't think you can bracket out any idea or ideal that you really hold — or that holds you. If you bracket out something that is central to your life, you become a shadow of yourself and your intelligence is not effective. There is no science without faith. Everything great is always a question of faith. Of course, I suppose you could speak of a kind of *kenosis* of faith, that is, emptying yourself of mimetic rivalry as you approach others and your intellectual work. This is a sort of *kenosis* from below, as contrasted to the *kenosis* of Christ from above according to Philippians 2. As your faith grows, the more you empty yourself of rivalry and self-aggrandizement and the more you feel impelled to communicate to others, *with* others, the truth you have experienced. This belongs to the essence of Christianity. The idea of silencing Christianity in the name of Christian humility is a Christian idea gone mad — as Bernanos used to say: *une idée chrétienne devenue folle,* like much of the madness in our world.

J.W.: So you would not agree with Mircea Eliade's advocacy of practicing *epoche,* the suspension of beliefs and assumptions in the approach to other religions?

R.G.: No, that is a Stoic term, and you can practice that if you believe in Stoicism. But it has nothing to do with being a Christian or with real Christianity.

J.W.: But isn't there an ethical impulse which goes with faith in Christ and becoming a disciple that involves trying to see from the other's point of view? Isn't the Christian directed toward the other, or through God to the others?

R.G.: That is true, but it doesn't mean espousing the other's mythology. It means trying to understand the other's situation, why he believes what he believes, and so forth. But I don't think there is any good sense in which a Christian could bracket out Christianity. Christianity based on the Gospels must be experienced as a twofold calling: to commitment of the whole person to God and to interpretation of the Gospel texts.

If you believe that Christianity is truth, including societal truth, you are not going to reach truth by bracketing it out. You can see the result of this method all around us, in the current academic debacle for instance. The biblical scholars who are still talking in terms of bracketing truth out are still thinking in nineteenth-century terms. They are on their way to a goal which the deconstructors reached long ago. If we must have nihilism, let us not dilute it with water and let us drink it full strength, with Nietzsche, Heidegger, and the deconstructors. In order to reach the end of the present crisis we must first experience it fully, we must not interminably repeat attempts which already failed a hundred years ago, like "the quest for the historical Jesus." Mine is a search for the anthropology of the Cross, which turns out to rehabilitate orthodox theology.

Glossary

Culture. Everything — assumptions and common ideas, roles, structures, etc. — which enables human beings to exist together without being overcome by chaos, violence, random murder. According to the mimetic scapegoat theory, culture is founded by scapegoating and maintained by a system of differences which is rooted in a nonconscious, concealed scapegoat mechanism (see Scapegoating). "Difference" here refers to the basic distinction arising from victimage and the beginning of culture (which of course may have actually taken place over hundreds of thousands of years). The originary distinction is the one between "here" or "us" by contrast to "it" or "that," the victim. This could have been originally a reflexive gesture or sign rather than spoken words. From this distinction all others stem: language, roles, rules, institutions, etc.

Dionysus. Known also as Bacchus, he was a wandering god, associated with wine and madness, and the bringing of culture. The myths of Dionysus include a version in which the Curetes, or Cretan warriors, encircle the infant Dionysus and save him from Zeus, while another version narrates that the Titans, predecessors of the Olympian gods, seduce him with trinkets, encircle him, cook him, and devour him. Dionysian ritual was associated with the dismemberment of a sacrificial victim, probably a ritual repetition of what was believed to have happened to the god/victim himself. Friedrich Nietzsche was fascinated with Greek culture and with Dionysus in particular. In one of his early books, *The Birth of Tragedy,* he maintained that music first emerged from the cult of Dionysus. In that early work "Dionysian" was a metaphor for the vital, passionate, sacrificial, and destructive side of human culture, whereas the "Apollonian," from the god Apollo, was a metaphor of human imposition of order and constraints. It was, according to him, a kind of veil covering the Dionysian abyss. Although Nietzsche came to modify this distinction between the Dionysian and Apollonian, Dionysus continued to be his paradigm of the concrete reality of life in all its fruitfulness and destructiveness, a paradigm that he opposed to Christ or "the Crucified." In *The Will to Power* no. 1052 Nietzsche wrote of "Dionysus versus the 'Crucified' " as the fundamental antithesis of his thought. After his mental breakdown he signed letters alternately as "Dionysus," "the Crucified," and a nonsense word that may have included part of

Cosima Wagner's name (the wife of the composer with whom he was probably infatuated).

Faith. The person's complete trust — or "existential" knowledge if faith is considered a kind of knowing — that s/he belongs to the God who sides with victims, with scapegoats; for Christians the trust or existential knowledge directed to God is based on Jesus Christ as model or mediator (see Model/Mediator). In mimetic desire (see Mimesis) the tendency is for the relationship between subject and model to become one of conflictual, potentially destructive rivalry. The tenor or "spirit" of the relationship is satanic (see Satan). But in faith the person enters into communion with others through the relationship of perfect love shared between God the Father and Christ the Son. The Spirit of the relationship is union, trust, self-giving.

Mimesis/Mimetic Desire.

A. *Mimetic Desire.* Mimesis is practically synonymous with mimetic desire. Mimesis evokes desire. Desire constitutes mimesis.[1] Mimetic desire is a kind of nonconscious imitation of others, but it is important to stress that the word "imitation" has to be joined with the adjective "appropriative" or "acquisitive." Mimesis seeks to obtain the object that the model desires. The function of culture is to control and channel this potential conflict over the object.

B. *Metaphysical Desire.* As mimetic or interdividual beings we associate being or reality with the other, the model or mediator. Our deepest desire is not for things or objects, but to *be*. In struggles with the model-rival, and particularly when the subject seems to come to a dead-end against the model-obstacle, it becomes apparent from a mimetic analysis that the subject wants the being of the model-mediator. This is the source of fascination, hypnosis, idolatry, the "double," and possession. The experience of the double occurs when the model-obstacle as overpowering other is so internalized that the subject does not experience a distinction of self and the model-mediator. The subject is thus "possessed" by the other. The extreme alternatives are suicide or murder of the model-obstacle. Other possibilities are schizophrenia, escape into a new identity, and liberation through the release experienced in love and forgiveness. This latter is the work of a good or conversionary mimesis.

C. *Mimesis as Good.* Girard does not hold that mimetic desire is inherently bad or destructive. It is the structure and dynamic enabling human beings to open themselves to the world and engage in loving

1. In the concluding conversation with Girard, he speaks of the need for another term than "desire" because it is so intimately associated with the influence of Freud's sexual theory; see p. 268.

relationships. It is what he has in mind in *Things Hidden since the Foundation of the World* when he speaks of "good contagion" and "nonviolent imitation." If it becomes effective in a fundamental change of personality through the imitation of God or Christ, it could be termed "conversionary mimesis" or "conversionary imitation."

Model/Mediator. The person, group, or human reality with which the individual is in a mimetic relationship (see Mimesis). We are never immediately conscious of mimesis and for the most part we are involved in mimesis unconsciously. The model *mediates* reality (world, experience, specific assumptions about life-settings, etc.) to the subject. We are thus always *interdividuals,* Girard's only neologism. It refers to our intersubjective make-up; as human beings we are not the other or model, but on the other hand, we are constituted by the other or model, and so the self is a set of mimetic relationships operative in the individual, both in the present and from the past.

A. *Internal and External Mediation.* In *Deceit, Desire, and the Novel* Girard distinguished between internal mediation, the situation when the subject's and the model's objects of desire overlap and become a matter of rivalry; and external mediation, where the model or mediator is removed from the individual (whether historically, ontologically, or however) and so there is no competition for an object of desire.

B. *Model-Rival.* Strictly speaking, if a model is a person in our immediate life setting (parent, authority figure, peer), then he or she is always potentially a rival. Likewise, a rival in this same immediate setting is always basically a model, although this may not be apparent to the subject. The model-rival is associated with an object of desire which the subject wants to obtain, but the important thing is not as much the object as the defeat of the model-rival. Continually putting oneself in situations of rivalry may be exhilarating if one is winning, but losing may lead to extreme depression. The situation becomes a crisis if the person is entrapped in a *model-obstacle* relationship.

C. *Model-Obstacle.* The model-obstacle is someone or something over whom the subject *cannot* win, or in some cases it would be accurate to say that the subject *will not allow himself* to defeat the model-obstacle, for to achieve that would be to lose the model. All sorts of self-defeating behavior, including addictions (so well described in Dostoyevsky's writings), stem from this predicament. From the standpoint of the mimetic theory, it can only be understood in terms of the mimetic, interdividual character of human existence. The person in this predicament could be described as stumbling over or being blocked by the *skandalon.* The *skandalon* of the Gospels is a an obstacle or stumbling-block (the older meaning of "scandal" in English and French, from the Latin and Greek). The *skandalon* is associated with Satan. This is seen particularly, e.g., in the Gospel of Matthew. Jesus has spoken of his suffering, death, and resurrection, and Peter rebukes him for saying he will suffer and die. Jesus in turn rebukes Peter: "Get behind me, Satan! You are a *skandalon* to me..." (Matt. 16:23). That is, "you are a scandal, an obstacle, a hindrance to me." Here Satan, usually named as the personification of the mimetic model-obstacle, is "deconstructed" or "demythologized" in that Jesus uses the name to express the mimetic rivalry that obsesses Peter. Peter wants to identify himself with a worldly winner and in anger he begins telling his master what he can and cannot do. Something quite similar is reported concerning James and John, who ask to be Jesus's chief lieutenants when he comes into his glory (Mark 10:35–45; Matt. 20:20–28).

Religion. Indistinguishable from culture in archaic societies. It is that generative and protective aspect of culture that serves to control mimetic desire and violence through sacrifice (see Mimesis and Sacrifice), which is at the center of ritual and closely connected to prohibition and myth (see both under Scapegoat/Scapegoating). The violence at the heart of the traditional sacred is therefore twofold: the negative sacred of the collective violence that is associated with the dangerous aspects of the god or the hero, which may become split off into a devil or demon or trickster; and the positive sacred that is associated with the formation and maintenance of order.

Ritual. See Sacrifice and Scapegoat/Scapegoating.

Sacrifice. see also Scapegoat/Scapegoating.

A. *Sacrifice* — its primary sense. Sacrifice stems from originary victimization or scapegoating. It refers first and primarily to the ritual immolation of a human or animal victim. Girard holds it likely that humans were the first sacrificial victims,[2] and only subsequently were animals substituted, and eventually various objects as gifts.

B. *Sacrifice* — its positive sense, primarily in the case of Christ. In recent years Girard has begun to affirm, or at least make explicit, a positive, derived sense of "sacrificial" as the willingness to give of oneself to others and to commit oneself to God, not for sadomasochistic purposes (i.e., to inflict injury on others or oneself, ostensibly for the sake of faith), but out of love and faithfulness to the other.

C. *Sacrifice and Atonement or Redemption.* The word "sacrifice," if retained in the derived, positive sense, should be understood as having its basis in faith in a God of love who does not make a secret pact

2. In French and German the word for victim is also the word for a human or animal sacrifice: *la victime* and *das Opfer.*

with his Son that calls for his murder in order to satisfy God's wrath.[3] The suffering and death of the Son, the Word, are inevitable because of the inability of the world to receive God or his Son, not because God's justice demands violence or the Son relishes the prospect of a horrible execution.

Satan. See also Model-Obstacle under Model/Mediator. Aside from the question whether Satan refers to an objective transcendent reality, in the mimetic scapegoat theory the name refers to the personification of the rivalrous mimesis, the mimesis engendering accusation and violence. But this is also the mimesis that is effective in subduing violence and maintaining order. Satan is thus the *archē,* the "beginning" in the sense of the spirit of rivalry and accusation responsible for the originary murder; and the *archōn,* the prince or ruler of this world. As the ruler of the world of order, as the principle of *Realpolitik,* he is elegantly and beautifully described by Dostoyevsky through Ivan Karamazov's Grand Inquisitor legend in *The Brothers Karamazov.* The Christian revelation exposes Satan as "the father of lies" by disclosing not only the innocence of one victim, Jesus, but of all victims. Satan attempts to cast out Satan through murder, especially collective violence, but he is defeated by the Cross. This defeat is accomplished because the disciples, with the aid of the Paraclete, the Spirit of God as defender of the falsely accused, break away from the mimetic consensus of the social order that is undergirded and constantly regenerated by the scapegoat mechanism.

Scapegoat/Scapegoating. The age-old way of gaining release from the violence or potential violence that mimesis produces is through nonconscious convergence upon a victim.

A. *Scapegoating and Culture.* As noted above (see Culture), culture stems from the disorder, the actual or potential violence that is experienced when mimetic desire gets out of hand and the hominids in the process of becoming human make the discovery that convergence upon a victim brings them unanimity and thus relief from violence.

B. *Scapegoating and Sacrifice.* Both sacrifice and rituals of scapegoating represent, in camouflaged form, the disorder resulting in the originary violence of immolation or expulsion of the victim and the order stemming from the newly found relief from conflict and violence.

C. *Double Transference.* This disorder and order are the function of the *double transference* of the originary victimization: those involved in the collective violence transfer the disorder and the offenses producing it to the victim, but they transfer also their newly found peace to the victim, ascribing to him or her the power that brings it about.

3. *Things Hidden since the Foundation of the World,* 184.

D. *Prohibition.* Prohibition in its basic, originary sense is the taboo of the alleged offense of the victim/scapegoat, the crime that is blamed for the mimetic crisis. The two universal prohibitions are parricide and incest, which are often attributed, whether spontaneously or more formally in ritual and myth, to gods, heroes, and supernatural beings, who represent the disguised form of the victim.

E. *Myth.* Myth is narrative centered in scapegoat events. Myth was probably developed much later than ritual and prohibition and offers the greatest possibility of displacement and disguise because its verbal, narrative character is a stage well beyond the reflexive imitation of the earliest forms of sacrifice and prohibition.

F. *Scapegoat Mechanism.* As Girard states in the concluding interview, "scapegoat mechanism" means basically and simply a generative scapegoat principle which works unconsciously in culture and society. He quotes Peter in Acts: "And now, brothers, I know that you acted in ignorance, as did also your rulers. But what God announced beforehand by the mouth of all the prophets, that his Christ should suffer, he thus fulfilled. So repent, and turn again..." (Acts 3:17–19a).

Skandalon. See Model-Obstacle under Model/Mediator.

Bibliography

Works by René Girard

This bibliography includes all of Girard's books, contributions to collective works, and articles in French and English as of May 1996.

Books

Mensonge romantique et vérité romanesque. Paris: Grasset, 1961.
Proust: A Collection of Critical Essays (ed.). New York: Prentice-Hall, 1962.
Dostoievski: du double à l'unité. Paris: Plon, 1963.
Deceit, Desire and the Novel: Self and Other in Literary Structure. Baltimore, London: Johns Hopkins University Press, 1966. (Trans. of *Mensonge romantique.*)
La Violence et le sacré. Paris: Grasset, 1972.
Critique dans un souterrain. Collection "Amers." Lausanne: l'Age d'Homme, 1976.
Violence and the Sacred. Baltimore: Johns Hopkins University Press, 1977. (Trans. of *La Violence et le sacré.*)
Des Choses cachées dupuis la fondation du monde: Recherches avec Jean-Michel Oughourlian et Guy Lefort. Paris: Grasset, 1978.
"To Double Business Bound": Essays on Literature, Mimesis and Anthropology. Baltimore: Johns Hopkins University Press, 1978.
Le Bouc émissaire. Paris: Grasset, 1982.
La Route antique des hommes pervers. Paris: Grasset, 1985.
The Scapegoat. Baltimore: Johns Hopkins University Press, 1986. (Trans. of *Le Bouc émissaire*).
Things Hidden since the Foundation of the World: Research Undertaken in Collaboration with Jean-Michel Oughourlian and Guy Lefort. Stanford, Calif.: Stanford University Press, 1987. (Trans. of *Des Choses cachées.*)
Job, the Victim of his People. London: Athlone Press, 1987. (Trans. of *La Route antique.*)
Shakespeare: Les feux de l'envie. Paris: Grasset, 1990. (Trans. of *A Theater of Envy.*)
A Theater of Envy: William Shakespeare. New York: Oxford University Press, 1991.
Quand ces choses commenceront... Entretiens avec Michel Treguer. Paris: arléa, 1994.
Resurrection from the Underground: Feodor Dostoevsky. New York: Crossroad, forthcoming. (Trans. of *Dostoievski.*)

Contributions to Collective Works

"Existentialism and Criticism." *Yale French Studies* 16 (1956): 45–52.
"Duc de Saint-Simon." In *A Critical Bibliography of French Literature* 3, ed. D. C. Cabeen and J. Brody, 332, 336–41. Syracuse, N.Y.: Syracuse University Press, 1961.
"General Studies on the Novel." In *A Critical Bibliography of French Literature* 3, ed. D. C. Cabeen and J. Brody, 125–29. Syracuse, N.Y.: Syracuse University Press, 1961.
"Introduction." *In Proust: A Collection of Critical Essays,* ed. René Girard, 1–12. New York: Prentice-Hall, 1962.
"Existentialism and Criticism." In *Sartre: A Collection of Critical Essays,* ed. Edith Kern, 121–28. New York: Prentice-Hall, 1962.
"A propos de Jean-Paul Sartre: rupture et création littéraire." In *Chemins actuels de la critique,* ed. G. Poulet. Paris: Plon, 1967.
"La notion de structure en critique littéraire." In *Quatre conférences sur la nouvelle critique,* 61–73. Turin: Società Editrice Internationale, 1968.
"Triangular Desire." In *Stendhal, Red and Black,* ed. Robert M. Adams, 503–21. New York: Norton, 1969.
"Explication de texte de Jean-Paul Sartre." In *Explication de textes II,* ed. Jean Sareil, 175–91. New York: Prentice-Hall, 1970.
"Une analyse d'Oedipe Roi." In *Critique sociologique et critique psychanalytique,* ed. Institute de Sociologie, Univ. Libre de Bruxelles, 127–63. Brussels, 1970.
"Tiresias and the Critic (Introduction)." In *The Languages of Criticism and the Sciences of Man,* ed. Richard Macksey and Eugenio Donato, 15–21. Baltimore: Johns Hopkins University Press, 1970.
"Stendhal et les problèmes de noblesse." In *Stendhal: Textes recueillis et présentés par J. P. Bardos,* 151–169. Paris: Firmin-Didot, 1970.
"La grâce romanesque." In *Les critiques de notre temps et Proust,* ed. Jacques Bersani, 134–39. Paris: Garnier, 1971.
"Introduction to 'De la folie.'" In *L'esprit moderne dans la littérature française,* ed. Reinhard Kuhn, 59–64. Oxford: Oxford University Press, 1972.
"Myth and Ritual in A Midsummer Night's Dream." In *Memorial Lectures,* ed. Harry F. Camp, 1–17. Stanford, Calif.: Stanford University Press, 1972.
"From The Divine Comedy to the Sociology of the Novel." In *Sociology of Literature and Drama,* ed. Elizabeth and Tom Burns, 101–8. Penguin Books, 1973.
"Preface." In *Structures romanesques et vision sociale chez G. de Maupassant,* ed. Charles Castella, I–V. Lausanne: L'Age de l'Homme, 1973.
"Critical Reflections on Literary Studies." In *Velocities of Change,* ed. Richard Macksey, 72–88. Baltimore: Johns Hopkins University Press, 1974.
"Preface." In *Mimesis Conflictiva,* ed. Cesáreo Bandera, 9–18. Madrid: Gredos, 1975.
"Differentiation and Undifferentiation in Lévi-Strauss and Current Critical Theory." In *Directions for Criticism,* ed. Murray Krieger and L. S. Dembo, 111–36. Madison: University of Wisconsin Press, 1977.

"Narcissism: The Freudian Myth Demythified by Proust." In *Psychoanalysis, Creativity, and Literature,* ed. Alan Roland, 293–311. New York: Columbia University Press, 1978.

"Postface." In *L'enfer des choses: René Girard et la logique de l'économie,* ed. Paul Dumouchel and Jean-Pierre Dupuy, 257–65. Paris: Seuil, 1979.

"Myth and Ritual in Shakespeare: A Midsummer Night's Dream." In *Textual Strategies: Perspectives in Post-Structuralist Criticism,* ed. Josue Harari, 189–212. Ithaca, N.Y.: Cornell University Press, 1979.

"Comedies of Errors: Plautus — Shakespeare — Molière." In *American Criticism in the Post-Structuralist Age,* ed. Ira Konigsberg, 68–86. Ann Arbor: University of Michigan Press, 1981.

"Narcissism: The Freudian Myth Demythified by Proust." In *Literature and Psychoanalysis,* ed. Edith Kurzweil and William Phillips, 363–77. New York: Columbia University Press, 1983.

"La contingence dans les affaires humaines: 'Debat Castoriadis — René Girard." In *L'auto-organisation de la physique au politique,* ed. P. Dumouchel and Jean-Pierre Dupuy, 279–301, 331–52. Paris: Seuil, 1983.

"La danse de Salomé." In *L'auto-organisation de la physique au politique,* ed. P. Dumouchel and Jean-Pierre Dupuy, 365–71. Paris: Seuil, 1983.

"Preface." In *The Secret Sharers: Studies in Contemporary Fictions,* ed. Bruce Bassoff, 9–15. AMS Ars Poetica 1. New York: AMS Press, 1983.

"Disorder and Order in Mythology." In *Disorder and Order: Proceedings of the Stanford International Symposium (Sept. 14–16, 1981),* ed. Paisley Livingston, 80–97. Stanford Literature Studies 1. Saratoga, Calif.: Anma Libri, 1984.

" 'The Ancient Trail Trodden by the Wicked': Job as Scapegoat." *Semeia* 33 (1985): 13–41.

"The Politics of Desire in Troilus and Cressida." In *Shakespeare and the Question of Theory,* ed. Patricia Parker and Geoffrey Hartman, 188–209. London: Methuen, 1985.

" 'To Entrap the Wisest': A Reading of The Merchant of Venice." In *Literature and Society,* ed. Edward W. Said, 100–119. Baltimore: Johns Hopkins University Press, 1985.

"La meurtre fondateur dans la pensée de Nietzsche." In *Violence et vérité: Autour de René Girard,* ed. Paul Dumouchel, 597–613. Colloque de Cerisy. Paris: Grasset, 1985.

"Violence et reciprocité." In *Les Cahiers de l'IPC 2, Sonderausgabe: L'Acte de violence,* 53–88. 1985.

"Generative Scapegoating." In *Violent Origins: Walter Burkert, René Girard, and Jonathan Z. Smith on Ritual Killing and Cultural Formation,* ed. Robert G. Hamerton-Kelly, 73–145. Stanford, Calif.: Stanford University Press, 1987.

"Bottom's One-Man Show." In *The Current in Criticism,* ed. Clayton Koelb and Virgil Lokke, 99–122. West Lafayette, Ind.: Purdue University Press, 1987.

"Des pestes médiévales au SIDA: le danger des extrapolations abusives." In *Proceedings d'un symposium sur l'AIDS, 20–21 juin, Annecy, France,* 138–46. Annecy: Fondation M. Mérieux, 1987.

"Jealousy in The Winter's Tale." In *Alphonse Juilland: d'une passion l'autre,* ed. Brigitte Cazelles and René Girard, 39–62. Saratoga, Calif.: Anma Libri, 1987.

"La mythologie et sa déconstruction dans 'L'Anneau du Niebelung.'" In *Structures et temporalités figures du désir, de la dette et du sacrifice,* ed. Centre de recherche en épistémologie appliquée, 57–201. Cahiers du CREA 12. Paris: C.R.E.A., 1988.

"The Founding Murder in the Philosophy of Nietzsche." In *Violence and Truth: On the Work of René Girard,* ed. Paul Dumouchel, 227–46. London: Athlone Press, 1988.

"Theory and Its Terrors." In *The Limits of Theory,* ed. Thomas M. Kavanagh, 225–54. Stanford, Calif.: Stanford University Press, 1989.

"Envy of So Rich a Thing: 'The Rape of Lucrece.'" In *The Scope of Words: In Honor of Albert S. Cook,* ed. Peter Baker, Sarah Webster Goodwin, and Gary Handwerk, 135–44. New York: Peter Lang, 1991.

"Origins: A View from the Literature." In *Understanding Origins: Contemporary Views on the Origin of Life, Mind and Society,* ed. Francisco J. Varela and Jean-Pierre Dupuy, 27–42. Boston Studies in the Philosophy of Science 130. Dordrecht: Kluwer Academic Publishers, 1992.

Anspach, Mark R. and René Girard. "A Response: Reflections from the Perspective of Mimetic Theory." In *Violence and the Sacred in the Modern World,* ed. Mark Juergensmeyer, 141–48. London: Frank Cass & Co., 1992.

"Job as Failed Scapegoat." In *The Voice from the Whirlwind: Interpreting the Book of Job,* ed. Leo G. Perdue and Clark Gilpin, 185–207. Nashville: Abingdon Press, 1992.

"Raison et folie dans l'oeuvre de Shakespeare." In *Autonomie et automatisme dans la psychose,* ed. Henry Grivois, 141–53. Paris: Masson/Coll. Histoire et Psychiatrie de l'Hôtel-Dieu, 1992.

"A Venda Myth Analyzed." In R. J. Golsan, *"René Girard and Myth: An Introduction,"* 151–79. Theorists of Myth 7. New York and London: Garland Publishing, 1993.

"How Can Satan Cast out Satan?" In *Biblische Theologie und gesellschaftlicher Wandel: Für Norbert Lohfink SJ,* ed. G. Braulik, W. Groß, and S. McEvenue, 125–41. Freiburg: Herder, 1993.

Articles

"L'homme et le cosmos dans L'Espoir et Les Noyers de l'Altenburg d'André Malraux." *Publications of the Modern Language Association of America* 68 (1953): 49–55.

"Les réflections sur l'art dans les romans de Malraux." *Modern Language Notes* 68 (1953): 544–46.

"Le règne animal dans les romans de Malraux." *French Review* 26 (1953): 261–67.

"The Role of Eroticism in Malraux's Fictions." *Yale French Studies* 11 (1953): 49–58.

"L'histoire dans l'oeuvre de Saint-John Perse." *Romanic Review* 44 (1953): 47–55.
"Marriage in Avignon in the Second Half of the Fifteenth Century." *Speculum* 28 (1953): 485–98.
"Franz Kafka et ses critiques." *Symposium* 7 (1953): 34–44.
"Valéry et Stendhal." Publications of the *Modern Language Association of America* 59 (1954): 347–57.
"André Suarès et les autres." *Cahiers du Sud* 42, no. 329 (1955): 14–18.
"Situation du poète américain." *Cahiers du Sud* 42, no. 336 (1956): 196–202.
"Saint-Simon et la critique." *French Review* 29 (1956): 389–94.
"Winds and Poetic Experience." *The Berkeley Review* 1 (Winter 1956): 46–52.
"Où va le Roman?" *French Review* 30 (1957): 201–6.
"Man, Myth and Malraux." *Yale French Studies* 18 (1957): 55–62.
"Voltaire and Classical Historiography." *The American Magazine of the French Legion of Honor* 24, no. 3 (1958): 151–60.
"Tocqueville and Stendhal." *The American Magazine of the French Legion of Honor* 31, no. 2 (1960): 73–83.
"Pride and Passion in the Contemporary Novel." *Yale French Studies* 24 (1960): 3–10.
"Memoirs of a Dutiful Existentialist." *Yale French Studies* 27 (1961): 41–47.
"Mensonge romantique et vérité romanesque." *La Nouvelle Revue Française* 98 (1961): 241–58.
"Les mondes proustiens." *Méditations* 1 (1961): 97–125.
"De Dante à la sociologie du Roman." *Revue Belge de Sociologie* (1963): 263–69.
"Marivaudage and Hypocrisy." *The American Magazine of the French Legion of Honor* 34, no. 3 (1963): 163–74.
"Des formes aux structures, en littérature et ailleurs." *Modern Language Notes* 78, no. 5 (1963): 504–19.
"Métaphysique du souterrain dans *Les possédés*." *La Table Ronde* 183 (April 1963): 73–76.
"Racine, poète de la gloire." *Critique* 205 (June 1964): 484–506.
"Camus's Stranger Retried." *Publications of the Modern Language Association of America* 79 (December 1964): 519–33.
"Monstres et demi-dieux dans l'oeuvre de Hugo." *Symposium* 29, no. 1 (1965): 50–57.
"De l'expérience romanesque au mythe oedipien." *Critique* 21, no. 222 (1965): 899–924.
"Réflexions critiques sur les recherches littéraires." *Modern Language Notes* 81 (1966): 307–24.
"Symétrie et dissymétrie dans le mythe d'Oedipe." *Critique* (January 1968): 99–135.
"Pour un nouveau procès de *L'étranger*." *Revue de Lettres Modernes* 170–74 (1968): 1, 13–52.
"Dionysos et la genèse violente du sacré." *Poétique* 3 (1970): 266–81.
"Perilous Balance: A Comic Hypothesis." *Modern Language Notes* 87 (December 1972): 811–26.

"Système du délire. Review of 'L'anti-Oedipe,' by Gilles Deleuze." *Critique* 28, no. 306 (1972): 957–96.
"Work in Progress." *Diacritics* (Summer 1972): 35–40.
"Vers une définition systematique de sacré." *Liberté* 87–88 (July 1973): 58–74.
"Discussion avec René Girard." *Esprit* 429 (November 1973): 528–63.
"Lévi-Strauss, Frye, Derrida and Shakespearean Criticism." *Diacritics* (Fall 1973): 34–38.
"The Plague in Literature and Myth." *Texas Studies* 15, no. 5 (1974): 833–50.
"Les malédictions contre les Pharisiens et la révélation évangélique." *Bulletin du Centre Protestant d'Études* 27, no. 3 (1975): 5–29.
"French Theories of Fictions, 1947–1974." *The Bucknell Review* 21, no. 1 (1976): 117–26.
"Differentiation and Undifferentiation in Lévi-Strauss and Current Critical Theory." *Contemporary Literature* 17, no. 3 (Summer 1976): 404–29.
"Superman and the Underground: Strategies of Madness — Nietzsche, Wagner and Dostoyevsky." *Modern Language Notes* 91 (1976): 1161–85.
"Violence and Representation in the Mythical Text." *Modern Language Notes* 92, no. 5 (1977): 922–44.
"Dionysus and the Violent Genesis of the Sacred." *Boundary* 2 (1977): 487–505.
"Mimesis and Violence: Perspectives in Cultural Criticism." *Berkshire Review* 14 (1979).
"L'an prochain à Jérusalem." *Le Nouvel Observateur,* May 7, 1979, 84–85.
"Rite, travail, science." *Critique* 380 (January 1979): 20–34.
"Interdividual Psychology." *Denver Quarterly* 14, no. 3 (1979): 3–19.
"Review of 'Ce que je crois,' by André Chouraqui." *Le Nouvel Observateur,* May 7, 1979, 84–85.
"Vers une nouvelle anthropologie. (Review of: Georges-Hubert de Radkowski: Les jeux du désir)." *Le Monde,* May 10, 1980.
"Shakespeare's Theory of Mythology." In *Classical Mythology in Twentieth-Century Thought and Literature,* ed. W. Aycock and T. Klein, 107–24. Lubbock, Tex.: Texas Tech University, 1980.
"Peter's Denial and the Question of Mimesis (Mk 14:66–72)." *Notre Dame English Journal: A Journal of Religion in Literature* 14, no. 3 (Summer 1982): 177–89.
"Derrière la modestie de l'approche, un projet vaste se dessine." (Review of: Jacques Attali, Histoires du temps). *Le Matin,* December 27, 1982.
"Job et le bouc émissaire." *Bulletin du Centre Protestant d'Études* 35, no. 6 (1983): 9–33.
"Le démolisseur de l'Olympe." *Le Nouvel Observateur,* February 4, 1983, 70–75.
"Un prétexte pour régler les comptes." *Le Nouvel Observateur,* February 26, 1983, 67.
"Esprit de concurrence: des vertus inaltérables." *Le Point* no. 553 (May 1983): 80.
"History and the Paraclete." *The Ecumenical Review* 35, no. 1 (January 1983): 3–16.

"Scandal and the Dance: Salome in the Gospel of Mark." *Ballet Review* 10, no. 4 (1983): 67–76.
"The Bible Is Not a Myth." *Literature and Belief* 4 (1984): 7–15.
"Generative Violence and the Extinction of Social Order (Dynamics of Mimetic Rivalry Exposed by the Gospels)." *Salmagundi: A Quarterly of the Humanities and Social Sciences* 63/64 (1984): 204–37.
"Review of 'Le 19e siècle à travers les âges,' by Philippe Murray." *Commentaire* 27 (Autumn 1984): 613–16.
"Exorciser la violence." *Le Figaro*, April 15, 1985, 2.
"La Différence Franco-Américaine." *L'Expansion*. Special issue entitled "Demain la France" (October/November 1984): 275–81.
"Faits divers et bonne nouvelle." *Autrement* 75 (1985): 180–90.
"Nietzsche and Contradiction." *Stanford Italian Review* 6, no. 1–2 (1986): 53–65.
"What Is the Question?" *The Stanford Magazine* 14, no. 4 (1986): 60.
"Dieu et l'esprit moderne." *L'Express*, April 11, 1986, 36–38.
"Le jeu des secrets interdits. (Review of Milan Kundera)." *Le Nouvel Observateur* 1150 (1986): 102–3.
"La morne vengeance de Hamlet." *Les Saisons de Saint-Jean* 15, 16 (1986): 23–38, 5–35.
"The Scapegoat Transformed: The Gospel Passion as Victim's Story." *Cross Currents* 1 (Spring 1986): 29.
"Quelques clés des désordres collectifs." *Le Figaro* 9, no. 10 (May 1987): 18.
"Serres, le philosophe en marche." (Review of Michel Serres, Statues). *Le Figaro Littéraire*, December 7, 1987, 3f.
"Ritual Killing and Cultural Formation." *Zyzzyva* 3, no. 1 (1987): 98–104.
"Un équilibre périlleux: essai d'interprétation du comique." *Les Saisons de Saint-Jean* 20 (1987): 5–21.
"Violence et société." *Revue des Deux Mondes* 12, no. 35 (1988): 91–98.
"Des chiffres et des hommes." (Review of: Georges-Hubert de Radkowski, Métamorphoses de la Valeur). *L'Express*, May 13–19, 1988, 186.
" 'Génie et démons du christianisme,' in 'Fanatisme: la menace religieuse.' " *Le Nouvel Observateur*, October 5–11, 1989, 20.
"Love Delights in Praises: A Reading of 'The Two Gentlemen of Verona.' " *Philosophy and Literature* 13, no. 2 (1989): 231–47.
"Do You Love Him Because I Do?: Mimetic Interaction in Shakespeare's Comedies." *Helios* 17, no. 1 (Spring 1990): 89–107.
"The Crime and Conversion of Leontes in 'The Winter's Tale.' " *Religion and Literature* 22, no. 2–3 (1990): 193–219.
"Innovation and Repetition." *SubStance* 62–63 (1990): 7–20.
"Religion et Démocratie." *Le Nouvel Observateur*, March 1990.
"Croyez-vous vous même à votre propre théorie?" *Le Règle du Jeu* 1 (May 1990): 254–77.
"Love and Hate in 'Yvain.' " *Recherches et Recontres* 1 (1990): 249–62.
"Collective Violence and Sacrifice in Shakespeare's 'Julius Caesar.' " *Salmagundi: A Quarterly of the Humanities and Social Sciences* 88–89 (1991): 399–419.

"L'apothéose des victimes." *Le Nouvel Observateur,* January 23–29, 1992, 54–55.
"Is There Anti-Semitism in the Gospels?" *Biblical Interpretation: A Journal of Contemporary Approaches* 1, no. 3 (November 1993): 339–52.
"Mythology, Violence, Christianity." *Paragrana: International Zeitschrift für Historische Anthropologie* 4, no. 2 (1995): 103–16.
"Are the Gospels Mythical?" *First Things* 62 (April 1996): 27–31.
"Eating Disorders and Mimetic Desire." *Contagion: Journal of Violence, Mimesis, and Culture* 3 (Spring 1996): 1–20.

Recent Books by Girardian Scholars

The following list includes works that explicate, apply, or criticize the mimetic scapegoat theory (English, French, and German only).

English

Alison, James. *Knowing Jesus* Springfield, Ill.: Templegate, 1993.
———. *Raising Abel: The Recovery of the Eschatological Imagination* New York: Crossroad, 1996.
Bailie, Gil. *Violence Unveiled: Humanity at the Crossroads.* New York: Crossroad, 1995.
Bandera, Cesáreo. *The Sacred Game: The Role of the Sacred in the Genesis of Modern Literary Fiction.* University Park: Pennsylvania State University Press, 1994.
Chilton, Bruce. *The Temple of Jesus.* University Park: Pennsylvania State University Press, 1992.
Golsan, Richard J. *René Girard and Myth: An Introduction.* New York: Garland, 1993.
Goodhart, Sandor. *Sacrificing Commentary.* Baltimore: Johns Hopkins University Press, 1996.
Hamerton-Kelly, Robert G. *Sacred Violence: Paul's Hermeneutic of the Cross.* Minneapolis: Fortress, 1992.
———. *The Gospel and the Sacred: Poetics of Violence in Mark.* Minneapolis: Fortress, 1994.
Kaptein, Roel. *On the Way of Freedom.* Blackrock, Co. Dublin, Ireland: Columba, 1993.
Livingston, Paisley. *Models of Desire: René Girard and the Psychology of Mimesis.* Baltimore: Johns Hopkins University Press, 1992.
McCracken, David. *The Scandal of the Gospels: Jesus, Story, and Offense.* New York: Oxford, 1994.
McKenna, Andrew. *Violence and Difference: Girard, Derrida, and Deconstruction.* Urbana and Chicago: University of Illinois Press, 1992.
Oughourlian, Jean-Michel. *The Puppet of Desire: The Psychology of Hysteria, Possession, and Hypnosis.* Stanford, Calif.: Stanford University Press, 1991.

Simonse, Simon. *Kings of Disaster: Dualism, Centralism and the Scapegoat King in the Southeastern Sudan.* Leiden and New York: Brill, 1992.
Smith, Theophus, and Mark Wallace, eds. *Curing Violence.* Sonoma, Calif.: Polebridge, 1994.
Webb, Eugene. *The Self Between: From Freud to the New Social Psychology of France.* Seattle: University of Washington Press, 1993.
Williams, James G., *The Bible, Violence, and the Sacred: Liberation from the Myth of Sanctioned Violence.* San Francisco: HarperCollins, 1991; Valley Forge, Pa.: Trinity Press International, 1995.
Wink, Walter, *Engaging the Powers.* Minneapolis: Augsburg-Fortress, 1992.

French

Dupuy, Jean-Pierre. *La panique.* Paris: Laboratoires Delagrange, 1991.
———. *Le sacrifice et l'envie: Le libéralisme aux prises avec la justice sociale.* Paris: Calmann-Lévy, 1992.
Lagrange, François. *René Girard ou la christianisation des sciences humaines.* New York: Peter Lang, 1994.

German

Baudler, Georg. *Töten oder Lieben: Gewalt und Gewaltlosigkeit in Religion und Christentum.* Munich: Kösel, 1994.
Dieckmann, Bernhard. *Judas als Sündenbock: eine verhängnisvolle Geschichte von Angst und Vergeltung.* Munich: Kösel, 1991.
Niewiadomski, J., and W. Palaver, eds. *Dramatische Erlösungslehre: Ein Symposion.* Innsbruck, Vienna: Tyrolia, 1992.
———. *Vom Fluch und Segen der Sündenböcke: Raymund Schwager zum 60. Geburtstag.* Thaur: Kulturverlag, 1995.
Palaver, Wolfgang. *Politik und Religion bei Thomas Hobbes: Eine Kritik aus der Sicht der Theorie Girards.* Innsbruck: Tyrolia, 1991.
Schwager, Raymund. *Brauchen wir einen Sündenbock? Gewalt und Erlösung in den biblischen Schriften,* 3d ed. Thaur: Kulturverlag, 1994.
———. *Jesus im Heilsdrama: Entwurf einer biblischen Erlösungslehre.* Innsbruck, Vienna: Tyrolia-Verlag, 1990.
———. *Dem Netz des Jägers entronnen: Wie Jesus sein Leben verstand,* erzählt von Raymund Schwager. Freiburg: Herder, 1991.

Index

OF RELATED INTEREST